THE ROOTS OF RESILIENCE

THE ROOTS OF RESILIENCE

Party Machines and Grassroots Politics in Southeast Asia

Meredith L. Weiss

CORNELL UNIVERSITY PRESS   ITHACA AND LONDON

First published 2020 by Cornell University Press

Printed in the United States of America

Library of Congress Cataloging-in-Publication Data

Names: Weiss, Meredith L. (Meredith Leigh), 1972– author.
Title: The roots of resilience : party machines and grassroots politics in
    Southeast Asia / Meredith L. Weiss.
Description: Ithaca [New York] : Cornell University Press, 2020. |
    Includes bibliographical references and index.
Identifiers: LCCN 2019039142 (print) | LCCN 2019039143 (ebook) |
    ISBN 9781501750045 (hardcover) | ISBN 9781501750052 (ebook) |
    ISBN 9781501750069 (pdf)
Subjects: LCSH: United Malays National Organisation. | Barisan Nasional
    (Organization) | People's Action Party (Singapore) | Political parties—Malaysia. |
    Political parties—Singapore. | Political culture—Malaysia. | Political culture—
    Singapore. | Democracy—Malaysia. | Democracy—Singapore. |
    Authoritarianism—Malaysia. | Authoritarianism—Singapore. | Malaysia—
    Politics and government. | Singapore—Politics and government.
Classification: LCC JQ1062.A979 W45 2020 (print) | LCC JQ1062.A979 (ebook) |
    DDC 320.9595—dc23
LC record available at https://lccn.loc.gov/2019039142
LC ebook record available at https://lccn.loc.gov/2019039143

In memory of Fred R. von der Mehden, who got me started.

Contents

Acknowledgments   ix

Terms and Acronyms   xi

1. Parties, Machines, and Personalities   1

2. Regimes and Resilience Reconceptualized   24

3. The Convoluted Political Path to Malaysia   48

4. Edging toward Sovereign Singapore   77

5. Competitive Authoritarianism in Malaysia:
    Consolidated but Challenged   108

6. Hegemonic Electoral Authoritarianism in Singapore:
    Firmly Entrenched   154

7. Drivers of Stasis and Change: Will the Pattern Hold?   200

Notes   209

Bibliography   241

Index   261

Acknowledgments

This book complements a comparative analysis of political networks and resource flows in the context of Southeast Asian elections, together with co-investigators Edward Aspinall, Allen Hicken, and Paul Hutchcroft. Primary funding for that project, which has overlapped with this one, has been from the Australian Research Council (DP140103114), supplemented for Malaysia's 2013 general election by a grant from Universiti Malaya, in collaboration with Edmund Terence Gomez and Surin Kaur. The University at Albany provided additional funds, particularly for my research in Singapore. I benefited immensely, as well, from time and space to think and write at the Australian National University's Coral Bell School of Asia Pacific Affairs in 2016 and Kyoto University's Center for Southeast Asian Studies in 2017, as well as from visiting stints for research at the Institute of Southeast Asian Studies (ISEAS–Yusuf Ishak Institute) in Singapore and Universiti Kebangsaan Malaysia's Institute of Malaysian and International Studies (IKMAS).

More difficult to specify are the extensive personal debts this project has incurred. I am immensely grateful to the scores of current and former legislators, local councilors, and activists who agreed to interviews or allowed me to shadow them or observe constituency events—this research would simply not have been possible had they been less forthcoming. Moreover, I learned *so* much from these interviews; these discussions confirmed my respect for the incredible dedication, thoughtfulness, and self-reflection of these extraordinarily hardworking public servants. (A note on how I cite those interviews: at key points—for instance, in describing the extent or character of constituency-outreach—I cite in blocs. Those who requested anonymity are identified only by party. My objective has been to balance research transparency with respect for my sources.) I cannot list all interviewees here, but especial thanks to those who seemed always ready to meet, chat, and share contacts and insights unreservedly—who were more sounding boards than mere respondents. In alphabetical order (and painfully aware that I *will* surely forget to mention someone), these individuals include Tian Chua, Daniel Goh, Kenneth Jeyaretnam, Liew Chin Tong, Bryan Lim, Ong Kian Ming, Janil Puthucheary, Saifuddin Abdullah, Sim Tze Tsin, John Tan, and Wan Saiful Wan Jan.

Then there are the many others, some of them overlapping the first category, who helped to facilitate those meetings, a significant share of which would not have happened without a personal plug or referral, and/or helped out in other ways—with feedback, ideas, criticism, and more. This list is a very long one; I could not name everyone if I tried. Among the friends and colleagues most central to the fact of my completing this book and disentangling the ideas in it are—beyond Ed, Allen, and Paul, mentioned above—Anna Har particularly (and her mother), Eileena Lee, Idzuafi Hadi Kamilan, Andrew Aeria, Terence Chong, Chong Ton Sin, Chua Beng Huat, Luenne Chua, Faisal Hazis, Terence Gomez, Francis Hutchinson, Suzaina Kadir, Surin Kaur, Sharaad Kuttan, Lee Hwok Aun, Joe Liow, Francis Loh, Loke Hoe Yeong, Sumit Mandal, Ngu Ik Tien, Ooi Kee Beng, Arnold Puyok, Mush Ridzwan, Ben Suffian, tan beng hui, Tan Seng Keat, Wong Chin Huat, and Kean Wong. Outside Southeast Asia (at least at the time), Thanet Apornsuvan, Coeli Barry, Ward Berenschot, Cheng Chen, Andrew Chin, John Funston, Eva Hansson, Carol Hau, Erik Kuhonta, Marcus Mietzner, Joan Nellhaus, Alysson Oakley, Michael Ong, Ayame Suzuki, and Ross Tapsell have been especially key.

And the debts mount still. . . . Yuko Kasuya volunteered herself for the amazingly helpful service of organizing a book workshop at Keio University; not only was the feedback I received there truly valuable, but I would likely still be drafting chapters today if not for having had that looming deadline. I am deeply grateful to my workshop discussants—Khoo Boo Teik, Nathan Quimpo, and Ed Aspinall—as well as those who attended and offered feedback, especially Mike Montesano, Hidekuni Washida, and Yuko herself. Loke Hoe Yeong and Faisal Hazis's read-throughs saved me from what could otherwise have been some truly embarrassing errors; Ooi Kee Beng likewise did a nerves-calming review on short notice. My thanks, too, to the Politics and History Workshop in my own department and to my colleagues who read and not only offered great comments, but also lent confidence that someone beyond Southeast Asianists might find these arguments of interest. Audiences at a series of talks on the project over the years offered excellent feedback, including at the Australian National University, Griffith University, Johns Hopkins–SAIS, ISEAS, Universiti Kebangsaan Malaysia, Kyoto University, the University of London (SOAS), Universiti Malaysia Sarawak, Northern Illinois University, and the University of Texas at Austin. Of course, the book would likely not be a book—and certainly would be far weaker—if not for Cornell's exceptionally encouraging and constructive reviewers, as well as Roger Haydon and the CUP staff. What faults remain are, of course, all my own.

Then there are all those people who have helped temper the inevitable weirdness of academic life, and especially a chronically peripatetic, jet-lagged version thereof. Particular thanks to Ruth Burdick, of course, as well as to Doug Tookey, Erin Shawn, Winifred Amaturo, Andy Rich, Joel Allen, Barry Trachtenburg, Jennifer Greiman, Harley Trachtenburg, Lynn Foley, Erszébet Fazekas, and Glenn Flanagan. Last, thanks to my Dad, who never seems to mind if I pretty much only call from airports (though granted, there are a *lot* of airports)!

Terms and Acronyms

1MDB	1Malaysia Development Berhad (state investment fund)
ADUN	*Ahli Dewan Undangan Negeri* (state legislator)
Angkatan Pemuda Insaf	Movement of Aware Youth
Barisan Nasional	National Front
Barisan Sosialis	Socialist Front
Bersatu	*Parti Pribumi Bersatu Malaysia*, Malaysian United Indigenous Party
BJP	Bharatiya Janata Party
BN	*Barisan Nasional*
BR1M	*Bantuan Rakyat 1Malaysia* (1Malaysia People's Aid)
CC	Community center
CCC	Citizens' Consultative Committee
CCMC	Community center management committee
CDC	Community Development Council
CDF	Constituency development funds
CEC	Central Executive Committee
Ceramah	Speech, election rally
CSO	Civil-society organization
DAP	Democratic Action Party
DPJ	Democratic Party of Japan
FELDA	Federal Land Development Authority
FIO	Federation of Indian Organisations
GRC	Group Representation Constituency
HDB	Housing and Development Board
JKKK	*Jawatankuasa Kemajuan dan Keselamatan Kampung* (Village Development and Security Committees)
Kaum Ibu	*Pergerakan Kaum Ibu UMNO* (UMNO Women's Section Movement)
Kesatuan Melayu Muda	Young Malay Union
Ketua kampong	Village head

KMT	Kuomintang
Kōenkai	Japanese politicians' personal support networks
LDP	Liberal Democratic Party
LF	Labour Front
LP	Labour Party
LPM	Labour Party Malaysia
LSP	Liberal Socialist Party
MCA	Malaysian Chinese Association
MCP	Malayan Communist Party
MES	*Merakyatkan Ekonomi Selangor* (Selangor's People-based Economy)
MIC	Malaysian Indian Congress
MLA	Member of the Legislative Assembly
MMM	Mixed-member majoritarian
MNP	Malay Nationalist Party (Parti Kebangsaan Melayu Malaya)
MP	Member of Parliament
MPKK	*Majlis Pengurusan Komuniti Kampung* (Village Community Management Councils)
NCMP	Non-constituency Member of Parliament
NEP	New Economic Policy
NMP	Nominated Member of Parliament
NTUC	National Trades Union Congress
PA	People's Association
Pakatan	*Pakatan Harapan* or *Pakatan Rakyat*
Pakatan Harapan	Alliance of Hope
Pakatan Rakyat	People's Pact
PAP	People's Action Party
Parti Islam seMalaysia	Pan-Malaysian Islamic Party (PAS, initially PMIP)
Parti Keadilan Rakyat	People's Justice Party
Parti Pribumi Bersatu Malaysia	Malaysian United Indigenous Party
PAS	*Parti Islam seMalaysia*
PBB	*Parti Pesaka Bumiputera Bersatu* (United Bumiputera Heritage Party)
PBS	*Parti Bersatu Sabah* (United Sabah Party)
PKMS	*Pertubuhan Kebangsaan Melayu Singapura*, Singapore Malay National Organisation
PKR	*Parti Keadilan Rakyat*

Parti Rakyat Malaysia	Malaysian People's Party
PMIP	Pan-Malaysian Islamic Party
PMLP	Pan-Malayan Labour Party
PPP	People's Progressive Party
PRD	Party of the Democratic Revolution
PRI	Institutional Revolutionary Party
PRM	*Parti Rakyat Malaysia* (Malayan People's Party, initially *Partai Ra'ayat Malaya*, then *Parti Sosialis Rakyat Malaysia*)
RC	Residents' Committee
REACH	Reaching Everyone for Active Citizenry @ Home
SATU	Singapore Association of Trade Unions
SDP	Singapore Democratic Party
SIT	Singapore Improvement Trust
SMC	Single-member constituency
SNTV	Single non-transferable vote
SPA	Singapore People's Alliance
SPP	Singapore People's Party
SUPP	Sarawak United People's Party
TC	Town Councils
UMNO	United Malays National Organisation
UNKO	United National Kadazan Organisation
USNO	United Sabah National Organisation
Wanita UMNO	UMNO women's wing (previously *Kaum Ibu*)
WP	Workers' Party

THE ROOTS OF RESILIENCE

PARTIES, MACHINES, AND PERSONALITIES

In 1996, Singapore's prime minister, Goh Chok Tong of the People's Action Party (PAP), cautioned voters before impending elections, "You vote for the other side, that means you reject the programmes of the PAP candidate, you won't get it. This is going to be a local government election. . . . If you reject it, we respect your choice. Then you'll be left behind, then in 20, 30 years' time, the whole of Singapore will be bustling away, and your estate through your own choice will be left behind. They become slums."[1] He could make these threats—and be assured of their sting—thanks to two key innovations: his party's prioritization since the early 1960s of public housing, such that over 80 percent of Singaporeans lived in Housing and Development Board (HDB) flats, and a structural change in the late 1980s that gave members of parliament (MPs), overwhelmingly from the PAP, managerial authority over HDB estates. Singapore's few opposition MPs played the same role, but without benefit of PAP machinery or access to the resources afforded ruling-party MPs. However assiduously they built rapport on the ground, opposition candidates for national office faced a stark disadvantage at the local-government level.

This dilemma highlights a comparatively little-remarked aspect of how Singapore's PAP has remained in office since 1959: not just coercion (though Goh's threat entails that, as well), but close management of *local* government specifically. Micromanagement of mundane aspects of citizens' lives, and particularly the municipal services on which they most rely—including public housing— undergirds regime durability and offers a highly granular indicator of the "performance" that accords a regime political legitimacy. In neighboring Malaysia, too, cultivated dependence on state and federal legislators at the local-government level personalizes politics and grants parties and politicians concrete relevance to citizens' lives.

In this book, I examine governance from the ground up in the world's two most enduring electoral-authoritarian or "hybrid" regimes—regimes that blend politically liberal and authoritarian features to evade substantive democracy. (As explained later, while elections in 2018 ousted Malaysia's dominant party, the regime arguably persists under new leadership.) I find that although skewed elections, curbed civil liberties, and a dose of coercion help sustain these regimes, selectively structured state policies and patronage, partisan machines that effectively stand in for local governments, and diligently sustained clientelist relations between politicians and constituents are equally important. While key attributes of Singapore's and Malaysia's regimes differ, affecting the scope, character, and balance among national parties and policies, local machines, and personalized linkages, the similarity in their overall patterns confirms the salience of these dimensions. Taken together, these attributes acculturate citizens toward the system in place. As the chapters to come detail, this authoritarian acculturation is key to both regimes' durability, although weaker party competition and party–civil society links render Singapore's authoritarian acculturation stronger than Malaysia's. High levels of authoritarian acculturation are key to why electoral turnover is insufficient for real regime change in either state.

The Terrain of Hybridity

In 1965, the tiny island state of Singapore became independent of the Federation of Malaysia after a stormy two-year marriage. The divorce marked the end of a geopolitical experiment but also signaled the beginning of the end for domestic political experimentation on either side. Until that point, uncertainty about the shape of these polities had left open a gamut of ideological and policy options; after parting ways, Singapore's and Malaysia's polities ossified. As late as 1968, political scientist Thomas Bellows (1967, 122) could write of Singapore over the preceding decade as having been "characterized by a relatively open and competitive party system," unlike its Southeast Asian neighbors.[2] By that point, we now know, Singapore's competitive political moment had passed; Malaysia's ruling coalition was similarly entrenched. As independent Singapore and independent, Singapore-less Malaysia pushed on through the decades, it was with the same governments in power as during their two-year union: the communal Alliance, later rebranded the National Front (Barisan Nasional, BN), headed by the United Malays National Organisation (UMNO) in Malaysia and the PAP in Singapore.

This book probes not just how these parties secured and sustained preeminence, but how they changed politics in the process, entrenching a particular style of contestation and outreach even among their challengers.

In order to become dominant, both UMNO and the PAP had to engage in strategic coalition building and careful institutional design and cultivate a conducive political culture. Both parties fought their way into power and still face rivals. Although both battled left-wing challenges in the 1960s, the PAP more effectively quashed its chief nemesis than did UMNO; some of the same parties from that era still contest in Singapore, however, joined by new ones. UMNO, too, has faced a mix of social democratic, Islamist, and other noncommunal challengers since Malaysia's first elections. Several of these parties consistently secured footholds at the state level—a tier unitary Singapore lacks—and the latest coalition bested the BN nationally in 2018. For both regimes, this formal contestation, repeated at regular intervals, has constituted a key prong in their assertions of legitimacy: both claim a popular mandate and call their polities "democracies." Yet both parties have used the power so gained to consolidate their own position, grading the playing field first laid out to a postcolonial British pattern with a pronounced slope. Democracy, yes; liberal democracy, no.

The chapters to come disentangle the ways these parties have restyled their respective environments to their own advantage. These polities are ostensibly similar, on account of their shared British heritage, illiberal political leanings, strong parties, and heavy reliance on performance legitimacy. However, it is the important divergences between them—the character of the nexus between state and society, the space for ideological competition, and the potential for a turnover in government—that sparked this investigation into what features of the political landscape matter, and in what ways, to how politics plays out on the ground.

Internationally, around one-fifth of contemporary regimes are electoral-authoritarian, but their extraordinary longevity distinguishes Singapore and Malaysia (Diamond 2002, 23). Singapore's PAP has held power since 1959, and the Alliance or BN, from Malaysia's inaugural general elections in 1955 until 2018. A simple structural explanation goes far toward explaining that resilience: both Singapore and Malaysia have sampled multiple items on Andreas Schedler's "menu of manipulation" (2002), from prolific gerrymandering of electoral districts to aggressive curbs on civil liberties. Yet over time, the governing parties have buttressed these structural features with less visible and less readily supplanted normative and cultural attributes, the legacy of long-term hybridity.

Most contemporary citizens in both states have never participated in anything but electoral authoritarianism. The parties that challenge the PAP and BN have likewise competed at least since the 1960s only in the framework of single-party dominance.[3] As Beatriz Magaloni notes of dominant-party regimes, "The 'tragic brilliance' of these systems is that the population plays an active role in sustaining them, often despite corruption, inefficient policies, and lack of economic growth. Citizens' choices are free, yet they are constrained by a series of strategic dilemmas that compel them to remain loyal to the regime" (2006, 19). Both Singapore's and Malaysia's dominant parties have informally institutionalized premises for accountability and loyalty oriented more around local outreach and management than national politics. How closely these efforts touch citizens' lives, as well as the resources they require, makes alternatives difficult for challengers to develop or citizens to trust; voters come to see the party in office not as modular and replaceable, but as built-in and inevitable.

Indeed, over decades, structure molds (political) culture, understood as "the attitudes, sentiments, and cognitions that inform and govern political behavior in any society" (Pye 1965, 7). Political culture, comprising ideals and norms inherited but incrementally transformed over generations, "gives meaning, predictability, and form to the political process," guiding individual political behavior and institutional performance (Pye 1965, 7–8).[4]

As Singapore's earlier electoral history suggests, its citizens are not naturally averse to adversarial politics, even if low levels of participation have, in fact, featured since early days. Recurrent heated electoral contests in Malaysia confirm that here, too, citizens embrace competition. However, since the 1950s, Singapore's and Malaysia's leading parties have trained citizens in both states to expect a reliable partisan machine and expeditious personalized outreach from the politicians they elect—even though many voters do still weigh heavily candidates' ideology or party programs. This relational, more instrumental than ideological approach to governance and accountability is difficult and slow to dislodge.

Rather than simply "electoral authoritarian" (fleshed out more fully later), these two perennially hybrid systems feature political machines: a well-organized party takes on and personalizes roles in political socialization, distribution, and governance normally left to the state. Strong grassroots machinery allows a party to identify supporters and opponents, monitor their behavior and leanings, and distribute rewards and punishments accordingly. To speak of a machine, though, indicates not just an operational electoral network, but an apparatus for governance. Machine politics leaves the average citizen little ground on which to distinguish clearly among party, state, and civil society. The ties between citizens and elected officials in a machine environment are structured substantially, if not around individual-level patronage, contingent on voters' reciprocated support—what Hutchcroft (2014, 177–78) labels "micro-particularism"—then around impersonally distributed, or "meso-particularistic," patronage, benefiting targeted blocs of voters. The drive to compete, especially once voters have become habituated to machine politics, presses opposition politicians and parties to replicate that approach. Through close analysis of Malaysian and Singapore politics over time, I argue that a linchpin to the extreme durability of electoral authoritarianism in these two states is their purposeful cultivation and maintenance of personalized, partisan political machines, sufficiently formally and informally institutionalized over time to shape political culture broadly.

In such a system, transforming the regime requires more than just electing a new government. I define the regime less in terms of elections than of broader, if fuzzier, dimensions of policy processes, access to decision making, and norms and metrics for accountability, as well as paths to public office (cf. Schmitter and Karl 1991, 76). This conceptualization helps particularly in understanding what happens between elections, making those aspects part of the central concept. Regimes include both formal and informal institutions, and regime actors respond to both formal and informal incentives and rules. Norms and other informal institutions are harder to pin down than electoral data or even party platforms, but help to structure behavior, with implications for representation, accountability, and governance; it is not analytically helpful to give these dimensions short shrift or simply assume they will transform postelection. Perhaps most important, meaningful democratization would normally entail a shift in bases for political legitimacy and accountability. While structural manipulation clearly helps a dominant party continue to win elections, the real staying power of electoral-authoritarian governance rests in the transformation of state-society relations. Hence, while an election has transferred power to new hands in Malaysia, regime change writ large lags that shift.

Adopting this lens on regime durability[5] requires a novel, historically grounded approach, moving away from a literature on political regimes and transitions heavily focused on how dominant parties win (or lose) elections (see chapter 2). My account centers around three primary arguments. The first concerns institutional makeup, particularly political parties and how they and their policies structure the political economy and society. Dominant parties are only part of this story; just as important to understanding regime persistence is grasping how opposition parties as well as groups within civil society organize, in turn. The second argument homes in on the primary interface between citizens and state: local government. The literature on regimes is overwhelmingly national in focus, yet it is at the lowest tiers of governance that we see better how citizens understand and engage with both states and partisan machines. My third and final argument addresses individual actors: the linkages between actual or aspiring politicians and their constituents. Exploring these three dimensions not only illuminates why UMNO and the PAP have remained so entrenched, but also how their challengers have adapted to their political environment, to the point of perpetuating some of its defining tenets. Throughout, I develop a concept of (authoritarian) acculturation, or the process by which citizens become acclimated over time to a particular mode of politics, conditioned by the nature of competition and the structure of both political parties and civil society. Singapore's higher level of authoritarian acculturation, propelled by political actors' accommodation to structural turns over time, I propose, is a critical factor in the greater resilience of its regime than Malaysia's.

Two primary analytical goals drive the work: to recommend a new way of conceptualizing regimes broadly and to present a new, empirically driven explanation for electoral-authoritarian persistence. While I delve into two specific cases in great detail, that exploration has wider theoretical significance. The study adds to a sparse literature on the "nuts and bolts" of politics in postcolonial polities, including "the everyday behaviour of politicians" (Lindberg 2010, 118). For Southeast Asia, apart from a minor flurry of behavioralist and related works in the 1960s–1970s (e.g., Scott 1968; Chan 1976a, b; Ong 1976), scholars have given these mundane workings of politics far less attention than they have more macrolevel institutional features—which is far less than they deserve. And scholars of any region still tend to study politicians' praxis from the perspective of the center, notwithstanding our awareness of its distance from the constituents who elect them.

The study also adds to a newly resurgent literature on clientelism and machine politics, adding an at least partly redemptive twist by homing in on the responsiveness and underlying accountability such politics fosters. Much of the literature on clientelism remains tightly bound to electoral processes, such as vote buying (e.g., Schaffer 2007), the role of brokers in securing votes (Stokes et al. 2013), and the balance of particularistic and other appeals in election campaigns (Aspinall and Berenschot 2019; Weiss 2014a). My wider focus, situating elections among larger institutions and longer-term, iterative relationships, gives a different picture. It suggests not only how electoral authoritarianism becomes embedded, but also what would need to shift for that regime truly to change.

My analysis draws on intensive and extensive interviews and observation, building on two decades' close study of Malaysian and Singaporean politics.[6] I have interviewed dozens of current, past, and aspiring politicians, visited service centers, attended constituency events, and observed election campaign activities from across parties in both countries. For earlier periods, I rely heavily on archival records, particularly the British National Archives and the remarkable Oral History Interviews collection in the National Archives of Singapore. To avoid reading past events through the lens of present-day assumptions, I have referred as much as possible, too, to contemporaneous academic, political party, media, and other accounts, rather than later retellings—though I do draw, too, on more recent scholarship. And throughout the work, I engage with theoretical literatures on patronage and clientelism as part of electoral processes, as well as a more varied literature on regime hybridity and transitions. These resources allow me to delve into the early foundations and initial development of political parties, electoral and other institutions, and politicians' strategies for outreach and service-delivery in Malaysia and Singapore. The specific steps identified in these states might be sui generis, or limited to tutelary transitions such as those under the British in Southeast Asia. However, the broader pattern should hold elsewhere—the stabilizing role of partisan machines and the premise that linkages among politicians, parties, and voters take on the character of informal institutions—as do key questions such as for what citizens look to the state versus elsewhere, as well as how representation is understood and structured.

Three Core Arguments

My discussion of Malaysia's and Singapore's political histories tracks three core arguments, representing three overlapping dimensions of the polity. I develop this analysis through a historical-institutionalist approach of considering configurations of institutions and processes, over time, and with close attention to context. By homing in across dimensions—from parties and policies at the national level, to local governance, to individual-level linkages between politicians and constituents—I am able to consider how politics actually happens, beyond elections, and the expectations and habits that praxis inculcates among citizens.

Parties and Structuring Policies

In this book, I seek to understand not just how parties secure their own dominance, but also how that position then shapes the terrain for opponents, transforming the regime broadly. I argue that at the macro level, dominant parties define themselves in ways that minimize the scope for coherent ideological challenges, retooling their own profiles along the way, and use state programs to reshape society to their own advantage. For instance, UMNO's massively expanding racial affirmative action programs in Malaysia in the 1970s gave the ethnic Malay majority added incentive to prefer communal politics, and the PAP's aggressive development of public housing in the 1960s rendered most Singaporeans clients of the PAP-led state. Both parties framed these programs as due to the party's foresight and concern. Through such strategies, dominant parties present themselves as the people's champions and core providers, even when what they are delivering are actually state, not party, resources.

To understand these efforts requires attention to the state's institutional makeup, for the broader backdrop to electoral politics; the development and attributes of the party system; and the ways public policies may be channeled strategically or "partisanized": made to appear to come from a party rather than from the state.[7] Under electoral authoritarianism, efforts to entrench the ruling party's advantage, including by rewarding supporters, may go further than under liberal democracy, as electoral-authoritarian governing parties face less compelling checks and balances. The longer they are in office, the more substantially dominant parties may mold the policy landscape—even as that landscape, in turn, shapes how all parties calibrate their goals and functions.

Parties and the rules under which they operate sit at the structural core of electoral-authoritarian regimes, even if these parties are personalized, nonideological, or otherwise sub-par. Whereas in democracies, legally secure, autonomous interest associations and social movements perform similar intermediary roles, aggregating individual preferences, linking these to government agencies and offices, and seeking to influence public policy (Schmitter 2001, 70–72), these organizations face curbs under electoral authoritarianism. The extent to which civil society organizations (CSOs) develop and connect with other political institutions and processes affects the extent to which parties alone define the political landscape. However, dominant and even challenger parties retain more such clout, including roles in political integration and socialization, as well as policymaking, in any electoral-authoritarian regime than under political liberalism.

In any context, political parties combine functions of control and representation, presenting candidates and platforms and channeling citizens' preferences and interests toward the policy process. However, the balance among their expressive, instrumental, and representative functions—that is, the extent to which they politically activate particular social cleavages or identities, translate social position into demands and claims, aggregate pressure, and strike bargains (Lipset and Rokkan 1967, 4–5)—reflects parties' relative expectation of policymaking authority. That provisional adaptation may become habitual and ingrained over time. Parties that begin life under electoral authoritarianism, with little hope of attaining office, may develop characteristics that endure into a more competitive era.

Yet other aspects of parties are mutable and change as strategy or demographics recommend. For instance, the defining qualities of Malaysia's ruling BN and its component parties have grown hazier since the 1980s, given changes in the population, political economy, and competitive landscape, and these parties' policy platforms have overlapped with those of challengers they hope to preempt. Partisan allegiance tends to be sticky, regardless, but may be even more so under entrenched electoral authoritarianism. Citizens' inability to distinguish the institutional regime from the current officeholders raises the stakes of pressing a challenge, as "any attack on the political leaders or on the dominant party tends to turn into an attack on the political system itself" (Lipset and Rokkan 1967, 4).

Particularly once a dominant party has been able to make programmatic distribution appear partisan, voters may fear losing selective benefits should the incumbent government be voted out, so remain loyal. Hence, considering patterns of party formation, differentiation, and policy frameworks offers a critical perspective on and explanation for how citizens navigate electoral authoritarianism and why so many voters continue to support dominant parties and their political praxis.

Local Government and Machines

This book's second major argument is that local government offers a key prop to electoral authoritarianism, both for maintaining the party in power and in shaping citizens' expectations of officials. It is at the local level that most citizens experience the workings of government personally and at which party machines play a direct governance role. Even if most power rests at the center, it is at the local level that parties render themselves visible and useful—both dominant parties vested with authority and resources, and challengers seeking to establish a reputation and base. Even when contingent extenuating circumstances upturn the dominant party—as with corruption scandals in Malaysia sufficiently massive to blame for perceived economic decline—that party's replacement is both primed and has incentive to sustain the pattern.

Although the British first introduced municipal elections across peninsular Malaya[8] and Singapore soon after the Second World War, to serve as late-colonial training grounds for democracy, both states phased out still-competitive local polls early on.[9] Levels of government became structurally fused: local with state in Malaysia and with national in Singapore. Nor have these states decentralized significantly, however common decentralization elsewhere in the region. Centralization and amalgamation of tiers of government shape both how citizens encounter the state and the arenas in which political parties operate. Absent elected authorities, local government became "a device of grass-roots control utilized by the center to stabilize the rule of the incumbent national leadership" (Rüland 1990, 462).

Even before these states abrogated local elections, then increasingly after that point, lack of government capacity offered an opening for political parties to provide services the local authority could not. Machine politics as it now exists in both states was thus really a bottom-up phenomenon. As detailed in the chapters to come, elected local governments began with a stacked deck. Local authorities in Malaya in the 1950s and 1960s faced an inflexible and inadequate revenue base, fragmented and incomplete geographic coverage, a shortage of competent staff, and a series of corruption scandals that had eroded popular confidence by the mid-1960s (Norris 1980, 17; Sim and Koay 2015, 13–14). The Alliance coalition that governed at the federal level also fared poorly in municipal elections; its communal model appealed less to the non-Malay majority in cities than to the Malay majority overall, dimming Alliance enthusiasm for these polls. In Singapore, the city council governed, but the purse strings–holding British were highly abstemious, plus the council's functions came to appear inadequately differentiated from those of the legislature. The PAP, therefore, had similarly weak incentive to maintain elected local government. Malaya phased out local elections starting in the early 1960s, and Singapore, after the PAP won nationally in 1959. This institutional reconfiguration served to depoliticize and demobilize the public and to deepen central control at a time of political clampdown and ambitious development plans (Rüland 1990, 474–75, 477). "Urban government" in Malaysia, according to Enloe, became "urban *administration*" (1975, 162).

Yet citizens still needed local governance. Urbanites in particular depend on public services and infrastructure. Even in rural areas, citizens seek agricultural inputs, emergency aid, and help in navigating a bureaucratic machinery that functioned initially largely in English, a language with little constituency in any community outside urban areas, and that has remained complex even once language came to pose less of a hurdle. The incapacity that debilitated local councils offered an opening for political parties: bureaucratic weakness at the local level proved essential to sustaining partisan machines. Now, choice of nominated, not elected, local councilors in Malaysia, intended to favor distinguished professionals and community representatives, came to prioritize party loyalty instead. Those chosen are accountable to the party, not the public. In Singapore, the nationalization of elected government happened even as the state extended its reach: citizens became deeply reliant on state services as public housing and social assistance programs exponentially expanded—pressing Singapore to reintroduce municipal authorities in the 1980s, but now headed by MPs.

As both states (and supplementary parastatal organizations) extended their capacity and developed programmatic remedies to citizens' concerns, such as social welfare policies from the 1960s on, they continued to channel services and supplements through parties' and politicians' service centers or outreach, maintaining a partisan cast. Indeed, Singapore's PAP and Malaysia's UMNO and partners have reinforced their profiles over the years, stepping up their efforts when their popularity slips by devolving yet more local intervention to party branches and partisan machinery. Instead of relying on a local government possibly dominated by a party different from that in power at the state or national level, citizens hence came increasingly to rely on the party itself for municipal functions. That mode of distribution and interaction, sustained over time, shaped citizens' understanding of how and where they access the state and what they should expect from their representatives. Opposition parties, for their part, came to build their own, competing machinery for local service delivery, especially in urban areas in Malaysia, even absent the opportunity to develop experience and secure access to public resources by holding local office.

Missing or low-quality local authorities likewise create a reason for higher-tier legislators themselves to intervene at the local level, working with and through those partisan machines, even if unremitting, resource-sapping constituency service distracts them from legislative work. The arrangement lets elected officials take credit for matters that touch citizens' lives most directly, keeping voters' attention fixed not on ideology or national governance, but on municipal services, and fostering dependence on, and gratitude to, what at least appears to be *party* or *private* rather than *state* funding and intermediation. In Malaysia today, legislators (and aspiring candidates) at both the state and federal levels support grassroots service centers and spend inordinate time handling local-government matters; in Singapore, MPs have doubled since the 1980s as heads of (appointed) town councils, responsible for the same sorts of mundane requests about streetlights and noisy neighbors. While their institutional details differ, both scenarios privilege a highly personalized, localized, machine-oriented politics that by now, voters expect of government and opposition parties alike. The end result is both entrenchment of the dominant party, helped by a clear advantage in party and state resources for local service delivery and enhancements, and inculcation among voters of a tendency to privilege narrow, short-term gains over ideological, normative goals requiring meaningful political liberalization.

Personal Linkages

Third and finally, I argue in this book for the importance of individual-level clientelism, in the sense of sustained and responsive, but hierarchical, mutually beneficial relationships, as an especially durable underpinning of electoral-authoritarian politics. In both Malaysia and Singapore, the fabric sustaining governance since the advent of elections—from national institutions, to local authorities, to the grass roots—has been a web of linkages among politicians and constituents. Despite some extent of diversification of or transition among forms, clientelist ties, established early on, remain clearly salient in both Singapore and Malaysia. These ties are personalized: voters know their MPs and expect to see them at neighborhood festivals or knocking on doors. Where prevailing rules and norms permit a permeable border between civil society and political parties—a key distinction between Malaysia and Singapore—it is at this level that politicians may especially capitalize, too, on links with non-party organizations. But the ties are also partisan: the teams supporting legislators are at least party centered rather than fully exclusive to individual patrons.[10] Moreover, and offering resource-strapped challengers a lifeline, these connections are not just about dispensing patronage, but also about mere physical visibility and personal interaction. More than straightforward constituency service, and fully compatible with simultaneous programmatic efforts, these efforts build long-term relationships, even with short-term electoral payoff unlikely. Such personal ties allow a form of direct accountability beyond elections, as voters keep track of who has at least been present and concerned.

In any electoral regime, we find a mix of charismatic, programmatic, and clientelist political linkages, or "structured or patterned transaction flows of influence, support, claims and information between allied and interdependent political participants" (Jones 1972, 1195–96). Charismatic politicians emphasize their own personality, not programs: "They tend to promise all things to all people to maintain maximum personal discretion" and build up their own factions rather than the organization (Kitschelt 2000, 849). Programmatic linkages are the obverse, emphasizing coherent organizational infrastructure, procedures for conflict resolution, and policy platforms rather than contingent selective incentives (Kitschelt 2000, 850). Clientelistic linkages favor investment "in administrative-technical infrastructure but not in modes of interest aggregation and program formation"; politicians maintain these linkages with voters via "direct, personal, and typically material side payments," supported by "multilevel political machines" (Kitschelt 2000, 849).[11]

Yet as Hutchcroft (2014, 176–77) describes, politicians need not deploy the personal relationships that define clientelism for distribution of material patronage. Nor are these linkage types mutually exclusive, even for a politician-voter dyad. Within one state, too, national party leaders may maintain programmatic ties with voters, representing the big-picture party, but be tied clientelistically to subordinates within their party, who themselves rely on charismatic or clientelist linkages with constituents. For instance, while Taiwan's then-dominant Kuomintang (KMT) remained ideologically pitched and programmatic at the central party level, local party factions took a more clientelist approach, trading individual- or community-level services and improvements for votes, playing key roles in voter mobilization and patronage distribution, and, ultimately, sustaining KMT control in the process (Bosco 1992, 160–61).

Clientelism is especially salient to electoral authoritarianism, but not unique to it. Even industrialized liberal democracies feature clientelist linkages, apparent when constituency service extends beyond what electoral considerations seem to warrant. Elected officials in the United Kingdom, for instance, have increased their time spent on constituency service dramatically since the 1960s (Norris 1997, 30), and legislators in the United States return frequently to their districts, adopting a "home style" in their allocation of personal and staff resources, presentation of self, prioritization of service requests, and explanation of their policy efforts (Fenno 1977, 890; Butler, Karpowitz, and Pope 2012, 475–76, 484). In all but the most party-centered electoral contexts (for instance, fully closed-list proportional representation systems), legislators stand to benefit by cultivating at least a supplemental personal vote. Hence, for instance, in Indonesia, where voters may select one candidate from within their preferred party's list, candidates differentiate themselves from party mates by personal appeals and gifts (Aspinall and Sukmajati 2016). Even in nondemocracies, public officials engage in constituency service, absent an electoral incentive, since doing so provides the government with other benefits (Distelhorst and Hou 2017). But clientelist linkages are especially important in electoral polities where endemic dominance by a catch-all party diminishes the space for substantive differentiation, as politicians need some way other than programmatic appeals to make themselves stand out to voters.

However fortified by side payments, these linkages extend beyond material patronage. The relationship centers around a personal, empathetic connection between politician and voter: the "personal touch," or being present at weddings, funerals, hospital beds, and more, often delivering clearly token gifts for the individual voter or community. Such gifts may serve to reinforce loyalty, clarify membership in a particular network, and demonstrate the seriousness of a campaign, but they differ in intent and how they are understood from payments to purchase votes a candidate would not otherwise win (Bosco 1992, 169–70, 172). These in-person interactions also offer opportunities for voters to adjudge a politician by nonverbal performance rather than words, to get a sense of their personality, and to build and maintain mutual trust. In this way, the politician allows for representation less in terms of policy preferences than access and confidence in themself as essentially decent (Fenno 1977, 898–89, 915)—a prospect especially germane where few politicians, and none from outside the dominant party, exercise significant policy influence.

Given that limited policy clout, it is hardly surprising if voters under electoral authoritarianism prioritize, not legislating, but "good old face time."[12] For instance, suggesting the extent to which they have been acculturated to this mode of politics, almost all respondents to a June 2016 national survey in Malaysia[13]—95.1 percent—said an elected official's "record of service in the community" was important to them, more than for any other factor; ability to "bring development projects," for which it helps to be in government, came a close second. A prominent Singaporean opposition-party candidate similarly explained, "you just cannot *not* interface personally" with voters; a politician must be at least physically visible to be credible.[14] This mixture of personal outreach and perks conveyed reflects the mix of "affective" (interpersonal) and "instrumental" (material) aspects of clientelism (Scott 1972, 99). Well-resourced dominant-party politicians may gain support for their greater generosity, but opposition candidates can at least compete on the affective dimension.

Most voters in both Singapore and Malaysia cast votes on party lines. However, despite sporadic upticks, the dominant party's share of the popular vote in both has been declining—the BN's more consequentially. The marginal difference between a strong and weak personal vote may make the difference in increasingly tight contests, meaning candidates from no party can afford to ignore the exhausting labor of working the ground, and the party may drop an incumbent whom voters deem lazy or absent, regardless. It is at this interpersonal level that we see long-term hybridity entrenched, as dominant-party politicians aggressively style themselves as effective patrons, challengers attempt to outdo them, and voters come to expect a more particularistic than programmatic framework.

Putting these arguments together: dominant parties stay in power through elections, not (solely) coercion. They use policy levers to tip the electoral scales in their favor but can only go so far. Having had the benefit of institutional and fiscal resources, these parties have constructed dense machines, reaching to the grass roots, which effectively stand in for the state at the local level, magnifying their own utility; opposition parties develop countervailing machines, but without the same resources or authority. Driving these machines on either side are party-loyal politicians, who build rapport among, and cultivate both affective and instrumental clientelist linkages with, voters. This model is not absolute: as explained in chapters to come, many voters do vote on programmatic grounds or favor normative premises for political legitimacy. But having experienced only one model of politics since independence, most voters have been acculturated toward this mode of governance and standard for accountability. As such, the imperative of securing the margins drives politicians on both sides to channel benefits strategically and partisanize distribution where they can, invest in machinery for de facto local governance, and cultivate clientelist relationships, through visibility and service if not generosity, lest voters defect to a more reliable choice.

Approaching Regimes

As this framework suggests, among my key analytical contributions is to recommend that we resist the urge to define regimes in terms of elections. A broader conceptualization draws attention to what happens between elections; those aspects are better situated as part of the central concept, *regime*, than as caveats. Other scholars have recommended a similar reframing. For instance, Jayasuriya and Rodan conceptualize regimes in terms of institutions and how they deal with conflict, including "access to and the distribution of political resources, author-ity, and legitimacy" (2007, 775). But the electoral tendency dominates the litera-ture. While acknowledging the importance of civil society and independent in-stitutions, Howard and Roessler, for example, offer a typically election-oriented definition, that "political regimes are the rules and procedures that determine how national, executive leaders are chosen" (2006, 366–67). Likewise, Greene defines a dominant-party authoritarian system as one in which one party has won at least four consecutive elections or governed for at least twenty years, amid "meaning-ful but manifestly unfair" elections (2007, 12–15). Yet should a dominant party fall without a real transformation in access to policymaking or politician-voter linkages, little about governance might change. Hence, my effort to shift the frame, to understand not just UMNO's or the PAP's staying power, but the extent to which they have entrenched regimes equipped to outlive their own dominance.

The common understanding of electoral authoritarianism as ending with a change of government—for instance, explorations of why Japan's Liberal Demo-cratic Party (LDP) or Mexico's Institutional Revolutionary Party (PRI) fell from their pedestals—tells us how and why a dominant party may lose, but not what happens next. These states may either experience limited policy shift after "tran-sition" (e.g., Lipscy and Scheiner 2012; Scheiner 2012; Bruhn and Greene 2007) or still exclude or coopt popular movements, trade unions, or other social forces (Shin 2012, 294–95), or clientelism and personalism may persist (Hilgers 2008).[15] For an opposition party to make parliamentary inroads, too, may not grant that party decision-making power, if the configuration of forces leads those legisla-tors to prefer the status quo to reform (Lust-Okar 2005, 5), if challengers "are trapped in investing in the survival of the autocratic electoral game" (Magaloni 2006, 16), or if the legislature lacks policymaking authority in the first place. Or-dinary citizens, too, far from mere "victims," may prove "important autono-mous and opportunistic actors in upholding the logic of hybrid regimes," as they respond to the rational incentives and forms of empowerment, however con-strained, those regimes offer (Persson and Rothstein 2019, 11).

Electoral authoritarianism both lures challengers into playing by the electoral rules and habituates both them and voters over time to a similar mode of politics as the dominant party's. Regime change may still happen—Malaysia and Singa-pore are not forever frozen in place, and any change of government, including in Malaysia in 2018, will surely usher in at least some important policy shifts. But substantial reform will take more than an electoral upset; by the same token, citi-zens may gain new access to and influence on policymaking absent a change of government (Weiss 2014b).

We might conceptualize this broader view in terms of what a focus on elec-tions might overlook or sideline. Among the most important such features are informal institutions and civil society. Because regime actors respond to both formal and informal incentives and rules, my analysis includes both among what constitutes a regime. Informal institutions include shared rules that carry with them an assumption of credible sanction if violated, and they may be embedded within formal state institutions; they are not just habit or tradition.[16] They help to structure behavior, with implications for representation, accountability, and governance—whether voters expect patronage from those they elect, or how parties negotiate power sharing in coalition, for instance—but may undermine or compete with, as well as complement, formal institutions (Helmke and Levitsky 2006, 5–12; Rakner and Walle 2009, 119). Indeed, strong informal institutions may suppress demands for services through formal channels and encourage actors to invest instead in preserving informal rules of the game (Helmke and Levitsky 2006, 16–18); we see this tendency in citizens' increasing reliance, not on formal institutions of local administration, but on partisan machines and personal intermediation in Malaysia and Singapore. My analysis considers the order electoral authoritarian fosters and what would be necessary to change both formal institutions and informal norms and praxis.

Second, I give civil society due billing. However much parties channel mobilization and participation, a diverse array of CSOs or networks, of varying political ambition or efficacy, play at least supplementary roles. Even where an illiberal regime curbs civil liberties, activity within civil society independently structures aspects of the terrain on which parties compete, as by activating or deescalating particular cleavages or exhorting the public to prioritize particular issues. However much we might differentiate conceptually between the domains of parties and civil-societal organizations, parties cultivate grassroots networks most efficiently by liaising with such intermediary organizations as trade unions, neighborhood associations, religious bodies, and nongovernmental organizations. Some of this effort revolves specifically around elections, including engaging well-networked brokers to coax or buy support (Aspinall 2014, 554). But especially to endure long stretches out of office and "reify" their party—to crystallize a differentiated, stable image of the party among the public (Randall and Svåsand 2002, 14), absent opportunity to govern—opposition parties benefit from longer-term, less purely instrumental connections permeating civil society. Limiting opportunities for challengers to develop such connections offers an oblique but effective strategy for preserving dominant-party advantage.

Examining what parties and politicians actually do among the public reveals clearly the potential overlap and reinforcement between party and nonparty layers of the public sphere under electoral authoritarianism. In Malaysia, for instance, opposition parties glean resources and supporters by allying with CSOs and, lacking formal policy influence, may engage in very similar sorts of issue advocacy and welfare provision to these partners. In Singapore, in contrast, formal rules and informal norms limit not only the density and vibrancy of civil society overall, but also the extent to which it overlaps with political parties. Isolating opposition parties weakens them by removing potential sources of funds, volunteers, and ideas, and making it harder for voters to discern who or what those parties represent. Teasing apart this dimension helps to explain not just why the PAP's control is more nearly hegemonic than UMNO's, but also why opposition parties in Singapore offer more anemic alternatives to electoral-authoritarian governance than do their counterparts in Malaysia.

Explaining Electoral-Authoritarian Persistence

A second, connected key analytical contribution of the book is to offer new insight into what makes electoral-authoritarian regimes durable—and specifically, how and why they become increasingly entrenched over time. I argue for a deeper dive into electoral-authoritarian governance than is common in the literature to examine not only how dominant parties win elections (for instance, by deploying public resources, as explained in chapter 2), but also how they mold voters' expectations. Being in office and largely unchecked for an extended period allows for substantial institutional innovation, such as both Singapore's and Malaysia's restructuring of local government. Parties such as the PAP and UMNO may thus exercise dominance and acculturate citizens to an essentially illiberal, if responsive, political praxis, from the ground up. My analysis of electoral-authoritarian persistence encompasses the remaking of political culture over the long term, as citizens adopt the norms of political legitimacy and standards for accountability that dominant parties cultivate and to which opposition parties increasingly conform.

A hybrid form of government situated along a continuum between democracy and authoritarianism, electoral authoritarianism is something of a catch-all category. Such regimes, which skew the playing field to advantage incumbents through "electoral manipulation, unfair media access, abuse of state resources, and varying degrees of harassment and violence," outnumbered full democracies by the 1990s (Levitsky and Way 2010). The literature on Southeast Asia is full of both examples of and labels for these regimes. For instance, William Case distinguishes between *semidemocracies*, which curb liberal participation more than electoral contestation, and *semiauthoritarianism*, which does the converse (1996, 438, 459); Harold Crouch offers the more descriptive *repressive–responsive regime* to capture the interplay between maintaining constraints to limit the scope for opposition electoral success while meeting popular aspirations enough to generate an electoral mandate (Crouch 1996). I favor the term *electoral authoritarian* here not to convey a normative judgment, but to align discussions of the region more closely with the wider disciplinary literature. That literature distinguishes between *competitive* and *hegemonic* variants as reasonably stable electoral-authoritarian subtypes, differentiated by the severity of challenge to, and vulnerability of, the government in power. Malaysia falls within the *competitive* category, in which challengers embrace elections as the path to power, even though incumbents' machinations leave them at a significant electoral disadvantage. Singapore fits among *hegemonic* cases, defined by greater controls on opposition groups and legal and institutional obstacles to opposition parties' contestation (Diamond 2002, 25; Howard and Roessler 2006, 366–67; Levitsky and Way 2010, 5).[17]

The difference these categorizations suggest relates not only to elections, but also to a deep-seated political-cultural orientation. Notions of political legitimacy, or popular acknowledgement of the right to rule and uncoerced compliance with that leadership, offer important indicators for that position. Even nondemocratic regimes may enjoy high levels of political legitimacy, but the bases for that assessment vary, from Weber's classic triptych of tradition, charisma, and legality to normative goals and economic performance. The pattern of legitimation "implies the basic organization of the political regime," as it reveals what claim elites make that is credible enough to ensure stability (Kailitz 2013, 40–41). At the micro level, below that of the regime as a whole, we can understand political legitimacy in terms of accountability: the standards to which voters hold politicians. I argue that a key way electoral-authoritarian regimes entrench themselves is by their leaders' acclimating voters to particular bases for accountability and, hence, political legitimacy. Electoral-authoritarian regimes cannot resort readily to coercion, as they face a real, if deflated, challenge at the polls. But over time, the dominant party may adjust the primary (never the sole) basis on which their candidates win—for instance, for Singapore's PAP, from anticolonial social-democratic ideology to municipal services—moving the bar for challengers and altering the normative backdrop to political contests.

Yet illiberalism complicates our assessment. Because dominant-party leaders have the option of coercion, they do not require voluntary compliance, even if they prefer it; the fact of the party's election does not necessarily mean it commands legitimacy. Nor can observers readily measure legitimacy, because citizens may prioritize different premises or assess different segments of the regime differently. Performance legitimacy at the subnational level, for instance, may either compensate for or filter up to bolster less secure normative legitimacy at the national level. Furthermore, curbs on civil society and media limit the circulation of negative evaluations. The difficulty of interpreting the depth and voluntarism of citizens' acquiescence nudges observers back to the legibility of elections as a measure of support for the regime, however unreliable an indicator.

Moreover, as we see in Malaysia and Singapore in the chapters to come, opposition parties gradually adapt themselves to the standards dominant parties set. What gives rise to a dominant-party system in the first place may be a "first-mover advantage" that allows the initial winning party to shape the rules under which they contest thereafter, yielding an asymmetry in partisan advantage that breaks down only incrementally (Templeman 2012). Indeed, as Davidson and Mobrand note, rule making is as much an issue as rule breaking among incumbent political elites, including efforts at "masking of their own malfeasance through incessant tinkering with the electoral architecture" (2017, 69–70). That power imbalance leaves nondominant parties limited ability to set the terms on which voters assess them—though they may try to sway voters' preferences toward normative premises (for instance, Islamism), leaders' personal charisma, or other grounds on which they outperform the incumbent. Yet as the party with a record, recognition, and resources, as well as the ability to tweak the rules, the dominant party in a longtime hybrid system retains the upper hand in shaping to what voters hold their representatives accountable. And even if voters do deem an opposition party more legitimate than the incumbent party, if the premise for that assessment is orthogonal or antithetical to the legal-rational standard we expect in democracies, electoral turnover need not indicate that citizens want a change in governance, beyond a new slate of leaders. Hence my concern for the extent to which long-term acculturation to electoral-authoritarian governance embeds this mode, not just institutionally, but also culturally.

Why Malaysia and Singapore?

Malaysia and Singapore present a particularly revealing comparison. Theirs are the only two electoral-authoritarian regimes currently in that category that have been so classified since the 1950s (though Malaysia may now be leaving the fold). Mexico's PRI endured longer as a dominant party—it held the presidency from 1929 to 2000 and a majority in Congress until 1997—but Malaysia and Singapore emerged directly from independence, which came long after Mexico's, to single-party dominance. That persistence means these two polities have ridden out subsequent waves of democratization, transnational financial downturns, and other exogenous shocks. Both countries have long-standing as well as newer opposition parties, within fairly well institutionalized party systems (Tan 2013; Weiss 2015)—in fact, these polities stand out in the region for their strong-party systems, whereas those of more politically liberal Indonesia and the Philippines (and pre-coup Thailand) are notably inchoate (Hicken 2006, 43–44). Their similarly robust partisan politician-voter linkages stand in contrast to more rudimentary and fragmented forms in these other states, yet the divergent specific attributes we find in Malaysia and Singapore offer analytical grist.

The states' intertwined roots suggest or rule out a range of potential explanations for current similarities and differences. Governed via a set of British colonial arrangements that overlapped current national boundaries, Malaya and Singapore merged briefly after independence, before separating permanently in 1965. Although the texture of colonial rule differed between Singapore and most of peninsular Malaya (excluding urban Penang and Malacca), British tutelage and other legacies were not radically different, and both states gained independence with Westminster-style parliaments and essentially liberal constitutions. Both states, too, faced cognate early threats, particularly communism and an insurgent left, on the one hand, and persistent, episodically flaring ethnic tensions, on the other.

While both states settled fairly quickly into electoral authoritarianism, their features differ notably; this comparison aims to capture not just why both regimes could remain so long emplaced, but why similar origins have produced divergent patterns. First, more so than Singapore, Malaysian opposition parties have consistently contested elections; Singapore's PAP is more nearly hegemonic. Singapore's share of opposition seats in parliament is lower, civil society poses less of a political challenge or partisan resource, and opposition parties offer less ideological challenge to the dominant party than in Malaysia. Elites in Singapore also remain more unified and cohesive than in Malaysia, limiting alternative ideas' or actors' ability to secure footholds (Abdullah 2016, 525–26). Yet still in Malaysia, for the opposition to win power required not only the breakdown of the BN, but also the incremental buildup of what had been weak and niche-oriented opposition alternatives.

Second, the character of dominant parties in each state is different, even if both parties have presented themselves ideologically as "the embodiment of the nation" to shape citizens' political identities and interests (Jesudason 1999, 134). British authorities ensured initial political parties in both Malaya and Singapore developed, had standing, and were fairly well institutionalized before they introduced fully elected legislatures or made serious efforts to socialize the masses toward electoral politics. They actively incorporated their preferred parties into preindependence governance. These cognate efforts, by the same colonial power, yielded different outcomes. Singapore's PAP—which the British did not initially favor, given its early radical-left leanings—is a cadre party[18] with tight top-down control over recruitment, minimal internal pluralism, and corporatist, nonethnic ties to the voting public. UMNO, which the British did favor, is an ethnicity-based mass party, with a broad membership and connections to society across classes and communities (Jesudason 1999, 128–29). British officials anticipated communal politics and worried about safeguarding minority rights in both states,[19] but they addressed that likelihood differently. In Singapore, electoral institutions, including compulsory voting, aimed to boost representation of underrepresented communities; in Malaya, the British encouraged a less formal solution, by which UMNO allied with Chinese and Indian communal partners in a multiracial coalition. (Financial exigency played a supporting role—UMNO was destitute as inaugural elections loomed in the early 1950s, with limited fundraising prospects; the Malayan Chinese Association proffered a financial lifeline.)

Third, civil society remains positioned differently vis-à-vis political parties in these two states. In both, key sectors, as organized in associations, held seats in nominated preindependence governing institutions. Chambers of commerce, for instance, were entitled to representation, joining party-based and specifically communal interests. As such, these associations developed not only a vested interest in governance, but a sense of a rightful place in that process. Malaysian parties, both government and opposition, retained links with such organizations, even as the latter's relative coherence or ability to deliver a bloc vote diminished. In Singapore, the PAP drew a sharper line between party and nonparty organizations, forbidding overlap—albeit exempting its own People's Association grassroots network. These points of difference between Singapore and Malaysia shape not just the conduct of campaigns and elections, but the dominant party's relative ability to mold political norms, expectations, and common praxis.

What Reform Requires

Given this complex, ever-evolving mix of formal institutions and policies, informal institutions and norms, and individual-level linkages, what would it take to seriously transform these regimes? However structurally distinct Malaysia and Singapore are, the prospect of renovating both the institutional framework and the premises for governing is similarly daunting in either state; the long history of electoral authoritarianism in both has changed the nature of politics through interventions in national policies, the structure of local governance, and the nature of linkages between politicians and voters. An opposition party's winning an election, as Malaysia's Pakatan Harapan (Alliance of Hope) coalition did in 2018, would likely be a prerequisite for that metamorphosis (though it is hypothetically plausible that a dominant party could itself initiate the process), but it is only the opening volley, given the deep entrenchment of electoral-authoritarian governance. The *duration* of hybridity matters: what has changed over time, and would need to shift again, is not only structure, but also acculturation to a mode of doing politics.

Most important, and driving voters' expectations and assessments: in both Malaysia and Singapore, clientelism has become embedded in and integral to legislative office (cf. Lindberg 2010, 136); together with machine politics, these linkages have served to suppress class consciousness and ideology (cf. Bosco 1992, 179). Clientelist, machine-oriented politics devalues programmatic parties, or those for which "well-structured and stable ideological commitments" undergird links with constituents, interparty competition, and policymaking (Luna, Rosenblatt, and Toro 2014, 1). A clientelist rather than programmatic orientation precludes responsible party government, in which parties aggregate and express, and citizens vote based on, substantive policy and ideological preferences—whether understood in terms of competing mandates, such that parties differentiate themselves in terms of constituents' preferences, or "accountability representation," in which voters retrospectively assess whether an incumbent party has acted in their interests (Luna, Rosenblatt, and Toro 2014, 2–4). And clientelist linkages are asymmetric and limiting, encouraging constituents to vote per what they have personally experienced or can reasonably expect, rather than on abstract ideals or amorphous promises. In these terms, clientelist politics becomes "the functional equivalent of the welfare state, appeasing the have-nots to abide by political orders that tremendously advantage the haves" (Kitschelt 2000, 872).

Yet this pattern has an upside: it entails a form of responsiveness and is mutually beneficial and voluntary, and voters are not mere pawns. Moreover, the social welfare implications of clientelist patterns should be compared not just against those of programmatic systems, but also more predatory ones: clientelism centers around and facilitates divvying up and distributing national public goods, even if with suboptimal efficiency (Hicken 2011, 302). Still, regardless of whether the interplay of formal and informal rules grants clients additional sanctions to deploy—not just defecting at the polls, but more "everyday tools" of embarrassment and social demotion of known patrons (Lindberg 2010, 136)—such empowerment is shallow and overwhelmingly reactive. And the accountability relationship may be reversed: politicians may hold voters liable for their behavior, rather than vice-versa; voters effectively trade political rights for distributive benefits (Stokes 2005, 316).

On balance, the implications of the entrenchment of nonideological, substantially clientelist, machine politics are suboptimal. Such entrenchment impedes real pursuit of new ideas or policy objectives by aligning voters' and politicians' interests in purposefully narrow terms. It perpetuates piecemeal and likely inefficient allocation of resources, from national policy initiatives to the grassroots level. It assumes that many or most voters should expect little from state policies, and thus not evaluate candidates in programmatic terms. And it may not only favor candidates with the status and wealth needed to establish a reputation as reliable and generous, but even more clearly, keep the advantage with the incumbent, dominant party that crafted this state of play in the first place. At the same time, the transactional premise this pattern entrenches encourages or requires favorable performance: politicians have to earn their support, through painstaking effort among at least enough voters or population segments to deliver a win. Meanwhile, these patterns become ingrained over time, to the extent that challengers are pressed to mimic the party and personal strategies of their rivals. That reinforcement, however instrumental or grudging, keeps genuine regime change elusive, even once a dominant party finally falls.

REGIMES AND RESILIENCE RECONCEPTUALIZED

In this book, I argue that the durability of electoral authoritarianism rests not just on one party's winning elections, but on that party's using the opportunity those successive victories provide to reshape the political landscape, institutionally as well as culturally. Macrolevel policy enactments build loyalty but also change citizens' incentives and approach to political legitimacy. At the subnational level, dominant parties magnify their own importance and opposition parties cultivate niches through partisan machines they deploy not just for elections, but also for tailored, ongoing service provision and outreach. And even in a strong-party framework, politicians foster a personal vote—simultaneously bolstering their party's machine—by maintaining clientelist linkages with constituents. Much of the prevailing literature focuses on dimensions that also matter but that present a different logic, oriented more around elections themselves as targets of manipulation and as indicators for regime classification.

My approach challenges and supplements the prevailing literature in four primary, interlinked ways: in reassessing the salience of electoral outcomes as markers of regime type, in taking electoral-authoritarian parties more seriously as institutions, in offering distinct reasons and ways electoral-authoritarian regimes endure or transform, and in adding nuance, and perhaps a redemptive cast, to our understanding of clientelism and its workings, including through its effects on political culture. The first of these contributions qualifies the others: most of the literature on classifying regimes and assessing transitions emphasizes the national level, and specifically the possibility or incidence of electoral turnover; my goal in drawing attention to parties, other indicators for regime status, and clientelism is to confirm the real muddiness of the too-stark conventional picture. I agree that a change of government is almost certainly important to regime shift—my goal is to enhance and nuance, not refute, extant excellent analyses of what makes such an election outcome likely. Yet that outcome is, at best, a necessary but not sufficient condition for more meaningful regime change. In Malaysia, we now have a change of government without yet a change of regime; in Singapore, we have yet to see either. As the chapters to come make clear, the latter shift will likely lag the former, for so long as it takes voters' preferences and politicians' praxis to adapt to new national leadership, formal institutions, and informal incentives.

The Relative Centrality of Elections

A key theoretical aim of this work is to decenter elections in the study of regimes and transitions; I deem elections part of, but not necessarily defining for, the regime. As noted in chapter 1, the literature on electoral authoritarianism tends to fetishize elections, especially at the national level. That emphasis overshadows attention to other institutions that matter as least as much to governance (e.g., Barkan 2008, 124, on legislatures). Existing scholarship offers compelling reasons elections merit attention but also hints at the risks of reading too much into the fact of competitive elections, if the goal is to understand governance more broadly.

The quality of elections clearly matters to the incentives driving politicians and parties, voters' expectations of accountability, and patterns of policymaking. In illiberal states that hold elections—that is, under electoral authoritarianism— these exercises serve multiple purposes. They may trigger political liberalization, offer "safety valves" to disarm societal grievances and monitor popular support, broadcast and consolidate incumbent elites' power, offer opportunities to distribute patronage and positions, force opponents to choose between system-legitimating participation or self-sidelining boycott, or prompt a turn toward authoritarianism (Brownlee 2007, 8; Schedler 2010, 1; Donno 2013, 703–5; Seeberg 2014, 1266–67). State capacity mediates elections' effects: high-capacity states tend to experience elections as more stabilizing than do their low-capacity counterparts, which may need to resort to fraud or coercion to maintain control (Croissant and Hellmann 2017). But given the advantage a ruling party in an electoral-authoritarian system enjoys over rule setting, regulations, and resources, as well as recourse to repressive fixes (in ways Schedler 2002 enumerates), opposition parties rarely win. Even if viewed, appropriately, "as symptoms, not causes, of regime change or regime durability" (Brownlee 2007, 9–10), lost elections do signal weakened ruling parties and/or strengthened opponents.

That pattern has rendered electoral turnover an attractive indicator among scholars of regime transitions. Most have come to take the threshold for when a polity has transitioned from the authoritarian to the democratic side of the regime continuum as when it meets Freedom House (or cognate) criteria of supporting a competitive, multiparty system, with universal adult suffrage, for regular, free, fair elections in which major parties have access to the public through media and open campaigns (Donno 2013, 708). Turnover by election is less part of a democratization process, in this reading, than the best signal that transition has happened (Lindberg 2009, 4–5). Indeed, some work uses *democracy* simply as shorthand for an authoritarian government's losing an election and accepting the result, rendering democracy effectively a residual category to authoritarianism (e.g., Magaloni 2010). Other work focuses on why a dominant party wins or loses but stops short of asking what happens next—whether the new ruling party, for instance, simply mimics its predecessor or governs differently (e.g., Greene 2010). However, elections alone cannot tell us the quality or depth of democracy or democratization, which may proceed unevenly across dimensions of governance (Morlino, Dressel, and Pelizzo 2011, 493–94), perversely empower old-guard elites or would-be autocrats rather than reformers (Aspinall 2010; Hadiz 2003; Kuhonta 2008), or fail to reconcile new democratic institutions with antidemocratic elements (Winichakul 2008).

My account does not ignore elections, but it keeps them in context. Elections are relevant to politicians and citizens, both for signaling a polity open to new interests, actors, and perhaps rules, and to shake up the structure of political opportunities facing reformers. These contests also reveal and permit introduction of curbs on civil liberties—further hallmarks of electoral authoritarianism—that limit the flow of information and exercise of association and voice essential to meaningful participation in elections and to civic life in general. When parties secure electoral dominance by winning repeated elections, they open the door to what du Toit and de Jager term "constitutional dominance" and "hegemonic dominance" (2014, 104–9). They define these conditions to mean, respectively, that parties can rewrite or selectively retain constitutional rules to strengthen their own position and disadvantage challengers, or control the state bureaucracy and authority to dictate national historical narratives, ideology, and symbols.

However, elections are only part of what makes a regime. Although highly significant for how they structure the system—particularly in fostering parties and determining access to office—elections tell us little about either the day-to-day nature of governance or how much political culture and citizens' expectations might constrain even a successful challenger. A deeper understanding of how electoral authoritarianism works requires attention to how it is enacted on the ground. This focus means paying attention to what the incumbent government does to build support without requiring coercion: how politicians organize themselves, curry loyalty, and preempt or undercut challenges before they become electoral threats.

Parties under Electoral Authoritarianism

The core actor in elections and governing alike is, effectively, the party. Moreover, what most clearly differentiates electoral authoritarianism from flat-out autocracy is the extent to which opposition to that government likewise organizes at least substantially in parties, which compete in elections. Yet scholars tend to read parties under electoral-authoritarian regimes largely as amorphous entities that exercise or resist dominance—in Cheeseman and Hinfelaar's words, "as being little more than the playthings of their leaders, on the one hand, and a sad reflection of the societies which give rise to them on the other" (2009, 52). Electoral-authoritarian parties warrant closer study. They cannot function quite as classic theories of parties would have us believe—as more than factional parts of a pluralistic whole and as channels for representation and expression of popular interests (Sartori 1976, 25–26). Regardless, parties still substantially structure and orient political participation even beyond electoral contestation and may themselves participate in governance.

A key starting point for analysis is how parties organize themselves and, in so doing, configure competition and integrate citizens into formal politics. Political parties aspire to the three "faces" V. O. Key (1964) detailed: parties-in-the-electorate, or members and activists who educate, socialize, and mobilize voters; parties-in-government, or elected officials who create majorities, enact policies, organize government and opposition, and foster stability and accountability; and parties-as-organizations that recruit and train leaders, articulate platforms, and aggregate interests. Under electoral authoritarianism, however, opposition parties lack opportunities to be parties-in-government, which restrains the profile they may develop. Although opposition parties may profit from negative retrospective assessments of the dominant party, to win more votes, they must usually also offer grounds for a positive prospective evaluation of themselves. This requirement, suggests Kenneth Greene, helps explain the delay in dissatisfied Mexican and Taiwanese voters' shifting their support from the dominant Institutional Revolutionary Party (PRI) and Kuomintang (KMT), respectively (2007, 19–21). Merely being unhappy with the dominant party is insufficient impetus. We can get a rough sense of the extent and type of regime change an electoral upset might facilitate by examining these proactive proposals to see if opposition parties are promising a new mode of governance or mere policy tweaks.

These faces are not highly malleable, however; institutional rules and sticky history limit the scope of institutional innovation. For example, Japan's Liberal Democratic Party (LDP), in office for all but ten months between 1955 and 2009, retained mobilizing, governing, and organizational structures that appeared geared to competition under single nontransferable vote (SNTV) rules[1] for fifteen years after Japan's shift to mixed-member majoritarian (MMM) voting in 1994 (Krauss and Pekkanen 2011, 6–7).[2] We cannot expect parties that develop under electoral authoritarianism to alter swiftly their orientation toward the electorate, approach to governing, or organizational form, even if the rules under which they operate change. To understand why a party system has the form it does thus requires a historical approach, to take into account path dependency as parties start off poorly or well, and the sequencing of decisions on party structure and system rules (Krauss and Pekkanen 2011, 9–13). The next four chapters thus track the formation of dominant and opposition parties and alterations in their efforts at and orientation toward elections, governing, and organizational maintenance to understand their role in reinforcing, maintaining, or subverting electoral authoritarianism.

When Electoral-Authoritarian Regimes Thrive or Fail

That same historical gaze, cast more broadly, offers insight into why a given regime endures or declines. Here the extant literature has made more headway, though I suggest conventional explanations miss key strategies, including those more pertinent to everyday praxis than elections per se. The dominant explanations for regime persistence focus on opposition disorganization or weakness and incumbent performance; those for regime failure focus also on the latter, as well as social cleavages and catalysts. I take these insights as useful starting points, but situate them in the larger context not just of winning elections, but also of policy approaches, governance, and politician-voter linkages to see both how dominant parties perpetuate their status and how challengers vie to improve theirs.

Opposition Weakness and Incumbent Advantage

While the extant literature does consider opposition parties, it is mostly in terms of their losing elections for failing to coordinate; my analysis supplements this perspective by exploring how these challengers adapt otherwise to electoral authoritarianism. The coordination problems opposition parties face at elections, however, are emblematic of their limited space for innovation at any point in the electoral cycle. Complicating collaboration may be ethnic cleavages, policy differences, personal rivalries, and the incentives electoral rules create (Magaloni 2006, 24–25).

Where dominant parties coopt the middle ground, as is commonly the case, challengers represent niche fragments; to pose an electoral threat, those segments must join forces. Indeed, middle-of-the road moderates' jumping toward the opposition may signal dominant-party decline (Greene 2007, 5–6). (On the plus side, parties' tendency toward niches facilitates seat distribution, assuming mutually exclusive catchments.) Preelection coalitions signal that the opposition vote will not be split, lending confidence that a vote for one of those parties will not simply help the incumbent (Gandhi and Reuter 2013, 138). Yet even where policy platforms are less decisive than identity or other appeals, coalition formation reflects parties' wish both for election and to advance a policy agenda (Wahman 2011, 643). For instance, in Malaysia, opposition coordination has been more likely when winning seems plausible, giving impetus to efforts to shift or surmount cleavages by finding some workable common-denominator platform; the fact that victory has been patently unlikely in Singapore since the 1960s (for reasons clarified in chapters 4 and 6) helps to explain opposition parties' endemic failure to coalesce.

It is because coordination is so tricky that the odds of what Howard and Roessler call a "liberalizing electoral outcome" increase more dramatically with formation of an opposition coalition than from any other factor (2006, 375–76). To overcome a dominant party's advantages, opposition leaders need to make strategic choices and ensure their parties and supporters remain united and resilient. As a stopgap measure, coordination under a "strategic coalition," short of full merger or agreement on leaders, may enable electoral victory, siphoning votes away from the incumbent regime by reducing its ability to coerce support through repression or woo it with patronage or divide-and-rule tactics and encouraging voters to see the opposition as a potential governing coalition (Howard and Roessler 2006, 370–71). However, such an instrumental pact leaves significant, stable change—"liberalization" beyond the fact of electoral turnover—dubious; merely being in office instead of on the sidelines does not itself resolve ideological, personalistic, or policy disagreements.

Indeed, political parties may not develop in such a way that coalition is feasible or reasonable. The cleavage structure in society, and which of these divisions coalesce as parties, may differ dramatically across time and space. Parties' scope for reinvention diminishes over time, too, as they have histories known to voters (Lipset and Rokkan 1967, 2). Notwithstanding the benefits of coordination, "the intensity of inherited hostilities and the openness of communications across the cleavage lines will decide whether mergers or alliances are actually workable"; if cleavages cut deep, trust among leaders and trust in fair representation and policy influence postelection may be in too short supply (Lipset and Rokkan 1967, 32). Electoral-authoritarian regimes intensify those difficulties by limiting parties' ability to communicate with counterparts or voters. We might expect that communications debility to ease over time, though, facilitating coordination, as reiterated elections themselves provide parties and voters with "informational cues" (LeBas 2011, 31). As such, it stands to reason that opposition coalitions might be easier to foster and promote under a long-standing electoral-authoritarian regime than earlier in the game.

But not always. Mexican opposition parties formed in opposition to the already long-standing, centrist PRI failed to coordinate in the 1980s, explains Greene: They occupied polarized, incongruent positions. The right-wing National Action Party (PAN) catered to the middle- and upper-class, with roots in Catholic social conservatism and classical economic liberalism; the left-wing Party of the Democratic Revolution (PRD) had its roots in communist/socialist predecessors, urban-poor movements, and the intelligentsia (2007, 9, 76–77). It was only as privatization and belt tightening sharply limited the PRI's recourse to patronage by the mid-1990s and new oversight mechanisms made competition more fair that voters looked seriously to alternatives and opposition parties broke out of their segregated niches to court the moderate masses. Similarly, in Japan, the issue of electoral rules drove previously intractably disparate opposition parties to unite against the LDP in 1993, under the leadership of two ex-LDP politicians. Their success allowed Japan finally to achieve electoral reform,[3] notwithstanding the LDP's quick return to power, and positioned the briefly empowered Democratic Party of Japan (DPJ) as a leading challenger (Krauss and Pekkanen 2011, 22, 25).

Even as a common opponent may nudge opposition parties into alignment, it may also encourage them to mimic that rival. The policy divide between government and opposition may already be less than that among marginalized opposition parties (Wahman 2011). A long-term, catch-all dominant party, coupled with constraints on political discourse and association, tends to sideline issue-based mobilization. If voters align with that dominant party based on expectations or receipt of patronage, for instance, opposition parties may see their best strategy as competing on those same lines—not asking voters to choose ideological commitment over material self-interest. Hence, over time, dominant parties' own approaches to cultivating legitimacy and support crowd out other alternatives. Even if parties' overarching messages differ, there are likely to be similar efforts in practice, including at the crucial level of politician-voter linkages. That convergence renders challengers less apt even to promise radical regime change, let alone pursue it if elected, among voters conditioned to support them as better guarantors of what the dominant party had previously provided. Hence, however difficult electoral turnover is to achieve, it may leave core aspects of the regime intact, at least until new leaders have been able to resocialize voters to hold them accountable to different standards.

Incumbent Performance: Works Both Ways

Indeed, building support through material patronage is dominant parties' default path, though never their sole strategy. A strong record of economic and security performance, particularly reinforced by patronage that shares out windfall resources, increases the chances of uncoerced support for an incumbent government—but also raises expectations. Performance legitimacy offers a material basis of support for regimes otherwise lacking in "moral authority" (Alagappa 1995, 22–23). Even citizens aware of, and perturbed by, illiberal features of their regime will often still back a government that delivers. Performance legitimacy is the criterion most clearly associated with the literature on authoritarian persistence in Asian developmental states of the 1970s–1980s through the late 1990s, with or without elections, but nearly all nondemocratic governments stress this dimension (von Soest and Grauvogel 2017).

Relying for support on macroeconomic indicators, patronage distribution, or both leaves governments vulnerable to economic downturns or resource constraints, however; being unable to measure up to past standards may trigger disillusionment or unhappiness among voters and erstwhile elite allies. The proposed mechanisms behind how economic decline yields regime breakdown vary, and plenty of economic crises do not result in regime upset, if challengers either cannot or choose not to take advantage of such shocks (Lust-Okar 2005, 2–4). Regardless, disruption in patronage may not just erode performance legitimacy, but also divide authoritarian elites and help to tilt the playing field to advantage the incumbent less, whatever other factors are simultaneously at play (Howard and Roessler 2006, 372–3, Haggard and Kaufman 1995). Examples include the speedy collapse of Indonesia's New Order regime once the 1997 Asian Financial Crisis deprived Suharto of capital to dispense as patronage to voters or wavering elites (Mietzner 2017, 92–93), or of Mexico's PRI once privatization and fiscal reforms cut the party's access to spoils for patronage jobs, collective benefits, and other spending after decades of splashing out on public goods (Greene 2010, 823–26). Pursuing economic globalization, meanwhile, limited the PRI's recourse to coercion in the 1990s, lest evident repression spook American or other Western trade partners (Levitsky and Way 2010). Depending on performance legitimacy, too, may prompt shortsighted policies for the sake of winning elections; "election budgets" feature across electoral regimes, but may be especially pivotal to incumbents without other strong sources of legitimacy.

Alternatively, economic frailty or transformation might reconfigure the salience of patronage by making its distribution more politically fraught. Popular perceptions that elites are protecting themselves in a recession and leaving the masses to suffer have been especially destabilizing to electoral-authoritarian regimes in Southeast Asia, including igniting mass protests (Case 2005, 224). Relative deprivation and distributional conflicts add theoretical nuance: those groups disadvantaged under conditions of inequality have incentive to press for political change, yet if disparities are wide, elites have especial cause to resist and repress those challenges; the causal relationship between inequality and transitions to (or reversions from) democracy is complex (Haggard and Kaufman 2012, 495). These considerations draw our attention to the policy decisions that shape efforts to develop and assess performance legitimacy throughout the electoral cycle.

Overarching economic policy frameworks, then, matter not just for how they affect growth and development, but also for how they define "success" (that is, performance legitimacy) and for the patronage resources they provide or withhold. Greene (2007, 33–34), for instance, highlights the distinction between state-led and private sector–led strategies: Greater state control over the economy gives an incumbent dominant party cash and bureaucratic jobs to distribute. Privatization renders the marketplace for votes more fair, enabling opposition parties to expand—even if what allows them to do so is drawing on different resources to mimic their opponent's patronage approach. Ethan Scheiner's explanation for the persistently unpopular LDP's endurance in Japan, despite free and fair elections, echoes Greene's logic in key respects. Combined clientelism and fiscal centralization leave each level of government reliant on the good graces of the center. That pattern makes it harder for opposition candidates to win even locally and gain experience and name recognition, while opposition parties struggle to articulate compelling goals, attract promising candidates, or garner donations to offset their resource disadvantage (2006, 2–4, 8). The centrality of patronage has thus aligned the interests of LDP politicians and voters and of both with a strong state sector. When the DPJ came briefly to power in 2009, it announced plans to reduce state spending, as on large-scale public works projects that embodied the connection between development strategy and clientelist electoral outreach—policies that had been mutually beneficial to national and LDP fortunes, and hence less controversial, in the growth years from 1955 until the economic bubble burst in 1990 (Pempel 2010, 229, 232–33). The party failed, however, to implement a substantially innovative policy agenda before being voted out in 2012 (Lipscy and Scheiner 2012, 313).

While constraints on supply are the most obvious mechanism for the decline of patronage advantage, a drop in demand may have the same effect. It is in this regard that opposition parties stand their best chance of whittling down the predominance of performance legitimacy in favor of normative or other premises on which they themselves fare better. India offers an example. In the late 1960s through early 1970s, the Congress Party government created a large pool of public resources to channel to voters and party supporters: it nationalized banks and insurance funds and introduced an array of inefficient but politically useful antipoverty programs. Other parties established cognate party-linked schemes at the state level. Although federal- and state-level politicians continue to lure votes with antipoverty schemes and by facilitating access to still largely discretionary public services, changing economic aspirations and capacities since the 1990s have weakened voters' reliance on patrons or parties (Wilkinson 2014, 269–72). Secular restructuring, not political strategy, is elevating support for programmatic policies and diminishing the salience of patronage. Middle-class voters can opt out of patronage networks and protest their shortcomings (even if the poor still have cause to prefer immediate, targeted handouts); a rising, educated middle class has greater access to information on the extent and negative effects of corruption and the benefits of reform; and these demands are simply increasingly difficult to afford, especially amid budget deficits (Wilkinson 2014, 274–76; 2007, 112). However, political participation and democratic buy-in may assume new ethnic and class dimensions, instead. Indeed, where the private sector is larger in India, lessening access to patronage resources, we do see parties' increasing recourse to an ideological politics of ethnic polarization (Chandra 2014, 169–70). A shift away from (patronage-supported) performance legitimacy does not in itself ensure emplacement of a specifically "liberal" substitute.

Social Cleavages and Catalysts for Incumbent Decline

Examining other common explanations for why dominant parties lose elections reiterates the importance of setting a new bar: changing how voters assess political legitimacy. Dominant parties structure the polity to favor themselves, which means privileging their own mode of politics. The norm is that voters become socialized toward that mode, hence the relevance of very local regime-citizen interactions. Dominant parties cannot anticipate or forestall all shifts, however. In choosing to prioritize one premise (e.g., economic performance), they deemphasize others. A range of gradually developing or sudden spurs can magnify some other dimension, benefiting opposition parties that contest on that premise and leaving the dominant party scrambling. The odds of some such recalibrations grow slimmer if opposition parties have adapted themselves to the same praxis as the incumbent over time—for instance, cultivating clientelistic linkages of their own, as necessary to compete. And some catalysts, such as an exogenous geopolitical change, may leave existing opposition parties as much in the lurch as dominant parties, benefiting whichever is more nimble in adapting.

One such change is movement along a key cleavage or zero-sum issue. Taiwan offers an exemplary case. An identity cleavage has always been apparent there, but both population proportions and partisan alternatives have changed since a dominant-party electoral regime replaced martial law in 1987.[4] That cleavage subsumes language, dividing mainlanders from "native" Taiwanese; nationalism, as feeling part of a Chinese or Taiwanese nation; and a policy question of whether Taiwan should move toward formal independence or reunification (Templeman 2012, 233–35). Having gained increasing salience since the mid-1970s, the identity question has come to subsume other political cleavages in Taiwan, demarcating camps among all significant parties (Templeman 2012, 38, 240–44). Initially broader-based, the opposition Democratic Progressive Party (DPP) came to emphasize ethnic politics and Taiwan's orientation toward China through the 1990s, energizing its core of proindependence native Taiwanese and alienating prodemocracy mainlanders and moderates. The dominant, basically centrist KMT also faced mainlander defections as it tried to play both sides. DPP leaders won local elections in the 1990s, securing experience and resources, then in 2000, nabbed the presidency (Templeman 2012, 246–63, 274). A declining KMT resource advantage played a role, too—given privatization and increasing pressure to be economically efficient for a globalized market in the 1990s, combined with candidate-centered SNTV electoral rules that amplified the effect of even slight decreases in patronage for a personal vote—as did embarrassing scandals and elite rivalries. However, the campaign really centered around the unification/independence cleavage (Greene 2007, 264–68; Templeman 2012, 222–27, 232–33, 280, 286–87). In this case, then, an opposition party was able to capitalize on its difference from the dominant party, given a shift among the electorate, rather than conform to the KMT model.

Abrupt or one-time catalysts—economic crisis, succession crisis, and so on—pose a different sort of opportunity for dominant-party challengers. While opposition parties may have more incentive than incumbents to adapt quickly and less baggage to stow, they may not be able quickly and credibly to reposition themselves. Particularly if opposition parties have come to focus more on building local support than proposing distinct national platforms, they may be unconvincing as new-model alternatives. Regardless, these moments may offer a chance for leadership change, even if the regime to follow remains uncertain.

For instance, the death or departure of a leader may enfeeble a dominant party, particularly if the leader is pushed out for weakness or an intended successor does not inherit the incumbent's personal base (Howard and Roessler 2006, 372). In Kenya, for instance, because term limits barred incumbent president Daniel Arap Moi from contesting the 2002 elections, opposition parliamentarians planned proactively to avoid splitting the opposition vote. (It helped that Moi's Kenya African National Union party also splintered.) With its share of the popular vote about the same as in previous elections but no longer divided, the opposition coalition won, launching a process of political liberalization. (Howard and Roessler 2006, 377–80). More broadly, such "open seat" elections are more likely to lead to a turnover in power than when an incumbent stands—the search for a successor may divide the party, a new contender may lack a record, or a lame-duck outgoing president may decide to allow a clean election—especially when combined with an economic slump, scandal, or other catalyst (Cheeseman 2010, 141–43). Again, though, an opportunistic electoral pact, especially formed quickly when opportunity arises, may not indicate sufficient opposition unity for significant change in aspects of the regime beyond its slate of leaders.

My analysis takes these factors common in the literature—opposition weakness and disunity, ebbs and flows of performance legitimacy, unsettling cleavage shifts and catalysts—as starting points. I agree that these factors tend to be behind dominant-party wins and losses. The weakness of this literature is in its too seldom looking beyond that point to see what change a loss ushers in or what praxis remains constant under new management. Having been shut out of national policymaking and lacking access to public resources, for instance, opposition parties may have come to focus more on countering dominant-party patronage with their own (largely affective) clientelism—meaning what support they command may not be based on macrolevel plans, but on microlevel outreach. A decline in patronage resources due to privatization or economic downturn may not change voters' expectations, but only who they think more reliable once staunched financial flows make the comparison less stark. If an invigorated social cleavage is what sinks a dominant party, the new government could simply replicate the order it replaces, to the benefit of a different segment of citizens. Nor does a national election shaken up by a succession crisis, for instance, necessarily mean subnational leadership transitions in tandem in a multitiered system. In short, these factors *are* important to a turnover in government, but not necessarily in the regime. The latter would require remaking formal and informal institutions for representation and accountability, generating adequate voluntary support to obviate coercion—most notably, change in underlying relations among parties, politicians, and voters.

Clientelism

Rather than focus on the political center as the linchpin of electoral authoritarianism, I turn toward the ground. What this regime type represents in practice is a way of satisfying popular demands enough to command loyalty at the polls and preempt destabilizing calls for democracy. Central-government constraints on civil liberties and fair elections offer the dominant regime a cushion, but cultivating positive support requires more. The party in power needs for the public to see it—and not a neutral state—as responsible for all good things, including politically targeted policies and patronage. Moreover, individual politicians benefit from building up their own base, the more readily to ride out electoral waves. On the ground, especially between elections, forms of clientelism nurture both electoral-authoritarian dominant parties and challengers, in calibrated guises. These patterns dig deep: pruning the upper branches of the system by an electoral upset may have little impact on the clientelist roots.

Understanding how clientelism functions as part of a given regime requires, first, a clear concept of what it is. While the literature is inconsistent, I take clientelism to refer to human relationships and networks: asymmetric, dyadic, mutual, usually enduring,[5] and normatively neutral rather than inherently good or bad. Political clientelism specifically contrasts with a rational, anonymous, universalist logic of bureaucracy, but may still entail complex transactions, echoing through the government hierarchy (Lemarchand and Legg 1972, 151–55). Among the material resources those networks channel is patronage, whether from public or private sources. This patronage includes both individual and collective goods and political influence; clients reciprocate with political support or loyalty, including votes. Such patronage entails, too, both carrots and sticks: its givers aim to cultivate political loyalty, not just dependence, so may exclude the disloyal from benefits (Hutchcroft 2014, 176–77; Brun 2014, 4; Magaloni 2014, 254). Distributive programs such as cash transfer schemes are ambiguous. They may be implemented universalistically or with nonclientelist political targeting, depending on state capacity, the nature of the regime, and the parties in power, but even broad-based policies, from disaster-relief to health-care services, may pass through a "clientelistic filter" or allow politicians' intervention (Brun 2014, 4–10; Lindberg 2010, 120). The result then is "morselization" of public goods, carving up and distributing them per political objectives (Cox and McCubbins 2001, 47–48), or partisanized distribution.

Both supply and demand considerations set the balance between clientelist and programmatic policies, overall and among particular communities. Parties' relative access to public funds and the state's provision of public goods help to determine the supply side: how reliant parties are or can be on access to and distribution of particularistic benefits. In a dominant-party system, this dimension is highly uneven, and ruling parties have strong incentive to make public goods at least appear tied to the party in power. A range of factors, though, encourage politicians to prioritize patronage over programmatic public goods, including political institutions and culture, partisanship and competitiveness, stage in the electoral cycle, and patterns of generating and spending revenue (Remmer 2007, 374). Parties lacking access to public resources are more likely to favor a programmatic strategy for voter mobilization (Hellman 2013, 662–63), though the evidence here suggests long-term electoral authoritarianism may temper those predilections. Meanwhile, voters develop expectations—shaped by past experience, assessments of parties, proximity to partisan networks, or relative policy distance—of the likelihood that parties will deliver benefits to them. These expectations forge the demand side and may differ from distributive *preferences*, which are more likely to reflect socioeconomic traits (Calvo and Murillo 2014, 18–21). Indeed, from a citizen's perspective, clientelist relationships may lend "calculability"; citizens may find that informal channels, including relying on known patrons and social conventions, lend greater certainty of outcomes than would recourse to formal institutions (Oakley 2018, 35–41). Given this mix of incentives, unless countries actively strive to combat clientelism, they tend to grow more deeply into it over time (Brun 2014, 12).

We can understand clientelism most usefully through three perspectives. The first concerns individual-level patron-client ties. The second is as a policy framework: a focus on particularistic rather than programmatic policies. The third is as a mechanism or structure for mobilization, particularly as embodied in political machines.

Patron-Client Ties

Patron-client relationships—informal institutions linking "two persons of unequal status, power or resources each of whom finds it useful to have as an ally someone superior or inferior to himself" (Landé 1977, xx)—are at the conceptual core of clientelism. Patrons may have numerous clients, but traditionally, most clients have a multistranded, "whole-person" relationship with only one patron, to whom they are linked pyramidally, via intermediaries or brokers (Scott 1972b, 95–96). Collective exchanges may scale up individual ties. For instance, an organization's leader may negotiate with a political party and the organization's base, brokering the exchange of members' votes (assuming some means of ensuring compliance) for group benefits (Holland and Palmer-Rubin 2015, 1195–96). The underlying economic relationship is of subordination and, potentially, exploitation—even if the relationship is materially advantageous to the client;

clients may thus be ambivalent, particularly if patrons' services are not essential or unique (Landé 1977, xx–xxvii; Scott 1972b, 100). Vote buying may likewise personalize political appeals, but even less securely. On-the-spot vote buying, absent an ongoing relationship to build a sense of moral obligation and at least conditional loyalty (plus the possibility of sanction), invites opportunistic defection (Magaloni 2014, 254–5). The uncertainties and costs of vote buying encourage candidates instead to "nurse" constituencies long term, as by sponsoring public works projects or providing jobs, to lock in a solid base of support. The result is not just better odds of securing office, but political machines (Scott 1972a, 99–101).

Despite decades' worth of definitions, the literature on patron-client relationships remains hazy. Quipped Carl Landé, surveying the lot, "One is tempted to conclude that to varying degrees in different political systems, dyadic interactions can be shown to promote, impede, or in some fashion shape almost any political process" (1983, 436). Indeed, the logic of this pattern, rooted in landlord-tenant relationships of a feudal, agrarian past, has persisted into an era of urbanization and economic transformation and is pervasive. Cognate relationships permeate such "modern" institutions as bureaucracies and parties, often with a quite instrumental premise and professionalized aspect (Landé 1983, 445; Brun 2014, 3; Machado 1974, 524–26). However less comprehensive or resilient than previously, though, these ties remain more affective than "the impersonal, contractual ties of the marketplace" (Scott 1972b, 107). Where clientelism shades into purely functional, "normal" constituency service is difficult to demarcate precisely.

The *kōenkai* system undergirding Japan's LDP exemplifies present-day, party-linked patron-client politics.[6] Kōenkai are permanent, membership-based personal support groups for specific candidates (who might have multiple, overlapping kōenkai organized by personal connection, geography, or function) and are active throughout the electoral cycle. Their activities span from political discussions to sightseeing trips, allowing politicians to connect with voters and socializing citizens into political society, but emphasize get-out-the-vote efforts as elections approach. Diet members recruit kōenkai members through personal attention and constituency service. In exchange, members vote for the candidate and mobilize others to do so. These "personal political machines" help candidates compete against members of their own and other parties, including by circumventing restrictions on campaign activities; moreover, local-level candidates' kōenkai combine to help national-level candidates, in return for reciprocal support and parliamentary access (Krauss and Pekkanen 2011, 17, 29–30, 33–39). Diet members themselves bear most of the cost of sustaining kōenkai activities, outreach, and gifts, which may run to hundreds of thousands of dollars annually, although campaign finance reforms encouraging dues collection help (Krauss and Pekkanen 2011, 42).

When kōenkai really took off, in the early 1950s, the personal vote dominated and weak electoral mobilization encouraged buying and selling of blocs of votes, coordinated by local notables or bosses. Kōenkai offered an appealing alternative, at the cost of party control and local-branch development, which still lag. That candidates with kōenkai performed better than those running just on party label discouraged aspiring politicians from investing in party strengthening when they could focus on their own base and machine, instead. The LDP helped by funneling "different flavors of pork" to its Diet members to help them distinguish themselves (Krauss and Pekkanen 2011, 31–32, 54–57, 60–67, 97–99, 276).[7] Being visible and delivering benefits still reinforce local power brokers' backing and reassure voters of a politician's ability to bring improvements (Scheiner 2007, 277–78). Although the DPJ's 2009 victory highlighted an increase in unaffiliated (especially younger, urban) voters and in the importance of both media and party labels, those LDP politicians who won still disproportionately had strong kōenkai (Krauss and Pekkanen 2011, 281–82; Lam 2011, 150–51). These support groups are not entirely anomalous; as later chapters demonstrate, Malaysia and Singapore offer close parallels.

More broadly, ongoing constituency service is a normal function for legislators anywhere, regardless of whether they actively cultivate a "patron" identity. Their efforts to provide services, material aid, and earmarked policies vary with individuals' priorities, institutional rules, and how much a marginal boost matters. While reliance on a personal rather than a party vote encourages such outreach, the correlation is imprecise. Legislators, especially backbenchers with a limited policymaking role, may gain satisfaction from service work, may see it as their best chance to build a reputation with voters and within the party (especially since constituency service reverberates up the chain also to benefit party leaders), or may deem it a core function, regardless of electoral payoff (Norris 1997, 30, 32–33; Heitshusen, Young, and Wood 2005). First-time MPs in the liberal-democratic United Kingdom, for instance, spend more time in "surgeries" (service centers) than rational calculations of payoff in votes would indicate (Norris 1997, 38–39), suggesting more relational than purely instrumental clientelist expectations. In contrast, legislators in authoritarian regimes of the Middle East have a minimal policymaking role but can pull strings to secure jobs, licenses, and more for constituents; elections there represent "competitive clientelism," with access to these resources as the prize (Lust 2009, 124). What makes such efforts patron-clientelistic is that they involve personal, mutual, long-term and not just election-focused exchange, with politicians themselves directly engaged. And as Miriam Golden notes, "voters are unlikely to be able to co-ordinate their efforts and successfully 'throw the rascals out' once an equilibrium based on the incumbency advantages offered by constituency service has fully emerged" (2003, 211).

Cues allow us to differentiate routine constituency service from more person-alized political clientelism. In Ghana, for instance, Lindberg finds the office of MP includes an expected role as "father figure," including "a moral obligation to solve problems for followers in need" and an incentive to flaunt wealth to appear more likely to deliver (2010, 125–26). However, whereas MPs feel obliged to meet nearly all requests in rural areas, where quasi-familial expectations remain rela-tively strong, they deny most in urban constituencies, where voters tend to be more instrumental in seeking benefits and less likely to reciprocate with their vote (Lindberg 2010, 127). We might consider only the former scenario to embody patron-client ties. Where the legislature has an unusually straitened policymak-ing role, as in Senegal, voters may expect more of an "advocate and intermedi-ary" role: MPs field requests for local public goods, individual assistance, and ad-ministrative intervention; cognate requests in Kenya may exceed representatives' salary (Thomas and Sissokho 2005, 99, 111). Senegalese expect legislators, qua patrons, to visit regularly to provide service and maintain support, as well as to lobby ministers for targeted public goods. Even representatives elected from a na-tional district are expected to look after their home community (Thomas and Sissokho 2005, 111–12).

Regardless, prioritizing constituency service—whether visiting the district to offer individual assistance or supporting targeted development projects—entails a tension between representation (advocating for particular concerns) and legis-lating (requiring bargaining and compromise), as well as between catering to the full nation or a small segment thereof (Barkan 2008, 126–27). Explains Golden, legislators who devote excessive resources to shepherding citizens through a bu-reaucratic morass the legislature itself created develop an interest in sustaining that bureaucratic bloat. Grateful voters reward their representative's bureaucratic navigation prowess. "Bad government" results (2003, 192). The economic out-comes of this pattern, especially when highly personalized, may be suboptimal. The particularism of patron-client ties entails inherent electoral accountability, yet individual voters have a clear incentive to remain loyal, lest they lose out if others do not also defect; the effect is to entrench incumbents and retard or dis-tort economic development strategies (Magaloni 2014, 259–60).

Still, patron-client linkages also activate affective ties. African survey data, for instance, suggest it is less aid delivered than voters' assessment of MPs' dedica-tion to the community that drives voting behavior (Young 2009). Voters under-stand that it is unlikely that an MP (or even intermediaries) could personally be-stow benefits upon more than a fraction of the constituency, and most grasp that they derive greater utility from development projects than from sporadic handouts—even if they do still request favors when opportunity arises and local public goods in the absence of national-level programs (Young 2009, 1–3, 9).[8] This emphasis on visible, ongoing commitment rather than purely transactional assessments represents a patron-client model, compatible with a measure of programmatic policies, and helps buffer against economic or other shocks.

Malaysia and Singapore demonstrate the particular value of this aspect of patron-client politics under electoral authoritarianism. Dominant-party politicians transmit public benefits directly to voters, encouraging buy-in to a party and system with which some might otherwise have qualms. However, challengers can siphon off personal support by being more useful and quasi-familial—better patrons—even absent equivalent resources.

Policy Framework

Clientelism also manifests as a policy framework, entailing particularistic and contingent rather than programmatic enactments. Understanding the balance among public policies requires attention to more than the electoral scrum, to wit, to whether the party crafting the policies developed with or without access to state resources and before or after mass mobilization into politics, and what sort of linkages with voters the party maintains, regardless of those voters' social characteristics (Shefter 1977, 405–6, 410, 415–17). In practice, this policy angle connects voters' expectations and legislators' efforts in complex ways. For instance, voter pressure for private goods may push legislators to produce collective goods that satisfy those needs more efficiently (for instance, national health insurance as an alternative to settling constituents' hospital bills), even to the point of undermining the conditions conducive to clientelism, or may encourage them to spend more time lobbying for "pork" than might otherwise be the case (Lindberg 2010, 127–28, 137). Where legislation is comparatively central to MPs' duties and voters' assessments, the balance of who benefits and who suffers from a candidate's policy decisions may follow a similarly strategic distributive logic (Cox and McCubbins 1986, 372–73). It is hardly surprising that clientelism today thrives especially where redistribution is unavoidable—in many contexts, for instance, in antipoverty and other social policies (Brun 2014).

Perhaps the clearest manifestation of how clientelism shapes policy arises with constituency development funds (CDFs), or increasingly common schemes to channel central-government infrastructure funds directly to constituencies, their disbursal largely determined by the local MP (Van Zyl 2010 [1]). CDFs' aims may include decentralization, local empowerment, or simply political advantage; they display varied levels of formality, regulation, and oversight (Baskin 2010, 2–3). Such funds are popular among legislators and constituents alike, since they simplify the task of securing resources for local public goods (Barkan 2008, 131). Around two dozen countries (including Malaysia, with a comparatively very high level of funding per legislator) have adopted or are considering CDFs, even though re-search suggests they bode poorly for accountability and service delivery (Van Zyl 2010 [2], Baskin 2010, 3–4).

CDFs *may* ensure projects get done, allow for community participation in planning for infrastructure development, and empower legislators to respond to community demands. Nonetheless, they breach the principle of separation of powers (since executing budgets otherwise generally falls to the executive branch) and may complicate oversight, limit state capacity for redistribution (e.g., if funds are divided equally across constituencies or per partisan considerations), obstruct both local-governments' efforts at service delivery or development and MPs' fo-cus on broader national issues and legislation, and shift (or cement) the relation-ship between MPs and constituents from a policy-oriented to a financial basis (Van Zyl 2010). Moreover, the approach raises questions about the roles of legis-lators and the public in setting development priorities and encourages voters to assess candidates in terms of how effectively they have spent CDFs, thus poten-tially strengthening incumbent advantage (Baskin 2010, 1, 6).

Taken to an extreme, beyond delimited CDFs, we approach what Kanchan Chandra labels *patronage-democracy*: a minimal democracy in which "the state monopolizes access to jobs and services, *and* in which elected officials have dis-cretion in the implementation of laws allocating the jobs and services at the dis-posal of the state" (2004, 6). She places India in this category for the extent to which "elections function as auctions for the sale of government services" and "the most basic goods that a government should provide" have become "market goods rather than entitlements" (2014, 155). A larger public than private sector enables elected officials' discretion across services and policies. The most socioeco-nomically vulnerable are most deeply affected, as they are least able to opt out of the electoral market through the private sector or emigration, as a growing share of the middle class may do (Chandra 2014, 156–62, 169). Electoral authoritari-anism is compatible with patronage democracy, although earlier, more extensive privatization in Malaysia and a programmatic welfare core in Singapore have of-fered buffers.

More broadly, patronage structures may significantly define not just relations between voters and politicians, but among tiers of government. Paul Hutchcroft (2014) tracks the conditions under which patronage comes to define central-local relations in terms of "political" versus "administrative" channels. Where coher-ent, national bureaucratic agencies and well-institutionalized parties—two of three linkages between "capital and countryside"—are weak or lacking, the third, patronage flows, may stand in to connect political regions with the center. In that case, we can expect a relatively greater proportion of public resources than otherwise to be allocated via clientelistic patronage and for local candidates to rely on patronage to convince voters of their access to the distributive core (2014, 175–79). As discussed in chapters to come, this framework captures how a polity like Malaysia or Singapore may build grassroots support through personalistic or impersonal patronage—micro- or mesoparticularistic strategies, in Hutchcroft's (2014, 177–78) terms—despite fairly programmatic policymaking overall and while largely resisting the fissiparous tendencies of such turf staking. The other two legs of the distributive stool keep the polity upright, if wobbly, and control of the central government remains key.

Mobilization and Machines

Last, the clientelism frame extends to structures for political mobilization and organization—structures especially important in an electoral-authoritarian context. Machine politics is a long-acknowledged facet of political life in Southeast Asia, albeit one that scholars in decades past teleologically assumed would fade away as states built capacity, parties matured, and, presumably, horizontal loyalties edged out patron-client ties. Despite its unsavory reputation, machine politics is not inherently egregious. James Scott notes that the infamous political machines of turn-of-the-century American cities, for instance, were able "to fashion a cacophony of concrete, parochial demands into a system of rule that was at once reasonably effective and legitimate" (1969, 1143). Since the advent of the form with New York's "Albany Regency" of the 1820s, shifts in machines' fortunes have been tied especially to changes in incomes and social homogeneity that altered the relative efficiency of patronage (Reid and Kurth 1992, 427–30).

Political machines vary in their details but have common features. The minimum requirements for one to emerge are elections to choose leaders, mass (usually universal) adult suffrage, and a relatively high degree of electoral competition (usually between, but sometimes within, parties). They arise where getting out the vote is essential, and usually in a context of rapid social change, social cleavages or disorganization, and widespread poverty, which makes short-run material inducements appealing (Scott 1969, 1143, 1149–51). Machines are not ideological but center around distributing income via particularism and "pork," on the one hand, and securing office, on the other; corruption in this framework is less about greed than maximizing votes. Machines cultivate a "vaguely populist image" based on manifestations of a party's "accessibility, helpfulness, and desire to work for 'the little man'" (Scott 1969, 1144). They emphasize informal bargaining, responsiveness, reciprocity, and particularistic distribution; voters support such parties on the basis of what they personally gain, however perverse the policy implications overall (Scott 1969, 1144–45). Other groups may work with and enable parties in machine politics—for instance, influential business groups. But the key actor is an empowered nonstate, but state-linked, apparatus.

The durability and reciprocity of machine politics means constituents may reap enduring benefits from it rather than being simply exploited for their votes. For instance, localized electoral pressures may push parties to prioritize rural development rather than more glamorous industrialization schemes, and even corrupt practices may generate political legitimacy and stability based on short-term particularistic gains that meet voters' basic needs and circumvent class conflict (Scott 1969, 1153–56). Early thinking was that once those services were no longer necessary or came to be performed by a higher-capacity state, or if the party lost access to resources, the size of the potential clientele dwindled, or elections were suspended, machine politics might decline (Scott 1969, 1156–57). Yet we see examples of machines that have endured much longer.

India offers compelling examples. Machine-based mobilization dates back to the early postindependence Congress, as the party, aided by local brokers, courted voters with employment, scholarships, permits, help with application forms, and other benefits. Machines were a rural phenomenon; cities were both more tied to the state proper and home to an increasingly militant, if suppressed, left. While national party leaders emphasized structural change and favored party-strengthening unity, those lower in the hierarchy—their wagons hitched to local power brokers and institutions—cared more about distribution and consumption, including through increasing decentralization and devolution (Scott 1972a, 132–42).

That pattern of locally pitched machinery persists. For instance, the upper-caste-based Bharatiya Janata Party (BJP) has worked to win support among lower-caste voters, despite differing preferences and interests, by allying with service-providing Hindu nationalist grassroots affiliates. Relying on "nonelectoral organizational affiliates" with an "apolitical" appearance allows the BJP to reach out to poor voters distrustful of the party's ideology without alienating elite ones resentful of pro-poor policies or obvious nonelite patronage (Thachil 2011, 435–36). To be effective, the linkages thus developed cannot be merely episodic or quid pro quo, nor are the intermediary organizations only or even substantially for the purpose of monitoring voters. Rather, the aim is that grassroots organizations' mobilizing will influence voters' preferences, generally over the course of multiple electoral cycles (Thachil 2011, 437). As such, the approach echoes the early machines Scott describes but highlights the potential for organizations in civil society to amplify or extend the party apparatus.

This strategy differs from more transactional exchanges of benefits for votes among parties, brokers, and voters. The activists in question are not only concerned with winning elections, but the time horizon of their welfare services also extends beyond an electoral cycle, although they have an interest in helping the BJP win (Thachil 2011, 442). Moreover, since the activists are embedded in communities, their welfare efforts earning them credibility, they influence even non-beneficiaries' votes, recommending service delivery be understood as effective beyond individualized material exchange (Thachil 2011, 443, 452–53, 464).

Such brokers are as central to machines as they are to individual patrons or more episodic vote-buying efforts. Studies of whom parties approach and with what inducements assume parties *can* effectively target and monitor voters. But far-distal staff or intermediaries are more likely than central party organizers to make those calls. Party bosses or candidates may develop elaborate tests to determine who is reliable or untrustworthy, since brokers may be more opportunistic than loyal (Szwarcberg 2012, 89–90; Aspinall 2014). Within an enduring partisan machine, brokers may or may not be party members; some may support a specific politician/patron regardless of party, and others may participate by way of affiliated organizations, such as the Hindu nationalist groups on which the BJP relies. All presumably expect some payoff, from access to parliamentary decision making, to preference in contracts, to ethnic group privileges.

As these alliances make clear, a political machine need not be subsumed fully within a political party, even if a party forms its hub. For India's BJP machine— or that of Singapore's PAP, tied symbiotically to the grassroots People's Association—the key is maintaining "quotidian social interaction": offering, explains Tariq Thachil, a seemingly "depoliticized framework through which activists can interact with ordinary voters." Such service provision "embeds parties within communities in ways that selective conditional cash transfers or public sector jobs and contracts do not" (2011, 465). This effort entails substantial organizational costs, however dependent it is on ideologically committed activists willing to engage long term, for minimal remuneration. But it leaves the party proper free to pursue policies calibrated to appeal to differently situated voters (Thachil 2011, 465–66), allowing for the sort of mix of strategies seen also in Malaysia and Singapore.

Such organizations as state-sponsored vehicles for "administrative grassroots engagement"—parastatal neighborhood or residents' associations (Read 2012, 3–4)—can be especially useful to sustaining a political machine. Operating as "an extension of the municipal government's administrative apparatus" even when formally autonomous (Read 2000, 808), these bodies work at a level at which office holders interact personally with a substantial portion of their electorate. While potentially useful for voter mobilization, their functions are much wider—and they may lack any electoral imperative altogether. These organizations help political leaders acquire and disseminate information, target policies, and embed state action within legitimizing face-to-face relationships, plus they offer a key channel for citizen input and building social capital (Read 2009, 122–23). Indeed, these organizations may perform the sort of two-way communication of programs and feedback that parties might aspire themselves to do. The nature of account-ability they offer likewise varies with the electoral context: proactive via elections, where available, or essentially preemptive, as nondemocratic institutions seek to nurture civic faith and participation by following through (Read 2009, 122; Distelhorst and Hou 2017, 125).

Such community associations may not be clientelistic themselves, particularly where participation entails only tenuous mutual obligation or dependency. However, as brokers, these associations' leaders allow sustained state-citizen interaction, including with hard-to-reach constituencies such as housewives and the unemployed, given their local knowledge and interpersonal ties (Read 2000, 810; 2009, 129–36, 148–50; 2012, 11). However many residents deem them intrusive or pushy, these institutions still generally enjoy strong popular support for their utility and rootedness (Read 2012, 9–11). In comparatively democratic contexts, they compete with other organizations for participants and support, whereas in less liberal polities, they may crowd out or constrain less state-favored alternatives. Yet across regimes in Asia, at least, these institutions tend to persist, thriving even after regime transitions (Read 2012, 7). These competencies make neighborhood associations attractive to party machines—including, for instance, at the heart of party outreach in Singapore.

Shifting the Lens

The discussion to come encourages one to rethink aspects of what has become conventional wisdom both on electoral authoritarianism generally and on Southeast Asian regimes specifically. The literature on political development would lead us to expect an early phase of clientelist politics, diminishing as state capacity grew and urbanization disrupted social ties in Singapore and Malaysia. Instead, early efforts to cultivate political machines, combined with curbs on electoral competition and civil liberties, reshaped structures of governance. In both states, elections are less than fully fair, even if substantially free. The reasons the PAP and, until recently, UMNO have remained dominant, as well as how the former might falter and the latter has fallen, are similar to what we see in other electoral-authoritarian settings. But however important continuity or change in the government, what is at issue here is what happens *after* a potential win. Real regime change in either state requires both alteration in power and a change in linkages and governance.

The first of these transformations does not necessarily entail the second. A catalyst could bring on a "rotten-door" transition, for instance, in which even limited opposition mobilization suffices to topple the ruling party fairly easily. Yet the circumstances of such a transition—possibly debilitating state frailty (or in the case of Malaysia in 2018, an exceptionally corrupt leader), a weak civil society and still-fragmented opposition, and elite defections rather than turnover, such that the same people return under different banners—would render even a superficial transition shaky (Levitsky and Way 2010, 354–56). Regime restructuring would be unlikely. Where the transition requires a more concerted press, which succeeds, formal democratization is more plausible (Levitsky and Way 2010), yet the parties that come to power will still have developed under the ancien régime, with the bad habits that history generates.

The historical process detailed in the chapters to come finds linkages among parties, politicians, and voters, planted in a more competitive foundational period, then cultivated over decades of single-party/coalition dominance, characterized by partisanized policies and active political machines, to be central to an explanation of electoral-authoritarian resilience. That centrality is not to reject the importance also of the usual suspects: performance legitimacy, opposition weakness and disunity, patronage, (lack of) catalysts. But shifting attention to how parties and politicians operate on the ground, to coax rather than compel support through sustained interaction and to differentiate themselves from challengers, keeps our gaze on governance and political culture: what the regime in power actually does and to what standards the public holds their representatives accountable. In so doing, we broach the question of how the *regime*—patterns of access to public office, who has or lacks such access, and how decisions are made (Schmitter and Karl 1991, 76)—rather than simply the cast of characters at center stage might change, and why that regime can or could remain so relentlessly stable in two cases with otherwise quite different political-economic patterns, institutional and ideological frameworks, party structures, civil societies, and state capacity.

THE CONVOLUTED POLITICAL PATH TO MALAYSIA

Contemporary mechanisms for representation and governance in Singapore and Malaysia date to the mid-twentieth century, when British and local leaders hashed out institutions appropriate to the emerging polities. By that point, eventual self-government, probably with full independence, was assured. However, the British wanted to remain on good terms with the states-to-be to protect their financial investments and military installations. At the same time, aspiring local leaders carved out distinct identities and bases of support, defining themselves not only against the colonial administration, but also vis-à-vis domestic challengers.

The overarching backdrop was the difficult reality of early postwar Southeast Asia following wartime destruction and displacement, including a harsh, order-upending Japanese occupation in the early 1940s and an aggressive Malayan Communist Party (MCP), newly armed and legitimated as a British-supported anti-Japanese force during the war. While most of the parties emerging in this primordial political milieu made clear their intentions to play by electoral rules, the MCP equivocated.[1] The anticommunist Malayan Emergency, a guerrilla war launched in 1948, made the question moot but constrained mobilization overall, as the British and the local right wing worried that even ostensibly moderate-left parties were actually MCP sympathizers or puppets.

Colonial authorities hence edged cautiously toward departure. Their local successors wrangled over not just a political pecking order, but the very parameters of the nation-state. After convoluted negotiations among a nationalist (mostly Malay) elite, the British, and nine state-level sultans (termed Malay Rulers), the four

Federated and five Unfederated Malay States, plus two territories of the former Straits Settlements (Penang and Malacca) combined as the Malayan Union from 1946 to 1948, as the Federation of Malaya in 1948, then as a unified, independent state, Malaysia, in 1957. Singapore, Sarawak, and British North Borneo (Sabah) joined in 1963, only to have Singapore leave the still-new Malaysia two years later.

Establishing boundaries raised fundamental questions about the state. The Malay-led Federation government had been chary of incorporating predominantly Chinese Singapore and thus shifting its own ethnic balance. However, a series of progressively more left-wing governments in their nearest neighbor, Singapore, was even more worrisome. The terms for merger left internal security in Federation-government hands. The Borneo territories, for their part, were politically and economically underdeveloped; both were ceded to the British Crown and brought under Colonial Office control only in 1946. Consequently, the British security and administrative apparatus had yet to penetrate deeply, nor had internal self-government made much progress. Yet by 1961, increased concern for stability in Borneo—both to protect Brunei's oil and stave off pan-Borneo leftist inclinations[2]—had rendered the territories more central to British plans for Malaysia (Poulgrain 2014, 114–17). These states' inclusion would also "balance out" Singapore's Chinese population. In 1962, the Commission of Inquiry on Sarawak and North Borneo, chaired by C. F. Cobbold, found local opinion mixed: about one-third of the population in each state strongly favored joining Malaysia; one-third were cautiously amenable; and one-third either insisted on independence first or preferred British rule (Cobbold 1962, 44–46). Without wide debate, the respective authorities negotiated a balance between central authority and states' rights—safeguards that started to erode almost immediately (Loh 2005, 93–96; Milne 1963, 76–79, 81; Chin 2001, 31–33).

The contours of the current order had emerged by 1965, then crystallized further in the years following Singapore's departure. Not just the parties still in government, but also the leading opposition parties date back to the fraught formative years of both Singapore and Malaysia—and strong new players in Malaysia, such as those spawned by protest movements, have tended to ally with more established counterparts (see Weiss 2006). The roots of this order in an anticommunist era contributed to the cooptation and emasculation of labor, undercutting a key resource elsewhere for building a cross-cutting opposition base (LeBas 2011, 16). And the dawn of electoral politics in a time of great need—for infrastructure, jobs, housing, training, health care—but limited state capacity or resources encouraged specific adaptations to build support. These adaptations, which formed the basis of a distinct machine politics, have long outlasted the conditions that produced them.

To understand this evolution, this chapter looks first to the institutional framework: the initial plans and justifications for local electoral politics and modes of governance and the extent to which members of the public oriented themselves toward the emerging formal politics. Next, it considers the structures of parties and political networks taking shape, including the identities and objectives around which they organized themselves and sought to structure the polity. Finally, the chapter considers how these early patterns laid the ground for the electoral authoritarianism that so swiftly and firmly took hold, institutionally and political-culturally, through the lenses of national policies, local governance, and individual-level linkages.

Establishment of Elections and Governance

Despite scattered initiatives prewar,[3] it was really only after rounds of constitutional consultations in the mid-1940s, then with the Federation of Malaya Agreement of 1948, that Malaya moved toward self-government (Cowen 1958, 52). The agreement included provisions for introduction of municipal, state, and legislative elections as soon as feasible, in that sequence, to replace nominated institutions and socialize the public toward democratic, noncommunist methods.[4] A postwar constitutional commission saw "few risks" to such devolution and deemed local government necessary to cultivating democratic habits (Norris 1980, 16). Even so, the Emergency nearly scuttled these plans: in early 1952, the Secretary of State for the Colonies "stated categorically that there could be 'no elections in Malaya until safety is assured'" (Carnell 1954, 220). Nevertheless, plans progressed.

Parties came first and helped to design the rules under which they would compete. Among preeminent local negotiators were early leaders of the United Malays National Organisation (UMNO) and the Malayan Chinese Association (MCA). British officials, meanwhile, sought both preservation of some extent of control and alignment with praxis in their other colonies.[5] Malaya's hereditary Rulers, the sultans of nine of eleven peninsular states (who rotate as king), agreed with elections in principle but urged caution.[6] A commission convened to draft a constitution in 1957 but included no Malayan representatives—just nominees from the United Kingdom, Australia, India, and Pakistan—though the Malay Rulers and Federation government had a chance to weigh in on and approve what became their constitution (Cowen 1958, 47).

Local Government

The transition to elections began at the local level. Until 1939, Malayan local administration was primarily via district and field officers, together with sultan-appointed, usually hereditary, subdistrict-level *penghulu*,[7] as well as various boards (e.g., for taxes or sanitation) in urban areas. Sanitary boards morphed into appointed town boards, and the Municipal Ordinance of the Straits Settlements was extended to the Malay States in 1948, yet town planning remained piecemeal and most local authorities' services, limited.[8]

The Local Elections Ordinance 1950 sketched a complex new architecture. Municipal councils (initially in Kuala Lumpur, Penang, and Malacca) would move toward two-thirds elected membership, while towns with over ten thousand residents would establish at least partly elected town councils.[9] Elections would extend also to rural boards, extending civic education.[10] The framework left details to localities, including requirements for the franchise—comparatively loose terms for conferral of which resulted in a substantially non-Malay local electorate (Hawkins 1953, 156–57). (Initially, states also administered local elections; jurisdiction transferred to the federal Election Commission in 1960.) The first of these elections were in 1951 in Penang, where the multiracial Radical Party swept six of eight seats. It was with Kuala Lumpur's Municipal Council elections the following February that UMNO–MCA coordination posted its first success, becoming the tripartite Alliance with the addition of the Malayan Indian Congress (MIC) in 1955 (Hawkins 1953, 157; Goh 2005, 51).

Colonial officials next moved to extend elections to smaller communities, building on a system of committees in many "new villages"—the roughly five hundred villages into which colonial authorities forcibly resettled over half a million Malayan Chinese (nearly one-tenth of all Malayans) between 1950 and 1953 to disrupt communist supply chains and networks.[11] The Briggs Plan represented the colonial government's effort to think not just in terms of military action, but of "destroying the morale and support infrastructure of the insurgents" and wooing rural Chinese via "social services and agricultural assistance" (Yao 2016, 100). Early new villages were "shanty-town-like," their mostly involuntary, settler-farmer residents sometimes forced to build their own huts upon arrival (Yao 2016, 100–2). As Souchou Yao describes the new village, "If it was not a concentration camp, it certainly took on the features of a prison or any place of incarceration or detention"—and government aid came always with the threat of its withdrawal and the reality of ongoing intimidation and submission, including harsh collective punishments (2016, 105, 108–9).

There, the government worked to incorporate the MCA and consultative mechanisms into local governance and outreach as part of a (poorly received) campaign of "realistic or materialistic propaganda," delivering welfare qua MCA patronage (Harper 1999, 187–88).[12] From the MCA's perspective, enthusiastic participation in the resettlement program allowed the party to prove the community's loyalty, despite the preponderance of Chinese among local communists (Yao 2016, 108). Initially, in line with plans for civic education and self-government, the District Office appointed a village committee to run new village affairs under a colonial resettlement officer's lead (Yao 2016, 106). But British planners noted the benefits of at least partly elected and financially viable village councils, not just for handling minor public works and matters of welfare, security, and education, but also for racial harmony, civic education, and as a bulwark against communism.[13] Elections for these committees as of 1953 aimed at "self-government from the ground up" (Yao 2016, 106). These concerns were pressing. However useful militarily, mass involuntary resettlement sharply exacerbated racial segregation and Chinese ghettoization and grievance. Malays, for their part, resented the amenities and consideration these communities received, pushing a shift to "benign neglect" by the 1960s, as the Malay-dominated government shifted focus (Strauch 1981, 128).

Meanwhile, deliberations over local government continued. In mid-1952, colonial authorities commissioned a report on Malayan local government from English town clerk Harold Bedale.[14] Bedale highlighted the need for uniformity in qualifications for election, accurate and complete voter registers, and particularly, financial autonomy for local authorities, including the ability to make and pursue long-term plans, exercise prudent management, and hire their own staff (1953, 12–20). He also advised giving local authorities greater responsibility for such policy domains as primary education, housing, and libraries (1953, 20–23). Simultaneously, the separate Committee on Town and Rural Board Finances advocated increasing these bodies' financial independence (Davis 1953).

The appointed Legislative Council duly enacted a Local Councils Ordinance in August 1952.[15] Within about eight months, over fifty fully elected local councils had been established, with another seventy in the works.[16] Town and village elections ensued annually from 1953 to 1958. Penang's George Town City Council was the most comprehensive, providing public transportation, water, electricity, clinics, drain inspection, rubbish collection, and even Malaya's first public housing—all helped by its being the country's wealthiest local authority, with a larger budget and more professional staff than the Penang state government (Sim and Koay 2015a, 13). The final phase was extending elections to North Borneo and Sarawak in the lead-up to merger in 1963, despite scarce local political organizations.[17] Sarawak held inaugural local elections in 1959—all but Miri had fully elected local governments by the early 1960s—and Sabah, in December 1962

(Milne and Ratnam 2013 [1974], 69; Aeria 2005, 125). All told, by 1965, Malaysia had 3,013 elected councilors and 500 appointees (Norris 1980, 17).

State and Settlement Councils

State-level elections came next. Planning was difficult. State leaders were unevenly enthusiastic about elections, however seemingly inevitable, and while they assumed the federal level would retain real power, those rules and procedures had yet to be set.[18] Johor was first off the mark, in 1948: its sultan pledged elections in conjunction with the Federation Agreement, then established a planning committee in June 1950.[19] The main push came in 1954, when state delegations met to hash out amendments to their constitutions to establish elections, coordinating on certain parameters (single-member districts, majoritarian voting, qualifications for electors) but leaving details such as the proportion of members elected up to each state.[20] Those details were thorny. At an early 1955 protest rally, for instance, Malacca's UMNO Youth League floated a copy of the Settlement Council Elections Bill down the river in a bamboo casket to protest the lack of an elected majority, while an *ulama* prayed for realization of UMNO's "true aspirations."[21]

Early elections saw some irregularities and violations—for instance, a "muddle, or worse" in Terengganu in October 1954[22]—but mostly smooth sailing and high turnout among registered voters. The well-organized Alliance was the clear winner nationwide, defeating challengers mainly from Party Negara and state-based Labour parties. A broad anti-Alliance electoral front failed to cohere, resulting in three-cornered fights, especially in party-rich Perak. Filling out the ranks in the state councils were nominated official members (e.g., financial officers, legal advisers) and unofficial members whom the high commissioner or sultan selected, favoring, for instance, underrepresented ethnic groups, women, organized labor, and chambers of commerce.[23] These groups remained salient as institutional bases and vote blocs for specific parties.

Federal Legislative Council

The postwar federal Legislative Council (renamed Parliament after independence in 1959) included fourteen official members and fifty unofficial members (mostly political and community leaders), all nominated, as well as heads of government from each of the nine states and two settlements. Civil servants stood in for ministers until 1950, when, looking toward self-government, High Commissioner Henry Gurney proposed what he termed the "Member" system: Council members would serve in a "quasi-ministerial capacity," joining the federal Executive

Council and administering government departments.[24] But as at the state level, determining the share of seats to be elected proved difficult.

Seizing the initiative from an April 1953 cross-party Malayan National Conference (MNC) to plan for a self-governing Malaya, as well as a plethora of supplementary proposals, the British appointed a large committee under M. J. Hogan that July (Carnell 1954, 224–25). Dominated by Alliance and MNC leaders who "virtually submitted their 'blue-prints' to themselves" (Carnell 1954, 226), the committee invited input from the public (ultimately limited) and from political and other organizations (more forthcoming). The committee rejected proportional representation as too likely to result in a raft of small parties and unstable coalitions and as too confusing for voters. After some equivocation, the committee recommended a legislature with a speaker and five official members, one representative per state, twenty-two nominated members to represent scheduled interests (commerce, mining, agriculture, trade unions, etc.) and three to represent minorities (Ceylonese, Eurasian, and a "European official to represent Aborigines"), fifty-two elected members, and five "nominated reserve" seats the high commissioner would fill in consultation with the leader of the majority party. Elections—to commence as soon as feasible—would be direct and majoritarian, in single-member territorial constituencies (with the possibility of multimember ones in urban areas), with added weight for rural, heavily Malay areas. Voting would be voluntary, but the election would be void if turnout fell below 25 percent. The Executive Council would include ex-officio members plus twelve to twenty-four other Legislative Council members, selected by the high commissioner.[25] Comprising an unelected upper house, the Senate, would be two members per state, chosen by each state's legislature, plus sixteen notables or minority representatives appointed by the king (Cowen 1958, 57–58).

The Hogan committee's initial proposals failed to satisfy UMNO or the MCA. The latter had initially been less committed than UMNO to elections, for fear of being swamped by Malays, given restrictions on citizenship; having found a way to share power via the Alliance seemed to quell those concerns (Carnell 1954, 222–23). The parties held a national convention on the committee's report, then lobbied the Rulers, the high commissioner, and other relevant authorities for concessions, including at least 60 percent elected members, allowing civil servants to contest, majoritarian voting, and early elections. They cited precedents ranging from Singapore's share of elected members to the Universal Declaration of Human Rights.[26] Colonial officials were unsympathetic, deeming the just-concluded process sufficiently consultative. An April 1954 Alliance delegation to the United Kingdom could secure only an unofficial meeting with the Secretary of State for the Colonies—the "three worried little men" from UMNO and the MCA found a more sympathetic ear in British Labour, then in opposition.[27]

It was Labour that suggested the compromise of expanding the slim majority of elected members by having the high commissioner allocate his nominated seats to the party winning the most votes.[28] Alliance leaders, especially from UMNO's left wing and Youth League, threatened to resign their government positions and boycott elections or not assume their seats should the government deny this proposed concession. Not only did the Alliance make good on the threat, but the MCA also pressured nominated representatives from Chinese chambers of commerce, mines, and the like to follow suit, even though these groups advocated for their interests through nominated positions.[29] The British caved,[30] seemingly swayed by the fact that there now was a cross-communal coalition ready to assume power (Carnell 1954, 229)—though a related request by the MIC, for reserved seats for Indian candidates, went nowhere. (The party rejected separate electorates as "political segregation" and nomination as unaccountable, but feared the Indian 10 percent of the population would be permanently unrepresented.)[31]

The fifty-two constituencies for the first federal elections in July 1955 "were drawn without regard for communal groupings, without being weighted, without electoral devices or fancy franchises of any sort" (Tinker 1956, 258). The Constituency Delineation Commission's main criteria were that federal constituencies approximate preexisting administrative districts and be about equal in population (Carnell 1954, 229–30)–malapportionment came later. Planners dominating the Federal Elections Committee, mostly from the noncommunal Independence of Malaya Party and the Alliance, rejected common, but problematic, expedients to ensure representation, including separate electorates, ethnic gerrymandering, or multimember constituencies in which voters might "plump" their votes for a single candidate (Tinker 1956, 260–65). That said, segregated living patterns allowed a sort of "unintentional 'honest gerrymandering'": the Alliance could run candidates from UMNO or the MCA where Malays or Chinese, respectively, constituted the majority (Tinker 1956, 264).

In 1957, the government tasked a new Election Commission (EC) with the conduct of elections, preparation of electoral rolls, and delineation of constituencies, replacing the Elections Committee. Unhappy with the EC's 1960 delineation, UMNO started almost immediately to whittle down the commission's independence. A 1962 constitutional amendment transferred the final decision on delineation to Parliament, allowing the prime minister first to revise the recommendations (Lim 2005, 252–53). Elections continued, but never again on such fair premises as initially; while Malaya's original institutional framework did not predetermine an electoral-authoritarian outcome, Alliance-government tweaks quickly set it on that course.

Orienting the Public Toward Formal Politics

Public enthusiasm for elections lagged behind interest in parties. Anticlimactically, one of the two first elections scheduled, in Malacca in December 1951, had to be called off: the nine available seats drew only nine nominations. Before 1952's three municipal elections, colonial authorities and local political organizations, including all the major communal associations and political parties, worked aggressively to register voters and encourage turnout, both to ensure meaningful results and to minimize the odds of enthusiastic radicals' outvoting lackadaisical moderates. Civic education initiatives included mock elections in schools, talks to Rotary Clubs and village headmen, songs, plays, and house-to-house visits. The Malayan Auxiliary Air Force even air-dropped leaflets.[32] Among the more creative measures were targeted Radio Malaya broadcasts. Two by Malay women, for example, reminded Kuala Lumpur housewives how "fortunate" they were to have been enfranchised from the outset and to pay attention to such municipal council issues as road drainage, refuse collection, and clean markets,[33] and a current municipal commissioner described the voter registration process and how a municipality functions.[34] In Malacca, a British Council–sponsored film series on British elections supplemented similar radio exhortations.[35] In the final days of registration, political parties, chambers of commerce, and community associations drew thousands to a "circus" of open air festivals, bands, and cinema shows.[36] These efforts continued as the scope of elections expanded.[37]

Yet registration figures remained disappointingly low. Part of the problem was eligibility: those qualified to vote included the subjects of Rulers (mostly Malays), federal citizens, and citizens of the United Kingdom or its colonies born in Malaya or Singapore. That ruling, explained a *Straits Times* editorial, served to "shut out the Indian, Ceylonese and European communities almost entirely, and, of course, the whole China-born community." Indeed, "the business and professional classes of Kuala Lumpur—classes which have so important a contribution to make to the successful running of any municipality—are for the most part debarred from voting in Municipal elections or standing as candidates."[38] A backlog of eight thousand citizenship applications awaiting approval in Kuala Lumpur as of early July 1951—more than double the number of Chinese registered to vote there[39]—forced the government to extend voter registration.[40] After six weeks, just about 1 percent of the city's population had registered in Kuala Lumpur, many of them not actually qualified. Municipal commissioners requested that the sultan of Selangor approve a more liberal franchise for the city, weighing residential criteria more than nationality, given that these elections concerned narrowly "parochial affairs." The *Straits Times* deemed the registration campaign "a conspicuous flop," and the electorate to be "farcical in its racially unrepresentative character."[41] Yet the sultan rejected the proposal, leaving at least six of sixteen incumbent commissioners themselves disenfranchised.[42] Emergency-era suspicion made matters worse. British reports noted not just unfamiliarity and disinterest, a "traditional Chinese" antipathy to government, and a "wholesome dislike of filling up forms," but also voters' fears that the register might become a communist blacklist or tax roll.[43]

Patterns varied, however. As of June 1951, reflecting Chinese reluctance to register, only 4 percent of the "potential electorate" was registered in Kuala Lumpur, but 35 percent were in Penang and 40 percent in Malacca.[44] Moreover, although eligible Chinese outnumbered Malays for Penang's first settlement elections in 1954, Malay turnout significantly exceeded Chinese. Malay women in particular turned out in droves for UMNO and other Alliance candidates, bolstering uneven MCA support for the coalition.[45] At the federal level, the electorate totaled approximately 2.2 million,[46] but fewer than 1.3 million had registered by 1955. Of these, 84.2 percent were Malay and 11.2 percent Chinese—all told, only about 12 percent of eligible Chinese registered. George Town and Ipoh were the only constituencies with a non-Malay majority among voters; in 37 of 52 seats, Malays exceeded 75 percent. Nowhere were Indians even 15 percent, and registered men outnumbered women overall for all ethnic groups.[47]

Regardless, the general election in 1955 saw contests in all but one of fifty-two peninsular constituencies, prefacing an enduringly competitive but lopsided framework. The well-prepared Alliance ran in every seat, Party Negara in thirty, and the Pan-Malayan Islamic Party (PMIP, or Parti Islam seMalaysia, PAS) in eleven. The National Association of Perak, Labour Party, Perak Malay League, and Perak Progressive Party each contested fewer than ten. Eighteen ran as independents. Elections went smoothly, held in one day, with almost 85 percent turnout. The Alliance won a resounding fifty-one seats, only barely losing the remaining one to PMIP.[48] The British high commissioner opined that the Alliance's "excellent" organization, unmatched by other parties, and "superior financial resources" had given it a decisive edge.[49] By 1959, with a larger, less heavily Malay electorate, challengers built up through intervening local elections, and strains within the Alliance, especially over seat allocations, the Alliance share declined to 74 of 104 seats, with 51.5 percent of the vote (versus 55.5 percent across preceding state elections). Coalition weak spots included large urban areas, Terengganu, and Kelantan (Smith 1960, 39–42, 46). Meanwhile, direct elections remained only at the local level in Sabah (until 1967) and Sarawak (until 1970). Elected district and town councils there selected some from among their number for divisional advisory councils, which in turn elevated some members to the state legislature; the state legislature then selected federal legislators in proportion to each party's share of state seats (Loh 2005, 75–78; Aeria 2005, 118–21).

Nationally, these early local, state, and federal elections both reinforced the salience of elections for an initially underenthusiastic citizenry and set a precedent for UMNO and Alliance dominance. Those parties most deeply involved in drafting electoral rules fared best under them, not surprisingly; these same parties continued to tweak formal and informal rules to their own advantage. Although Malaya's initial framework presumed liberal democracy, the British-favored Alliance quickly occupied the middle ground and center stage. From there, the Alliance consolidated its advantage via policy enactments and retail politics, even as challengers retained both niches at the local level and wider ambitions.

Parties and Political Networks

As their early activism indicates, Malayan political parties played an outsized role in the 1940s–1960s: coherent parties, particularly UMNO, preceded and helped to structure emerging electoral institutions, rather than vice-versa. These parties' approaches and foci differed (see Vasil 1971); a different initial winner might have set the electoral stage, from guiding ideology to patterns for mobilization, differently. At the most basic level, they remained tied to their territorial unit (Federation, Singapore, Sabah, Sarawak), though they made efforts to coordinate and individuals from across parties maintained personal ties; part of the challenge of merger lay in coordinating among parties.[50] The scope of variation suggests the extent to which the Alliance's 1954 victory set Malaya's course.

UMNO

Malayan electoral politics developed in UMNO's image above all, particularly in the entrenchment of communalism. It was opposition to the Malayan Union, which would strip authority from the Malay Rulers, centralize power in British hands, and extend equal citizenship across races,[51] that galvanized Malays both to identify more as Malayan than with a particular state and its Ruler and to launch UMNO, inaugurated in 1946. The party merged state-level progenitors— previously discrete entities lacking central coordination—and other Malay groups.[52] The national leadership, particularly the decision-making Supreme Council, grew increasingly assertive as of the 1950s; state executive committees disbanded altogether in 1960 (Hutchinson 2015, 117).

With nineteen associations initially affiliated at least tenuously with the party,[53] UMNO began, per John Funston, "more as a mass movement than a political party." Although authority centered in the chairman, the rank and file had influence. Regular assemblies offered infrequent but important plebiscites on party leaders' decisions. Leadership remained largely aristocratic—second chairman Tunku Abdul Rahman's older brother was the sultan of Kedah—despite a falling out with the Rulers in mid-1949 (Funston, 2016, 31–33, 39, 119; Tunku Abdul Rahman is commonly referred to simply by his aristocratic title: "the Tunku"). As branches formed across Malaya and Singapore[54] and the party anxiously sought fee-paying members, UMNO absorbed ex-members of the left-wing Parti Kebangsaan Melayu Malaya (Malay Nationalist Party)[55] and Angkatan Pemuda Insaf (Movement of Aware Youth), some of them former political detainees. The British worried about infiltration given MCP plans for a cross-party, postwar Malayan Democratic United Front.[56]

The party started small, attracting still only about 1 percent of the Malay population in some areas by 1950. Late that year, membership stood at seventy-one thousand, including merely eight thousand women.[57] UMNO fragmented on policy lines, and Onn Jaafar complained of the "difficulty of getting any competent young Malay leaders to do anything constructive."[58] The party's base was not only firmly rural—every Malay village soon had a branch—but "basically traditional, feudal, conservative, and religious"; through the 1960s, primary schoolteachers and traditional leaders such as *penghulu* were powerfully influential.[59]

The party launched sections for youth, labor and peasants, and social welfare almost immediately.[60] A women's wing, Pergerakan Kaum Ibu UMNO (UMNO Women's Section Movement; later renamed Wanita UMNO, UMNO Women), followed shortly thereafter.[61] Particularly under the forceful Khadijah Sidek from 1954 to 1956 (before she was expelled from the party), Kaum Ibu not only recruited women to UMNO, but pressed for better women's representation in party leadership and as candidates—only one of thirty-five UMNO candidates in 1955 was female (Ting 2007, 77–78). But the youth wing took on particular prominence. Formalized in 1949, UMNO Youth siphoned members from the Malay Nationalist Party and Angkatan Pemuda Insaf. It became comparatively militant, subordinated to and supported by UMNO proper, but not always ideologically in step (Mustafa 2004/5, 20–21). When, in 1950, Onn Jaafar appealed to the feisty wing to "arm the kampongs [villages]," British authorities worried, "With its uniform, parades and oaths of allegiance, U.M.N.O. youth is beginning to take on something of a Fascist tinge."[62] After independence, the wing goaded party leadership—for instance, criticizing the government's extravagance and pro-West stance—to the extent that UMNO expelled Youth division leaders in Johor and Negeri Sembilan in 1957–58. Drafting the Alliance constitution (on which the Youth wing felt inadequately consulted) revealed an ideological rift: whereas UMNO Youth advocated a socialist coalition, the Tunku argued that UMNO needed to be a "rightist party" to ensure safety and prosperity, and most members prioritized Malay communal interests.[63]

Regardless, UMNO's first priority was staying afloat: the party was penurious. British officials estimated UMNO's bank balance in mid-1950 to be all of $35. The party urged state branches to enroll new members and brainstormed fund-raisers. Among the most persistent ideas were lotteries, which UMNO Kedah first introduced in early 1950.[64] Their model was the MCA, which had been raising millions of dollars thus for welfare efforts and other patronage in the new villages (Harper 1999, 188). When opponents protested at a 1951 UMNO general meeting that lotteries contravene Muslim law, Onn bluntly retorted that UMNO's "religious scruples must be set off against its ability to survive as an organisation."[65] He sought funds, too, from the British. Complaining that colonialism had done much for Malayan development, but less for Malays, in 1948 and 1950, he pressed British leaders for a financial gift to the Malay people. It would be "as a mark of friendship and appreciation for their loyal support," particularly during the ongoing Emergency.[66] Presumably, Onn and UMNO would take credit. The Tunku revived the lottery idea in 1952, bemoaning the party's "sad financial position," as well as suggesting that state branches hold "fun-fairs, etc." to support a building fund.[67] Still in 1957, as the Tunku prepared to travel to London to seek independence, members of Kaum Ibu and then men, as well, donated gold jewelry, watches, and more to fund his trip.[68] The real solution, though, was alliance with the wealthier MCA. However Malay nationalist, the Tunku was also strategic; joining forces was expedient—and though only two of fifteen MCA candidates stood in Chinese-majority seats in 1954, all were elected (Tinker 1956, 265–66, 271). That opportunistic decision set Malaya on its quasi-consociational path.

Even before that point, how much the British relied on UMNO to staff the nominated Legislative Council already magnified UMNO's position—while also bolstering the legitimacy of the colonial administration. In 1950, Onn proposed allowing UMNO as well as the MCA and MIC to fill a certain number of unofficial seats, and in the process increasing the proportion of local members relative to Europeans. Onn expected at least that UMNO should be able to choose most Malay members and insisted he would only accept a seat if elected to it by his party. High Commissioner Gurney scoffed that the idea was "so obviously objectionable, with [its] emphasis on communal politics."[69] Yet just a month later, Gurney proposed that UMNO choose six legislative councilors to represent Malay agriculture and husbandry. He justified the proposal as introducing aspects of elections (since UMNO members would, per the plan, select these individuals by secret ballot) and planned to offer the same to the MCA for two Chinese agricultural seats.[70] Later that year, colonial officials asked UMNO to submit seven names for the upcoming legislative session, planning to seek nominations for the remainder from states and other groups, following prior practice. Onn instead demanded that UMNO be able to nominate at least two-thirds and preapprove others, with states to be replaced by functional categories in seat allocations. The party resolved that if the high commissioner refused any name without proper cause, none would accept nomination.[71] These early skirmishes foreshadowed UMNO and MCA's coordinated 1954 push to expand the share of elected seats, amid negotiations on electoral rules.

A self-important UMNO also took on the Rulers and challenged elements of customary law, suggesting the party's readiness to diminish rivals. Onn in particular—whose personality dominated the young party[72]—engaged in a power struggle with the Rulers and the Persatuan Melayu Semenanjong (Peninsular Malay Union), with which they allied. For instance, Onn pushed for a central religious body under UMNO to undercut the Rulers' influence, and UMNO opposed local inheritance customs (*adat perpateh*) as contrary to Islam and as undermining traditional officials' power to appoint local headmen.[73] These brusque actions made clear that UMNO proposed a different basis for political legitimacy and loyalty than Malay custom mandated.

Throughout, UMNO changed institutionally. As the party grew more involved in the economy and party office increasingly offered access to government boards and appointments, intraparty competition increased. Vote buying for party elections started, however modestly, in the 1950s (Funston 2016, 120), notwithstanding the passage of the Election Offenses Act in 1954. The law did not constrain parties' campaign spending, only candidates' own, and even those limits (uniform across constituencies, regardless of size) applied only to expenditures between nomination day and polling day (TI 2010). The party made initial, strategic forays into business: in 1961, UMNO took over *Utusan Melayu*, a then-independent, critical newspaper, foreshadowing further media takeovers and investment ventures (TI 2010, 95). These shifts both increased political aspirants' incentive to remain with the party (albeit while defending their own niche within it) and launched UMNO as an economic rather than merely political force.

Other Communal Parties

UMNO's early establishment and an already existing panoply of communal organizations rendered communal parties an obvious option, but non-Malays, as minorities, had less motivation than Malays to pursue communal politics, and other alternatives vied for support. Neither the MCA nor the MIC, UMNO's Alliance partners, ever matched UMNO's community-wide support. The MCA, launched in 1949, brought together existing communal organizations, including Dong Jiao Zong (the United Chinese School Teachers and School Committees Association) and the English-educated professionals' Straits Chinese Business Association, yet struggled to find its niche (Heng 1996, 36–37). The party and its coalition were to the right of most Malayan Chinese ideologically; the party also suffered rifts from early on, including over the Tunku's "dictatorial attitude" in the Alliance. The MCA had to cope, too, with the hasty addition of hundreds of thousands of Chinese to the electoral rolls upon independence, most of them left-leaning, underprivileged voters from towns, mining areas, and new villages.[74]

Indeed, a key reason Chinese elites founded the MCA was to stave off "class-based ethnic demands from below"; the party's strategic position within the Alliance allowed it to secure rewards for the community, which leaders presumed would ensure support (Hilley 2001, 90–91). Although the community's economic profile was stronger than Malays', most Malayan Chinese were *not* wealthy, but wage earners in tin mines, on rubber plantations, and in unskilled urban jobs (Heng 1996, 35). Nonelite Chinese immediately rebuked the MCA for its compromises with UMNO over the Federation constitution, especially on issues of education and language, condemning party leaders as self-interested lackeys (Cowen 1958, 56). Subsequent MCA concessions on the 1961 Education Act and the 1967 National Language Bill further alienated Chinese associations as well as the Chinese press, benefiting further-left opposition parties that championed communal interests (Heng 1996, 37–38, 41).

The MIC's position within the Indian community was even more tenuous. Vying for influence was the Federation of Indian Organisations (FIO), inaugurated in 1950 (with, the MIC alleged, British sponsorship), which aimed to coordinate the activities of about 160 organizations devoted to Indians' social, economic, and political welfare and to represent the community.[75] Regardless, as the 1955 elections approached, only 50,000 Indians had registered as voters. Not only were their allegiances fragmented, but Indians accounted for no more than 20 percent of the electorate in any constituency. Nevertheless, the UMNO–MCA Alliance partnered with the MIC at the last minute, completing its communal triptych. The candidates in the MIC's two allotted seats both won (Tinker 1956, 268).

Meanwhile, the PMIP and Onn Jaafar's repackaging of his multiracial Independence of Malaya Party (launched after he left UMNO) as the communal Party Negara in 1954 offered Malays alternatives to UMNO. Both these parties touted a "racialist and Islamic line" and prospered mainly on the east coast and in rural areas. Party Negara failed to thrive, but the PMIP won control of Kelantan and Terengganu in 1959 with a communal platform and direct appeal to Islam, including having religious teachers stand for federal and state office. These wins shocked the Alliance: UMNO read them as rejection of multiracial-coalition politics, and the MCA (presciently) feared they might inspire more Malay-nationalist policymaking.[76]

PMIP proved especially salient as an ideological foil to UMNO; while the parties' approaches overlapped in practice, PMIP stressed a less performance-based, more normative premise for legitimacy. The party emerged out of the Persatuan Ulama Se-Malaya (Ulama Association of Malaya), first launched under UMNO's aegis in 1950; it then became the independent Persatuan Islam Se-tanah Malaya (Pan-Malayan Islamic Association) in late 1951 before registering as a party in 1955 (Liow 2006, 23). PMIP aimed at both "moral development," including through its youth wing, launched in 1953, and, like UMNO, rural community development (Liow 2011, 669–70). PMIP used Islam to discredit the Alliance, telling Malay voters it was *haram* (forbidden) to vote for non-Muslims—worrying the Alliance, since a religious leader could sway the votes of a village (Tinker 1956, 277). Over time, that tactic served to nudge UMNO toward layering normative over developmentalist appeals.

Parties of the Left

However powerful the pull of a communal framework, the 1950s–1960s was also the heyday of the Malayan left, operating on a divergent premise. The two key national-level contenders in peninsular Malaya were the Pan-Malayan Labour Party (PMLP), renamed the Labour Party of Malaya (LPM) in 1954, and Partai Ra'ayat Malaya (Malayan People's Party, later Parti Sosialis Rakyat Malaysia, then Parti Rakyat Malaysia, or PRM). The leading smaller contenders were the Perak-based People's Progressive Party and the Penang-based United Democratic Party, but neither had national impact.

The PMLP replaced a confederation of state-based labor parties headed mostly by English-educated Indians and Malays from public service unions. While all emphasized democratic socialism and multiculturalism, in the mold of the British Labour Party, the parties' priorities differed, including that regarding independence (Tan K. H. 2008). The British initially barred geographic extension; regardless, the Penang, Selangor, and Singapore Labour Parties forged the PMLP in June 1952, accepting organizational, not individual, members to contest municipal elections. Its initial platform included provisions for both agricultural and industrial workers, as well as social welfare policies and economic reforms (Tan K. H. 2008). The PMLP maintained an anticommunist, largely pro-British stand—colonial authorities deemed it a safe alternative to the MCP—but grew increasingly critical of British policies.

By the mid-1950s, the party began to call for more "radical socialist reforms," including public ownership of the means of production, then even recognition of the MCP and (briefly) abolition of Malay special rights and the Rulers' position (Cheah 2006, 639–40). Reorganized as the LPM (Labour Party of Malaya), the party edged away from its earlier program of gradual economic nationalism and welfarism toward uniting workers and peasants to pursue independence, democracy, and socialism (Tan K. H. 2008). On the ground, working-class Chinese saw the MCA as the party of the rich, and the LPM as the party of workers and the poor, particularly as middle-class leadership yielded to a working-class orientation.[77]

PRM shared the LPM's leftist ideology but developed a different profile. The party emerged in 1955 as successor to the Kesatuan Melayu Muda (Young Malay Union), launched in 1937 and popular especially among Malay-educated teachers and journalists. The PRM, however, was less staunchly socialist and eschewed the Kesatuan Melayu Muda's links with the MCP (Rustam 2008, 7–8; Khong 2003, 24, 30–31). Some from the Malay Nationalist Party and Angkatan Pemuda Insaf also joined, following the lead of party founder and former Angkatan Pemuda Insaf leader Ahmad Boestamam.[78]

In August 1957, the LPM and PRM joined forces in the Malayan People's Socialist Front, under the initial leadership of Ahmad Boestamam. Interparty tensions, such as between the People's Progressive Party and the LPM, confounded expansion, although Singapore's Workers' Party and People's Action Party welcomed the Socialist Front, whose constitution promised cross-Straits cooperation to advance socialism.[79] The Socialist Front established its first branches in Penang and prepared to contest December 1958 town council elections.[80] A loose agreement assigned the PRM primary responsibility for rural, Malay areas, especially farming and fishing communities, and the LPM responsibility for more urban, Chinese areas, including new villages (whose negative experience of government inclined them leftward). The LPM outperformed the PRM in local-government elections; rural areas were harder to penetrate, given not just a "feudal mentality," but also rural development schemes that reinforced Alliance support.[81] The Socialist Front secured control of the George Town city council and a number of other local councils, as well as 8 (of 104) parliamentary and 15 state seats in 1959—all in predominantly non-Malay constituencies (Tan K. H. 2008; Cheah 2006, 640–41). The coalition struggled to draw Malay support even after former Malay Nationalist Party leader Ishak Haji Mohamed became LPM chairman in 1959, leaving both parties led by Malays.[82] That record suggests the traction UMNO's rural development emphasis afforded the Alliance, even before UMNO stepped up communalism-reinforcing preferential policies in the 1970s.

Moreover, suspected communist infiltration and resultant arrests almost immediately debilitated the Socialist Front.[83] Merger in 1963 brought matters to a head. The LPM accepted merger "in principle," deeming it unavoidable, by 1962. However, detentions earlier that year of Singaporean left-wing leaders with whom LPM leaders had ties, as well as of Socialist Front leader Ahmad Boestamam, embittered the Front's base and further soured the coalition's relationship with the Alliance regime—the more so when the Alliance and the People's Action Party attacked the Front as a "fifth column" of Indonesia during *Konfrontasi*, Indonesia's assault on the expanded federation, launched in 1963. The federal government detained hundreds of Socialist Front leaders and members under the Internal Security Act (Tan K. H. 2008; Cheah 2006, 641–42).

Repression spurred radicalization. New leadership pressed the LPM in a more Chinese-chauvinist direction in 1966 and the two parties diverged particularly on issues of Malaysian language and culture, plus whether Chinese-owned firms or only foreign-owned ones should be nationalized. Strained to breaking, the Socialist Front collapsed (Heng 1996, 41; Tan K. H. 2008). LPM ideology and tactics then radicalized further, extending to regular street demonstrations, a *hartal* (mass boycott) in Penang in 1967, then boycott of the 1969 elections. The government responded with waves of mass arrests, bans of party divisions and branches, and other repressive measures, finally deregistering the party in 1972 (Tan K. H. 2008). PRM persisted, though it was never strong. The Alliance's blend of positive appeals to woo support with coercion to suppress a key rival signaled the regime's turn from mere single-party dominance to electoral authoritarianism.

Parties of Sabah and Sarawak

Meanwhile, party politics developed along a separate track in Sabah (North Borneo) and Sarawak. Most parties in Sabah were loosely communal, but defined more by their founders than fixed platforms.[84] Sabah's population at the time—before Islamization efforts starting in the 1970s—was mostly non-Muslim, from various ethnic groups; the largest share were Kadazan.[85] Almost one-fourth of the population was Chinese; community business leaders, aware of their minority status, leaned initially toward forming a noncommunal party (Lee 1968, 306). The strongest party in the 1960s was the United Sabah National Organisation (USNO), led by Tun Mustapha Datu Harun. Others included the United National Kadazan Organisation (UNKO), under Mustapha's rival, Donald (later Fuad) Stephens; the Chinese-based United Party and the Democratic Party, which soon merged into the Borneo Utara National Party (renamed Sabah National Party, SANAP); the United Pasok Momogun Organisation; and the Sabah Chinese Association.[86] Under Stephens's direction, UNKO and USNO formed the crux of the Sabah Alliance.[87]

Sarawak was especially unprepared for independence. After taking control from the paternalistic "white raja" Brooke family postwar, Britain had "vigorously suppressed" even trivial political movements through the late 1950s (Lockard 1967, 111). Not only was the state economically underdeveloped, but the various communities had little interaction, mutual sympathy, or sense of shared nationalism, and a mostly Chinese local communist presence tarred the Chinese community (Lockard 1967, 111–13). Nevertheless, the Sarawak Alliance formed in the early 1960s among pro-Malaysia parties, winning the 1963 state elections. (A subsequent power struggle culminated in a federal declaration of emergency in 1966.) The coalition included two Malay-Muslim parties, Parti Negara Sarawak (inclusive of some prominent Dayaks) and Barisan Rakyat Jati Sarawak; two non-Muslim indigenous parties, the Iban-led Sarawak National Party, headed by first chief minister Stephen Kalong Ningkan, and Parti Pesaka; and the Sarawak Chinese Association. The two Malay-based parties and Parti Pesaka then merged to form Parti Pesaka Bumiputera Bersatu in 1973, which dominated the Sarawak Alliance thereafter. The substantially Chinese Sarawak United People's Party, especially strong at the grassroots, affiliated with the Sarawak Alliance only later, having survived near-collapse by 1965 over divisions between pro–People's Action Party moderates and more militant, anti-Malaysia leftists. Communal rivalries, particularly over the place of the Chinese in Sarawak, stymied the Sarawak Alliance's early progress, and a genuinely multiracial opposition party, Machinda, formed in 1964 but started unraveling within two years. Nonetheless, all Sarawak parties accepted at least some degree of multiracial membership and accommodation (Kaur 1998, 175; Lockard 1967; 114–21; Tilman 1963, 508–11). It was only later, after the Alliance had become the Barisan Nasional, that the peninsular communal-developmentalist model took deeper root in both Sabah and Sarawak (as detailed in chapter 5), driven by particularly aggressive patronage-based strategies.

Parties as Interest Protectors, Ideologues, or Vehicles

This varyingly ethnic-based, class-oriented, and state-specific array of parties proposed alternative ways to orient and practice politics. Although most early parties in Singapore and Malaysia may be characterized ideologically as communal, left wing, or right wing, understanding the cleavages parties activated and the strategies they deployed requires attention to how parties understood their own role. Some saw their purpose as protectors of specific, exclusive group interests; others, as advocates for an ideological order, with attendant programmatic goals; and still others, as vehicles to advance certain leaders or factions. These roles recommend different policy processes and outputs—hence the extent to which, in office, the Alliance wrought a specific type of regime.

Ethnicity, distinct from class interests, took on greater salience in Malaya than in Singapore; a communal framework was always a possibility. By 1921, after aggressive British labor importation, Malays were in the minority nationally and immigrants were settling down (Rustam 2008, 14). By 1947, almost two-thirds of the Chinese in Malaya had been born there (Tinker 1956, 259). Colonial classification and praxis codified and reified racial categories (Hirschman 1986), but the political and economic implications of this mix remained hazy: for instance, whether Malays' primary loyalty should be to their sultan, the place of Islam and Malay language in national identity, and on what basis one could claim citizenship (Shamsul 1997, 242–43; Milner, Abdul Rahman, and Tham 2014, 8–9). Indeed, until the 1930s, Malay organizations' nationalism was "more a reaction to the immigrant populations in their homeland, than a reaction to an alien colonial rule" (Rustam 2008, 16–17).

Once launched, UMNO made access to citizenship and Malay dominance core issues—hardly surprising for a party that grew out of opposition to the Malayan Union and its liberal citizenship provisions. Attention-grabbing UMNO campaign speeches starting in the 1950s played up "communal sensibilities and emotions" (Smith 1960, 44). Yet the party's position was not fully consistent. Onn Jaafar cautioned Governor Gent in 1947, for instance, that if the British diminished Malays' "special position" or engaged in "undue pandering" to noncitizens, "frustration and despair at British hypocrisy" would impel Malays into an anti-British coalition.[88] Belying that vehemence, three years later, UMNO itself permitted non-Malay associate members.[89] (That move, plus UMNO's leftward mien at the time, disrupted plans for a newly seemingly redundant Labour Party.[90]) Onn left UMNO in 1951 after the party rejected his plan to rebrand it as the United *Malayan* National Organisation, premised on a single, multiracial nationality.

But parties still diverged even on whether and when to seek independence, reflecting both communal anxieties and differing priorities. Before Japanese occupation, only the MCP and Kesatuan Melayu Muda had clearly nationalist, sovereign aspirations (Khong 2003, 24, 30–31). Postwar, UMNO hesitated even to adopt the slogan *Merdeka* (Independence).[91] While UMNO Youth resolved in February 1951 that *Merdeka* replace the party's original *Hidop* [sic] *Melayu* (Long live the Malays), some members thought it too radical or worried that a term derived from the Arabic *mendeheka*, implying revolt against tyranny, would encourage subversives.[92] The Tunku assured High Commissioner Gurney that independence would be less a "main feature" for UMNO than securing "practical advantages" for Malays.[93]

Similarly, Onn Jaafar's new social-democratic, pro-Commonwealth Party Negara preferred only incremental steps toward independence "as the country becomes fit for self-government," with the Rulers' remaining heads of state and minimal expansion of the franchise.[94] Onn complained in a 1955 radio address that since "Malaya is to the Malay his only Home," Malaya's substantial Chinese and Indian population required controls, lest Malays become "a back number in their own country."[95] Conversely, the LPM protested to the Alliance Merdeka Mission that maintenance of nine constitutional heads of state might foster an "oligarchic state with local feudalists and capitalists replacing the Colonial exploiters." The LPM preferred republicanism and a common federal nationality, contra the British "well-known predilection for puppet princes and feudalistic mumbo-jumbo in the Colonial world."[96]

Launch of the Alliance effectively settled the question and set Malaya on a multiracial-but-Malay-dominated course. Beyond financial exigency, what pushed UMNO toward the MCA was a British requirement that all races "combine politically" before independence. Special Branch records suggest Tunku Abdul Rahman considered UMNO's alliance with the MCA, then MIC, temporary to meet that rule. He worried about MCA motives, especially if UMNO became more financially indebted to the party.[97] For their part, Chinese and Indian voters understood that as (substantially disenfranchised) minorities, they needed Malay votes to win seats.[98] The Alliance struggled—the more so since the Tunku seemed only fully to trust Malays.[99]

Institutionalizing elections rendered enfranchisement more divisive. The MCA decried holding polls with the question of citizenship still unsettled. Strong communal sentiment and the "vast number" of non-Malays not eligible for federal citizenship, the party argued, rendered it "almost impossible" for a non-Malay to win an election beyond the local level, at least outside Penang and Malacca, where those born locally were British subjects, so could vote.[100]

The foil of women's enfranchisement suggests how fraught ethnicity was: the debate over gender was far more quickly settled. Women's suffrage was not a foregone conclusion—Puteh Mariah, inaugural head of UMNO's Kaum Ibu, pushed for it (Dancz 1987, 169)—yet the new constitution did grant women the vote. In fact, in Kuala Lumpur, where the majority of voters registered in 1951 were Indian (despite an immense backlog in applications for citizenship), most Indian voters were female. A well-coordinated Selangor Regional Indian Congress registration drive had targeted women specifically, assuming they would need more persuading than men, resulting in an unusual skew.[101]

This early identification of parties as champions of communal interests, including as primary interlocutors in debates over the terms of independence and citizenship, etched lines of partisan cleavage. It presented the Alliance less as a class- and development-based coalition than as one inspired by and oriented around power sharing, but readily tipped toward Malay interests. In reality, ethnic, religious, and class identities overlapped substantially, but the Alliance's framing both dilemmas and proposed solutions in communal terms resonated readily and penetrated deeply among the public.

Distinct but not dissociated from these identity-based premises were the ideological claims in much early politicking, particularly communism and Islamism. The MCP's active presence made radical-left ideologies particularly fraught in postwar Singapore and Malaya. The British worried the MCP would be even more subversive if legalized, extending its influence and exploiting Chinese frustration to embarrass the government and challenge still-consolidating Alliance leadership.[102] Meanwhile, concern about communist infiltration into other parties both presented genuine cause for concern and offered a convenient, multipurpose political bludgeon. PMIP offered a very different, but similarly normative premise for governance: Islam. PMIP's defense of Muslims' interests overlapped with a defense of Malay interests. However, the PMIP, more than UMNO, insisted on Islamic administration, including elevation of the Qur'an and Sunnah as bases for Malaysian law, *dakwah* (proselytization) to extend Islam within Malaya, and promotion of religious values in all spheres (Liow 2006, 23–25). Over time, UMNO and the Alliance largely suppressed class cleavage–activating left-wing challenges and coopted more communalized Islamist ones to shore up their own position.

All early parties served to a significant extent also as vehicles for their leaders. The personalization of politics sidelined issues, with long-term implications for linkages between parties and voters. That party leadership conferred both policy influence and rewards from so early on perhaps made opportunism inevitable. As the British negotiated with UMNO over appointments to legislative seats in 1951, for example, Onn Jaafar not only wielded the specter of angry Malay masses under his command,[103] but also tried to coerce Gurney into selecting Onn's relatives.[104] That by midyear Onn had announced his own departure from UMNO suggests the conditionality of his partisan commitment.[105] Once elections began, partisan and personality contests overlapped. Terengganu's first state council elections in 1954, for instance, saw "a battle of personalities rather than policies," despite efforts otherwise.[106] These foundational patterns helped ensure an enduring element of patron-client loyalty, within parties and between politicians and constituents, and personal as well as party-line voting.

The Emerging Partisan Political Economy

The early years after independence saw the Alliance government's first steps toward restructuring the economy, both for development generally and to benefit Alliance supporters specifically—particularly UMNO's core Malay constituencies. In the mid-1950s, half the labor force was employed in agriculture, while rubber and tin together constituted 85 percent of export revenue (Cowen 1958, 50). The government's rural development strategies, intended to cultivate Malay support, were its most ambitious, extending late-colonial efforts under the Rural Industrial Development Authority (RIDA), an affirmative-action program launched in 1950 to help rural Malay small- and medium-scale entrepreneurs access capital and training. Independence brought a comprehensive rural development program under a new Ministry of Rural and National Development, complemented by the National Investment Company, established in 1961 to assist Malay would-be shareholders; the Malay-focused Organisation for the National Timber Industry, launched in 1963; and other institutions. More targeted still were efforts to distribute land to poor Malays under the Federal Land Development Authority (FELDA), launched in 1956;[107] provision of infrastructure such as clinics, roads, schools, and irrigation; and initiatives to boost rural productivity and incomes (Shamsul 1997, 246–48; Jomo and Gomez 2000, 284; Lafaye de Micheaux 2017, 120–21).

Overall, however, Alliance development strategy was not highly interventionist. The government defended British and Chinese business interests, while making "modest attempts" to nurture a Malay business community. Initial forays into import-substitution industrialization favored British investors and local subsidiaries of foreign firms. However, the small domestic market pushed a transition toward export orientation by the mid-1960s, together with efforts to diversify crops and manufacturing (Jomo and Gomez 2000, 284–85).

Already by the 1960s, income inequality was worsening between rural and urban areas, among ethnic groups, and especially within the Malay community, motivating a new approach. The Malay community had transformed from the least unequal at independence to the most by 1970, but the fact of communally structured political mobilization encouraged UMNO to portray inequality as racial, particularly as a new Malay middle class became more assertive and dominant as of the mid-1960s (Jomo and Gomez 2000, 287). A version of "ethnopopulism," or fusing ethnic and populist appeals (Cheeseman and Larmer 2013, 23), gained ground. Yet until the 1960s, a coherent Malay economic-nationalist agenda, centered around displacing immigrant and British economic control and reinvigorating Malay commerce and agriculture (Shamsul 1997, 244–45), remained hazy, notwithstanding rural development schemes that presaged 1970's New Economic Policy (see chapter 5). In the process "UMNO politicians became not only more interested in the business of politics but also increasingly knowledgeable in the art or the politics of business . . . generating income, wealth, and influence from projects related to the rural development programs" and benefiting both UMNO politicians awarded tender and Chinese subcontractors (Shamsul 1997, 248).

A Malay entrepreneurial class took shape among Malay peasants, petty traders, and cottage industrialists who benefited from "endless development projects" for infrastructure and capacity building, either directly from the government or channeled through UMNO (Shamsul 1997, 249). By the late 1960s, urban and rural Malay entrepreneurs were able to articulate and press a more concrete

Malay-nationalist agenda under UMNO, transforming the guiding ideology of "Malay dominance" to "Malay hegemony" (Shamsul 1997, 250)—even though Tunku Abdul Rahman had promised MCA negotiators that the government would review, then phase out Malay special rights after fifteen years (Heng 1996, 37).

In this climate, partisan control of federal resources became a political tool. In particular, the Alliance federal government used its fiscal leverage to undercut state-level competitors. Hence, having won control of the Terengganu and Kelantan state governments in 1959, the PMIP struggled to govern with "no more than the constitutional minimum" in federal development funds (Smith 1962, 153). These patterns of politically expedient economic policymaking and distribution persisted and intensified.

Local Government and Party Machines

What perhaps most clearly came to shape the emerging order was the knitting together of the interest-oriented and personality-oriented sides of parties' mandates, as ideology (for the increasingly dominant Alliance, largely centered on communalism) flickered and faded. As parties institutionalized—especially Alliance component parties—they did so clientelistically, building support among voters with an instrumental, distributional rubric at a time of limited state resources or capacity. What emerged in both Malaya and Singapore was a form of machine politics, the timing and extent of which shaped parties' presentation, voters' entry points into and identification with the political system, and the ways in which the state met citizens' needs.

The genesis of the wider state helped set parameters. For instance, that the British launched a Malayan civil service, with provisions for recruitment and training, before the establishment of political parties or mass enfranchisement diminished the space for patronage jobs (Shefter 1994). Early parties still worked to connect constituents with employment, but more often with private-sector than civil-service positions. The later enhancement of pro-Malay affirmative action—the public sector grew by a factor of four in size and about twenty in expenditure from the mid-1960s through the mid-1990s (Ho 1998, 8–9)—muddied this pattern, suggesting a possibly heightened patronage function. Even then, though, hiring criteria remained arguably noncontingent.

How colonial authorities developed local government proved particularly consequential. Wary of ceding too much ground (especially to left-wing Chinese), the central government hobbled local authorities in key ways—most important, fiscally—leaving gaps for machine intercession. The postcolonial government sustained and extended that pattern, most notably, by doing away with local elections altogether in the 1960s (e.g., Rabushka 1970, 346). These maneuvers redirected politics. For instance, as of 1960, state governments had to consult a new National Council for Local Government, half its members representing the federal government rather than the states, regarding changes to local government–related legislation (Hutchinson 2013, 5). And increasingly, party offices came to serve as access points to state resources and programs. This shift toward central control and party intervention contrasts with the bureaucratization that supplanted storied American urban machines. Once "cleaned up," those cities embraced "the power of professionalized agencies," their independence entailing new bases of power and career paths (Lowi 1967, 86).

From the outset, Malayan town and municipal councils lacked the budgets and support needed to work effectively.[108] Demographic differences between mostly non-Malay cities and Malay-majority rural areas—in a country listing sharply toward communal politics—exacerbated these weaknesses; the federal government had little incentive to redistribute fiscal and other resources. (That bureaucrats were overwhelmingly Malay and local councils were frequently the reverse also hindered communications.) Many state-level politicians saw little value to local authorities, whose activities often required extensive coordination with state agencies, were inherently difficult (like collecting taxes), overlapped with state efforts, or (particularly in state capitals) might mar the Alliance's record (Norris 1980, 24–28). A series of corruption charges against local authorities in Penang, Seremban, and elsewhere before merger also eroded public confidence and offered states impetus to suspend local elections (Sim and Koay 2015a, 13–14).[109]

Two main factors foretold a denouement. First, the Alliance only barely won the 1959 general election; its urban linchpin, the MCA, was especially weak. The coalition fared relatively poorly in key cities, including Kuala Lumpur and George Town.[110] Second was the communist threat and (the official reason) *Konfrontasi* (Norris 1980, 23). Kuala Lumpur's 1959 local election was the first casualty. The committee that made the decision to suspend elections faulted delays in completing the electoral roll and indecision over whether to move to a fully elected council, but critics allege they feared an all-elected council would have a Socialist Front, Chinese majority. Kuala Lumpur then shifted to an appointed commissioner and advisory staff with the Federal Capital Act of 1960, the precursor to its becoming a federal territory in 1973 (Rabushka 1973, 74–75; Goh 2005, 55–56). The federal government suspended local elections overall in March 1965. Incumbent councilors remained in place; parties filled vacancies as they emerged. From July 1965 through September 1966, state governments took over at least five major local authorities, and Johor dissolved one local council altogether; justifications ranged from allegations of malpractice (later disproved) to subpar performance (Sim and Koay 2015b, 17; Tennant 1973, 79).

The Alliance government's elimination of local elections showed its willingness to undercut electoral institutions to maintain its dominance (even if other factors also mattered) and fundamentally reshaped the terrain for political parties. Municipal elections in particular had helped to consolidate "power centers" for opposition parties unable to make much headway at the state or federal level (Rüland 1990, 476; Enloe 1975, 161–62). By 1964, the Socialist Front had been nearly wiped out otherwise; city councils were its only lifeline (Tennant 1973, 80). UMNO faced the reverse situation: while it was strong at the state and federal level, only 15 percent of Malays lived in cities as of 1970 and the federal government seemed inclined to slow urbanization pending job creation (Enloe 1975, 158–59). Nor could the MCA rescue the Alliance. As Democratic Action Party secretary-general Lim Kit Siang taunted in 1971, the MCA's only hope of a foothold in local authorities was "through the backdoor system of government appointment" (Lim 1971).

In essence, partisan machines supplanted elected local governments. The ruling party at the state level came to appoint councilors in each local area, effectively collapsing the distinction among tiers of government; from the outset, appointments prioritized "political affiliations instead of merit and experience" (see chapter 5; WDC 2008, 27–28). The party gained a range of offices to distribute, comprising a broad partisan web with assured adherence to a party whip. Moreover, continuing bureaucratic weakness and incapacity validated ever more extensive party machines as service-providing, mobilizing apparatuses.

Overlapping this transition, in 1962, the federal government introduced Village Development and Security Committees (JKKK, *Jawatankuasa Kemajuan dan Keselamatan Kampung*) in about fifteen thousand villages, headed by the *ketua kampung* (village head, usually chair of the local UMNO branch[111]), to expand its reach. Modeled on a new village innovation, and with a similar surveillance edge, JKKK were to be the government's "eyes and ears" on security matters and aid in poverty eradication. Their responsibilities expanded to include broader administrative, developmental, and patronage-channeling roles among rural communities (Funston 2016, 41, 133n22; Hunter 2013).[112] Although JKKK are funded mainly at the federal level and housed administratively at the village level, state governments appoint their members (who receive a small allowance) with advice from local party leaders; members usually include party activists.[113] JKKK came to serve as party-aligned village-level governments, further consolidating clientelistic party machines.

The overall pattern at the local-government level, then, was of increasing party control, absent the mediation of an electoral check. With the Alliance securely entrenched (and enfeebling key rivals) at the federal level and in most states by the mid-1960s, regime leaders could be confident these changes would benefit themselves. Having parties choose local councilors and JKKK members, and having these appointees administer government programs, facilitated casting even programmatic welfare policies as though they were party patronage, effectively partisanizing them and ensuring the ground-level officials with whom most voters interacted were Alliance loyalists.

Connecting with Voters

Indeed, Alliance and opposition politicians alike, independently or with their party apparatus, nurtured close ties with citizens, only partly fueled by concrete benefits. The niche each groomed reflected his or her specific orientation and base. Their common premise, though, was direct accountability and well-maintained relationships to reassure constituents that the politician and party would take care of them.

Especially after 1957, UMNO cultivated its rural Malay base. Early UMNO leaders were tied to the *kampung*, involving themselves with funerals, religious observances, and other village occasions. For a politician to be accepted, especially if not from that village, required careful adaptation to local culture and comportment, from dialect to posture. Humility and proper behavior, especially in public, were essential. The party's role, too, intertwined with broader village socio-economics. (Later, legislators' allocations allowed local leaders and villagers to secure contracts for rural development projects, allowing more distinct, financialized connections.)[114] UMNO built mosques, schools, and health facilities, supplementing national rural development schemes. When its efforts also to woo non-Malays and city dwellers cost UMNO rural support in 1959—particularly concessions on the language of instruction in schools, which alienated Malay teachers—UMNO responded not just with measures to restrict opposition and media, but with stepped-up, hyperlocal rural patronage: small-scale contracts, scholarships, land allocations, village development projects, and payments for helping UMNO campaign. UMNO branches, party leaders, ordinary members, and localities all benefited (Funston 2016, 39–40). At the same time, Kaum Ibu, the women's wing, ensured a deeply personal interaction between party activists and local families, as its members provided door-to-door ongoing civic education, persuasion, and mobilization (Manderson 1977, 175–76).

More urban-based politicians, in contrast, focused on organizational ties; these connections augmented parties' roots in communities and illustrated the party's profile. Associational life was especially dense among the Chinese community, which had enjoyed a degree of autonomy under colonial rule and had transplanted from China clan associations, secret societies, and locality-, dialect-, or occupation-based organizations and established hundreds of community-supported schools (Heng 1996, 33–34). In Sabah, for instance, behind emerging Chinese parties were North Borneo Chinese Associations, with branches in almost every town. Through affiliated clan organizations, these bodies wielded "considerable influence" on the community.[115] The local Chinese Chamber of Commerce sought nevertheless to insulate commerce from politics, until the rise of *towkay* politicians blurred the lines; dialect associations, in which these same politicians were prominent, were less constrained (Lee 1968, 322). Peninsular Chinese guilds and associations were similarly important, especially for the MCA. Penang in particular had a concentration of these bodies (for instance, the Chinese Town Hall, *wushu* organizations, and Hungry Ghost Festival committees), which were politically powerful and influential from the 1950s until at least the 1980s.[116] The 1952 Barnes Report on Malayan education's antipathy to vernacular schools particularly pressed Chinese education-related organizations (a central node in the Chinese association landscape) to ally with the MCA in 1953 to facilitate negotiations with UMNO (Ho 1992, 10–12)—notwithstanding the fact that "men somewhat detached from the Chinese cultural milieu" dominated MCA leadership (Ho 1992, 24). On the left, as well, labor unions allied with the MCP, granting the party exceptional influence in an "intensifying climate of industrial unrest" in the early postwar period (Chin Peng 2003, 196).

As this galvanizing of party activists and targeting of voter clusters on the assumption of a bloc vote suggests, individuals could exercise outsize influence in a population with fairly broad franchise and relatively little interest in formal politics. A British report on Sabah was especially scathing, noting that voters "make no pretence of understanding the issues at stake and are content to let some recognised leader to do their thinking for them. . . . It is less true to say that political leaders 'represent' their followers than it is to say that the leaders have followings who are prepared to accept their lead uncritically."[117] The combination of politicians' personal intermediation with individuals and groups, provision of welfare and other services through party channels, and government control of information, all streamlined by the fusing of tiers of government, fostered similarly pragmatic politics nationwide.

Hands-on service—the "personal touch"—came to be the mainstay of politicking, not just at elections or only for the Alliance. PRM leaders and activists, for example, visited constituencies regularly, their activities ranging from offering courses on the country's political and economic situation, to helping New Villagers acquire identity cards, to washing dishes after *kampung* wedding feasts. By being actively involved in society, they got to know villagers and had time to chat; such outreach was more effective than rallies at drawing people into the party. The party was thus strongest where it had a sufficient pool of members for such work—for instance, in parts of Pahang and Johor.[118]

The LPM likewise emphasized "mass work" such as fixing damaged roads or houses and cleaning rubbish and drains; the party roped both party members and nonmember supporters into "contact" efforts and supporting the poor. They offered sewing and literacy classes as well as discussion sessions, tempering socialist theory with songs and literature. Party-based clubs and dances drew in young people, at least several times a week—these cultural activities, and the social network they fostered, were important in attracting recruits. Selling the party newspaper door-to-door also combined training in outreach for members, maintaining contact, propaganda, and fundraising. And like UMNO, LPM established branches at the village level, each with elected leaders, forming a hierarchy stretching to the national level. Also, as for UMNO, even the highly educated professionals among party leaders needed to maintain good relations with party members: "attitude" mattered.[119] This emphasis on the "personal touch" built connections; it was less about dispensing resources or funds than demonstrating sincerity and service.

More broadly, while practiced by government and opposition alike, it is this deep, everyday penetration that came to maintain the electoral-authoritarian regime by acculturating citizens toward a particular mode of engagement with their government. Over time, citizens came to expect and rely on patron-client relationships, nested within party machines, albeit reinforced by carefully structured distributive and development policies. Reflecting on their political efforts starting in the 1960s, one politician dates contemporary social media assessments to "traditionalist" practices, in which local notables, from village heads to schoolteachers, scrutinized his performance and "service" trumped loyalty to party leaders, while another credits his start as a district officer—the omnipresent "face of government" at the grass roots—as readying him for elected office, when citizens expected him to be always accessible and focused on their basic needs.[120]

However inefficient and labor-intensive the approach, the Alliance preferred clientelism, which clearly favors a well-organized incumbent, to regularizing access to programmatic benefits under a "neutral" bureaucracy. Even opposition parties with a more ideological premise came to replicate Alliance behavior—and key opposition parties began with cognate strategies of outreach and assistance, regardless—adapting to evolving norms and voters' expectations, as well as structural shifts. As discussed later, the result remains a lukewarm commitment at best among opposition parties to transform the regime—and among voters, a persistent source of legitimation for, dependency on, and sense of indebtedness to the now fully mature electoral-authoritarian party state.

EDGING TOWARD SOVEREIGN SINGAPORE

As in Malaya, political institutionalization in Singapore proceeded on parallel local and national tracks against a backdrop of postwar reconstruction, anticommunism, ethnic tension, and uncertainty about the benefits and disadvantages of independence and uniting with Malaya. Yet Singapore presented a different environment: it had a more solid Chinese—and hence substantially settler—majority (though with an uneasy mix of Chinese-educated and English-educated), a much smaller land area, a population less inclined toward Indonesia or pan-Malayism, and, postwar, a fully separate administrative structure. That the People's Action Party (PAP) would become dominant was not initially clear; the party formed after elections were under way, its growing pains were severe, and the British were decidedly chary of it. Nor was it initially apparent what cleavages—for instance, communal, ideological, class—would define the party system as parties emerged in the late 1940s.

Tumultuous rivalries both within and among parties, amid British and local concerns about communists, communalists, and Singapore's viability, cast long shadows. The Emergency began in June 1948, three months after Singapore's first elections. Threats of unrest, real or trumped-up, yielded institutional constraints still important to regime maintenance, worry over infiltration encouraged parties to adopt cadre structures rather than embrace a mass base, and bitter contests inspired habits of laboriously maintained clientelism. Singapore's distinctive regime, combining hegemonic authority, pragmatism over ideology, and a near-compulsive service orientation rests on this early foundation, as competition gave way within only about a decade to firm one-party dominance.

Basic issues of how to structure the institutional framework proved daunting for British and local planners. The details of merger were especially fraught: Singapore's regime reflected a different ethnic and ideological legacy from Malaya's. The solution devised was an unequal, incomplete (and ultimately unsustainable) partnership between polities (Milne 1963, 76–77, 80). Tumult notwithstanding, the years before separation in 1965 saw a remarkably durable system emplaced. Notwithstanding important tweaks in later years, the regime's premises for accountability and legitimacy fast solidified, with party machines and substantially clientelistic linkages central.

Institutions and Elections

Small though Singapore is, self-government began with a two-tiered administrative structure of local and national government. As in Malaya, colonial officials assumed local government important for civic education and countering communism. Yet local government developed somewhat disjointedly, then was soon scotched altogether. At the same time, messy initial elections sparked strong reforms, shaping parties' strategies and broadening participation.

Local Government

That self-government began at the local level reflects colonial-era demography: at the turn of the twentieth century, over 80 percent of Singapore fell outside the city limits. The Municipal Ordinance of 1887 first separated town from city, with an appointed Rural Board to handle basic utilities and administration alongside an also appointed, mostly European, Municipal Committee (Quah 2001, 5–6). In 1946, six months after the postwar resumption of civilian government, the head of the Rural Board proposed adding village (renamed district) committees to foster civic responsibility and facilitate cooperation and communication between government and people. Security was a key impetus: committee members would be sufficiently well-acquainted with their areas to note "strangers." The idea took off. Seven committees, each representing seven villages, were soon swamped with requests and seeking space for public meetings, adult night schools, and other functions.[1] By popular demand, colonial authorities moved to replace the board-and-committees system with elected district councils. Boundaries for three electoral divisions were formalized in January 1958; the electoral roll was confirmed by mid-April; four parties announced plans to contest. But the process then stalled, pending the recommendations of the Elias Commission, discussed below.[2]

Urban government developed simultaneously postwar through piecemeal legislation. A part-elected Municipal Commission (renamed City Council when Singapore gained city status in 1951) took office in 1949. With self-government imminent in 1951, colonial authorities commissioned a report on local government from Dr. L. C. Hill.[3] He recommended renovating city government machinery and reallocating responsibilities to prepare for more complex welfare-state needs under a fully elected council and mayor.[4] Singapore's new Labour Front government rejected a proposal to merge the national Legislative Council and the City Council.[5] Instead, the 1955 McNeice committee advised maintaining local government for opportunities to participate at the local level, as a training ground for legislators, and for greater efficiency. The 1957 Legislative Council enactments settled on an expanded, elected city council and the aforementioned rural district councils (Quah 2001, 6–7).

But the newly elected PAP government eliminated City Council two years later, fulfilling a campaign pledge, then the 1963 Local Government Integration Ordinance dissolved both it and the Rural Board and distributed their functions among government ministries (Tan K. Y. L. 2015, 73–74). By the time of merger, local government was dead—although partly resuscitated with the launch of town councils in the 1980s (see chapter 6).

Legislative Council

National government was simultaneously in transition. A nominated Legislative Council, launched prewar for partial self-government, regrouped in 1946. However, as Governor Gimson acknowledged, the war had awakened political consciousness; the British could "no longer expect the general mass of the people to accept the benevolent bureaucratic government which existed previously."[6] Colonial authorities appointed a committee to propose a new legislative framework. Building on these recommendations, the final plan included two urban two-member districts, two rural single-member districts, three members elected by the Singapore, Chinese, and Indian Chambers of Commerce, plus up to four additional nominated members from otherwise unrepresented constituencies.[7] In practice, since so few Chinese registered to vote, those extra seats ended up going primarily to them after inaugural elections in 1948.[8] The initial model, then, presumed a fairly ethnicized politics.

Once elected, the legislature amended the 1947 Legislative Council Elections Ordinance almost immediately, in late 1948. Some changes were fairly trivial, such as allowing candidates to choose their own ballot symbols and share them among party members. (Supervisor of Elections G. Hawkins worried that partisan displays might spark a last-minute flood of "party favours" and "mass hypnotising and mental cruelty to electors.") Others were more controversial. For example, the amendments converted two-member constituencies to single-member ones, removing the possibility of double voting for minority candidates such as Indians, Europeans, and Jews.[9] Three years later, a member system modeled on Malaya's (see chapter 3), put legislative councilors in control of government departments.[10]

The Legislative Council was short-lived. In 1953, colonial authorities convened a constitutional commission (poorly coordinated with Federation planning) under George Rendel.[11] The resultant 1954 constitution extended self-government under a now majority-elected, renamed Legislative Assembly (again renamed Parliament in 1965), with automatic voter registration and no longer special representation for chambers of commerce (Carnell 1954, 219–20). Full, and fully elected, self-government followed in 1959.

The final legislative arena was the federation one, for the brief period of merger (1963–65). On this stage the PAP stumbled: the party decided, contra a tacit agreement between Lee Kuan Yew and Tunku Abdul Rahman, to contest beyond Singapore in the 1964 Malaysian general election. Several Malayan-born PAP ministers led the charge; Lee acceded, noting that UMNO leaders had already breached the agreement with appearances during Singapore's elections. The PAP fared terribly in peninsular contests: it lacked ties with local organizations and community leaders, its message and candidates remained unfamiliar, and its aims in engaging in the Malay heartland were unclear. Nonetheless, the large rally turnouts alarmed UMNO leaders and gave PAP leaders false hope. The PAP won one seat of nine contested, against the Socialist Front.[12] Though the latter was as much the PAP's target as the MCA (Poh 2016, 289), PAP participation still irked the Tunku's Alliance.

Orienting the Public toward Formal Politics

As both the franchise and the range of offices contested expanded, low registration, weak turnout, and electoral malfeasance sparked concern. Popular response to the first registration exercise in 1947 was "sluggish," stalling at about 20 percent of those eligible (British subjects at least twenty-one years old, resident for at least the preceding year, regardless of sex, literacy, or means). Reasons for not registering included distaste for filling out forms, the novelty of the procedure, distrust among those whom the Japanese had made to register on official lists, confusion over district boundaries and eligibility, and apathy. The Supervisor of Elections described local perceptions of voter registration as being "for an abstraction . . . as impersonal, bloodless and unattractive as a proposition in Euclid."[13] Neither trade unions nor parties were of much help, and a boycott by the left-nationalist All-Malaya Council of Joint Action and Pusat Tenaga Ra'ayat (Centre of People's Power) likely deterred would-be registrants.[14]

Legislative Council elections commenced, regardless, in 1948, initially with only independent and Progressive Party candidates. (The left-wing Malayan Democratic Union boycotted.) Turnout was a decent 62.3 percent, but only 22,334 were registered to vote, from a population exceeding 940,000.[15] The next round of elections, in 1950, saw little improvement, despite "energetic canvassing" by the Labour Party (LP) and the Progressive Party, since registration was still just about 49,000 for the Legislative Council and 22,500 for the Municipal Commission, of electorates estimated at 250,000 and 160,000, respectively. Still, colonial authorities deemed turnout "reasonably satisfactory," given parties' limited policy differentiation or ability "to achieve any real 'rapport' with the non-English speaking masses."[16] Still in 1951, only about half of all adults were eligible to vote for the Legislative Council, 20 percent of whom registered; about half those registered voted—that is, about one in twenty adults (Carnell 1954, 217). The municipal elections of 1951 also "did not attract a great deal of attention"; "political consciousness" and trust in democratic institutions remained low, except among Indians, who were heavily overrepresented among both candidates and voters.[17]

By 1957, the municipal electorate had increased about tenfold since the preceding City Council election in 1953.[18] Yet turnout remained just under one-third, dampened by inaccurate registers and incessant rain.[19] The upstart PAP took on the rightist Liberal Socialist Party, explained the governor, by trying to make the election "a straight-forward fight between Workers and Capitalists," while "older and more responsible citizens" yielded to youthful leftists. "The majority of the voters," he groused, "seemed to be housewives and illiterates who had been prodded by persistent young canvassers."[20] Indeed, with over half Singapore's population then under twenty-one (Curless 2016, 56), nearly all candidates in 1957 were young and inexperienced, their backgrounds ranging from architect to dressmaker to lorry driver (Comber 2012, 27). The PAP's candidates were exceptionally so, with an average age under twenty-seven, versus around thirty-five for candidates overall.[21] Still in 1959, the youngest PAP legislator was merely twenty-two and a "25-year old girl" vanquished a former Labour Front (LF) minister.[22]

The inchoate politics of the 1950s supported rampant malfeasance. The *Straits Times* described the efforts of "organised gangs of racketeers" to interfere with the 1953 city elections: hired children tore down posters overnight, thugs threatened candidates, and voters demanded payments. Several candidates reported that they were offered blocs of one hundred to one thousand votes for sale and rebuffed with calls of "No money, no votes" when they canvassed house-to-house.[23] For 1955, "every trick in the book was applied," with "so many ways" of buying votes.[24] Helping the PAP's Devan Nair, Lim Hock Siew met voters, he recalled, who acknowledged having accepted five-dollar payments and moved in a group when canvassing, in case of marauding gangsters.[25] By 1957, secret societies aligned with all parties as well as independents, sparking minor clashes.[26] Students, particularly from Chinese middle schools, likewise participated actively, especially for the PAP and the Workers' Party (WP). The British worried that at least some of their involvement might be communist inspired or organized and contemplated holding elections during exams as a deterrent.[27] Still, the governor conceded that the students involved were "well disciplined and pleasantly attentive to voters."[28]

Colonial authorities sought remedies. The 1952–53 Blythe Committee had recommended increasing registration rates to make vote buying untenably expensive.[29] Now the Elias Commission convened to examine "corrupt, illegal or undesirable" electoral practices. The commission found evidence of secret-society efforts to coerce support or obstruct voting, aggressive polling-day canvassing and bribery, and simple apathy[30]—as of 1958, an estimated 75 percent of those registered had never voted (Comber 2012, 33). Ensuing electoral law amendments barred parties and supporters from canvassing, displaying party symbols or flags, or transporting voters to polls on polling day, plus banned schoolchildren and secret-society members from electioneering. No one could campaign without a candidate's written authority, and space was to be allotted equitably and without compensation for banners and posters.[31]

But the centerpiece of the commission's recommendations was compulsory voting. The proposal made the rounds of British colonial offices, whose staff considered the few examples globally.[32] Opinion split on whether compelling participation was preferable to stronger efforts to encourage voluntary turnout.[33] The thorniest details were whether to allow voters to cast a blank ballot, whether electoral rolls and polling-station access could be improved sufficiently by the next election, how to ensure administrative capacity for enforcement, and what the penalties for not voting should be.[34] A select committee decided that those who failed to vote without adequate excuse would have to pay five dollars to be restored to the rolls but would not be actively prosecuted; those expunged would, however, be disqualified from certain social services and facilities, possibly including medical, unemployment, education, and housing benefits, as well as from securing passports and civil service jobs.[35] (These penalties echoed in PAP threats to potential opposition voters decades later.) Critics decried these measures as unduly punitive and likely to hurt the poor.[36] However, mandating voting might otherwise "play straight into the hands of those who wish to intimidate their political opponents from voting"[37] and disenfranchisement would simply ensure nonparticipation.[38]

Although PAP leader Lee Kuan Yew eventually came around, he initially (and with reason) had "jeered at the Government for adopting compulsory voting as a device to beat the P.A.P."[39] The WP rallied against the proposal, seeing it as both intended to force "white-collared" moderates to vote and an imposition on already-overburdened workers.[40] Labour Front Chief Minister Lim Yew Hock was unsure whether the additional voters would lean toward moderate parties and initially opposed the measure. He then reversed course, apparently hoping that, compelled to vote, more conservative, older voters would support Labour or the Alliance rather than the worrisomely strong PAP.[41] His party pushed to extend compulsory voting to rural elections, too.[42] The Liberal Socialist Party (LSP) agreed, lest an organized minority dominate the "lethargic" majority.[43] Only UMNO resisted. Full turnout would swamp the Malay minority.[44] Their threats of mass demonstrations or an electoral boycott failed to stall passage but ensured less punitive enforcement.[45] Governor Goode was likewise unconvinced that higher turnout would water down extreme-left influence,[46] and even some politicians in favor of compulsory voting balked at stripping nonvoters of welfare benefits; they rationalized that parties would now work harder and optimize their machinery.[47] The proposal passed in 1959 for both local and national elections. Legislative elections that year—the first experiment in compulsory voting—saw nearly 90 percent turnout, producing, interestingly, a disproportionately non-Chinese legislature, including about 10 percent women. The British declared a "complete success."[48]

The last genuinely competitive election before PAP dominance solidified was held in 1963. Despite a strong challenge from the beleaguered Barisan Sosialis (Socialist Front, but not to be confused with the peninsular coalition of the same name), the PAP won thirty-seven of fifty-one seats. By the time of separation from Malaysia in 1965, the PAP government had effectively quashed Barisan and the far left by extending the 1955 Preservation of Public Security Ordinance and the 1960 Internal Security Act, adopted in Singapore in 1963, detaining "subversives," curbing mass media and left-wing publications, deregistering dissident unions, and crowding out alternatives through its own "near saturation of the political arena" (Chan 1976, 202–6). These formative initial polls and phases in electoral lawmaking ensconced elections as reasonably fair and legitimate, with assured high participation. However, they also validated policymakers' tweaking the rules to their own presumed advantage.

Parties and Political Networks

Singapore's early political parties aligned themselves more on ideological than communal axes, leaving specific constituencies less clearly defined than in Malaya. Governor Goode noted that "points of emphasis and organisation" more than policies distinguished the five parties in Singapore's foundational 1959 elections: all were for "general social betterment," a welfare state, merger with Malaya, and racial harmony; all largely ignored international issues. Their platforms differed mostly in their attention to local businesses, administrative reorganization, and the like.[49] The PAP's stunning win that year of forty-three of fifty-one seats (thirteen with just a plurality), with 53.6 percent of the popular vote, owed as much to its opponents' incoherence as its own prowess. Allegations of corruption, reluctance to ally, and imperfectly aligned supporters forestalled cross-party collaboration, "bewildered" moderate voters, and "hopelessly split" the anti-PAP vote.[50] Yet the extent of common ground also facilitated the PAP's evolution into a catch-all dominant party.

"Moderate" or Right-Wing Parties

That parties of the political right—lukewarm toward independence, with a pro-business, pro-British orientation—emerged first laid the ground for this ideological mapping. Leading this camp were the Progressive Party and the Democratic Party, which merged in 1956 to form the LSP. The "practical and pragmatic," non-communal Progressive Party, its base among English-educated, locally born professionals and white-collar workers, favored increased investment, social services, and incremental progress toward self-government. A member noted that it was never a "tub-thumping crowd";[51] the party faced little initial political challenge or incentive to be more than "just laissez-faire," per a Labour Front opponent.[52] By 1955, a vastly expanded electorate pressed the party to develop a mass organization, but lacking "real contact" with non-English-speaking, lower-income voters, the party was routed.[53] The Democratic Party, in contrast, although ostensibly noncommunal, aligned with the Chinese Chamber of Commerce and emerged in part from business community efforts to make Chinese an official language. It favored jus soli citizenship, multilingualism, social services, freer trade, and improvements for labor.[54] Its leaders built support by maintaining simultaneous roles in clan, dialect, and other associations and a "paternalistic image" (Bellows 1967, 128).

After rivalry between these two parties enabled "extremists and opportunists to fluke a victory" in 1955, as the Progressives' secretary-general put it, the two parties forged the LSP. Its broad goals included a higher standard of living, racial harmony, multilingual education, orderly progress toward independence, Malayanization of the public service, and equal partnership in a Confederation of Malaya.[55] Yet whereas the Progressives and Democrats polled over 45 percent total running separately in 1955, as the LSP in 1959, they received only 11.3 percent (Bellows 1967, 124). The PAP had found what became a defining niche in promising probity. One of their top campaign gimmicks was brandishing a broom—to sweep City Council clean—and new PAP mayor Ong Eng Guan proved "a terror to the staff" once in office.[56] He complained that the City Council he inherited from the Progressives "was a cesspool of maladministration, corruption and inefficiency."[57] Opponents also charged the LSP with including among its ranks secret society leaders or "nominees of wealthy interests."[58] The party soon collapsed.[59]

Parties of the Left

Anticolonial sentiment propelled the left toward the limelight, but establishment disregard, then internecine competition, pushed these parties to innovate in connecting with voters, birthing patterns of personalized, consistent outreach. In this camp were the Labour Front (formed in 1954 of the merger of the Labour Party, Socialist Party, and Malay Union), the WP, and the PAP, plus later the Barisan Sosialis. The communal UMNO and MCA—branches of the Malayan parties, which contested as the Alliance as of 1953—also tended to align with the left.[60]

Welfarism, trade unionism, and nationalism offered sufficient common ground that left-wing parties might have allied, especially since "perambulatory politicians" (as a PAP minister branded party hoppers) limited differentiation.[61] Nevertheless, fractiousness prevailed, ultimately clearing the PAP's path to office. Attempts at electoral pacts accomplished little. In 1957, when the LF negotiated with both the PAP and the Alliance to avoid splitting the anti-LSP vote (Comber 2012, 22), for instance, the already-confident PAP "called the tune," claiming left-leaning wards for itself and relegating the LF to middle-class LSP bailiwicks.[62] LF members, meanwhile, considered themselves the key player, however perturbed by the PAP's solidifying ground[63] and aware that some of their own members of the Legislative Assembly (MLAs) were ineffective or "doubtful."[64] The LF swore off aligning with the PAP thereafter.[65]

Trade unions played key roles in several parties. Unions pressed parties to select candidates committed to workers' welfare and not to challenge prolabor rivals,[66] plus supplied both candidates and campaign support. (Indeed, trade unionists and manual workers constituted significant blocs among MLAs, although white-collar workers, especially teachers and journalists, comprised nearly half the 1959 Legislative Assembly.[67]) The PAP especially tapped this lode. Writing in the PAP magazine *Petir*, J. J. Puthucheary termed Singapore's unions the "industrial wing of a working class movement of which the P.A.P. is the political wing." With the PAP in office, union leaders could "swim with the current they control."[68]

Plans for independence proved more fraught, despite shared anticolonialism. Installed as mayor in 1957, the PAP's Ong purged the City Council chamber of

Union Jacks, ended hiring preferences for graduates of British schools, and limited compensation for retired expatriate staff.[69] But specific plans, especially whether or not to merge with Malaya, fractured the left decisively; the PAP emerged firmly dominant, but also more centrist and ruthless.

It was the amalgamated LF, though, that initially dominated, supplying Singapore's first chief ministers: David Marshall (who resigned in 1957 after failed constitutional talks in London) and Lim Yew Hock. The LF tended toward "middle-of-the-road Socialist." Its organizers, not working class themselves, pitched appeals to the English educated. The party sought expedited self-government, liberal citizenship, multilingualism, Malayanization of the public service, repeal of emergency regulations and banishment laws, a united Malaya, and tax-funded, expanded social services.[70] British assessments found the LF riven by "internal schisms"; the Malay Union pulled out almost immediately and "personal bickering" remained endemic.[71] Moreover, the LF's "very casual and amateur approach to the realities of politics" offered entry points to gang and secret society members, inviting police action (Thomas 2015, 32, 38–39). The disorganized LF "sort of staggered from crisis to crisis," recalled secretary-organizer Gerald De Cruz.[72]

The party lacked resources, administrative capacity, or a fully articulated platform. Its unexpected win in its first election in 1955, when the party had probably fewer than two hundred members, was largely because the still-new PAP, unprepared to contest widely itself, backed Labour candidates.[73] Few LF candidates had grassroots followings, nor could the party provide substantial campaign support—willingness to cover their own election expenses screened out opportunists. The party remained consistently in a precarious financial position, despite some campaign-time fundraising and (usually anonymous) contributions from small businesses and personal supporters.[74] By mid-1958, bracing for staff layoffs and bankruptcy, LF officials had to threaten Lim Yew Hock with legal action if he did not repay borrowed party funds (Thomas 2015, 55, 58, 165–70). The LF worked to build institutional capacity, nonetheless, encouraging its MLAs to "nurse their constituencies" with weekly meetings and "little branch offices."[75] MLAs contributed part of their salary to party expenses, plus usually maintained these branches out-of-pocket, though the party opened some where it lacked representation. Central control was weak.[76]

So dismayed were the British at the LF's surprise victory in 1955 that the high commissioner did not want to give Marshall an office as chief minister. Already, he had scored free campaign exposure by capitalizing on the English press's bashing him.[77] Now, relegated to a small room under the stairs of Assembly House, Marshall colorfully proposed to set up shop "under the old apple tree" at Empress Place—the sessions were essentially weekly publicity stunts, but still provided a genuine forum for service delivery.[78] (More on these efforts below.) His quixotic approach to building a reputation helped Marshall to sidestep British disregard and launched a new standard for politicians' outreach.

Three years later, seeking stronger footing against the PAP, Marshall's successor, Lim Yew Hock, proposed a United Socialist Front together with the LSP and the WP, soon rebranded as the Singapore People's Alliance (SPA). It would set aside "personal and political differences" to unite "to save Singapore from fear, slavery and dictatorship."[79] This collaboration against "extreme leftists"[80] created a centrist administration when four LSP MLAs crossed the aisle to join Lim's now-SPA government (Bellows 1967, 124). Rejecting the rightward shift, a rump LF remained independent but dissolved after bombing in 1959.[81]

Just in time to contest in 1957, Marshall emerged from short-lived political retirement to launch the WP, soon Singapore's leading opposition party. The WP sought full independence, parliamentary democracy, socialism, and racial equality.[82] Marshall aimed that the party, which targeted trade unionists, be more a "goad in Parliament" than an enduring vehicle; its only long-term objective was independence[83]—yet it persists today. To win over reluctant unions, Marshall, a lawyer, offered legal services for $1 per year, but the party also drew (sometimes opportunistic) dissidents from other parties.[84] Marshall worried about the risk of communist or secret society penetration and even requested police help in vetting applications, confessing to the commissioner of police that he had inadvertently accepted a secret society's headquarters as an election office and now felt obligated to the society.[85] The WP won four city council seats (of five contested) in 1957, only to experience mass resignations the following year. Marshall himself lost in 1959, returned in a by-election in 1961, then resigned from the WP in 1963. The party declined after two other top officials were detained that year, reviving only in the 1970s.[86]

Rounding out the left wing (apart from the PAP and Barisan, detailed below, and generally short-lived, smaller parties such as Partai Rakyat Singapura[87]) were the MCA and UMNO (reregistered as Pertubuhan Kebangsaan Melayu Singapura, Singapore Malay National Organisation, in 1961), communalism's only real foothold in Singapore. The MCA sought expanded political rights, better working conditions and welfare policies, and protection of local industries, agriculture, and trade.[88] However, it was so closely tied to its Malayan parent that the latter drafted the MCA's 1955 platform and Singapore's Chinese Chamber of Commerce withheld support, seeing the party as mostly about selling lottery tickets in Malaya.[89] UMNO's goals were similar, but it stressed also pro-Malay policies. A Singapore UMNO/MCA Alliance performed poorly in initial elections.[90] But UMNO fared better on its own. Its heydays were around the time of merger: it reached fourteen thousand members and eighty-one branches and joined its parent party in actively pushing for Malay privileges and standing. That even earlier, though, the party fared fairly well, winning all Malay-majority constituencies in 1959, suggests why the PAP proved so keen to eliminate ethnic enclaves in restructuring Singapore's electoral landscape in the 1960s (Chan 1976, 207–10; Yap, Lim, and Leong 2009, 276–77; Mutalib 2003, 200–3).

The PAP

Initially the PAP saw itself as part of a larger left-wing movement. A cluster of mostly English-educated "young intelligent anti-Colonial dissidents" formed the party in 1954.[91] Distrusting Lim Yew Hock and deeming his party too much mere election vehicle, PAP adherents hesitated to align with the LF, despite British encouragement;[92] Marshall deemed them "crypto-communists." The party was "patently populist," inspired by a "combination of Fabian socialism and communism" (Chan 1989, 32). The PAP agreed on a basic program—repeal of the Emergency Regulations and Trade Union Ordinance, a fully elected legislature, unification with Malaya, subsidized housing, free education, and opposition to proposed restrictions on schools—before it even had a name.[93] The PAP painted itself as a social-democratic reprieve from either communism or "right wing dictatorship."[94] The party advocated vehemently for political and economic independence and equality; state support of the ill, young, aged, and unable to work; rights to free expression, association, and peaceful assembly; and improved labor laws, including a Workers' Charter, which would guarantee a minimum wage, equal pay for women, a forty-hour week, and paid leave.[95]

The PAP presented a clear policy platform. Economics loomed large, including plans for tax revenue–generating economic expansion to fund moderately redistributive social welfare policies.[96] Also, as Lee Kuan Yew noted in a 1959 rally speech, while the party encouraged unionization and collective bargaining, it discouraged allowing "tussles" with capital to damage economic prospects.[97] PAP messaging emphasized clean, efficient, fair government; a responsive, Malayanized administration; accessibility to constituents; eliminating detention without trial; and supporting four official languages, but with Malay as the national language.[98] It also touted the fact that its candidates were from varied professions, racially mixed, and included more women than any other party.[99]

The party attracted primarily Chinese support, especially from students (followed by their parents) and trade unions—more so than the LF. Unionized drivers and conductors, for instance, kept buses running late and discounted fares for PAP election meetings,[100] and though prohibited, the PAP engaged middle-school students—"matured" ones who "looked like workers"—for campaigns.[101] Unions helped to bridge English-educated party leaders and the Chinese-speaking masses and helped reinforce the party's preferred image as "for the working class" and "mass-based."[102] English-educated voters, though, tended to be "slightly fearful" of the party.[103] Lee Kuan Yew blamed the "diabolical" English-language press for "smearing" the PAP as near-communist extremists, scaring off English-speakers who might otherwise help counterbalance communist appeals.[104] Courting that segment, but implying his own class position, PAP Central Executive Committee (CEC) member (and inaugural Minister of Finance) Goh Keng Swee offered that the English-educated minority merited protection as citizens and skilled professionals; English-educated leaders, too, could be gracious service providers for "people like hawkers, labourers, mechanics and such types with whom one does not normally associate."[105] The party also courted Malays, promoting Malay language, pursuing development programs in heavily Malay areas (UMNO's turf), and including nine Malays among its 1959 slate, with only limited success.[106]

The PAP's backing by left-wing unions (known as "Middle Road unions" for the street on which their offices clustered), the rise of party leaders such as Chinese-educated firebrand Lim Chin Siong, and its advocacy of women's rights and independence—annual meeting attendees shouted "Merdeka" instead of "aye" on resolutions—gave the PAP a radical cast.[107] It aimed, though, to cast a broad net.[108] The party soon developed two factions: one Chinese- educated and working class; the other English-speaking and better off. While the PAP's CEC touted collective decision making[109] and Lee Kuan Kew purportedly defeated Ong Eng Guan in the CEC vote for prime minister in 1959 by only one vote,[110] Lee dominated from the start (Cheah 2006, 646). (The PAP investigated and expelled Ong the following year, eliminating one of Lee's key rivals.[111])

Branches tended to emerge out of election campaigns, with initiative and funding from the PAP candidate or councilor, although the party soon made efforts to streamline and manage activities. Branches persisted even where PAP candidates lost, supporting cultural activities, kindergartens, publications, film screenings, sewing and language classes, current affairs discussions, and more. Face-to-face constituency service boosted political awareness and the PAP's profile, wooing members and sometimes funds. Some branches included women's, fundraising, education, and other subcommittees.[112] Branch workers (and unions) recruited party members through person-to-person contact, attracting all kinds— "illiterates, semi-illiterates, women . . . a temple medium"—but mostly Chinese-educated "underdogs."[113] The PAP launched a central Education and Cultural Committee in 1957, too, to coordinate branch-level social functions, publications, study groups, and more—though it increasingly clashed with the party hierarchy (Poh 2016, 165–67). Shortly thereafter, the party restructured its administration in terms of districts, adding paid district secretaries in 1959, most with union ties. Still then, though, some constituencies lacked full PAP branches,[114] and lack of central control proved a near-fatal flaw.[115]

The PAP first contested in 1955, seeking just a legislative voice. Three of the party's four candidates won; a fifth, trade unionist Ahmad Ibrahim, stood as a PAP-backed independent.[116] In 1957, the party again contested only fourteen of thirty-two City Council seats, likely partly for lack of funds, but explained its strategy as not seeking to govern for another five years—a harbinger of the opposition "by-election strategy" of the 1990s, discussed in chapter 6.[117] They won a thirteen-seat plurality and the mayoralty.[118] The PAP's promised Malayanization and anticorruption efforts then worked to the party's advantage: civil servants joined as "job insurance" amid the restructuring and cleanup.[119] Meanwhile, the PAP's councilors "were determined to endear themselves to the public" within six months, launching an Information Bureau, Public Complaints Bureau, and weekly meet-the-people sessions (detailed below, Pang 1971, 5–6).

In 1959, the PAP took an aggressively programmatic approach, announcing a separate policy statement at each of a series of preelection rallies, covering all major fields of government activity. Collated and published in three pamphlets, the proposals sold nearly one hundred thousand copies, while circulation of the monthly, then weekly, party newspaper, *Petir*, topped sixty thousand. Street-corner meetings, too, were "jammed by three, four and even five thousand listeners or more," with as many as thirty thousand at mass rallies.[120] The PAP used these opportunities to tout its record and plans, supplemented by house visits and leafleting at morning markets, where party cadres would chat with residents about their concerns.[121] The PAP emerged victorious. Party membership surged postelection, from about 4,860 midyear to 8,245 by the end of 1959 (Pang 1971, 6).

As for other parties, finances bedeviled the early PAP—though at least it had ample volunteers. In 1958, for instance, the party kicked off a campaign for a building fund with ticket sales for a postelection "Thanksgiving Party."[122] Campaign expenses from 1956 on nearly exhausted the PAP's meager resources; to contest all fifty-one seats in 1959, the party had to borrow funds for the $500 perseat deposit from one of Lee's law firm's clients—luckily, all got their deposits back—and the party obliged its MLAs to contribute at least part of their salary and allowances to the PAP. (The rule deterred some candidates who needed that income.)[123]

Worries about subversion also dogged the PAP. British intelligence equated its anticolonial objectives with "those of the terrorists in the Jungle."[124] Colonial authorities kept Middle Road unions and political parties under heavy surveillance,[125] and Lee Kuan Yew complained of the police's denying permits for rallies and meetings. He insisted on the "democratic right" to peaceful assembly and association.[126]

The ideological rift within the party widened through the 1950s. Presumably procommunist nonmembers packed the PAP's 1957 annual conference, including hundreds of Chinese-school students and prominent trade unionists. The assembly voted three of eight moderate CEC incumbents out, while Middle Road representatives made headway.[127] Lim Yew Hock's government then arrested five CEC members (along with thirty others) under the Public Security Ordinance, and PAP secretary-general T. T. Rajah resigned. Lee Kuan Yew called for unity, and an Emergency Council nominated new candidates for a special party election that October.[128] That same year, the Special Branch identified four of fourteen PAP candidates as connected with subversive activities.[129] Upon their arrest, whether detainees could contest elections became an issue in constitutional deliberations. Lee insisted that no PAP MLA would assume elected office so long as their colleagues remained in detention.[130] However, he confided to a British official that Lim's actions were "absolutely right and necessary," even if they lacked the "moral basis" to have been handled by the British, and observers assumed the arrests to be at Lee's request.[131]

Tension mounted. By early 1958, Lee and his faction struggled against extremists' efforts to capture PAP branches.[132] The party reregistered all members that March to reconsolidate—a controversial step that itself sparked protests[133]—then set up a Selection Committee, with final vetting by the CEC, to promote only certain members as cadres. Would-be cadre members needed to meet age, literacy, citizenship, and party loyalty requirements and exhibit "outstanding performance" over one year's initial probation.[134] Membership topped fifteen thousand by the mid-1960s, but with fewer than four hundred cadres (Bellows 1967, 131).

Lee's support of merger with Malaya brought the party's crisis to a head. Eight PAP assemblymen and a substantial part of the trade union movement, worried about right-wing Federation-government control of Singapore, conditioned their support of the PAP candidate in a July 1961 by-election on the PAP's pursuing full internal self-government. Lee stood firm. His candidate lost to the WP's Marshall; five more PAP MLAs then also defected. A motion of no confidence later that month on the question of merger left Lee with a whisker-thin majority, but his government survived the vote. In the course of debate, Lee blamed the British, claiming they had tried to force the "extremists" into open conflict to compel repressive action.[135] Thirteen PAP MLAs abstained; the PAP promptly expelled them, including Lim Chin Siong, whom the *Economist* labeled "the PAP's near-communist secretary-general [sic]."[136] Those ousted quickly regrouped as the Barisan Sosialis.

The PAP moved to reconstruct its base and vision. Lee's 1962 series of radio broadcasts, "The Battle for Merger," laid the ideological ground for the PAP as a popularly elected, anticolonial force to lead a multiracial, noncommunist, developmentalist nation (Chua 1995, 14–16). But by the time of the 1963 elections, the PAP-as-organization remained weak: it had yet to rebuild its branches and many candidates scrambled to find campaign staff and facilities, to gain access to certain groups, and to whittle away at Barisan support.[137] As detailed below and in chapter 6, the PAP restructured its grassroots outreach to accommodate an attenuated party base, supplemented by partisanized programs, to take advantage of resources only the PAP controlled, complemented by selective coercion.

Barisan Sosialis

Barisan Sosialis served as the PAP's key foil, forcing it to hone its strategy on the ground and in office. The key players at Barisan's founding in 1961 were the thirteen MLAs dismissed from the PAP (but still in office), prominent union leaders, and ex-PAP branch leaders who had resigned or been expelled. Chairman Lee Siew Choh and Secretary-General Lim Chin Siong helmed the party. Most leaders were young and Chinese-educated; few were university graduates. Already having established branches allowed Barisan to leap into wooing the grass roots, while trying to coax more PAP MLAs over and using the Assembly as a platform to raise issues, especially concerning merger. Where Barisan had MLAs, they were responsible for organizing in their constituency; otherwise, trade unions, old-boys' (alumni) associations, and farmers' associations took charge. A share of MLAs' salary covered some expenses, supplemented by member donations and yearly fees. Sales revenues made the party's English and Chinese publications (self-published, since no printer would take the job) self-sustaining—the *Plebeian* routinely sold out, with over thirty thousand copies weekly.[138]

Barisan's launch crippled the PAP machine. At least twenty-four of twenty-seven PAP organizing secretaries joined Barisan,[139] and thirty-five of fifty-one PAP branch committees resigned en bloc, followed by a mass exodus of members; up to 80 percent of PAP members resigned, were expelled, or let their memberships lapse in 1961. Barisan took over the PAP's major ancillary organizations, including the People's Association and Works Brigade; most members of the PAP's Women's League, self-initiated in 1955, also jumped ship. By the end of 1961, Barisan had about one thousand members, but gave the impression of being larger, especially given the crowd of around ten thousand at its first rally that August.[140] (PAP branches reported rampant pilfering amid these movements; a journalist wondered snidely if Barisan were launching a political movement or "opening a junk shop."[141]) The trade union movement divided, too. Replacing the original Trades Union Congress in 1961 were the pro-Barisan Singapore Association of Trade Unions, with about fifty unions (including the powerful Singapore General Employees Union), and the PAP-linked National Trades Union Congress

(NTUC), with initially about fifteen—though the PAP aggressively courted moderate unions.[142] By December 1965, Barisan controlled twenty-nine unions, comprising 21 percent of union members; 74 percent of members (in fifty-nine unions) had joined the NTUC (Bellows 1970, 109).

Although to the left of the PAP, Barisan denied British and PAP charges of being, as the PAP's Goh Keng Swee put it, an "open-front organisation of the Communist movement."[143] Barisan statements attacked "despotic" PAP governance as marred by "bureaucratism, arrogance and intransigence" and by failed promises to support unions and political rights. Barisan, in contrast, promised to support workers and the exploited or oppressed, end foreign domination, unite races and religions, pursue economic equality, and seek union with Malaya and Borneo on suitable terms.[144] Party leaders promised more consultative, democratic governance, including incorporating all parties' interests in constitutional negotiations.[145] They claimed Lee Kuan Yew had become paranoid and suspicious of dissent, ginning up tension as an excuse to suppress criticism within the party and civil liberties outside.[146] Having a small number of people select cadres, who then set party policy, Barisan leaders suggested, was problematic.[147] Barisan itself had only ordinary (not cadre) members, organized into branches; each branch elected delegates who elected a central committee.[148]

Barisan set out to build support, particularly through the branches it had across Singapore by 1963. Branch-funded kindergartens were a linchpin, currying parents' favor and teaching children antigovernment jingles (Seah 1973, 35; Bellows 1970, 103). Branches also provided classes (especially Malay language), social and cultural activities, and service centers to handle complaints, especially from rural and resettlement areas. These services aimed to link citizens' issues with structural attributes such as colonialism to promote Barisan's ideological line. However, the party had not really thought through how to frame its appeal after independence and remained stronger in rural than urban areas, particularly post-merger.[149]

What most differentiated the PAP and Barisan was their stances on political detentions and anticolonialism; what made Barisan such a threat was its proximity otherwise in posture and base to the PAP. Indeed, critics suggested the British came to support merger when they did, having opposed it previously, to give Lee an issue with which to launch himself above his challengers. Both parties sought allies, in both Singapore and Malaya. Most of Barisan's support came from trade unions, the student left, and the Rural Residents' Association, which helped with problems of land and housing (and had initially aligned with the PAP[150]). Barisan's strength was among poorer voters, across ethnic communities.[151] Supporters of Singapore's Malay left, then more anticolonial and pan-Malay-nationalist than socialist, were more likely to join Partai Rakyat Singapura than

Barisan, but the parties were on friendly terms. And Barisan leaders maintained close links with leaders of the Malayan left, although arrests on both sides disrupted ties.[152]

Debates over merger framed Barisan's rise and fall. The PAP continued full steam, shutting the opposition out from negotiations. All opposition parties but the Alliance walked out of a 1962 Assembly vote on the government white paper on merger—so it passed, thirty-three to zero. However, with the Tunku insisting that the Borneo territories enter simultaneously (which would slow the process), Lee decided to put the proposals to popular referendum.[153] Meanwhile, "secret discussions" weighed preemptive left-wing arrests. The Federation government strongly preferred firm action under Britain's watch. Lee initially agreed with the British on the wisdom of restraint and maintaining calm; he changed his stance both to appease the Tunku and for his own interests, agreeing to measures to harass, provoke, and hobble the extreme left.[154] The Tunku had reason to dislike Barisan: Lim Chin Siong proclaimed his confidence that, together with Malayan counterparts, Barisan could oust the Alliance government "by constitutional means."[155] Meanwhile in Singapore, Lee worried about losing his legislative majority—one PAP MLA was terminally ill and another resigned in protest against the referendum rules—so hoped the Tunku would move against Barisan in the name of internal security.[156] On edge, Lee's government refused permits for opposition rallies; Lee announced he would arrest even Marshall, should he still organize any. Although the PAP had sufficient Alliance support to pass the referendum bill, popular sentiment was genuinely divided. Merger would need to happen before the government collapsed or resigned, leaving the British to "deal with it."[157]

Seen from the Alliance perspective: the PAP had a strong majority in the Assembly when the Tunku started formulating the Malaysia proposal, but that changed; Barisan was sufficiently well-organized nationally, and the PAP sufficiently weakened, that Barisan might win the next election. Federation leaders apparently seized on the idea in late 1961 or early 1962 of selective arrests to neutralize Barisan as an effective force. Still, the Tunku balked at preemptive detention—it would be hard to defend in the House of Commons and the UN.[158] The British ran interference, reassuring the Tunku that Lee was "their best bet." By mid-November, Lee himself contemplated resigning as prime minister after federal elections to concentrate as PAP secretary-general on rebuilding the party's base and "be absolved from any personal responsibility for the arrests."[159]

The arrests, termed Operation Coldstore, came in February 1963 on the eve of a proposed general strike. The government detained over one hundred activists from Barisan, the Singapore Association of Trade Unions, rural associations, and Nanyang University, holding some without trial for well over a decade (Pang

1971, 17–18; Amnesty 1980, 14–15). Barisan was nearly paralyzed, especially after another five party leaders' arrest two months later, though it still won thirteen seats in September (Mutalib 2003, 98–101). An internal crisis and rash of resignations in mid-1964 left the party in disarray, then all eight remaining Barisan MPs resigned in October 1966, having declined to take up their seats since separation; three others had been arrested before their swearing-in, and two fled Singapore. Barisan exited the parliamentary fray (Mutalib 2003, 103; Chua 1995, 17).

Barisan's formation had excised the PAP's left, securely empowering Lee's moderate faction; its collapse removed the final remaining challenge to PAP dominance. However brief and stormy, merger proved especially consequential for Singapore in providing the pretext and context for this entrenchment, delegitimating left-wing ideology, diverting blame for coercion from Lee to the Tunku, and enabling Lee and the PAP to capitalize on Singapore's sudden vulnerability in 1965 as reason to consolidate their control. That the PAP had to claw its way up, in other words, fundamentally shaped the party and its approach to governance and helps explain its deep aversion to challenge, its resistance to alliances between parties and civil-societal organizations (including unions), and its tightly closed structure.

Parties as Interest Protectors, Ideologues, or Vehicles

Most Singaporean parties through the mid-1960s were disorganized and unfocused. The LF, then the PAP, won unexpectedly and unprepared; the latter pulled itself together better to govern. Parties struggled to differentiate themselves and define their niche. This inchoate landscape allowed the PAP to pitch its appeal broadly; unlike UMNO, the PAP never tied itself to any specific social group (Jesudason 1999, 149). Moreover, although the PAP defined itself as left wing, that label remained capacious and malleable.

Communalism in Singapore, with a population around three-fourths Chinese,[160] manifested differently from that in Malaya and offered a less clear scaffold for the party system. Through the 1950s, Singapore was racially highly segregated, compounded by an intraethnic divide between Chinese- and English-educated Chinese, overlapping substantially with class. Regardless, UMNO and MCA aside, all parties aimed to be multiracial and broadly inclusive. The PAP's earliest publications, for instance, conspicuously gave about equal space to each of Singapore's four major languages; over time, English crowded out the rest. Other parties did the same, plus published newsletters in multiple languages: sales from Barisan's English- and Chinese-medium publications, for example, subsidized a less successful Malay edition.[161] Candidates in the 1950s–60s considered the ethnic makeup of their constituencies (extending to Chinese dialect groups) in assessing their odds. For instance, Progressive Party candidate Chan Kum Chee recalled holding nightly rallies, distributing manifestos and voting cards, and still losing in 1950. He blamed the fact of being in a largely Indian constituency and credited his win in 1951 to having moved to a more heavily English-educated Malay and Chinese area.[162] Particularly after serious Malay-Chinese ethnic riots in July and September 1964 (see Leifer 1964, 1115), the PAP stepped up efforts to establish shared norms and a common identity. In particular, its housing policies broke up ethnic enclaves and its network of purpose-built grassroots organizations encouraged integration (Seah 1979, 279; 1985, 173–74). These moves also effectively ended UMNO's electoral chances and positioned the PAP to succeed nationwide. More broadly, early parties' inclusive orientation kept ethnicity in Singapore from moving beyond the level of criterion for matching candidates with seats to communal premise for party organization, as in Malaya.

Ideology presented a keener, but overlapping, cleavage. The specter of communism shaded the political left of the 1940s–60s, region-wide. After the PAP's startling success in 1957, Governor Goode expressed his strong suspicion that the communists had "revived to the full their infiltration of P.A.P. branches," as well as of Marshall's WP.[163] Later that year, Chief Minister Lim—whose suppression of riots in 1956 had fed criticisms of his being suspiciously procolonial (Chua 1995, 13)—repudiated rumors that he planned to ban the PAP on such grounds.[164] Yet in 1959, his SPA campaigned on the theme that a PAP government "would spell economic ruin and Communist dictatorship for Singapore."[165] A few years later, party leaders' arrest for alleged procommunism eviscerated Barisan, thereby eliminating the preeminent hurdle to PAP dominance. Hence, perceived threat and the mantra of "survival," even at cost of democratic freedoms, validated consolidation of single-party dominance prior to the PAP's economic achievements (Khong 1995, 109, 114; Chua 2010, 338–39). Unlike in Malaya, then, the PAP prospered with an ideological, not identity-based, premise—in a context of anxious anticommunism ripe for a savvy "protector."

Yet even as he angled to push ideology off the table, Lee Kuan Yew struggled to keep the PAP *his* vehicle. Those efforts illustrated a wider pattern: with less basis for differentiation than identity-oriented Malayan parties had, and with most falling within a fairly narrow band on the ideological spectrum, Singaporean parties defined themselves substantially by their leaders and key issues—particularly, through the mid-1960s, the pace of independence and merger. Lee vied to keep upstart challengers (especially Ong Eng Guan, then Lim Chin Siong) in line. The LF, the WP, and other parties, too, struggled to build identities beyond, and overcome the foibles of, their iconic leaders. But with the exception of UMNO and MCA, neither ever potent in Singapore, parties tended to chase the same mass of citizens, notwithstanding the salience of subcommunal, class-tinged catchments.

Parties hence functioned more to mobilize voters broadly than to aggregate a given subset of interests. First under Marshall, then under the PAP (and Barisan), the process of partisan mobilization came to define parties—and indeed, politics—ever more, through carefully tailored policies and outreach strategies.

The Emerging Partisan Political Economy

Singapore's postwar economy—promising, but troubled—left ample room for intervention and shaped the PAP's approach to governance. The PAP amplified the government's role in economic development, making not just the state, but also the PAP, appear responsible for economic progress in ways directly relevant to people's lives. When the PAP assumed power, housing and social services were in short supply. The British retained economic power. Organized labor was still regrouping. Unemployment hovered at an estimated 15 percent of the labor force in the mid-1960s as Singapore struggled to develop industry and trade (Bellows 1967, 122–23). Within its first decade, the PAP made economic growth its raison d'être, undergirding a host of policies to keep the population organized, unified, orderly, and oriented toward the national interest (Chua 1995, 18; Curless 2016, 60–61).

The PAP moved immediately to expand the state's economic role. Central to that effort was an array of statutory boards to implement development and industrial policies, starting with the Public Utilities Board in 1959, then the Housing and Development Board in 1960 (Chan 1989, 76). Unencumbered by bureaucratic procedures, parastatals took on key government programs, preparing the way for increased state involvement in commercial and industrial ventures (Seah 1976, 57). The inherited civil service, though, was suspicious of the PAP's pro-communist, anti-English-educated reputation. The new government recruited more Chinese-educated graduates, pressed a "mental revolution" among ministries, and established the Political Study Centre in 1959 to counter bureaucratic elitism and hesitancy toward PAP programs (Chan 1976, 20–23; Vasil 1988, 127–32). The effort combined bureaucratic "re-socialization and politicization" with transferring local government functions to the central government (Chan 1989, 75–76).

Trade unions were another linchpin in PAP plans. The PAP claimed in 1955, "we respect too much the independence of the Trade Union movement to ever think of having a hand in the running of the Trade Unions much less controlling them."[166] That hesitancy waned, especially after the Barisan-induced split in the trade union movement. The PAP government deregistered the Singapore Association of Trade Unions and its affiliate unions and limited allowable industrial actions, established the state-funded Labour Research Unit in 1962 to reinforce the NTUC's link with the PAP, incorporated NTUC leadership into government and vice-versa, and encouraged unions to leave capacity building to a government fixated on rapid industrialization and job creation (Bellows 1970, 109; Chua 2017, 35–37). Strikes declined dramatically, from over four hundred thousand person-days lost in 1961 to seven hundred *hours* lost in the first half of 1968, and unions hemorrhaged political influence (Bellows 1970, 112). A system of tripartism began with labor representation on statutory boards, enhanced in 1972 with the National Wages Council (Chan 1989, 77); PAP policy sought to align workers' interests with those of the larger economy and its own development goals (Seah 1978, 17–19).

Perhaps politically most consequentially, the PAP expanded its role in service provision, especially in housing. These efforts met welfare needs while broadening political support and developing reliable local leadership (Ooi and Shaw 2004, 68–69; Hill and Lian 1995, 117–18). Public housing was not new; the Singapore Improvement Trust, established in 1927 following a 1918 housing commission on urban blight, pioneered improvements to low-cost housing. Yet 1947 and 1954 reports showed conditions still substandard and cramped (Hassan 1976, 241–43). The population had increased sharply postwar, with 70 percent crowded into the urban core in "appalling conditions" and unable to afford housing on the open market. The Singapore Improvement Trust could not meet demand. The HDB began in 1960 with basic, affordable urban rental accommodation, then introduced ninety-nine-year leasehold public housing flats in 1964, emphasizing quantity over quality (Chua 2000, 47; Vasoo 1994, 27–50).

Yet resettlement schemes, structured to accommodate development plans and force ethnic mixing, drew near-immediate resistance. The Housing and Development Board moved residents from the flexibility of informal, if poor-quality or congested, housing, sometimes permitting gardening or livestock, to standardized, contractual arrangements in high-rises, entailing financial, physical, and social adjustments (Chua 2000, 47). Leading the charge against resettlement were the Singapore Rural Residents' and Country People's Associations (both banned in late 1963 as communist-front organizations) and Barisan Sosialis. Their efforts ranged from bargaining over compensation to blocking bulldozers. Anger at squatter-clearing efforts cost the PAP at least one seat in 1963, and Malay suspicions of urban renewal plans took on racial overtones, sparking riots in mid-1964. The opposition only died down—or at least, grew more diffuse—with the crackdown on the left in 1963 and as quality and services improved, underscoring the benefits of the new developments (Chan 1976, 165–68, 176, 185–86, 196–97; Chua 2000, 47–48). The PAP's focus on housing, however, illustrated keenly its use of programmatic economic policies to build political support. Mass resettlement, along with efforts to direct industrialization and coopt unions, did not just inculcate loyalty, and hence performance legitimacy, but also undercut or eliminated ideological and organizational alternatives.

Local Government and Party Machines

By the mid-1950s, parties were fast coming to structure the political order, from voter mobilization to service provision. Local government offered a key site, initially for parties to prove themselves, then for the PAP specifically to make itself useful. First, to improve efficiency and accountability, PAP mayor Ong Eng Guan devolved City Council tasks to standing committees and departments.[167] He simultaneously developed a form of "Tammany Hall politics," in which, "if you supported him and you voted for him, he would give you all kinds of blessings, licenses and all that sort of things."[168] License-reliant hawkers, taxi drivers, and others were beholden to Ong, reciprocating with political support. That exchange entrenched a politics of instrumental, personal relationships. Then in 1959, the PAP dissolved City Council, declaring it redundant: most city councilors doubled as MLAs and much council work entailed issuing licenses.[169] The unofficial reason was that the council had become a key political forum, enhancing the PAP's reputation—but allowing Ong too-substantial authority.[170] Reorganization eliminated a potential rival power center and consolidated policymaking and administration under Lee's faction. The Local Government Integration Bill of 1963 formally transferred specific City Council and Rural Board roles to the central government or Public Utilities Board. But the following year, the PAP devolved key local government functions to the People's Association (PA)—a parapolitical body tied closely to the party—creating a new sort of local machine (Quah 2001, 7–8; Ooi 2009, 176).

Organizational life already represented a key channel for party outreach. British authorities had validated chambers of commerce's taking political roles, for instance, by reserving nominated legislative seats for them and encouraging them to "go in for Party politics."[171] Trade unions also offered political leaders and channels for mobilization. Harbour Board workers, for example, mobilized for Lee Kuan Yew's 1957 Tanjong Pagar by-election campaign: he was their union's adviser.[172] When rupture in 1961 encouraged the PAP to allow its ground structure to atrophy thenceforth (Chan 1976, 101–2), the party turned to extraparty props. At the time, the PAP hesitated even to develop ancillary bodies such as a youth wing (Mustafa 2004–5, 19); only much later did the PAP revivify party life proper.

Branches remained active, but the party's organizational structure discouraged horizontal linkages among them or vertical connections between the CEC and members (Chan 1976, 105).

Most important for the PAP was an expanding network of organizations under the PA, established in July 1960 and fully operative by late 1962. The PA's board included individuals and representatives of social organizations appointed by the prime minister as chairman (Seah 1973, 20–21). With an overall objective of "controlled mobilization and participation" (Quah 2001, 8), the officially nonpartisan PA aimed to provide educational and recreational amenities, organize citizens through neighborhood-oriented activities, encourage multiracial community building, train leaders, cultivate national identity and a service orientation, combat communism, and increase loyalty to and identification with the government (Bellows 1970, 101–2; Choo 1969, 100). The PA network allowed the PAP to be increasingly active on the ground, absent robust party machinery. Publicly funded PA organizations took over and expanded functions the PAP previously handled directly, including local government–type tasks, working in tandem with PAP structures to coopt public space and convey "the ubiquitous presence of the party" (Chan 1976, 133, 186–87). Working outside its own partisan structure allowed the PAP to strengthen its reach and control (Chan 1976, 226); the approach "deliberately confused the roles of government and party so that the people tended to praise the party for activities undertaken by the government" (Kimball 1968, 48).

Building on a postwar British community development initiative, the newly elected PAP reinforced a previously loose, recreationally oriented set of community centers (CCs) to channel government communications, train future community leaders, and promote better welfare through sports, classes, cultural activities, and more. The PAP situated CCs under the Department of Social Welfare, abolishing management structures that members of other parties dominated and improving facilities (Seah 1973, 17–20; 1985, 176–77). Anxious to counter Barisan influence, the PAP rushed to build CCs under the PA umbrella: 103 by September 1963; over 180 by mid-1965, mostly in rural and resettlement areas, or where blank referendum ballots and Barisan-linked organizations recommended the PAP make more effort. A PAP leader or MLA officiated at each CC launch. CC offerings aimed to reduce the appeal of Barisan organizations and activities—and ensured that citizens would not be deprived if Barisan services ceased (Chan 1976, 155–56; Bellows 1970, 102–4; Seah 1973, 31–32; Choo 1969, 100). For example, the PA introduced nominal-cost kindergartens in 1964, focused initially on rural areas, specifically to compete with Barisan ones deemed likely to sap the PAP of support (Seah 1973, 35–36; People's Association 1973).

MLAs in the early 1960s visited each CC in their constituency every three to six weeks, allowing for "sustained interaction" and quick response times and consolidating support (Bellows 1970, 104–5). Especially as the PAP struggled to regain lost ground and build support for merger, CCs took on a greater role in political communication and allowed the government to sidestep a bureaucracy it found inflexible and indifferent (Seah 1985, 175–79). Absent elected local governments through which to work, the PAP came to feed national health, social, and environmental campaigns, which started in 1958 with antispitting, antipest, and other initiatives, through CCs (Quah and Quah 1989, 115–16). In 1964, the PAP also tasked CCs with organizing vigilante groups—civilian patrols in which almost fifteen thousand men enrolled—to support the resistance against Indonesia and build nationalist pride. Postseparation, CCs helped promote civic responsibility and the citizen-soldier ideal, fostering support for compulsory military service (Seah 1973, 33–37).

Even as CCs offered platforms for PAP MLAs "to cajole, praise, or inform" constituents and "inextricably entwined" CC, government, and party (Kimball 1968, 50–51), the PAP denied their partisan bent. In 1964, the PAP introduced management committees to helm each CC (CCMCs),[173] purportedly to reduce the too-close identification of CCs with the government and to ease the PA's logistical and financial burdens. Yet the local (PAP) legislator's recommendation guided the PA's selection of members. Most of those willing to serve were younger, Chinese-educated businessmen, active in community affairs, self-identified as social elites, and seeking government ties; as PAP demographics shifted, the party worked to recruit English-educated professionals and women (Chan 1976, 158; Seah 1973, 58–61, 64–79; Choo 1969, 102–3). The PAP's K. M. Byrne explained the overlap between PAP and CC leadership as merely due to the PAP's "roots in the masses."[174] Yet an increasing share of staff were PAP members or supporters, both given the selection process and because appointment served as a way "to distribute 'spoils,'" in the form of status and perks (Seah 1973, 23).

The same patterns applied as the PA network expanded to include Citizens' Consultative Committees (CCCs), launched in each district in 1965. Whereas CCs targeted individual needs, CCCs addressed more resource-intensive collective concerns—municipal matters like bus shelters, drains, and roads. Each constituency could recommend public works projects for funding from a designated allocation under the Prime Minister's Office, although communities themselves also contributed.[175] Except in opposition-held areas, the prime minister appointed the local MP as CCC adviser, who then recommended community leaders to serve as members. Again, most were Chinese-speaking traders and businesspeople, with limited education and literacy—although here, too, the PAP sourced new talent to cultivate a more professional, better-educated profile. The PAP screened all appointees for "political reliability and social integrity," though nearly all were from the party (Seah 1979, 279–80; Hill and Lian 1995, 165–66).

Early strains illustrated the extent to which the PAP intended the PA as a partisan machine and pseudo local government. A disruptive, ten-month strike in 1961–62 over irregular dismissals and political pressure increased public and opposition-party pressure to depoliticize the PA or close the CCs for concealing party machinery. After 1963, *Konfrontasi* and the Malaysian central government further pressed the PAP to shift to truly merit-based selection and train staff better (Seah 1973, 28–29, 32–33), including through a National Youth Leadership Training Institute, established in 1964.[176] However, the public largely still saw the PA "as one and the same thing as" the PAP, hindering PA efforts to attract professionals averse to partisan engagement (Choo 1969, 104). The language in which the PAP speaks of PA organizations in early publications reveals a perceived remove between masses and leaders, too, suggesting a PA brokerage role. By the mid-1960s, it remained the case that a CC client might be "unable to tell whether he owes its presence to the ruling party, the government, or the private sector," ambiguity the PAP enhanced by dispensing government services—welfare payments, health services, agricultural extension services—at CCs when possible (Kimball 1968, 53–54).

The PA quickly became a key node in the PAP's governing apparatus. The arrangement empowered a de facto partisan machine while excluding opposition parties far more assuredly than could still-elected local government bodies. Even though Barisan coopted much of the PA's infrastructure in its strongholds in the early 1960s, no other party could match the PAP's extended reach (Chan 1976, 163). Channeling Singaporeans' grievances and engagement toward PA "alternative avenues," rather than to opposition parties or even the PAP proper, contributed to parties' "declining position" within the polity (Bellows 1970, 101). Moreover, shifting responsibility from an electoral to an administrative apparatus nurtured a focus on performance legitimacy, or on politics as "framed in terms of efficiency and effectiveness rather than on what constitutes a good government and what role citizens have in the shaping of the country's future destiny" (Mutalib 2003, 4).

Connecting with Voters

Throughout, personalized outreach remained essential for candidates and legislators (including qua PA functionaries). One reason for low turnout in Singapore's elections through the mid-1950s was parties' tenuous connection with voters—and with many close contests, turnout could be pivotal. The Progressive Party attributed its loss of four seats in the 1951 City Council elections, for instance, to incumbents' complacency in not communicating to voters what they had achieved.[177] The *Straits Times* editorialized that to be reelected, councilors needed "careful stewardship," accounted for "loudly, personally and often."[178] At that time, though, politics remained "a tight little game played by a small number of persons, largely English educated and more or less confined to the upper socioeconomic strata"; some house visits and leafleting aside, candidates relied on prestige, networks, and wealth, rather than coherent platforms or meaningful parties (Bellows 1967, 127–28). Still in 1957, an election official reported that while the PAP and the WP were relatively "more active and better organised" than other parties, all had given short shrift to "nursing the constituency."[179] They got better.

From the start, when candidates reached out to voters, it was usually with personal service. Progressive Party candidate John Ede recalled having "worked like a beaver for months" before the 1955 election, "stomping round the constituency" and convincing clan heads, Muslim leaders, and influential others to support him by "being able to do something for them," like getting a bridge fixed or electric lights put in, or forwarding complaints to government agencies. He explained, if "you showed signs of doing things for people . . . they'd say, 'Oh, this chap seems a good chap to vote for.'"[180] Similarly, Jumabhoy Mohamed Jumabhoy, first elected as an independent in 1950, would offer five or ten dollars to needy constituents on walkabouts and fretted at the difficulty of rounding up cars to transport voters.[181] Even after he joined a party, his branch members "were more for me personally than for the Labour Front as such. . . . I had helped them in many cases, legally, through official channels—writing letters and bashing my head during the City Council days." His interventions were often superfluous. People presumed his "chit" made the difference, when it really did not; "that was a little trick of the trade, you use something which is available because he doesn't know, he feels obligated to you." Over five years on City Council, he built up hundreds of such cases, of people "personally grateful to me for the assistance they were given," and therefore loyal.[182] Or as the LF's Francis Thomas concluded in 1958, in Singapore, "one joined a party for protection and a big brother as well as to support its politics" (Thomas 2015, 80).

In this vein, the PAP's early campaigns were exceptionally labor-intensive. Beyond rallies and house-to-house canvassing, PAP outreach, explained a 1950s branch official, included politicians' "distribution of welfare aids, things like that" when calamities occurred and helping voters petition the government for assistance.[183] He explained, people "will of course vote for the man who is easily approachable and who will be able to assist them one way or another."[184] Goh Keng Swee, later deputy prime minister, published a charmingly self-deprecating account of his first campaign, in Kreta Ayer in 1959. The party held up to forty mass meetings weekly—up to twelve in one evening at the campaign's peak—since these were among the PAP's "most powerful" tools, especially to reach "marginal constituencies and difficult areas." They might have over one hundred street corner meetings, too. Individual campaigns elaborated on the CEC's "broad strategic plan." Goh's own team included a core of about twenty party members plus thirty occasional volunteers—mostly mechanics and factory workers. The area was a PAP stronghold, yet Goh still trudged, sweating profusely, door-to-door, up and down steep, poorly lighted staircases in his compact constituency. Since many constituents were hawkers, his division leader also paraded Goh around in the morning, "hailing every other hawker, as if he or she were a long lost relative . . . and proclaim[ing] to the multitude the superlative qualities of the party candidate." For a week after Goh's victory, branches organized victory processions, thanking his electors. His LSP opponent, the principal of a local Chinese school, merely offered a Cantonese "chauvinist" line without a clear policy message and played up Goh's being Baba Chinese (Peranakan) and lacking Chinese-language fluency.[185]

As Goh's hands-on slog suggests, persona mattered, beyond services rendered. Barisan's Lim Chin Siong, for instance, "was a standard unto himself" in Hokkien, enthralling crowds; his rapport helped him convince the masses he was incorruptible and ready to champion their interests.[186] Indeed, English-educated PAP leaders, including Lee Kuan Yew and Goh Keng Swee, learned Mandarin (then also Hokkien) after entering politics to connect more effectively with voters (Bellows 1967, 134). Meanwhile, the PAP used television to "personalize leadership" and publicize "incidents of thuggishness" by communist elements against Lee Kuan Yew and others, since "people don't remember arguments."[187]

A controversial 1961 by-election in which ousted PAP leader Ong Eng Guan successfully recaptured his seat confirmed, too, that, as PAP legislator Peter Low put it: "If you want to get support from the masses it is not only during election time. It must be worked all along to maintain the relationship, the approaches to the masses, mix with the masses, get along with the masses, then you will have a real understanding of the masses."[188] Yet candidates did not always have much time to prepare. The PAP's Othman Wok, for instance, learned only a few days before Nomination Day where he would be contesting in 1963. Luckily, he had spent time in that constituency previously, and his branch committee had already started groundwork.[189] And some candidates found the sort of anonymous-but-intimate rapport expected of a politician uncomfortable; S. Rajaratnam, for instance, notes that he had to learn how to put himself "in somebody else's shoes"— shoes that did "not fit at all."[190]

Most consequential among these outreach strategies was one David Marshall pioneered as chief minister, combining service delivery with simple presence. In June 1955, he inaugurated weekly "meet-the-people" sessions. Intending to bridge the gap between his English-educated, European-looking (Iraqi Jewish) self and ordinary Singaporeans, Marshall held forth in the Singapore Public Relations office, surrounded by reporters who eagerly recorded his giving a few dollars to poor people in response to "sob stories."[191] He had promised while campaigning to dedicate one day per week to meeting Singaporeans to hear their problems and assist where he could (Tan, K. Y. L. 2008, 295).[192] Cabinet ministers and others held similar sessions on different days, following the same format of recording details of complaints, then taking action on the spot to resolve them (Tan, K. Y. L. 2008, 298–99). Marshall also established the Public Advisory Bureau (PAB) in 1955 at his own expense; the PAB took requests for assistance daily except Sunday, primarily from job seekers, but also those needing help with immigration, social welfare, and housing (Tan, K. Y. L. 2008, 299–300; Comber 1994, 107). Marshall averaged sixty-eight supplicants each Saturday; the PAB, nineteen daily—some expecting "miracles" (Comber 1994, 107–8). At times, part of the PAB's remedy entailed ensuring press coverage of heartstring-tugging cases to generate public donations (Comber 1994, 111–12).

Before winning office, the PAP scoffed at such efforts. One early PAP activist noted the "novelty" of Marshall's outreach but suggested he was "reducing himself condescending to meet the people that way" and was not able to solve most problems anyway.[193] Yet once elected, the PAP embraced Marshall's innovation. Since December 1956, PAP legislators have held at least weekly meet-the-people sessions; for instance, Mayor Ong promised weekly sessions upon his inauguration in 1957. These sessions keep the legislator present, even if not all-powerful; involve and educate politically large numbers of people; and both assist constituents and apprise the party of current concerns.[194] Some likely candidates-to-be launched meet-the-people sessions even before their nomination to establish working relationships in the branch—especially helpful in distinguishing friends from foes after the Barisan split.[195] (Abbreviated campaigns were an early innovation, recommending advance work: 1963's campaign, coinciding with the proclamation of Malaysia, was the legal minimum, nine days [Pang 1971, 17–18].) Legislators also made a point of monthly door-to-door visits and spent significant time looking after the branch, dealing with local problems.[196] The PAP's K. C. Lee's rural constituents, for instance, treated him "like a godfather," seeking help with "everything under the sun"—from stolen chickens to gangster intimidation to chasing down an absconded spouse, though the majority of inquiries involved jobs, followed by housing, schooling, and immigration.[197] These activities established "a new political style in Singapore—one which stresses the accessibility of government for the ordinary citizen" (Chan 1976, 108).

Political discussion rarely featured in these interactions. According to city councilor, then cabinet minister Jumabhoy Mohamed Jumabhoy, "It was always personal difficulties," for which people came by "tens and scores" to have their

MLA send a letter (or in some cases, to request money for rice). Although only 10–20 percent of interventions secured a positive response, and however "silly" for a government minister to be writing such missives, he still "humored them" and promised to try. In the process, Jumabhoy made the constituent feel part of his circle and developed politically precious "personal gratefulness."[198]

The PAP also came to embrace club goods and photo-ops they had earlier scorned. In 1959, *Petir* mocked the alacrity with which the LF government re-housed fire victims, "for reasons not unconnected with the [upcoming] elections," and poked fun at newspapers' images of the chief minister with a bucket of water.[199] The PAP soon followed the LF's lead. In late 1962, the embattled PAP labored to build rural support, purportedly by diverting funds intended for industrial development to a "welfare services" strategy, offering roads, piped water, and housing subsidies to foster—argued a PAP defector to Barisan—"docile citizens."[200] One British report mentioned PAP leaders' personally inviting resettled smallholders to government agricultural courses; a skeptical farmer scoffed that Lee was "only buying our hearts for the next election."[201]

But presence itself mattered. In 1963, Lee engaged in listening tours of eight rural constituencies over several months; he acknowledged that these areas—Barisan strongholds—had prospered less than urban ones. His tours were on Sundays for maximum visibility, from morning until late at night, stretching to fifty or more stops at villages, schools, community centers, and associations. Garlanded by local leaders, and with media watching, he might participate in a small ceremony—opening a community center, turning on a new water standpipe, watching traditional dancing—and offer a short, tailored address in English, Chinese, or Malay, promising to look into their requests (on which a committee followed up), and sometimes citing government policies. Noted a British observer, "Lee goes out of his way to project his person. He pauses to shake the hands of all who show the least inclination, and many who do not. He maintains a warm smile and exudes an air of confidence. . . . Lee is never slow to grasp an opportunity of creating bonhomie," even among less-than-animated attendees.[202] Another time, Lee met with a largely Indian crowd of over four thousand at the British naval base. He affirmed he supported maintaining the base as a key employer[203] and attacked "hot heads" in its labor union, plus Barisan, for their anti-British sentiments. The crowds were "deeply touched by his simplicity and willingness to listen to minor problems of the masses."[204] These efforts helped the PAP, even though "no-one finds it more difficult than Lee to put on a false smile and the whole performance goes against the grain with him."[205]

All told, this formative early period saw more reactive innovation than proactive strategy as the PAP clambered to dominance. However, it revealed the PAP's tendency toward centralization of power, penetration into society, and bureaucratization, laying the ground for a depoliticized, clientelist order, with active repression only secondary and supplemental. Whereas Malaysian parties catered to defined constituencies, blending identity politics and ideology through similarly partisanized or particularistic strategies, the PAP took advantage of a more inchoate field to capture the middle ground, then abrogate challenge, through targeted coercion, political-economic restructuring, a pervasive machine, and the personal touch.

5

COMPETITIVE AUTHORITARIANISM IN MALAYSIA

Consolidated but Challenged

The same questions of ideology, identity, and institutions that complicated Singapore's integration have remained pertinent throughout Malaysia's development. Structurally, state, economy, and society have all changed significantly over time. Most important, installation of the Barisan Nasional (National Front, BN) coalition in the early 1970s, together with new illiberal constraints, signaled Malaysia's firm embrace of electoral authoritarianism. Yet it is underneath that institutional carapace that the real work of regime building happened, through policies, local machines, and ground-level linkages.

The Alliance, Socialist Front, and Pan-Malaysian Islamic Party (PMIP or PAS) sparred, offering ideological alternatives, until episodic ethnic unrest peaked with riots following the 1969 elections. Tunku Abdul Rahman used the violence as justification to suspend the nearly completed election and declare emergency rule. When parliament reconvened twenty months later, it was under a reconfigured Alliance, encompassing most opposition parties and relaunched as the BN in 1974. Politics became more centralized, elections more skewed, and the range of allowable action, for parties or individuals, narrowed.

Stark challenges have since roiled the system, particularly in the mid-1980s, late 1990s, and since 2008, yet the regime battened down and persisted, unseated only amid a massive corruption scandal in 2018. Malaysia's distinctive cleavage structure, the limited international pressure to change, scarce elite incentives toward moderation, and the distribution of power within UMNO over time all contributed to the BN's endurance. More salient still, the BN's mode of politics has taken root, particularly a heavily service-oriented, personalized rather than programmatic approach to governance and accountability, coupled since the 1960s with emphasis on performance rather than rational-legal legitimacy (Maryanov 1967, 109). These political habits have come to color even non-BN parties' alliances, messages, and strategies.

Institutional Makeup

Postmerger, the Malaysian state consolidated. Elections have continued unabated, apart from 1969–71, when the National Operations Council and the National Consultative Council governed. Although the National Consultative Council included representatives from religious and business associations, mass media, unions, and even opposition parties, the National Operations Council functioned as a "semi-martial law colonial government" (Cheah 2002, 132). Legislation developed then, including enhanced affirmative action and sedition laws,[1] significantly reshaped Malaysian politics.

Since 1969, nearly five dozen constitutional amendments[2] and supplemental legislation have buttressed the federal government, bucking a regional devolutionary trend. The states now name only twenty-six of seventy members of the Senate (Dewan Negara), seconded federal officials fill key positions in state administrations, and the central government regulates local governments and keeps states on tight financial tethers. Central government revenues were only four times those of combined state-level revenues in 1985; state expenditures are now less than one-tenth of federal levels. In 2010, distributions to states totaled only 2.48 percent of the federal budget and states raised an average of 80 percent of their own revenue (Yeoh 2012, 20–22, 141–42, 146; Hutchinson 2015, 117). Party hierarchy intensifies these patterns: national-level BN leaders approve candidates for state-level seats and party discipline carries central directives down the chain (Hutchinson 2015, 114–15). Moreover, the prime minister now appoints the attorney general and the speaker of parliament,[3] and the prime minister's department continued to swell until Pakatan Harapan (Alliance of Hope) came into office in 2018. From 2003 to 2011 alone, staff nearly doubled; the budget grew even faster, from MYR2 billion in 2005 to over MYR18.6 billion in 2011 (Funston 2016, 73). Also, especially after the courts declared UMNO an illegal organization after a messy row in 1987, Prime Minister Mahathir Mohamad pushed through constitutional amendments to limit judicial powers and prerogatives (Cheah 2002, 217).

Although Pakatan Harapan now promises change—for instance, instituting bipartisan parliamentary select committees and procedural tweaks to enhance debate[4]—legislating remains an overwhelmingly top-down process. No government bill has been defeated; no opposition bill has been passed; no member of either chamber has defied the party whip. Malaysia's very first bipartisan constitutional amendment passed only in 2019, under Pakatan: a measure to lower the voting age to eighteen and automate voter registration.[5] Seldom has a policy *not* originated with the Cabinet.[6] Moreover, since the first parliament (1959–64), the government has disregarded opposition views on changes to standing orders and procedural complaints (Ong 1987, 42–43, 45–52). Even intra-BN consultation was minimal: budget details caught component parties unawares at times.[7] Key ministries have traditionally fallen to a given component party, but individuals' assignments have commonly been independent of specific skills or preference.[8] BN MPs rarely took positions that might jeopardize their standing or annoy a minister,[9] and debates have frequently ended for lack of a quorum, given sparse attendance. Across parties, MPs confront minimal time to study bills, abbreviated question time (and incomplete or evasive answers), no parliamentary privilege in debating "sensitive" issues (e.g., Malay rights), an Official Secrets Act that limits MPs' access to relevant information, and rules that have, for instance, forestalled development of a viable committee system (beyond "housekeeping" matters and the reasonably empowered Public Accounts Committee) (Siddiquee 2006, 48–49; Kua 1994; Case 2011, 42–46; Muhamad Fuzi 2008; GCCP 2015). Only now are these debilities starting to change. Senate seats remain essentially patronage appointments, "parking spaces" entailing minimal effort—sittings totaled merely twenty-five days in 2011—for politicians who lack places in the lower house, or are conferred solely to make the holder eligible for appointment as a minister ('Abidin 2012, 11–14). Confirms a former member, senators "play almost no role,"[10] nor is meaningful revamping assured under Pakatan Harapan.

Securing its grip, the BN stepped-up electoral manipulation, relying on the Election Commission (EC), which was neither "mere puppet" nor fully independent; the government sought both compliant election management and seemingly legitimate wins (Lim 2005, 262–63, 277).[11] Constituency delineation is particularly imbalanced.[12] The number of votes an opposition party has needed to match 1 vote for the BN has ranged from 12.3 for the Socialist Front in 1964, to 26.1 for Parti Keadilan Rakyat (People's Justice Party, Keadilan) in 2004, to 40.4 for PAS in 1986 (Wong, Chin, and Norani 2010, 933). Amendments in 1962 codified a 35 percent cap on variation from average constituency size (versus 15 percent initially planned) and gave the prime minister power to modify EC proposals. Further amendment in 1973 removed limits on rural weighting—justified as compensating for the communication and other difficulties of rural areas (Lee 2015, 68, 76). In 1959, the largest constituency was 3.5 times the smallest; in 2013, the largest was over 9 times the size of the smallest at the federal level and over 11 times larger among states. BN-won parliamentary seats have been

40 percent smaller, on average, than opposition ones (Wong, Chin, and Norani 2010, 932; Welsh 2013, 146–47). Moreover, Sabah and Sarawak are overrepresented in parliament and traditionally opposition-leaning states are underrepresented (Chin 2002, 213). Gerrymandering is also rampant; initially it was designed to favor majority seats for *bumiputera* (Malay and indigenous groups), then also to boost mixed seats, since the BN's advantage in vote pooling tended to push opposition parties toward "ethnic outbidding" (Lee 2015, 71–76; Lim 2005, 267–71). Redelineation also reflects "packing and cracking," or shifting voters to concentrate or dilute opposition supporters. For instance, new boundaries transferred 8,000 "presumed hostile" voters from a Democratic Action Party (DAP) stronghold to neighboring Lembah Pantai, a district DAP partner Keadilan held tenuously in 2013.[13]

The electoral rolls, too, are suspect. Commonwealth observers in 1990 noted discrepancies affecting almost 4 percent of the electorate. Removal of mostly Chinese names after the 1969 election increased the Malay share of the electorate by over 2 percent; in 1999, EC delays left over 680,000 citizens who registered that year unable to vote. Other criticisms relate to issues such as improbably many voters at one address or unusual numbers of centenarians (Lim 2005, 272–73; Ong 2005, 294–300, 312–14). A population surge in Sabah of 285 percent from 1970 to 2000 (versus 113 percent for Malaysia as a whole) fed outcry over "Project IC" (the improper issuing of identity cards) and prompted a royal commission of inquiry in 2012 (Chin 2014, 115–16, 119). Declaring most criticisms outside its jurisdiction, inherent to a mobile and aging population, or unfounded (Election Commission 2013), the EC offered only minor adjustments.

BN regulations muted but did not stifle civil society. Just under one-third of Malaysians claim membership in at least one organization: most common (11.5 percent of the population) are political parties, followed by residential associations (4 percent), then religious ones (3.2 percent) (Welsh, Ibrahim, and Aeria 2007). Limiting civil-societal influence are curbs on political space, but also organizations' divergent goals and composition. A "limited but divided civil society," unable significantly to transform or deepen democratic engagement, let alone influence the judiciary or legislature, may ultimately help to legitimize the regime (Giersdorf and Croissant 2011, 10–15). That said, mobilization outside parties has served to amplify identities and ideas useful to parties, including advancing ideologies and policies oriented around axes other than the BN's guiding communalism, without regard to what wins votes, while offering space for coalition building (Weiss 2006).

Ethnicity remains a core lattice for Malaysian politics across institutional forms, but one politics itself changes. Most obvious is the strategic elision of *Malay* and *bumiputera* since the 1970s. Already in September 1968, the Tunku cautioned that the "keg of gun powder" of race called for moderation,[14] yet BN efforts have entrenched ethnic hierarchy. UMNO has always been a party of and for Malays—founder Onn Jaafar's effort to tweak that vision pushed him from the party in 1951. That premise became more explicit as a basis also for the state in 1969, when UMNO's Ghazali Shafie insisted Malaysian politics must rest upon *kebumiputeraan* (indigenism). The bumiputera frame helps bridge peninsular and East Malaysia—even as non-Muslim Dayak and Kadazandusun East Malaysians protest their lesser priority (Loh 1997, 3–4)—and undergirds regime policies. The bumiputera (really, Malay) share of civil service positions, for instance, has increasingly outstripped population share: Malays held 60.8 percent in 1969, but 78.8 percent (and other bumiputera another 10.9 percent) by 2014.[15] Such patterns exemplify both efforts to shape a bumiputera identity and the ethnicization of the state.

Yet communal mobilization is not all top-down. Islamist organizations, for instance, structure and amplify Malay organization and influence. Among the most effective long term has been the nonpartisan Angkatan Belia Islam Malaysia (Malaysian Islamic Youth Movement, ABIM). ABIM supports members interested in entering politics, regardless of party, and maintains ties with alumni in elected office (around thirty currently, in UMNO, PAS, and Keadilan). Although most ABIM activity does *not* center on politics and one cannot hold ABIM and party office simultaneously, ABIM sees these efforts as important toward advancing an Islamist agenda.[16] More overt Malay rights activism has been more clearly partisan—for instance, by the Pertubuhan Pribumi Perkasa Malaysia (Indigenous Empowerment Organization), formed in 2008 and with about two-thirds UMNO members.[17]

Chinese networks and identity are similarly politicized. The MCA, in particular, campaigns largely on the basis of concessions it has secured for the Chinese community, although the party has vied with the Parti Gerakan Rakyat Malaysia (Gerakan, Malaysian People's Movement Party) and the DAP since the 1970s for Chinese guilds and associations' backing. Among around eight hundred such bodies, the most prominent have been Malaysian Chinese Chambers of Commerce, the education-related bodies comprising Dong Jiao Zong (DJZ), and the umbrella Selangor Chinese Assembly Hall (Ho 1992, 9; Hilley 2001, 92). Most initially eschewed opposition parties for their lesser policy influence, until a 1987 crackdown, Operation Lalang, targeted Chinese educationists (Ng 2005, 195–97). By the 1990s, dueling networks supported and opposed the BN, advocating either a confrontational "politics of pressure" approach or a more conciliatory "politics of internal negotiation" (Ng 2005, 184–91; 2003, 92–94). Mobilization has been episodic but potent—and only partly coopted by the BN's MCA or Gerakan, however much these parties' (and other BN candidates') strategies centered around

Chinese organizations. Efforts have ranged from a popular Chinese National Unity Movement in the early 1970s sufficiently chauvinist to worry UMNO and MCA leadership;[18] to the DJZ's shifting alliances in the 1980s–90s, including an "Enter BN, Rectify BN" campaign; a 1985 Malaysian Chinese Union Declaration 5,000 groups endorsed; and a seventeen-point set of election demands (*Suqiu*) 2,095 organizations signed in 1999.[19]

Other grassroots bodies play similar connective roles. For instance, residents' associations (RAs) feature prominently, if unevenly, in politicians' outreach across parties. One UMNO MP, for instance, described a council he established for sixty to seventy RAs in his district, together with leaders of mosques, neighborhood *Rukun Tetangga*, and the paramilitary volunteer corps, *Jabatan Sukarelawan Malaysia*; he also met regularly with individual RAs and supported programs.[20] A former Keadilan state legislator (*ahli dewan undangan negeri*, ADUN) courted dissatisfied RAs, organizing committees and funding initiatives, until he "turned them" from BN.[21] School parent-teacher associations—essentially "government-sponsored NGOs" with wide networks—likewise represent ready partners.[22] UMNO's rural base also encourages the party to cultivate organizations for farmers and fishers. Such organizations require resources only UMNO could readily provide over the years; members knew opposition parties would be of limited help, for instance, in securing credit or subsidized seedlings.[23] Not surprisingly, Pakatan Harapan now courts similar support. While on assuming office in 2018, Mahathir discontinued a "one-off 'doubtful' incentive" the BN had given members of the Penang Fishermen's Association, for instance, his agriculture minister affirmed that the government would grant their request to restore MYR300/month payments—not a "bribe," the association insists![24] Hawkers represent a cognate constituency, particularly for Gerakan and the DAP. Gerakan even formed a hawkers' cooperative but remained unable to lean securely on their network; the influential Hawkers' Association of Penang has backed both Gerakan and the DAP.[25] And all sides seek to organize and mobilize youth, sponsoring sports teams, playing fields, and tournaments since at least the 1970s.[26] Collaborating with or fostering such associations and initiatives builds reputation and networks, buttressing party machines among identity- and place-based communities.

Development of Political Parties and Coalitions

Above all, political parties structure, and are themselves structured by, Malaysian electoral politics. While electoral rules—single-member districts, majoritarian voting—and the incentives these present clearly matter for how parties organize and function, so do the challenges facing parties anywhere, from participatory alternatives in civil society to ever-evolving media (Shefter 1994, 13). Yet Malaysia's main parties and party system as a whole remain highly institutionalized, constraining political change (Weiss 2015).

UMNO's Evolution

At the system's structural and symbolic center has always been UMNO. In late 1968, Secretary General Khir Johari claimed a membership of 160,000;[27] the party now counts over 3.6 million members.[28] Its organization permeates society: 191 divisions subdivide into over 20,000 individually registered branches (each with at least 50 members), then subbranches down to the village level, though relatively less abundant in cities. Wings for women (*Wanita*), young men (*Pemuda*, less militant than initially), and since 1999, young women (*Puteri*) mimic that structure.[29] MPs generally run their UMNO branch (the level individuals join) and division.[30]

UMNO began with an elitist core but significantly empowered rank and file. It was committed to liberal democracy, a secular state, and common nationality but prioritized Malays' language, rulers, and religion. After 1969, the party drifted increasingly toward a stronger executive, partisan bureaucracy, and only limited democracy or state secularism (Funston 2016, 30), coupled with a shift toward "extremer factions" among leaders and concern increasingly "exclusively with the Malays."[31] Preparation for the 1969 campaign had revealed internal squabbles. In Malacca, for instance—and with echoes in Kedah, Perlis, Kelantan, and Perak—eighty branches refused to cooperate with Chief Minister Ghafar Baba in July 1968 over his handling of division elections and formed their own divisions. UMNO headquarters initially balked but was forced to capitulate and agree to recognize separate "sections" in Malacca after the elections.[32] By the mid-1980s UMNO was no longer dominated by rural interests but by professionals and businesspeople with different expectations of the state; schoolteachers alone declined from 40 percent of UMNO delegates in 1981 to 19 percent in 1987 (Funston 2016, 54). The role of aristocratic elites likewise declined.

UMNO transformed structurally after 1969. Amendments to the party constitution in 1971 elevated the Supreme Council (Majlis Tertinggi); it now dominates candidate selection and party discipline and may initiate or approve government policies. Members and officers are now elected every three years rather than annually, although the party president may choose up to twelve members (Funston 2016, 50; Abdullah 2016, 533–34). Efforts since the 1950s, but especially since 1969, have tightened central supervision of state- and division-level activities and offices, shortening the leash of even comparatively powerful states

(Hutchinson 2015, 117–19). Moreover, Mahathir, in particular, further centralized authority in the executive. After UMNO's 1987 rift, for instance, Mahathir redirected fundraising: donors now give to the president to distribute, not the party,[33] and the prime minister's policymaking role is "paramount," from new economic initiatives to foreign relations (Milne 1986, 1379). Yet factions have also grown ever more salient, as "warlords" claim turf and back would-be party leaders. Disunity has fed splinter parties and vendettas and complicated sustaining a uniform ideological line (Abdullah 2016, 526, 529).

After 1969, anxious no longer to depend financially on the MCA (Gomez 2012, 1382), UMNO added to its media holdings by purchasing the [New] Straits Times and Berita Harian, and party treasurer Tengku Razaleigh Hamzah established a fund to invest in the stock market. By 1974, UMNO could meet its own electoral expenses and subsidize its partners' (Funston 2016, 50–51). The affirmative action New Economic Policy (NEP, detailed below), introduced in 1970, developed simultaneously and symbiotically, particularly as Mahathir and then-treasurer Daim Zainuddin expanded UMNO's economic role in the 1980s. The NEP obscured the line between legitimate policy implementation and patronage and fostered "business-backed political factions": UMNO division and branch leaders appropriated rents and a new bumiputera business community came to rely on projects secured through personal or political connections, reciprocating with campaign donations and other support (Jomo and Gomez 2000, 296; Ufen 2015, 568–69). As UMNO's institutional wealth grew, achieving party office became increasingly "a stepping stone to material riches" (Funston 2016, 42). Scandals proliferated, costing an estimated USD100 billion since the 1980s (Gomez 2012, 1383) and ticking upward under Prime Minister Najib Razak in the 2010s.

In part due to these higher stakes, before the hemorrhage starting around 2016, UMNO had ruptured in 1986–87 and 1998. Both times, Mahathir thought his deputy prime minister was challenging him. Musa Hitam resigned the post in early 1986, citing the impossibility of working with the suspicious Mahathir; he joined others in a Team B to challenge Mahathir's Team A in party elections. The spat extended to a purge of cabinet members, a judicial challenge to UMNO, reconstitution of UMNO Baru (New UMNO), and a crackdown on over one hundred dissidents (mostly from opposition parties and NGOs, but including four from Team B). Before long, though, Team B members seeped back into UMNO, wooed by concessions from the Supreme Council, the collapse of splinter party Semangat '46 (Spirit of '46), and the pull of patronage (Brownlee 2007, 138–45; Funston 2016, 54–56). A decade later, Mahathir ousted Anwar Ibrahim amid 1997's financial crisis. Mahathir's camp painted Anwar as a pawn of the International Monetary Fund and ethnic pot stirrer, adding charges of corruption and sodomy for maximal reputational damage. Meanwhile Anwar galvanized an opposition movement and electoral coalition, as thousands of UMNO members defected to his new Keadilan (initially Parti Keadilan Nasional, National Justice Party) or PAS. That Mahathir and Anwar joined forces to take on UMNO in 2018 is, hence, acutely ironic.

Moreover, increasing spoils—Tengku Razaleigh suggested Najib awarded UMNO division heads and MPs patronage worth at least MYR50,000 monthly (Funston 2016, 111–12)—perverted party functioning. Until the mid-1970s, voting in party elections tended to be by state, influenced by chief ministers even after elimination of a bloc vote system (Milne 1986, 1371). In 1981, Mahathir broke with precedent and left the choice of his deputy to the General Assembly; Musa Hitam defeated Tengku Razaleigh amid allegedly over $20 million spent (TI 2010, 75–76). Since then, rules for election to party leadership have changed repeatedly, including to shield the prime minister from challenge, favor candidates with broad-based support, and curb vote buying (TI 2010, 76–79). Money still permeates party elections, however. Mahathir declared his own 2006 bid to return to the General Assembly as delegate for Kubang Pasu, the division he had headed for over a quarter century, foiled by MYR200 payments to many of the five hundred voters.[34] (A cabinet minister rejected the allegations, claiming votes could not be bought so cheaply.[35]) Three years later, UMNO's disciplinary board charged fifteen with money politics, though the charges seemed more to influence party elections than to address corruption (Funston 2016, 111). Observers estimated payments in 2013 at around MYR300 per delegate, supplemented by contracts, letters of recommendation, and other assistance.

UMNO's balancing of identity, targeted benefits, and broader performance was already shaky; disempowerment now magnifies the challenge. The party's premises, core constituencies among Malays, methods, and messages have changed dramatically since its founding—it is hardly the same UMNO. Yet over time, UMNO has increasingly structured the regime.

Constituting the BN

Changes in UMNO and the party's increasingly hegemonic stature have defined the BN.[36] Only Sarawak-specific parties retained meaningful ability to dictate the terms of their cooperation, since it was only there that UMNO never dominated.[37] Otherwise, UMNO has held the coalition reins ever more securely since Alliance days, and leadership has always been fairly top-down. Even within UMNO, as early as 1969, allowing branches to submit nominations was primarily "an exercise in public relations"; a small national committee and the Tunku had final say on the full Alliance lineup.[38] Since then, complaints of UMNO's—and specifically, the prime minister's—interference in coalition partners' internal affairs, as well as UMNO's appropriating seats or portfolios, have been rife, but its partners have been unable to push back against "big brother" UMNO.[39]

Nor have these component parties remained static, as they also balance communal and other priorities. Support for the BN's Chinese partners, the MCA and Gerakan, has tapered downward, notwithstanding periodic upticks, diminishing their clout. Already in 1969, the MCA's Michael Chen had acknowledged his party's inability to command sufficient Chinese support to coax UMNO to risk Malay support by conceding non-Malay demands.[40] Internal challenges—including the MCA's own "Team A" and "Team B" split, between party president Ling Liong Sik and deputy Lim Ah Lek, respectively, in 1999—inflicted further damage (Chin 2006, 72–75). The Malaysian Indian Congress (MIC) has likewise battled claims of being elitist and unresponsive to community grievances and has fragmented along class, caste, and ethnic axes (Shekhar 2008, 25).

However, following UMNO's lead, both these parties have established corporate empires. Like UMNO's, their portfolios include media: The MCA's Huaren Holdings secured majority interest in *The Star* in 1977;[41] the MCA and the MIC came to control most Mandarin and Tamil dailies. The MCA launched cooperative society Koperatif Serbaguna Malaysia (KSM) in 1968, then Multi-Purpose Holdings in 1975, as a publicly listed investment company (with the KSM its largest shareholder)—"mired in corruption," yet the second-largest holder of Malaysian corporate stock by 1982 (TI 2010, 85–86; Heng 1997, 272).[42] The MIC similarly raised funds among the Indian community to launch Maika Holdings in 1984 as an unlisted investment holding company, supplementing cooperatives and educational institutions (TI 2010, 86–87).

Increasingly strident calls for Malay preeminence since the 2000s, at a time when non-Malay voters inclined increasingly toward noncommunal opposition coalitions, made plain the coalition's precarious keel and limited ideological valence. UMNO has blamed Chinese defectors for the coalition's declining fortunes and reasserted its role as ethnoreligious champion, including through an increasingly Islamist, unilateral posture (Mohd Azizuddin 2009, 103–6). For PAS to re-ally with UMNO as in 1970 (when, too, UMNO scoffed at the idea, until it happened[43]) was not only plausible, but, given collaboration starting soon after the 2018 elections, came quickly to seem imminent. The UMNO–PAS Muafakat Nasional (National Consensus), announced in late 2019, runs alongside (for now) the UMNO–MCA–MIC BN. Either the current BN formula or the "Malay unity" alternative rests on a fundamentally communal premise: ethnic power sharing or ethnic dominance. Regardless, economic prosperity—understood in terms of performance legitimacy or shared access to patronage—is the essential glue. As detailed below, increasingly wealthy and entrenched BN parties operationalized communalism and retained support by selectively distributing spoils, oiling their own machines in the process.

Challenges by and for the Opposition

Opposition alternatives have developed over the decades, navigating interrelated hurdles: structural constraints that impede mobilization and contestation and the difficulty of forging effective, let alone coordinated, appeals, given the distribution of issues, voters, and parties. These parties' profiles, composition, and pacts have changed with shifts in BN strategy and political openings, but most fit within broadly social-democratic, post-UMNO, and Islamist categories, alongside a complement of states' rights–oriented East Malaysian parties.

On the social-democratic side, the Labour Party faded, then folded in the early 1970s; some leaders shifted to the new DAP,[44] successor to the PAP in Malaysia—and initially still so associated with Singapore that its future seemed uncertain, though it outperformed the MCA or Gerakan from 1974 to 1990 (Maryanov 1967, 103; Heng 1996, 42, 46). The DAP has traditionally had a thin presence on the ground, though it has pushed increasingly to ramp up presence, activities, and coordination.[45] Gerakan, formed among multiethnic, English-educated moderates in 1968 (and always strongest in Penang), offered a similar profile to the DAP, but joined the BN after its first election (Cheah 2002, 135). Party Rakyat Malaysia (PRM) persisted, though most of the party merged with Keadilan in 2003. Cadre-based Parti Sosialis Malaysia sits farther to the left. With about fourteen hundred members, the party is small, but it helps anchor a much wider network of people's committees and front organizations, focused more on socioeconomic transformation than elections.[46] Trade unions have not figured significantly in left-leaning parties' efforts, given legal constraints, low union density (about 6.5 percent), and the fact that most unions incline toward the BN.[47]

Offshoots from UMNO emerge periodically. Launched in 1999 amid a broad *Reformasi* movement, Keadilan now has around five hundred thousand members (though data are imprecise) and a progressively stronger organization. Yet it is bedeviled by "UMNO 2.0 working culture," including messy party elections, and struggles to present a coherent, distinct, noncommunal brand.[48] Still, it has moved farther from the UMNO model than Semangat '46, which billed itself as "more UMNO than UMNO" and coopted entire UMNO branches.[49] Like Semangat, which galvanized opposition efforts in 1990 by bridging two otherwise-irreconcilable coalitions, Keadilan anchors Pakatan Harapan (Alliance of Hope; previously a partly differently constituted Pakatan Rakyat, People's Pact)—perhaps at the cost of clarifying its own identity. The latest UMNO splinter parties are Parti Pribumi Bersatu Malaysia (Malaysian United Indigenous Party, Bersatu), launched in September 2016, and Parti Warisan Sabah (Sabah Heritage Party, Warisan), launched the following month. Mahathir, his son Mukhriz, and ex-deputy prime minister Muhyiddin Yassin launched Bersatu to "bring back the original" UMNO, in coalition with Pakatan.[50] It is through this vehicle that Mahathir, improbably, returned as prime minister in 2018, luring enough UMNO MPs to "hop" postelection to raise concern that Bersatu would simply replicate UMNO. Meanwhile, UMNO vice president Shafie Apdal, at odds with Sabah's then-chief minister and irked by the 1Malaysia Development Berhad (1MDB) sovereign wealth fund fiasco, resigned and formed Warisan, absorbing disgruntled UMNO members, touting Sabah autonomy, and allying informally with Pakatan (Suffian and Lee 2020).

Paramount within the Islamist camp is PAS, consistently active and strengthened by a post-1969 *dakwah* (Islamic proselytization and revival) movement across Malaysia. Like UMNO, PAS has morphed over the decades: from left-wing anticolonialism, to Malay ethnonationalism, to Islamic internationalism and *ulama* leadership as of the early 1980s, to the rise of reformist "professionals" by the late 1990s, to a more hardline Islamist resurgence. These turns reflect not only PAS's capacity for reinvention, but also its sparring with a shifting UMNO (Farish 2014; Liow 2006, 184–87). PAS has endured, too, not just fluctuating electoral fortunes, but structural ruptures—most recently, the splintering off of Parti Amanah Negara (National Trust Party), taking about 20 percent of PAS branches, in 2015.[51] Although PAS has remained strongest in Malaysia's northeast, the party mobilizes nationally, especially through its youth wing, to develop cadres and leadership and promote its agenda (Liow 2011, 666–69). Recalibrations notwithstanding, PAS usually orients appeals toward rural Malays and recent rural-to-urban migrants, including through propounding a vision of political Islam sufficiently "extreme" to differentiate itself from UMNO (Thirkell-White 2006, 426, 431).

That the BN has occupied such broad terrain has pressed opposition alternatives into disparate niches, but secular-leftist and Islamist parties have pursued alliances since the late 1980s. They have aimed, effectively, to shift the axis from communalism and compete on different grounds. Hence, 1999's Barisan Alternatif (BA, Alternative Front), then Pakatan (launched in 2008 and reconstituted in 2015), challenged the BN's ethnic concept, albeit still allocating seats per ethnic composition. Echoing BN, opposition parties have pursued preelection pacts. These require especial discipline: usually, the party that is strongest in an area competes, shutting out partners' candidates.[52] Intracoalition battling over seats has been harsh and multicornered fights persist. New networks, online and in civil society, have eased communications—hampered otherwise by legal curbs on speech, press, and assembly—and socialization toward shared objectives, centered broadly around good governance, anticorruption, and social justice. Yet ideological disputes persist, too, as over the extent of Islamism and Malay dominance.

Regime roadblocks have posed daunting impediments. Setting the stage for the postseparation order was a crackdown shortly after the May 1969 elections.

Detainees included the DAP secretary-general, organizing secretary, and Labour Bureau chair. Arrests continued, including of two Parti Rakyat Malaysia state assemblymen in January 1970.[53] Early the following year, four more DAP members, including Fan Yew Teng, MP and editor of the DAP's *The Rocket*, were arrested under the Sedition Act; only on successful appeal did Fan retain his parliamentary seat.[54] Yet more members of the DAP and Parti Rakyat Malaysia were detained in the mid-1970s for alleged revolutionary aspirations and ties with a communist underground (Syed Husin 1996, 66–67, 132, 160–62). The DAP worried such harassment might itself radicalize party members or make non-Malays see parliamentary politics as pointless, even with Chinese officials in government.[55] Over time, the BN met a larger opposition presence in parliament with increasing harassment and detention of opposition politicians and activists. While in 2012, the government repealed the anticommunist Internal Security Act 1960, commonly used against opposition activists and other critics (Loh 2008), investigations and arrests continued, including under the Security Offences (Special Measures) Act that replaced it.

But the more prevalent grind has been coping with a range of manipulations that, as described in chapter 1, brand the regime as electoral-authoritarian. Tight curbs on campaigning in Sabah and Sarawak in the mid-1970,[56] for seats not filled before polling was suspended, signaled a trend. Constraints include the gerrymandering and constituency maldistribution detailed above, the brevity and unpredictable timing of campaigns, and the BN's until now vastly greater resources. BN candidates routinely exceed the low spending caps the Election Offences Act of 1954 emplaces for federal (MYR200,000) and state (MYR100,000) legislative contests. Only funds the candidate spends directly (not the party, nor in-kind donations or labor) count toward the limit, and only during the campaign period proper, making the cap "virtually non-existent" (and rarely monitored, regardless). No one has yet been jailed or fined for "treating" voters or exercising undue influence, as through bribery or intimidation (Wong 2012, 22–24). Cases verge on surreal: USD12 million smuggled into Malaysia in late 2012 was acceptable because it was a contribution to Sabah UMNO rather than for the chief minister himself; again in 2015, authorities declared USD700 million deposited into Najib's personal accounts legal, as a campaign donation (Ufen 2015, 564–65). The latter case demonstrates a larger trend of concentration of access to funding among a few politicians, who use those resources to maintain or improve their political stature (Gomez 2012, 1372). Although vote buying is relatively scarce in Malaysia (albeit higher in spots, Aeria 2005, 133–35)[57] and more routine campaign "goodies," from transportation money to dinners and performances, may carry no explicit directive to vote accordingly, BN resources have clearly helped (Wong 2012, 23–27).

But the core challenge for Malaysian opposition parties, as elsewhere, has been convincing voters to accept the risk of losing out on what they have—benefits from race-based affirmative action, targeted development grants, access to a generous MP—to pursue abstract goals of "democracy" or "Islamism" or "good governance." (Voters obviously cannot know for sure, too, the extent to which once in power, parties will pursue those objectives.) These entreaties require, essentially, a moral appeal: to make voters comply because the action, successful or not, is meaningful to them, or because they feel their own identity and conscience leave them no choice (LeBas 2011, 47). That the BN's promise has *not* been solely ethnic privilege, but also premised on performance legitimacy, has made the challenge greater. Francis Loh suggests that a new political culture of "developmentalism" had taken root by the early 1990s, valorizing economic growth, consumerism, and the political stability these require, "associated in the minds of most Malaysians with the BN," as the coalition theretofore in office (2003b, 261). Economic downturns and corruption scandals from the mid-1990s on called that premise into question, but without confirming that an alternative model could better satisfy aspirations, especially given the extent to which the BN, over decades in power, had turned the state to its own advantage.

State, Party, and Political Economy

Alongside these electoral-political developments, the BN radically reshaped Malaysia's political economy. These efforts have had long-term and pervasive effects, given the extent to which institutions—in Malaysia, especially those governing the labor market and state economic intervention—do not merely "supervise," but "kindle and shape" markets and growth (Lafaye de Micheaux 2017, 13–14). To some extent, 1969's outburst was "a blessing in disguise" for Malay politicians looking for a chance to advance a nationalist economic agenda (Shamsul 1997, 250). As UMNO reconsolidated, it foregrounded redistribution, embedding partisan advantage within an overtly programmatic policy framework. Before that point, Majlis Amanah Rakat (MARA, Council of Trust for the People), launched in 1966 (following a 1965 Bumiputera Economic Congress) as successor to the Rural Industrial Development Authority (RIDA) of the 1950s, already funneled benefits to bumiputera.[58] A second congress in February 1968 proposed an UMNO-based national finance company: UMNO established a new investment cooperative that year, issuing shares to members and directing proceeds initially toward housing projects.[59] Scaling up these precedents was the New Economic Policy (NEP) of 1970–90, followed by the New Development Policy (1991–2000), the New Vision Policy (2001–10), and then the New Economic Model (2011–20).

These initiatives institutionalized partisan patronage as state programs, cementing loyalty both within and to the party. "Money politics," understood in Malaysia to mean less vote buying than parties' and politicians' direct or indirect control of companies, skewed distribution of rents such as contracts and subsidies, and interference in the corporate sector (Gomez 2012, 1371, 1374), has become essential to political praxis.

Expanding existing preferential policies, the NEP allowed "a massive transfer of state funds to Malays" and to a lesser extent other bumiputera in the name of tackling poverty, redistributing wealth, and reducing the identification of ethnicity with occupation (Funston 2016, 44, 46). Its provisions tallied to "an almost unlimited source of patronage," channeled indirectly—for instance, requirements that government-linked corporations (GLCs) favor bumiputera, that bumiputera service all smaller and many larger government contracts, and that housing developers reserve discounted units for bumiputera (Funston 2016, 47–48). The 1975 Industrial Coordination Act, which increased a 30 percent bumiputera participation requirement for pioneer status firms enacted in 1968 to 55–60 percent, then extended minima to nonpioneer firms, was especially important, even after the MCA secured amendments to protect Chinese firms (Lafaye de Micheaux 2017, 254–55; Jomo and Gomez 2000, 289–90). Although Chinese capital was less a target than foreign ownership, the community was negatively affected, including in sharply reduced access to local tertiary education. Ensuring non-Malays' general acquiescence were growth rates averaging 6.7 percent throughout the NEP, opportunities for joint ventures (as well as "Ali Baba" arrangements, in which Malays were largely passive rentier capitalists), and later the NDP's recalibration and improved accommodation of minority educational and cultural interests (Heng 1997, 262–63, 274–78; 1996, 47). Resource rents also helped, especially once Malaysia became a net oil exporter in the mid-1970s. The 1974 Petroleum Development Act gave federal authorities jurisdiction over petroleum—states otherwise control natural resources—proceeds from which enabled public sector expansion and state spending in the 1970s–80s (Jomo and Gomez 2000, 280–82).

Starting early in the NEP years, the government established a range of public enterprises, both government owned and public/private joint ventures, and took over existing firms; by 1979, the government owned about 557 public enterprises (Ng 2001, 165). (BN MPs became chairs or board members, securing additional income, perks, and access to projects.[60]) The public sector share of GNP—29.2 percent at the NEP's launch—peaked at 58.4 percent in 1981, then dropped to 25.3 percent by 1993 (Jomo and Gomez 2000, 288–89). Public sector employment swelled to comprise an estimated 15 percent of total employment by 1986, representing a 66 percent increase in jobs since 1971 (and possibly significantly more, given classification errors) (Lafaye de Micheaux 2017, 251). Currently, despite three decades' privatization (but having expanded since 2009), the civil service employs 1.6 million, or 11 percent of the labor force—relative to population, the world's largest civil service, absorbing 40 percent of the government budget and with low productivity, given also unselective hiring.[61]

Economic downturns spurred course corrections in the mid-1980s and mid-1990s. With a state-led heavy-industrialization strategy clearly underperforming, Mahathir announced his "Vision 2020" plan in 1991, emphasizing modernization, industrialization, and growth over inter-ethnic redistribution (Jomo and Gomez 2000, 292–94). Under the NEP, the Malaysian state had played "trustee" for bumiputera would-be investors, acquiring and managing shares on their behalf, increasing Malays' share of investment in Malaysian companies from 1.5 percent in the 1960s to 18.7 percent in 1983. At that point, trust agencies held 61 percent of Malay capital, a proportion that dropped by almost half by 1990 (Lafaye de Micheaux 2017, 252–53). The state divested itself of public enterprises, giving not just trust agencies (particularly Amanah Saham Nasional, National Unit Trust Scheme), but also individuals holding assets on UMNO's behalf and pro-UMNO Malay capitalists, first dibs on shares (Ng 2001, 170). From 1991 to 1995, 204 projects from across sectors were privatized, often for less than their real value (Jesudason 1997, 156–57). By the mid-1990s, most of the largest bumiputera-controlled firms were linked to top UMNO politicians (Gomez 2014, 251–53). Yet an increasingly neoliberal approach hardly impeded provision of selective support. For instance, Najib announced the Bumiputera Economic Empowerment program in 2013, extending benefits in shares, housing, and GLC projects, including MYR20 billion annually in contracts.[62]

Effects have been mixed. Increasing federal economic involvement in Sabah under the NEP, for example, saw near-immediate returns, including a 100 percent increase in secondary school enrollments by 1978, a huge jump in tertiary education, and jobs for bumiputera in the expanded bureaucracy and statutory authorities. But those with the "right political connections" fared best; still-limited opportunities frustrated others' newly stoked ambitions (Loh 2005, 84–86). More broadly, mechanisms for accountability have fallen short; mirroring complaints of abuse of power, unfairness, and other problems have been poor scores on international assessments of transparency and corruption. Weak legislative oversight or ministerial responsibility, a politicized bureaucracy, and curbs on media and monitoring efforts leave few effective checks (Siddiquee 2006, 56–59). The Malaysian Anti-Corruption Commission, established in 1967, although fairly active (and increasingly so under Pakatan), has thus far investigated fewer than 7 percent of reported cases, favoring petty rather than higher-level allegations and seemingly targeting opposition politicians under the BN; the auditor-general, too, has limited capacity or authority to investigate irregularities in government accounts (Siddiquee 2006, 49–53; Loh 2010, 139). A spate of scandals have grabbed headlines: among recent others, revelations of improper channeling of funds and contracts related to the Port Klang Free Trade Zone in 2009; mismanagement and graft in a state cattle farming initiative in 2010 and smallholder scheme FELDA in 2017; and the hugely complex—and simply huge—1MDB debacle that broke in 2015, entailing massive debts and misappropriation.

Pathologies notwithstanding, by the 1980s, the BN had embraced features of developmentalism. Rather than technocratic management, though, this framework entailed a state with "the ability to siphon off and generate resources in society," internal controls sufficiently strong to resist social pressures, and "the ideological ability to inculcate national consciousness among large sections of the population" (Jesudason 1997, 159). State decision making responds to market signals—growth remains the overarching goal—but tempered by political considerations of whose interests warrant protection, and more reactively and slowly than in other developmental states (Jesudason 1997, 152–54, 160–63).

The increasing alignment of political and economic power has changed politicians' incentives. Previously, UMNO dominated via demographic might, so needed to cultivate and sustain support among economically marginalized voters, for instance, through pro-Malay education policies (Thachil 2011, 487–88). NEP restructuring created new distributional coalitions motivated to safeguard their own interests, including the military and religious establishment (by way of schemes such as the Armed Forces Provident Fund and the Tabung Haji pilgrimage fund), new bureaucratic cliques, and parties (Jesudason 1997, 155), while also entrenching UMNO "warlords" to be bought off in party elections (TI 2010, 78). Indeed, much patronage stayed within UMNO or "sticks to a few hands at the top"; as elsewhere, patronage furthers "intra-elite accommodation" as well as courting voters (van de Walle 2003, 312–13). Hidekuni Washida, for instance, tracks the extent to which distribution of ministerial portfolios and legislative seats has induced elites to do more with less to mobilize votes and has been "effective grease in coalitional politics" (2019, 2, 9, 109–10, 127–31).

But partisan patronage permeates the system. Especially key are constituency development funds (CDFs). Only ruling-party MPs receive full (or under BN, any) legislative CDFs; the government has channeled funds for opposition-held seats instead to a ruling-party *penyelaras* (coordinator).[63] The *penyelaras* system allows the party to test out possible candidates and for those individuals to lay the ground for a potential campaign or comeback.[64] As opposition, Pakatan did the same at the state level where it governed, albeit offering a (declined) token payment to BN ADUN in Selangor and Penang. That these funds are used for partisan purpose is clear. Notes a critical report, CDFs "are often used by both Opposition and Government MPs to treat their constituents and in some cases results in a form of vote buying" (GCCP 2015, 11–12).

The base parliamentary CDF increased under Najib from MYR1 million to MYR5 million,[65] and (only) BN MPs could request supplemental funds relatively easily.[66] In BN-held states, BN ADUN received an annual allocation from the PM's department, as well as project-specific support from relevant ministries. (The most sought-after ministerial portfolios are those that carry not prestige, but funds—especially rural development and education.)[67] The state development officer, a federal appointee under the jurisdiction of the Implementation Coordination Unit in the PM's department, held BN allocations; the MP or *penyelaras* submitted projects there for approval and funding. The Implementation Coordination Unit commonly approved requests, then engaged a BN-connected private firm or the public works department as needed. ADUN access CDFs via their constituency's district officer, who administers the substate district land office.[68]

With the BN still in power at the federal level, the Pakatan state governments in Penang and Selangor provided Pakatan ADUN with MYR500–900,000 in CDFs, and Pakatan MPs from there with around MYR150–300,000 in state funds to support their efforts in-state. About 40 percent was to be spent on projects (usually minor infrastructure); the rest was for donations, T-shirts, and so on. The PAS-led government in Kelantan granted other-opposition (e.g., Keadilan) ADUN allocations of MYR150,000 and other-opposition Kelantan MPs MYR50,000. State-appointed local councilors and senators in Pakatan-held states at the time also received CDFs: about MYR50–100,000 for councilors and MYR100–150,000 for senators.[69]

However much Pakatan complained of BN injustice in denying opposition MPs CDFs, the practice is equally useful to the new government, and largely sustained. Explained the newly installed head of Pakatan's Johor state government, in language redolent of the BN previously, "Why should we give BN assemblymen who had opposed us any allocations? It will be like giving bullets so they can shoot back at us."[70] (He soon came around and agreed to give all representatives a modest MYR50,000 annually for operations and staff.[71]) At the federal level, too, Pakatan has hardly jumped the BN track. The new government announced in 2018 that its own MPs would receive a MYR500,000 allocation, plus MYR200,000 for service center expenses—increased to MYR1.5 million plus MYR300,000 for expenses in 2019—and opposition MPs, only MYR100,000. The latter cried injustice; Pakatan MPs retorted that the BN gave them nothing, so fair's fair—although opinion within Pakatan remained sharply divided.[72] Pakatan's resistance to reform, on a dimension both readily retooled and so seemingly in line with its own manifesto, is testament to the coalition's adaptation to long-term BN praxis of spinning state resources to their own maximal advantage.

In fact, across parties, politicians use CDFs for concrete, visible, loyalty-building purposes, however token. CDF-funded projects echo (or fulfill) campaign-period promises. Even in 1964, the Alliance outspent other parties about threefold, for logistics as well as strategically timed development grants and other handouts (Ufen 2015, 571). BN expenditures have thus far well exceeded opposition parties'. In fact, DAP candidates have paid their party MYR10,000 for kits of party merchandise (including to sell) and campaign swag.[73] The BN has provided its candidates with the maximum funds the EC allows them to spend; opposition candidates have received a fraction of that amount, at best (although more than previously, when parties could not routinely cover even deposits[74]). In contrast with financially diversified BN parties, other Malaysian parties rely mainly on "grassroots financing": (token) membership fees, sales of publications, fundraising dinners, levies on legislators' salaries, (limited) contributions from businesses, and individual donations. Additionally, some PAS members pay *zakat* (the mandatory tithe on Muslims) to the party instead of the state, though technically disallowed,[75] and the DAP generates some income from rental properties (Gomez 2012, 1383–84; TI 2010, 96–99). PAS may also have built support through timber concessions in Kelantan and Terengganu; after the 1969 election, UMNO's Syed Ja'afar Albar (presumably biased) suggested as much, but indicated that PAS officials were "clever enough not to demonstrate their affluence openly while they were in office."[76] (Allegations still swirl of such practices, as of crony state-level contracts under Pakatan.)

All Malaysian parties rely on "covert funding" (TI 2010, 81–84). Political finance reform is pending; for now, political parties are under no obligation to disclose sources of donations. As registered societies, they submit annual audited accounts, but these may be highly obfuscatory (TI 2010, 119, 123; Ufen 2015, 575). UMNO discloses little regarding either transfers from its corporate holdings to the party or purportedly thousands of internally handled ethical breaches (Gomez 2012, 1385). BN partners follow UMNO's lead. The links between Sarawak's Parti Pesaka Bumiputera Bersatu (United Bumiputera Heritage Party, PBB), in power since 1981, with cement, steel, logging, exports, financial services, and a range of government projects, are especially substantial and murky. Former PBB chief minister Rahman Yakub allegedly distributed logging concessions worth USD9 billion, plus banking licenses and other benefits, to relatives and clients who then supported Sarawak BN campaigns (Aeria 2005, 129; TI 2010, 92). In contrast, then-Gerakan president Lim Keng Yaik, concerned about both proper accounting and candidates' differing fundraising abilities, collected donations in a common party fund for distribution.[77]

The BN has also benefited from incumbency, blurring the lines between state and party spending. Most blatant has been government officials' launching projects during campaigns—not technically illegal—and drawing on public resources for transport, staff, and other costs (TI 2010, 120–21). In 1970, when the Alliance faced poor odds in imminent elections in Sarawak, an observer noted that "never have so many buildings and bridges been opened as during the past week."[78] The pattern continued: the 1996 state election campaign alone tallied MYR7.68 million per constituency in "'electoral goodies' under the guise of official development patronage" (Aeria 2005, 131–32).

Beyond elections, parties claim credit for state spending. Most development initiatives are state, not party, programs, but hazy lines leave opposition parties challenged to convince voters that they will not lose vital state programs by voting opposition. Confusing the appearance of patronage are carefully pitched programmatic transfers—especially Bantuan Rakyat 1Malaysia (1Malaysia People's Aid, BR1M), an unconditional cash transfer program launched in 2012. Qualification for benefits—initially a one-time payment of MYR500 to households with monthly incomes under MYR3,000, then later extended and enhanced—is on "neutral," publicly known terms, and not contingent on one's vote. However, BR1M represents a partisanized programmatic policy: BN party offices (and sometimes MPs themselves) originally commonly dispensed payments, giving the impression of a party, not state, grant. Indeed, the official BR1M website credited the "Barisan Nasional Government" specifically.[79] The government switched to direct deposit, purportedly due to concerns of the PM's department oversight office, Pemandu (Performance Management and Delivery Unit), about avoiding the appearance of corruption.[80] One BN MP noted that about twenty thousand initially claimed their payments from his party office; he considered that chance to meet the people a core purpose of BR1M. With direct deposit, "there's no political mileage."[81] Regardless, a fellow MP maintained a database of constituents receiving BR1M (among other benefits) and directed his machinery to focus on them.[82]

Nor was it only BN, even though Mahathir announced mid-2018 that Pakatan would phase out BR1M, so as not to "mollycoddle the people," lest "they become weak."[83] The BN purportedly modeled BR1M on opposition state-level programs.[84] On coming to power in Penang in 2008, Pakatan introduced a cash transfer program designed to eliminate poverty in the state. Bundled under the Agenda Ekonomi Saksama (Equitable Economic Agenda), comprising 12 percent of the state budget, the program ensured a minimum monthly household income and included targeted grants for groups, including housewives, single mothers, senior citizens, students, and the disabled. Individuals needed not apply at a Pakatan service center, yet one such center alone processed fifteen to twenty applications daily.[85]

Selangor's People-Based Economy program (Merakyatkan Ekonomi Selangor, MES), rolled out in phases starting in 2008 (and maintained, though rebranded[86]), likewise offers various forms of insurance, education assistance, and allowances or programs for single mothers, housewives, and newlyweds. Additional programs support people with disabilities, healthcare and screening programs, and death benefits, plus offer economic stimuli and combat poverty. Aid is personalized: an ADUN may offer condolences in person while delivering the death benefit for a constituent's burial expenses, for example, or may invite recipients of higher-education benefits to enroll as voters or join the party. One Keadilan ADUN held a monthly MES distribution event; the event de-emphasized party brand, yet volunteers wore Keadilan T-shirts and the ADUN's photo embellished souvenir filtered-water jugs (a signature initiative).[87] But when a PAS ADUN added his photo and party logo to envelopes with state healthcare assistance payments in 2017, after PAS had exited Pakatan, legislative colleagues chastised him for making the state-government program appear a PAS initiative. He countered by noting how common such personalization was: "We've done this before."[88] Individual MPs run flagship programs, as well—for instance, Keadilan MP Wong Chen's Bulan Kebajikan (Welfare Month). He and his staff collect requests from needy constituents, submitted in person with an interview, then distribute checks (at their office) to recipients, funded by his allocation.[89]

Beyond such transfers, federal government development initiatives combine economic, social engineering, and political goals. FELDA, introduced in chapter 3, is exemplary. By 1990, FELDA had resettled nearly 120,000 families and developed over 900,000 hectares in settler smallholdings or commercial plantations. FELDA areas today account for around 9 percent of the electorate, approximately 1.2 million voters (Khor 2015, 91–92). Every FELDA scheme has an UMNO branch (and the UMNO-linked Majlis Belia FELDA Malaysia, FELDA Youth Council, has around 100,000 members). PAS also has branches on most FELDA schemes (Rashila 2005, 133; Khor 2015, 98–99). Until the combination of Bersatu's emergence and revelations of a "dubious" and costly FELDA land deal (C4 Center [2018]) tipped the scales in 2018, Pakatan made little headway among FELDA voters, stymied in 2013, for example, by UMNO's promises to youths of houses and resettlement land, alleged rounds of cash and hampers for each household, and payouts (about MYR15,000 per settler, equaling about six months' income) from a FELDA Global Ventures initial public offering (Khor 2015, 92, 99–105, 111–12). Maznah Mohamad sees in the BN's near-complete dominance within FELDA schemes a "politically driven economic geography" of UMNO support (2015, 146). FELDA creates not "traditional" rural villages, but "corporatised" ones, in which UMNO has been both patron and government. Voters are not independent cultivators, but work for, and are perennially indebted to, FELDA; that dependency rendered them a "crucial vote bank" for UMNO (Maznah 2015, 149–51).

But it was in East Malaysia that the BN truly nurtured dependency. Both states (Sarawak and Sabah) remain significantly underdeveloped, despite gains under the NEP. In 1992, Sarawak's longtime chief minister Abdul Taib Mahmud (1981–2014) announced a "politics of development" strategy: "a total commitment to development by using the power of politics to make sure that we achieve our development objectives" (quoted in Aeria 1997, 59). Purposefully vague, the policy lacked measurable targets and excluded opposition-supporting communities (Faisal 2009, 96). Subsequent BN campaign promises upped the ante—for instance, of MYR29.9 billion in projects in 2013, following MYR32.2 billion spent on roads, water, electricity, housing, and healthcare since the prior election (Faisal 2015, 12). Urban voters less in need of infrastructural and other investment resisted these appeals, amid concerns over corruption and state autonomy (e.g., Loh 1997, 9–10; Mersat 2009). But BN support increased among groups likely to be swayed by patronage, such as poor minorities, some of whom also enjoy benefits as bumiputera (Faisal 2015, 13–15). BN expectations for these targeted grants were clear. Distributing MYR18 million in government allocations to Chinese educationists in Sibu in 2010, days before a by-election, for example, Najib proposed, "I help you, you help me. . . . We will do what we should to give you what you want. And you know what I want."[90] Or as a Sabahan MP explained, if you show you can deliver "some gifts, goodies," such as low-cost housing or infrastructure, constituents will "cut you some slack."[91]

In Sabah, too, economic expansion, especially after discovery of oil in the early 1970s, generated funds for rural development. It was under Sabah BN anchor Berjaya, with Harris Salleh as chief minister (1976–85), that patronage peaked: he brought dramatic development, transforming the state, but tied projects explicitly to political support. After BN member Parti Bersatu Sabah (United Sabah Party, PBS) quit the coalition days before the 1990 elections, then won, the federal government froze several large infrastructure projects, banned export of timber logs (the source of almost half of state revenue), excluded the chief minister from state executive development-planning meetings, and rerouted funds beyond constitutionally mandated grants through the BN-controlled Federal Development Office and federal agencies rather than through the state government. PBS still narrowly won the next state election, but the BN coaxed sufficient ADUN defections to secure a majority. Once in power, the BN poured federal funds into the state under the "New Sabah" package of rural development, housing, schools, and industrialization (Chin 2001, 41–43; Loh 2005, 98–101). Ever since, at each election, the BN has reminded voters of what it has provided, launched infrastructure and other projects midcampaign, promised substantial new investment if returned to power, and warned of the costs otherwise. Coupled with the EC's ability since the 1990s to pinpoint microlevel voting patterns, such promises and threats encouraged voters to see the BN as their only sure conduit to resources (Lim 2008, 81–89; Aeria 1997, 59–60, 63–64, 67–72; Loh 1997, 8–9; Faisal 2009).

Peninsular states are not immune. After PAS secured control of Terengganu and Kelantan in 1999, the BN federal government removed Terengganu's petroleum royalty payments, worth over MYR810 million annually—guaranteed under 1975 and 1987 agreements and paid since 1978 (Funston 2016, 68)—and rechanneled federal projects through federal officers, bypassing state officials. A "political recession" resulted (Chin 2001, 48). Again after 2008, the BN rushed to shift control over or redirect federal development funds in opposition-won states, denying the authority of non-BN state governments (Loh 2010, 134–35). The BN also targeted individual constituencies, for instance, starving Bukit Mertajam, Penang, of resources from 1978, when its voters first elected a DAP MP, until 1995, when their return to MCA garnered "special discretionary development funds" for local infrastructure and amenities (Nonini 2015, 225).

These measures' objective is clear: to make voters fear economic penalties should they vote opposition. This "bullying" had become less tenable, however—notwithstanding hang-ups still in these states' securing federal resources—particularly with more states opposition led, including wealthy, industrialized ones (Penang and Selangor) that not only depend less on federal funds than Kelantan or Sabah, but whose decline could damage the national economy (Loh 2010, 136–39). Indeed, the extent to which the federal government could withhold necessary funds for cities' maintenance and development was limited, especially since UMNO touted its modernizing record; the BN's challenge was to maintain its opposition-led urban core, without letting the opposition take credit.[92]

Communicating policy achievements may be easier in rural areas. Post-1969 restructuring included remaking the adult education agency as the Social Development Division (Bahagian Kemajuan Masyarakat, KEMAS), under the Rural Development Ministry. KEMAS runs thousands of nurseries and kindergartens, but also connects closely with community organizations, monitors local developments, and delivers community programs while promoting the ruling party (Funston 2016, 48; Faisal 2015, 17–18). Supplementing KEMAS from 1982 through 2018 was the National Civics Bureau (Biro Tata Negara), which worked mainly "to indoctrinate participants with a chauvinistic justification of Malay dominance, and support for UMNO" (Funston 2016, 56).

Yet, much as we see with CDFs now, opposition parties have increasingly been competing on similar terms. In a 1999 campaign speech, a PBS candidate in Sabah, for instance, asked voters to review which party had distributed more rice, sugar, and coffee and to think back on the development her party had brought—roads, churches, mosques, flood relief—when in power previously.[93] More recently, the DAP and Keadilan nurtured support in Sabah and Sarawak through Impian (Dream) projects.[94] They worked with local bumiputera communities in the underdeveloped interior, providing small-scale infrastructure (solar panels, irrigation, roads), plus medical checkups and other services. Funding and volunteers were from the party and (often peninsular) churches and other supporters, as well as politicians. The goal was to demonstrate Pakatan's ability to provide development, even without access to federal funds. (The BN stepped up its efforts, in response.)[95] But funding remained a critical constraint. Pakatan's East Malaysian MPs and ADUN received no CDFs, state governments could not channel resources to out-of-state politicians, and Pakatan parties lacked resources to maintain *penyelaras* in BN-held states.

All told, these practices left the BN reliant on continued access to patronage resources, yet pressed challengers to respond in kind. Development promises, partisanized programs, and patronage-based appeals are now systemic rather than BN specific, discouraging a focus on ideology or issues, however clearly unequal the scope of spending and rent seeking.

Local Government

Beyond partisan-tinged economic policies and patronage, the system in place keeps parties pervasive and potent as mobilizing, service-providing machines—in turn stabilizing the regime status quo. Malaysia's post-1969 restructuring included the full abrogation of local elections. Notwithstanding expanding state capacity, politicians and party service centers (*pusat khidmat*) have taken on substantial municipal and welfare functions, rather than leave these to (appointed) local authorities. Malaysian politicians are not unique in stressing constituency service, but the fact of nonelected, subpar appointed councils makes this work particularly consequential, for both accountability and actual governance. Meanwhile, that focus has acculturated voters to expect federal and state legislators to prioritize municipal functions over higher-level policymaking.

Eliminating local elections provided a critical opening. In June 1965, the federal government appointed lawyer Athi Nahappan to chair an inquiry into allegations of local-government malpractice. Having surveyed all 373 local authorities and solicited political parties' input, in its December 1968 report, the commission recommended a new framework to overcome structural weaknesses in local government: larger authorities with wider functions, greater delegation to the local level, and uniform and better conditions for staff. It proposed, too, that all municipal councilors and two-thirds of district councilors be elected (Norris 1980, 40, 46–51; Sim and Koay 2015b, 18; Nahappan 1970, 3–7).[96]

Following the 1969 elections, the National Operations Council turned to the Nahappan report. Despite internal disagreement, worried about undue risks, the National Operations Council ultimately rejected its recommendations and eliminated local elections as "redundant," structurally complicated, costly, and unhelpful for national unity, development, intergovernmental relations, or efficiency (WDC 2008, 23–24; Norris 1980, 51–58; Goh 2005, 60). When Parliament debated the issue in 1972, opposition MPs' protestations had no effect (Norris 1980, 59–61). Prime Minister Tun Razak declared democracy at the state and national levels sufficient; at the local level, services, efficiency, and clean governance, which appointed authorities could provide, mattered more (Norris 1980, 61–63). Indeed, suspending local elections had drawn "no visible discontent or protest"; a contemporaneous survey showed most respondents "not aware" or "not concerned" (Cheema and S. Ahmad 1978, 589).

The key laws structuring local government remain the same today: the Local Government Act of 1976, the Town and Country Planning Act (TCPA) of 1976, and the Street, Drainage and Building Act of 1973. Additional laws apply in Sabah and Sarawak. Kuala Lumpur falls under the Federal Capital Act of 1960 and a 1973 constitutional amendment excising the federal territory from Selangor (eradicating its opposition-leaning residents' state-level representation). Local authorities include twelve city councils (*majlis bandaraya*, for urban centers of over five hundred thousand and MYR100 million annual revenue, led by *datuk bandar*, mayors), thirty-nine president-headed municipal councils (*majlis perbandaran*, for cities of at least one hundred thousand), and ninety-eight district councils (*majlis daerah*, for less-populated rural areas).[97] All fall under the purview of the Ministry of Housing and Local Government, established in 1964, and the coordinating National Council for Local Government, established in 1960. Terms of office vary, including minimum qualifications, duration of appointment, and salary—though remuneration is invariably low.[98] Local councilors (*ahli majlis*) are unelected legislators, with sizeable budgets and substantial authority in areas such as town planning.[99] However, while local-government functions have expanded, especially for planning, acquiring land, and development, the state approves zoning, budgets, and appointments and may transfer local-government functions to the chief minister, and prevailing laws do not facilitate public consultation or seriously redress overlapping functions and fiscal constraints (Norris 1980, 97–102, 111–14; Cheema and S. Ahmad 1978, 583).

The Local Government Act aimed to reduce the role of political parties; states are to nominate councilors with "wide experience in local government affairs or who have achieved distinction in any profession, commerce or industry, or are otherwise capable of representing the interests of their communities in the local authority area."[100] In practice, state governments have chosen councilors overwhelmingly for party loyalty, not merit; their competence varies significantly, with underperformance rarely penalized.[101] When parties do look outside the usual channels, recruiting qualified professionals is challenging—the workload can exceed an ADUN's, with far lower pay and benefits (Sim and Koay 2015a)—though status and access to contracts or rents may lure some.[102] Also, local authorities are winner-take-all: state governments eschew entirely councilors from the state-level opposition, eliminating a pathway for smaller parties to gain a foothold and experience.[103]

Councilors are not legally accountable to state governments or voters. Rather, the positions tend to be "political handouts"—party divisions or branches initiate nominations, mostly of local party functionaries—so councilors generally defer to the ADUN who backed them. Many councilors and even mayors have only a vague grasp of what their powers, responsibilities, and available resources *are*, let alone the skills or training to analyze the zoning maps and budgets civil servants draft. Although increased competition for nominations and stepped-up language and educational prerequisites have improved quality, some councilors remain "quite dirty" or lackadaisical.[104] The DAP has faced especial challenges, as it remakes its image from Chinese to multiracial: older, Mandarin-speaking grassroots party activists grumble at being sidelined in favor of non-Chinese, younger nominees.[105] Even for UMNO, while an MP can conceivably push through a young, new person from outside the party hierarchy for a position, doing so bucks convention.[106] Absenteeism is high in council meetings—and residents are excluded from the committee meetings at which most decisions are made (WDC 2008, 52–54; Goh 2005, 64–65). Malfeasance is endemic: a deputy minister in 2005 cited corrupt practices in all 146 local authorities, from abusing positions for personal benefit, to nepotism, to negligent enforcement. Yet councilors enjoy substantial immunity (WDC 2008, 55–58).

These weaknesses notwithstanding, states and parties lack incentive to reinstate local elections. Though Pakatan had previously promised to do so and some coalition leaders remain committed, that pledge fell away amid coalition compromises. States' paltry resources[107] render local authorities' budgets alluring, and, as, Kedah's Pakatan *menteri besar* (chief minister) admitted, "It's easier to get things done as councillors are our own people" (quoted in Rodan 2018, 197). Those pushing for change have been largely NGO activists lacking strong social bases, not the mass of voters—NGOs' concentration in certain opposition-held states helps explain the pattern of pressure for elections (Rodan 2014, 836–37). A resource-starved opposition state has especial incentive to support the status quo: the roughly two hundred local councilors in PAS-led Kelantan, for instance, each receive a monthly allowance, helping PAS "take care of [its] people."[108]

JKKK (Jawatankuasa Kemajuan dan Keselamatan Kampung, Village Development and Security Committees, introduced in chapter 3), likewise unelected, have also taken on increasing importance. Their salience to what Benjamin Read calls "administrative grassroots engagement" (2012, 3–4) is particularly clear in Sabah, where the BN's Berjaya introduced JKKK to address rural poverty under the NEP. While Berjaya framed JKKK as community-based organizations, led usually by a village headman or traditional leader, they functioned as fairly empowered village-level governments. Berjaya accepted official requests (for scholarships, licenses, replanting grants, and so on) only if transmitted via JKKK and used JKKK both for political surveillance and to determine who in the village should receive aid, on partisan grounds (Lim 2008, 93–97).

The system has since expanded. Both BN and Pakatan state governments came to support JKKK in constituencies their opponents held, as conduits for influence. Nor are JKKK confined now to villages: Pakatan changed the final *K* to *Komuniti* and the BN added counterpart *Jawatankuasa Perwakilan Penduduk* (Residents' Representative Committees, JPP) for urban areas in 2015 (overlapping local councils). After the 2008 elections, the BN also added a network of JKKKP (*Persekutuan*, Federal) to help BN MPs monitor and address issues in opposition-held *parliamentary* constituencies; lack of suitable candidates stymied plans to expand JKKK participation in rural development planning and implementation.[109] Here, too, minimal compensation deters skilled personnel. The BN particularly could draw on retired civil servants, and either side might lure representatives who welcome access to their ADUN—for instance, from public housing management committees. While most appointees are party members, and some are attached to a particular "warlord" or have (usually unrealistic) expectations of service as a stepping-stone to elected office, many serve from commitment to volunteerism.[110] Effective JKKK are legislators' hands, eyes, and ears—enough so that Penang increased their number by almost half in 2008, granting each MYR10,000 in CDFs.[111] Nonetheless, both sides tend to see JKKK largely as tools to attack adversaries and look after "their" voters (Hunter 2013).

Rather than discard the BN model, almost immediately upon coming to power, Pakatan abolished only the JKKKP, due to political influence, and renamed JKKK as Majlis Pengurusan Komuniti Kampung (Village Community Management Councils, MPKK). After the Rural Development Minister initially implied that grants would be distributed only to MPKK in Pakatan states, the deputy prime minister quickly clarified that opposition-state villages would also receive allocations for "beautification and well-being programmes"—but delivered through state development offices there rather than via opposition leaders (though at least not via local Pakatan officials).[112]

That the civil service, which implements local-authority directives, is under federal control helped sustained BN clout in opposition-controlled states (a distinction less apparent in BN-held states). When Pakatan took over Selangor in 2008, for instance, an immediate concern was that bureaucrats steeped in BN "political culture" would obstruct the new administration (Leong 2012, 32), particularly since their career prospects followed federal, not state, criteria.[113] Over time, BN interests had become the "behavioral norm" for the civil service, institutionalized in development planning and implementation (Washida 2019, 77). Opposition legislators in Penang even spearheaded development of a smartphone app to shame municipal civil servants into action.[114] Should civil servants disappoint, the state generally cannot fire them, but can only reshuffle them or put them in "cold storage."[115] Not only has local bureaucrats' performance been persistently subpar (WDC 2008, 47–54, 68–85)—one frustrated MP displayed photo after photo of illegal dumping in her constituency that she could not get addressed[116]— but political expedience, such as announcing necessary improvements only when a cabinet minister visits, has trumped systematic decision making (Goh 2007, 89–90). The result is a "blurring of the separation of roles between the state and local government" such that "state government leaders are beginning to treat local authorities as state departments," in which they feel justified intervening (Goh 2005, 66–67).

Tiers of government intertwine for partisan advantage. Lacking federal CDFs, for instance, some Pakatan MPs from opposition-held states liaised with local councilors to distribute at MPs' offices benefits that councilors fund.[117] More broadly, limited powers leave ADUN relatively little to do. Constituency service helps to "justify their existence" and "under-performing" local authorities "keep the States relevant" (Wong 2015, 28–29). Rather than simply establish systems for routine maintenance, legislators seek to appear involved in "direct service to the people," lest they appear "non-caring or worse, lazy" (Goh 2007, 11–12). As a former local councilor puts it, MPs have "no chance to shine in front of the people" if they merely fight in parliament, however much they replicate or obstruct the efforts of local councils and civil servants by intervening locally.[118] Logically, it would seem that poorly managed local councils would damage the reputation of the party in charge—and ADUN from the party in opposition at the state level may wrestle with uncooperative councilors.[119] But solving endemic local problems gains legislators from across parties "political mileage": they can serve as "longkang [drain] politicians" or highlight councils' shortcomings, capitalizing on blurred accountability to exculpate themselves (Goh 2007, 41, 273, 326). Importantly, while this intervention verges on micro- or meso-particularistic party-mediated patronage (Hutchcroft 2014, 178), its focus really is on what governments *do*: less opportunistic handouts than maintaining infrastructure, connecting residents with public goods and offices, and so forth.

From an autonomous third tier, local government has become parties' way of connecting directly with the ground, channeling public goods and services through party-loyalist councilors and JKKK and fostering dependency rather than legislating remedies. Politicians and partisan machines coordinate to fill the service provision gap. UMNO has always provided constituents with a range of goods and services—for instance, agricultural supplements for its historically rural base. In the 1970s, UMNO MPs submitted monthly reports of their programs and progress to party headquarters (however rarely scrutinized) and signed undated letters of resignation when they accepted nomination; Tengku Razaleigh warned in 1974 that MPs and ADUN could be expelled for not fulfilling service obligations (Ong 1976, 410–11). That same year, the BN secretariat established state and division levels and moved MPs' constituency offices, theretofore typically in the MP's home or office, to divisional headquarters. Those offices became both service centers and gathering places (Ong 1976, 410). In 1964, before the party's official founding, the DAP, too, established constituency offices (Ong 1976, 421). Contemporaneous research found Chinese MPs even more service oriented than Malay colleagues, especially in interceding with civil servants on constituents' behalf; Malay MPs emphasized explaining policies and resolving local conflicts (Musolf and Springer 1977, 126–30). With urbanization and intensified developmentalism, this model of "social-worker politicians"[120] took deeper root across parties, including in cities.

The *expansion* of service functions is most apparent in the MCA, Gerakan, and beyond the BN. By the early 1990s, the BN's Chinese-based partners had become "extensions and instruments of the state at the local level, not merely to assist in the maintenance of the status quo, but to deliver public goods and services" (Loh 2003b, 262–63). Anxious to build support despite the BN's pro-Malay national drift, the MCA and Gerakan increasingly emphasized not just targeted infrastructure development, but also brokering access to state and federal agencies and services (Nonini 2015, 224–25). Lower-income Chinese constituents in particular came to party service centers, rather than government agencies, for matters ranging from applying for official documents, to school enrollments, to road repairs (Loh 2003b, 262–63). That praxis bolstered the BN, as, the NEP notwithstanding, it allowed "ordinary Chinese, quite apart from Chinese business interests, to receive benefits and to identify positively—for many ordinary Chinese for the first time—with the BN government" (Loh 2003b, 263). Despite retaining few elected seats, the MCA has been able to sustain some legitimacy through service centers, as well as by serving as BN local councilors; the community has come to view the party more as a service provider than as representing their political interests (Chin 2006, 72–73).

The pattern extends to Gerakan. For instance, Gerakan's Chia Kwang Chye established a service center after being elected MP in 1995 to help constituents access state benefits and facilitate minor public works. Funds came from CDFs, plus election-time supplements; that the ADUN within Chia's district included the chief minister and the head of Penang's municipal council ensured ample additional resources.[121] All three relied on their service record in 1999 and promised more such benefits if reelected. Providing services "became the principal activity, even the *raison d'etre* for the local branch" (Loh 2003a, 171–73). The DAP's Lim Kit Siang, running against Chia, focused on social justice, democracy, corruption, and resisting developmentalism; neither he nor the DAP had a local record of service provision (Loh 2003a, 174–75). Lim lost.

Opposition parties adapted. Until recently, only PAS had a strong grassroots organization, drawing on its long history (including in state government) and ties to rural communities, religious schools, Islamic NGOs, and university-based organizations, initially geographically localized, but spreading nationally especially as of the late 1990s. The DAP, reliant on unaffiliated and less reliable mass support—particularly as Chinese associations became uncertain vote banks—tended more toward a cadre structure. But by 1999, the DAP could no longer count on "free votes" from Chinese irritated with the NEP and had failed to explain convincingly "why it is the government's job, not that of any political party, to provide goods and services" (Loh 2003b, 276–77). The party had to bolster its physical presence. In the 2000s, and especially after 2008, the DAP gained sufficient credibility, funding, and volunteers to expand their service center network.[122] The then-new Keadilan took similar steps, though it initially borrowed PAS infrastructure (Khoo 2016, 88–89).

Today, knowing voters' expectations, nearly all MPs and ADUN, plus *penyelaras*, maintain party-branded service centers.[123] Aspiring candidates may even establish them independently to prepare for a future run; most start working intensively months in advance, if they know where they will stand.[124] These offices reassure constituents of the candidate's and party's goodwill and machinery. Explained one MIC MP, the community does not vote for municipal councilors, but since they elect their MP and ADUN, they feel the latter should serve them.[125] Savvy voters may play both sides, seeking assistance both from their ADUN and the other party's *penyelaras*; some then-opposition Pakatan MPs encouraged such behavior to allow voters both material benefits and a protest vote in Parliament.[126]

The scope of parties' and politicians' investment in these efforts suggests their centrality. BN legislators' CDFs have covered service center costs,[127] estimated at

MYR10–20,000 monthly, as well as initiatives for the constituency and welfare outreach. Party branches have supplemented with (modest) budgets. Still, even UMNO MPs have fundraised. The party disallows dinners as too time-consuming, but an MP might, for instance, approach a friend or business (or a businessperson might approach an MP) to sponsor a specific initiative or donate "not great sums." Pakatan-held states gave their own ADUN a small subsidy for expenses, but most opposition legislators fund service center costs at least partly out-of-pocket or from donations; investing also in policy research or supralocal outreach may be impossible (on these costs: Koh 2011). Ad hoc or ongoing cash and in-kind donations from individuals, businesses, and organizations supplement fundraisers such as dinners; Pakatan also tithes its elected officials. Some, but not all, representatives avoid seeing donor lists, cap amounts contributed, or eschew benefactors from their own constituency to avoid feeling obligated.

Service centers offer hands-on intervention. They usually have a designated day—often Friday or the weekend—when the MP and/or ADUN is present (sometimes also with coalition-partner representatives and local councilors), though staff are there daily.[128] Constituents queue to see their representative: community organization leaders, to issue invitations or request allocations; village heads, for letters supporting applications for project funds; individuals, for letters of support for schools or jobs, financial assistance for medical or household bills, help with divorce and custody cases, guidance in applying for state and federal assistance, or random needs like removing bees' nests. Legislators rarely distribute jobs, though they may, for instance, refer a constituent to a friend's company. In adjudicating among requests, legislators consider how many they will reach and pressing need, but also their own priority areas, such as education, music, or sports. One MP sighed that each constituent's request is "the world's biggest problem" and something he "must fix right now." Another deemed the need for "nudges" to get the structure of government to work a "paternalistic, Asian feudal thing," complaining that however much a politician may try to institute systems for smoother functioning, civil servants decide what gets done, when.

In reality, politicians' letters of support seldom carry much weight. (When success does follow, though, the constituent is likely to credit the letter.) Explains a former ADUN, "the strategy is to be seen to have tried." Some MPs reinforce letters with occasional phone calls, or customize a particularly important appeal to a ministry, perhaps even delivering it by hand. A letter might push the bureaucracy to act; speeding the process helps in "demonstrating political value."

Legislators and service center staff also frequently direct constituents to, or intercede with, government offices. Simply navigating the system can be difficult: those in villages must direct concerns over issues like poor roads or flooding to the *pejabat tanah daerah* (district land office), while complaints from more de-

veloped areas go to the local council; some streetlights are under the local council, and others, federal; and so forth. An ADUN can help citizens lodge complaints
and can assign local councilors to look into them. Until now, BN representatives
have tended to get a better response with federal agencies, making it harder for
opposition parties to penetrate areas where poverty or need for specific programs,
like off-season agricultural credit, makes such assistance essential. Some opposition legislators bargain with district officers to get jobs done, promising not to
take credit (though voters still would know they had intervened), or assiduously
cultivate good relationships with departments with which they have to work. Yet
regardless of party, municipal service dominates: one Keadilan leader estimates
80 percent of his requests relate to garbage or clogged drains. Voter expectations
displace governance from state to partisan machine. An UMNO ADUN suggests
voters expect her to be "Mrs. Fix-it"; a Pakatan one says voters see him as an "op-
erator" more than a legislator.

Constituency service is multifaceted, overlapping more systematic policy initiatives. Candidates on both sides, for instance, paint high-density low-cost flats
as elections approach, or an ADUN might present residents with dustbins, or mobilize party workers to repair a community facility. Others have championed free
buses or environmental campaigns, or run mobile service counters or online com-
plaint systems. Behind this focus on service centers and piecemeal, ground-level
efforts is an understanding that such "bite-sized initiatives" tend to win more
votes than less tangible national policies—plus the fact that social welfare services
remain limited and local authorities are insufficiently proactive (cf. Scott 1969,
1143–44).

The machines enabling such intervention extend beyond parties to include
politicians' own networks. Affiliated individuals or organizations may support the
politician more for personal than partisan reasons; others rally behind the party.
Some support is episodic: for instance, "1Malaysia supporter clubs," which supplied meals, concerts, and other perks to energize BN mobilization in 2013 (their
extravagant costs drew even BN criticism). Overall, partisan networks are wide
and varied.

The upshot of these practices is that tiers of governance have merged for all
parties, with the local disproportionately defining. Appointed local councils answer to the party, not voters, anchoring parties' quasi-governmental functions.
Even voters who care about policy still expect their MP and ADUN to double as
de facto, all-hours local government, backed by a partisan machine, and may vote
accordingly. Meanwhile, state governments augment (as through access to city-
level programs) their limited resources and authority, entangling the party increasingly tightly in the lives of residents, through this tier—benefiting from an
undemocratic, but convenient, system.

Linkages with Voters

It is not just structural features rendering legislators relevant that matter; so do voters' relationships to politicians. Deep, everyday penetration acculturates citizens toward perceiving and assessing legislators not as policymakers or even party functionaries, but as dependable patrons, and keeps a personal vote salient notwithstanding strong parties. Politician-voter linkages remain heavily clientelistic, de-emphasizing platforms and policies but accentuating accessibility, responsiveness, and simple presence. This pattern is pervasive. By the mid-1970s, opposition MPs had learned to counteract the BN's resource advantage by providing "services to the little man," broadcasting effectiveness "by the number of people who approach him, the services he provides, and the appreciation shown to him" (Ong 1976, 419). Specifically, *affective*, not merely material or functional, patron-client ties remain part of the "modern" party-political system, absorbing traditional leaders and operating symbiotically with the machine-oriented governance described previously.

Clientelistic linkages operate within parties, too, particularly UMNO, helping explain how leader-led the party is and when personalization fosters stability. Intraparty contests determine access to resources and nomination for election. Consequently, it is ingrained among UMNO aspirants to consider fellow members as potential rivals.[129] Those chosen to stand owe loyalty to the party president—but they need to convince the local branch to accept them and not sabotage their candidacy had the branch preferred someone else.[130] Branch-level gatekeepers may block worrisomely competent applicants from joining the party; their desire to keep perks for themselves—including the around MYR800/month for leading JKKK—has led some branch leaders to deny applications to join the party (submitted at the branch level) if applicants seem potential threats, diluting the party's talent pool.[131] Across all parties, activists note having been recruited by a particular party leader—a personal approach that builds capacity but can also solidify "camps." Factionalism in UMNO and other BN parties—for instance, the MCA, periodically riven by succession crises and splits (Heng 1996, 45)—empowers regional "warlords" and makes maintaining the loyalty of midlevel power brokers key. Even amidst the massive 1MDB corruption scandal, an internal October 2015 poll found that 154 of 191 division heads backed Najib; 147 divisions signed a declaration of support in March 2016. Branch chiefs, closer to the ground, seemed less committed—several demanded Najib's resignation (Funston 2016, 118). However, with divisions in line, the prime minister could (he thought) relax.

What most clearly signals persistent clientelistic linkages—and marks these as inefficient, but not nefarious—is the extent to which the personal touch matters across Malaysia, beyond what a given politician delivers.[132] A politician's presence makes "the government" seem approachable and concerned. Such appearances often involve money, but less welfare payments on behalf of or in lieu of the state (though those also feature) than gestures to demonstrate generosity, reliability, and cultural probity. Regardless of distance and other duties, MPs return to their constituency as frequently as possible; when they cannot come in person, they send a trusted political secretary or assistant. Being truly local—not just from the state or a nearby town—is a clear advantage; an "outsider" may struggle to establish credibility. Typically, MPs stress that they are available at any time, at least by phone, and make door-to-door visits throughout their term, not just at elections. (Particularly at campaign time, however, state-appointed village and longhouse heads—generally leaders of party branches—are critical gatekeepers. Though not dictatorial, they may obstruct other parties' door-knocking access.[133]) Even for PAS, explained a women's-wing leader, "What's important is personality."[134]

Malaysian politicians devote enormous time to attending events and making themselves personally useful. Opposition legislators previously complained that the BN's greater resources forced them to make even more of an effort to drum up goodwill through visibility, since they would invariably be outspent. As one put it, while few constituents understand MPs' legislative work, "we are superman on the ground"; another grumbled that these activities wear one down and leave little time for policy work. That said, backbenchers in Malaysia, lacking policy influence, may devote little time to legislating. Parliamentary sittings last only two to three months per year, for four days a week (fifty-seven days in 2017[135]). Many MPs see outreach as where they can have greater impact. Those in national leadership face different imperatives: if the average MP spends 70–90 percent of the time on constituency work, this stratum might spend 30 percent, with the rest on party and policy matters.[136]

Polls suggest the extent to which these efforts define politician-voter linkages as clientelistic: the extent to which constituency service is not just something politicians do as a matter of course, but what determines Malaysians' assessments of legislators and tempers their vote choice. A June 2016 national survey found that the activity respondents most commonly ranked their first priority for ADUN was serving the people (19 percent), followed by going "down to the ground" (15.5 percent). No one ranked "lawmaking" first; only 0.7 percent ranked it second. MPs fared similarly: 0.4 percent ranked lawmaking first; the greatest share, 22.7 percent, prioritized "taking care of local constituents who need assistance," followed by going "down to the ground" (16 percent).[137] MPs' own survey responses, too, indicate usually greater concern with how they appear to their immediate constituency than to the broader public or as national leaders. Many care more about their service provision than their legislative role, even when they fault local authorities for requiring them to take on tasks that pull them away from policymaking (Loh and Koh 2011, 61; Koh 2011, 81–83). Moreover, the majority of Malaysians see political leaders as "like the head of the family" (Welsh, Ibrahim, and Aeria 2007, 17).

Apropos that "head of family" expectation, the most ubiquitous constituency events are weddings—one ADUN had attended fifteen in a day. Many legislators referenced an ethnic pattern, transcending urban-rural lines: Malays invite everyone for weddings and gain face if an *orang besar* (VIP) makes an appearance, generating "lifelong loyalty." Even better if that visitor eats, lest they appear superior. Weddings entail a cash gift (in most cases, out-of-pocket): MYR20–100 for an ordinary MP; MYR100–200 for a cabinet member or if the spouse also attends. Much the same pressure to appear, and with a token gift, applies for funerals (and the payment may be higher, perhaps a coffin) and visiting sick constituents. Some decisions are strategic: a PAS MP, for instance, prioritizes nonmembers' and fence-sitters' family events, knowing the party will take care of its members. Religious observances also call for appearances. Even non-Muslim legislators sponsor or attend *sahur* (pre-fast) and *buka puasa* (break-fast) meals throughout Ramadan—and during Aidilfitri, a legislator may attend over two dozen open houses in a day. The gamut of legislators likewise attend Chinese New Year, Deepavali, and other celebrations; they may spend a full day distributing oranges, sugarcane, or other holiday-specific treats. In Penang, an MP might attend (proffering requisite donations) fifty dinners over the thirty-day Hungry Ghost festival. A Council of Churches Malaysia Christmas function drew politicians from the deputy prime minister to opposition leaders, all posing for photos with a new archbishop (and one of whom, not Christian, laughed that he had been to eight masses in two days).[138] And, of course, Muslim MPs attend Friday prayers with constituents.

The personal touch—visiting regularly, recalling constituents' names, asking about their families, sharing meals with them, being humble and approachable—matters apart from the gift or benefit presented. Regardless, cash assistance is an important part of outreach, sometimes overlapping service centers' efforts but focused more than the latter on handouts, as opposed to connecting voters with more regularized public goods and services.[139] The practice is long-standing. In 1970 in Sabah, for instance, two incumbent cabinet ministers found the otherwise-muted campaign distinguished mainly by "a marked increase in the number of persons visiting their offices for the purpose of seeking favours."[140] And as of the mid-1970s, urban BN MPs needed "private income," since parliamentary allowances were insufficient to cover not just office rent and staff salaries, but also donations "befitting their status in the community"; opposition MPs were spared, since the public knew their parties lacked funds (Ong 1976, 411). At issue are both formal distributions from CDFs or other allocations and informal personal hand-outs; many of these expenditures are *not* from public funds. In either case, accounting is largely up to the legislator, although the process of CDF disbursement ensures at least some check.

Legislators tend to give annual subsidies—sometimes a standard flat amount, often delivered in person—to all places of worship, festival committees, and other groups in their constituency. On the opposition side, especially those legislators without state CDFs can ill afford the funds, but they know their opponent *will* give and do not want to risk breaking what is now a decades-old pattern. Associations apply for subsidies: a school PTA might ask their MP for funds for a new photocopier, if petitioning the Ministry of Education will take too long, for example. A legislator can also offer welfare assistance—for instance, identify a shop that sells school uniforms, direct needy children there, and cover the cost. Many reach out systematically to clusters of constituents with medical devices, water tanks, or other items. Even impecunious Parti Sosialis Malaysia crowd-sourced funding for micro loans for constituents. At least one former MP confessed a (resisted) temptation to prioritize projects in areas that voted for him. But an ongoing barrage of requests makes systematic planning difficult. Referring to these haphazard efforts to plug spending gaps, then-Penang chief minister Lim Guan Eng sighed that there are "lots of potholes to be filled," and temples do need more money.[141]

Individuals also come and simply request funds: for bus fare, lunch, home repairs, medical bills, or whatever else. Some requests are opportunistic, but many are genuine, and securing government welfare payments can be slow, even when the requests are within the scope of what might be covered. One opposition MP described feeling held "at ransom" by the imperative of not seeming stingy, however unproductive the payments; another said she feels like a "mobile ATM." Yet another noted that constituents find the small amounts he can afford "funny," but if they ask, he feels he must give. *Bantuan segera* (on-the-spot assistance) is usually paid out-of-pocket, though some legislators claim reimbursement from allocations, or are deterred only by tedious paperwork. One UMNO MP, noting that he spent "quite a sizeable amount" on these requests, said there is really no choice; that the only rule is not to promise and not deliver. Another lamented that his "office has become more like a welfare office," with the disabled, elderly, and poor coming for help, none of which assistance might actually win votes. One notes that he visits communities with contractors in tow to estimate costs for home repairs. An ADUN who shifted from BN to opposition finds voters sympathetic to the ideal of good government, by good people, but he still has to give when asked; his standard handout is MYR200. One senior opposition MP said all that differentiated the MCA from the DAP on this dimension is that DAP will still also speak up in parliament. Laughed a BN staffer, for an MP to appear in a Malaysian-made car might worry voters who rely on their MP's being rich.

Supplementing payments are personal services; here, opposition politicians compete on more equal footing.[142] Keadilan's Baru Bian, for instance, maintains strong support, despite his party's weakness in Sarawak, by championing native customary rights land cases in court. Another Keadilan MP, also a lawyer, provides free legal aid in his party office. Others organize roving health clinics or similar services. An Amanah MP serves as an *ustaz*: when he recites prayers or sermons, he does not discuss politics, but "they know" your affiliation. A DAP ADUN renegotiated constituents' rental agreements with shophouse landlords, albeit clinching the deal by subsidizing improvements.

Party activists enhance these personalized outreach efforts. Tens of thousands of party branches, individually registered, pepper Malaysia; it is through these that parties mobilize their base, but also keep legislators personally informed of issues, local births and deaths, and so on. UMNO dominates; other parties covet its density of branches, but only PAS comes close, and only in some states.[143] Branches help to consolidate a power base for the party—and sometimes for specific factions—even where the party is unlikely to win: they are where party machine and personalistic linkages intersect. In Sabah, for instance, UMNO has established 25 divisions and over 5,000 branches since arriving in the 1990s, while erstwhile BN-partner Parti Bersatu Sabah also has divisions in every state constituency. Grassroots activity facilitates ongoing recruitment, keeping tabs on community members' political loyalties, relaying information upwards, and channeling (or withholding) benefits. During campaigns, that same party machinery organizes thousands of *ceramah* (speeches or rallies) and meet-the-people sessions, canvasses door-to-door, and transports voters to polling stations. Where branches are too weak to engage beyond elections or feuds limit their reach, the BN has relied on federal and state machinery, instead, to sustain their grassroots presence, blurring the lines between party and state, and buys the support of influential community leaders to secure blocs of rural village and longhouse votes (Faisal 2015, 16–17).

The same logic applies on the opposition side, but branch-building success varies. With more supporters than active members, the DAP, for instance, has typically launched branches only when they contest or win in an area, though aspiring to more.[144] In contrast, Keadilan's efforts at both rapid expansion and intraparty democracy have spawned proliferating branches (albeit also factionalized, fraught party politics).[145] The party realized they needed branches to organize supporters for elections and to demonstrate a strong presence in areas during intra-coalition seat distribution.[146]

Party wings similarly personalize the party among voters. Women's wings in UMNO (Wanita) and PAS (Muslimat) work the ground especially actively; their efforts to build individual connections with voters mimic those of the legislators they support. Members can unthreateningly knock on doors and enter homes, plus effectively block competitors' canvassers from entering their territory.[147] That Muslimat could not "get past the kitchen door" or entice women to PAS political events in FELDA areas in 2013, for instance, hurt the opposition, especially given reports that UMNO's Wanita and Puteri went house-to-house, distributing rice with a warning to stockpile it against inevitable shortages once Chinese (e.g., Pakatan's DAP) took over (Khor 2015, 110). More commonly, Wanita UMNO trains members to identify political leanings among households assigned to them, engaging in months of "slow talk" to swing women in "grey" households toward BN. Muslimat takes a similar approach, but also relies on more "indirect" religious classes and meetings, such as weekly *yasin* (prayer) sessions in women's homes and *usrah* (discussion groups), and stresses not just wooing votes, but also educating on faith and rights.[148]

These wings help parties and candidates beyond election campaigns, too. For instance, Wanita has enticed women to UMNO to the point that some branches are 90 percent female.[149] Puteri has refined UMNO's social-media campaigning, and both Pemuda and Puteri not only serve as intra-party pressure groups, but recruit promising young leaders and members.[150] Key party leaders—for instance, Najib—may also have personal "shadow" youth and women's wings.[151] MIC and MCA now have cognate youth wings, with similar outreach and leadership-development foci.[152] PAS's Pemuda echoes Muslimat's outreach efforts,[153] and DAP and Keadilan have worked on developing similar wings to increase engagement, train activists and candidates, and enhance machinery on the ground.[154]

However useful a party's wings, the branch level is the pedestal on which the party rests. Instability or skew here, given Malaysia's personalized, clientelistic order—for instance, if a branch chair focuses more on consolidating their own "empire" than building a broader grassroots foundation[155]—may be damaging to the party, including to local councils and JKKK, the crux of the party machine, which recruit from this level. Across parties, competition introduces petty turf wars, infighting, and uncooperative branches.[156] That problem can be especially keen for a relative newcomer like Keadilan that has had little time to build a grassroots organization: personalities outshine the party. Strong personal votes may win seats, but undermine party cohesion.[157] Even in PAS, despite traditionally firm party loyalty,[158] members tend to follow and support a particular leader and their branch, including donating to that individual directly; relying on personal accounts sidesteps auditing requirements, but it raises risks if the party splinters and those holding funds leave.[159]

Indeed, most politicians sustain a personal base. An UMNO MP describes his campaign team as largely personal backers from residents' associations, religious groups, traders he has helped, and others, most neither party members nor interested in joining.[160] A Gerakan councilor-turned-MP credits his legal work among trade associations and guilds—he sat on 20–30 boards—with building his political base in Penang; members came to support his campaign and service center.[161] A Sarawak United People's Party state candidate acknowledged the elaborate team sketched on a board in his party office, then admitted that the team he trusts is of friends from outside the party; a "huge part" of his campaign finances also come from non-party sources.[162] In Selangor, the DAP's Hannah Yeoh ran with help and funding from her own network, mostly church-based; local churches continued to support welfare work.[163] PAS candidates, backed by formidable party machinery, may nonetheless establish their own supplemental team of NGOs and individual backers.[164] Of course, some party leaders ensure their personal pull benefits the party as a whole—for instance, much-beloved Kelantan PAS *menteri besar* Nik Aziz Nik Mat, who waited until the day *after* the 2013 elections to announce his retirement (Afif 2015, 240–42).

Where the balance between party and personalities is most tense is in nominations for office. The party leader determines the lineup. A skillful or potent party president might convince branch leaders to accept a candidate who is not their first choice, but the nominee's path may be rocky. Early on, party faithful assumed any UMNO candidate nominated by the center to be good—yet candidates still had to develop relationships, adapt to minutiae of local culture and customs, be present in the community, and be humble.[165] More commonly in UMNO, one climbs through the ranks, putting in hours and building support, until obviously the next in line. Because sitting leaders may be averse to threatening upstarts, to reduce the chance of "sabotage," candidates may be notified last-minute of their nomination—but may then race to demonstrate to voters their personal touch; party votes alone may not suffice.[166]

Among other parties, too, just as voters want their elected officials on the ground, party gatekeepers judge up-and-coming party activists by their assiduity and engagement with the party grassroots. An MCA leader explained that core to his party's efforts to rebuild its base is choosing candidates earlier and getting them working the ground, rather than centering campaigns around national leaders.[167] Another noted that divisions want their own people, even if they know they will "hit the wall," pressing the party to seek a new mechanism to select candidates who connect with voters.[168] In Keadilan, proposed candidates generally filter up from divisions to party leader Anwar Ibrahim, who has had the final say. Some of his decisions to "parachute in" or drop candidates have reflected or exacerbated factional cleavages.[169] Likewise for the DAP, being parachuted or substituted in at the last minute makes one seem there by party-leader fiat, and can antagonize the local party base.[170] Increasingly, too, the DAP has selected candidates new to the party and politics—including in pursuit of its 30 percent target for women—not only unknown to (and possibly resented by) the branch, but also in need of more support than the party can readily provide. One such candidate estimates that 95 percent of her campaign machinery ended up being not just non-members, but people "usually indifferent to politics."[171] Regardless, smaller parties, regardless of coalition, can contest only few seats, so need to situate "stars" in strategic or safe ones; parachuting may be unavoidable.

On the one hand, party matters immensely, not only for the platform each side presents, but also for party-branded benefits. On the other hand, Malaysia's system is highly candidate-centered: a candidate who is not known and visible faces steep odds, even if party leaders vouch convincingly for a promising neophyte. The head of the BN in Penang suggests the personal vote may be declining—that at least by 2013, voters chose by "logo," to the BN's detriment.[172] Others from BN, aware of its declining support, suggest the reverse: that party loyalties are weakening, so a proactive MP "goes direct," nurturing loyal supporters, including by providing "tangible, physical help."[173] A former MCA MP from a well-off, well-educated Selangor constituency is the rare legislator who thinks she lost because she spent too much time on constituency service rather than legislating.[174] Even if support is overwhelmingly party-based, not having made an effort to solve people's problems could cost an incumbent a tight race—and many races *are* tight. Hence, each politician still strives to be first on the ground when crises strike.[175]

Indeed, while a certain share of voters support a party for ideological, communal, or development reasons, the rest back whoever is more likely to deliver on voters' immediate needs.[176] That uneasy balance between personal and party vote helps to explain a striking anomaly: even on the BN side, candidates and novice legislators have usually received little guidance or support on how to do the job, beyond basic procedural rules. One newly elected MIC MP worked from his car for three months, until he located a suitable office and set up shop, nor did anyone guide him on how to pose questions in parliament.[177] And however much legislators castigate ineffective local councils, states and parties still provide little training. One tier's weakness is another's opportunity—but so is any legislator's failure an opening for a rival in the high-pressure, bottom-heavy party machine.

Candidates clearly represent their party and benefit from its machinery, yet they also curry a personal vote. What enables the dominant party to weather downturns and offers resource-starved opposition parties a lifeline is the nature of the clientelistic linkage in Malaysia. Patronage is part of it, but so is the sense of being a reliable, known champion, present and ready to help. That turn, too, renders clientelism not inherently bad, notwithstanding its reputation as a poor substitute for programmatic politics; vote-seeking politicians have incentive to be inclusive, and their intercession can both do concrete good and build faith in "the state." The strong parties of Malaysian electoral authoritarianism cloak a complex network of diligent politicians, building and drawing upon personal connections, and sustaining Malaysians' acculturation toward prioritizing direct intercession and local fixes over policy remedies. Those habits themselves constitute an especially resilient element of the electoral-authoritarian regime, deflecting expectations, interaction, and intervention from state to individual politicians, backed by personal supporters and party interlocutors.

Vectors for change

These patterns suggest the challenge of reform: mere change of leadership, as happened in 2018, neither necessarily revamps nor reflects transformation of deep-set norms and practices across parties and voters. Upholding the current system is a thick matrix of structural features, modes of governance, and individualized linkages. We might conceptualize possibilities for change accordingly, in terms of premises for legitimacy and parties' appeals, reasserting distinctions among tiers of government to deemphasize party machines, and retooling clientelistic linkages.

Even if their practice on the ground is similar, opposition coalitions since the 1990s *have* differentiated themselves ideologically from the BN, beyond encouraging voters to value programmatic policymaking. Whereas the BN's ideological premise is of "Malay-led multiracialism," centering development around a core of Malay supremacy, Pakatan (if not always PAS formerly or Bersatu now, as more specifically identity-based coalition partners) privileges Malays and Islam symbolically, but prioritizes class and equal citizenship over race. The BN has had to adjust its rhetoric and proposals in response (Abdullah 2017, 495–500). Yet the dust still swirls—Bersatu verges closer to UMNO than Keadilan in this aspect. Nor may ideological positions align tidily with current party configurations. Religious freedom, for instance, presents an increasingly galvanizing vector, yet one no party neatly captures, even if certain politicians take up the mantle.

Moreover, the political process *is* different under Pakatan, being at least moderately more consultative, participatory, and transparent, suggesting a drift toward rational-legal legitimacy. A Pakatan ADUN takes budget meetings as an indicator: the BN's go quickly and quietly; Pakatan's are "noisy and long," even if nothing gets changed.[178] Others describe increasing formal or informal consultation with interest groups, partnering with local NGOs on programs, introducing participatory budgeting, or empowering community task forces more than under the BN.[179]

Yet while NGOs and activists in Penang readied wish lists on gender, disability access, child care, governance, and other issues for their new state government upon Pakatan's win and promises of intensive collaboration in 2008, meetings soon tapered off.[180] The relationship between the state government and NGOs deteriorated, given different priorities and approaches, plus a less-than-enthusiastic chief minister.

Still, efforts persist, now also at the federal level. Experiences with participatory initiatives have been mixed—from NGOs that expect an MP to listen only to them; to voters who see attending meetings as a burden rightly borne by the person they elected; to activists frustrated by pro forma consultation that falls far short of collaboration. The issue is not only government inexperience with opening up policy processes, but also voters' unfamiliarity with or resistance to participatory governance. One ADUN distributed thousands of fliers for a dialogue on a hotly contested traffic redirection; two people came.[181] Nor has the BN been bereft of reformers. Then-UMNO MP Saifuddin Abdullah launched a "mini-parliament" in his constituency, bringing together heads of district departments, local BN and business leaders, and representatives from civil society. While the unfamiliar format (and too large group) entailed an awkward start, discussions became increasingly constructive.[182]

Meanwhile, Pakatan campaigns against patronage without eschewing it entirely, both within the coalition and vis-à-vis the public. Within Pakatan, lack of clear change in the practice of appointing senior party leaders to GLC and subsidiary boards has proved especially controversial, especially as GLCs have shifted to fall under new ministries in ways that seem tuned, for instance, to keep the prime minister problematically involved in financial decision making or to increase the odds of graft. While GLC management is part of carrying out the state's developmental agenda, argues Terence Gomez, ongoing praxis is open to abuse; Pakatan has made little effort "to dismantle the patronage-based political system institutionalised by Barisan Nasional."[183]

Nor has Pakatan fully forsworn more run-of-the-mill patronage politics. One Pakatan strategist explained, for example, that while open-tender for government contracts is the goal, it is too soon: should Pakatan move too quickly to preclude discretion, the small contractors prepared to snatch up projects would all be linked to UMNO. Pakatan needs to funnel projects to its "own" contractors for now to ensure they are able to compete and keep these contracts in Pakatan's camp.[184] More bald still is a paean to electoral authoritarianism by Bersatu vice-president—and Electoral Reform Committee chair!—Abdul Rashid Abdul Rahman, who proclaimed at his party's 2018 General Assembly that Pakatan "must win by hook or by crook." For Pakatan not to take advantage of opportunities to grant Bersatu members contracts and positions and to give Bersatu division chiefs "activities" would be "stupid," however little he liked the idea of using government resources in this way. For himself, he was "lucky that the prime minister gave me a job with a big salary so that I can support my division." Moreover, he urged Pakatan to restore the just-abrogated BN system of appointing parallel village chiefs in opposition-held states: Pakatan "cannot fight them by helping them" so should channel all development projects through its own party divisions. Although the party's Youth chief expressed dismay, a cheering crowd gave Abdul Rashid a standing ovation.[185]

However instrumental, participation in patronage politics reinforces the norm. Moreover, some of Pakatan's strongest supporters are those who have felt marginalized from BN largesse; their support may simply mean they accord Pakatan greater (promise of) performance legitimacy than BN. Other voters might have qualms with the system but still require development assistance, so hesitate to jeopardize what access they have (e.g., Faisal 2015, 19–21). And if support for alternatives surges as a vote *against* UMNO and the BN—as with the anti-Najib turn in 2018—how much and what positive ideological or policy commitment to a new mode those voters share is unclear.

A separate dimension of change is to renovate local authorities, obviating partisan machines. Most Malaysians have limited grasp of the jurisdiction of each tier of government; they bring the same issues to their MP, ADUN, and local councilors. Complicating matters, the person in office may be the same across tiers: a politician may serve simultaneously at some combination of federal, state, and local levels. The previously common practice of standing for both federal and state election has diminished, though, and some parties no longer allow ADUN to double as local councilors.[186]

Some Pakatan politicians, in particular, have encouraged voters to differentiate among their MP, who should handle national issues; their ADUN, who should address lower-level concerns; and their local councilor, who is responsible for municipal matters. One Keadilan MP distributes refrigerator magnets with public utilities' phone numbers, nudging his constituents to call *them* instead of him, yet he and his staff still make those calls on request; another notes that to deny such requests, however misdirected, would be "political suicide"; yet another emphasizes educating councilors themselves to reach out proactively.[187] Such efforts to encourage voters to value legislative activity above private benefits and to recognize the cost of failing to provide collective goods have borne fruit elsewhere, so might in Malaysia (e.g., Lindberg 2010, 129–30).

For now, MPs, ADUN, and partisan machines pick up local authorities' slack. Several initiatives have pushed procedural alternatives, including citizens' groups' advocating more participatory, accountable, and adept local governance in such cities as Petaling Jaya, Ipoh, Penang, and Kuantan (WDC 2008, 93–98). The electoral reform movement Bersih has sought restoration of local government elections, as did the People's Declaration before the 2008 general elections (Yeoh 2012, 11). Initiatives such as the Coalition for Good Governance, launched in 2008, likewise press state governments to improve operations, engage the public, and ensure at least a bloc of independent, competent councilors.[188]

A few parties have joined the local elections chorus, but inconsistently.[189] First to take up the call was Gerakan, in 1969. A year later, in control of Penang, Gerakan instead suspended its remaining elected local governments, all under other parties' control, citing administrative efficiency (Tennant 1973, 85). The DAP has been most persistent, its recent efforts dating back to a 2005 "Bring Back the Third Vote" campaign (Goh 2007, 352). Although the DAP and Keadilan called for restoration of local elections in 2008, PAS was less committed; the demand did not make it into Pakatan's 2013 or 2018 manifestos (Lee 2013, 5). For PAS, not just questions of party patronage, but anxieties over ethnic representation[190] limit commitment (Rodan 2018, 197–98).

Under Pakatan, the Selangor government commissioned a report from the Coalition for Good Governance on how local elections might be implemented; Penang convened a counterpart, the Local Government Elections Working Group. Both groups submitted reports in 2009, ultimately to little effect (Rodan 2018, 193). That year, Penang requested unsuccessfully that the National Council of Local Government take up the issue of local government elections. With the premise that reintroducing local elections was within the state's power, Chief Minister Lim asked the EC to oversee elections to Penang's two local councils; again: denied.[191] The state legislature passed the Local Government Elections Enactment in 2012, exempting the state from the relevant portion of the Local Government Act, then petitioned the EC again. Instead, the federal Court of Appeal rejected the state government's jurisdiction to enact the exemption.[192]

In the meantime, both states' stopgap remedies were ambivalent, and the issue hardly arose in PAS-dominated Kelantan and Kedah (Rodan 2018, 193–95). Both the Penang and Selangor governments introduced informal measures in 2008 to select quotas—never fully met—of independent councilors. Penang's method entailed mock elections under the independent Penang Forum for NGO representatives to forward to the state government to fill seven seats for each of two councils. Finding people willing to stand proved difficult—many activists lack interest or requisite patience, will not participate in a system they oppose, or are party members—and the scale of the election was too small to be fully representative.[193] The process in Selangor, for one-quarter of council seats, was more haphazard: a group of NGO activists met soon after the 2008 elections and submitted CVs to the state government; a tri-party Pakatan committee then produced a list. Commitment started to erode after the first year. The allotted seats not only declined in number,[194] but developed a party tinge: some of the NGO councilors were party members, and even NGO members adhered to party discipline, having been nominated by one of the three Pakatan parties. Pressures increased to replace independent councilors with party loyalists, particularly as Selangor started divvying geographic wards, each within a particular ADUN's jurisdiction, among councilors.[195] In both states, legislators tended to have closer ties with party than NGO councilors, rendering the former more in touch and effective, and those councilors participated at ADUN' service centers—blurring the lines between constituency service and party work.[196]

Inaugural Pakatan prime minister Mahathir is blunt: "No council elections."[197] Should elections be restored, however, although recent voting trends suggest urban voters would lean Pakatan, all parties have incentive to maintain the status quo. A strong-willed mayor and council could limit the capacity of a state even under the same party to intervene in or overrule local policies, or state and local policies could clash. Moreover, truly effective, accountable local governments would diminish a key way MPs, ADUN, and their parties make themselves needed.

Finally, we might think of change at the level of voters: shifting away from clientelistic linkages. A proportion of voters have always voted at least for federal *or* state representatives along ideological or programmatic grounds, including both Islamist voters, particularly in Kelantan, who support PAS notwithstanding federal government penalties, and Chinese voters, understood to split their vote to secure both state-level developmental benefits and a critical voice in parliament (e.g., Lai 1997). Since the 1980s, too, NGOs have highlighted discourses of democracy, participation, and good governance, consolidating these threads initially under the Reformasi movement (Weiss 2006). That focus remains one of several options as voters weigh discourses and practices of participatory democracy, ethnicism, Islamism, and developmentalism.

Constituency service has never been sufficient to ensure renomination or election; "a surprising number" of MPs found it not decisive, though important, even over four decades ago (Ong 1976, 420). But few politicians have been willing to risk abstaining. Demographic change might shift the odds. The emphasis parties and politicians place on service belies the fact that ever more voters do not live where they vote. Urban (or overseas) workers who *balik kampung* (return home) to vote may be more likely to prioritize party or ideology. One former MCA MP assumed 90 percent of those coming home to vote in 2013, especially from abroad, opposed the BN.[198] This pattern helps explain PAS's staying power in Kelantan: "outstation" voters care little about bridges and potholes, nor seeing their *kampung* change.[199] An estimated 150,000 urban voters returned to Kelantan to vote in 2013, most presumed unmoved by UMNO's campaign promises of a highway, stadium, and public housing (Afif 2015, 237, 239). Meanwhile, younger and/or urban voters, often comparatively well-educated and media savvy, might be more likely to vote in line with their ideology—including, for many, norms of governance and democracy—rather than according to more tangible targeted goods or services intended to coax their support.[200] One Gerakan leader sighed that, in 2013, knowing that someone had served the community well no longer mattered.[201] The issue may well rest at least in part on how increasingly mobile voters understand that community: as their home constituency or the wider polity, and hence which indicators or achievements they value most.

These trends suggest the possibility—perhaps even inevitability—of eventual regime change, beyond the current change in leadership. However, the game of patronage, machine politics, and clientelism that all contenders now play resists easy or quick upset. Overarching patronage-tinged policy frameworks, local-level partisan machines in lieu of elected local governments, and affective, effective clientelism cultivated through the personal touch, sustained and enhanced over the course of decades, combine to shape voters' expectations and politicians' behavior. The parties now in power may genuinely prefer a different system, but function in the one they are in. Their playing by established rules, however grudgingly or instrumentally, only reinforces the preferences and political culture BN-led electoral authoritarianism cultivated.

HEGEMONIC ELECTORAL AUTHORITARIANISM IN SINGAPORE

Firmly Entrenched

Like Malaysia, Singapore has transformed dramatically since the 1960s, yet its politics still rest on foundations Lee Kuan Yew laid. Under his increasingly consolidated leadership, Singapore regrouped quickly after 1965. Crackdowns had largely neutralized the far left; Barisan Sosialis never recovered from 1963's Operation Coldstore and subsequent harassment. Lee and his People's Action Party (PAP) could now claim the added legitimacy of being founding parents, charting Singapore's independent path. Interlinked imperatives of stability and growth offered increasing ballast, especially as Malaysia became more foil than sibling. And yet as Singapore's regime became far more hegemonic than Malaysia's, it came to rest—after a more technocratic approach proved infirming—on similar pillars of partisanized policies, party machines, and clientelistic linkages, fostering performance legitimacy and narrowing challengers' options to facilitate long-term, minimally coercive maintenance of illiberal rule.

Singapore throws into sharp relief the patterns seen in Malaysia, as opposition parties have had far less chance to make their mark. Not only has the PAP, like UMNO, changed over time, but it has changed Singapore's political culture, including how voters understand politics, assess politicians, and approach the regime. That shift has nudged challengers toward a common model. As in Malaysia, they have adapted to terms of a game almost impossible to win, stunting conceptualization of a genuinely different regime. Hence, as in Malaysia, we see a shift over time from a politics of ideology and policy to one of cultivated dependency and parochial, short-term, instrumental assessments, fostering calculations that favor the dominant party.

The PAP made "survival" the guiding motif for newly independent Singapore, urging citizens to subordinate personal or sectional interests to the common good. The decades following separation saw a subtle but systematic depoliticization and rise of an "administrative state" as the PAP consolidated. The bureaucracy exercised increasing authority, legislators lost importance, and political leaders pressed citizens to trust their judgment and capacity to bring continued economic progress (Chan 1975, 53–54). Lee Kuan Yew, prime minister from 1959 to 1990, then successors Goh Chok Tong (1990–2004) and Lee Hsien Loong (2004–present), claimed Singapore's economic and social accomplishments justified the PAP's continuation in office, even as they still craved the validation of absolute electoral wins.

It was only in the mid-1980s that more than a fringe of citizens, disenchanted with PAP policies, paternalism, and blindly "rational" style, came openly to question the need for such strict control. The PAP's earlier emphasis on cultivating personal rapport had waned as social safety nets reduced the need for individual assistance and the party favored technocrats over mobilizers. Opposition parties made headway, raising the possibility of more pluralist policymaking and nudging the PAP to refocus on the "personal touch": to couple its commitment to "meritocracy" with more clientelistic outreach. The PAP restructured local government, empowering party machinery and changing how opposition parties, too, had to function to compete. And throughout, the PAP government put a partisan spin on development policies and state spending. These steps not only fortified hurdles against opposition challenge, but reshaped citizens' expectations and both PAP and opposition politicians' behavior. As in Malaysia, the result has been increasingly deeply rooted electoral authoritarianism. Not only is a PAP electoral loss unlikely, but key aspects of the regime would surely persist, regardless.

Institutional Makeup

The years since separation have seen important innovations in Singapore's institutional and legal framework. Those changes reflect both the realities of governing an increasingly complex, now fully sovereign, polity and measures at least substantially tailored toward sustaining PAP dominance. Changes to structures of governance and administration, as well as to socioeconomic organization and mobilization, have reshaped not only opposition strategies and odds, but also how Singaporeans relate to their government.

Beyond adding ministerial portfolios—for example, foreign affairs—Singapore's institutional framework, centered around a unicameral legislature and unitary state, remained initially stable after separation in 1965 (Nam 1969–70,

468–71). Elections continued without interruption, but with enhanced curbs on information, expression, and association. A 1967 enactment, too, eliminated non-Chinese-majority seats; all would roughly reflect Singapore's population—effectively requiring catchall parties (Bellows 1970, 117–18).[1] Over time, though, the PAP expanded the array of outlets for nondisruptive participation and voice, operationalizing Lee Kuan Yew's preference to "nip it in the bud."[2]

Party and state became tightly entangled. The PAP's S. Rajaratnam cautioned in 1970, "When a party becomes a ruling party, you should not think of government and party as two separate entities" (quoted in Yap, Lim, and Leong 2009, 391). Singapore's "nanny state" is unusually pervasive, centered around a bureaucratic core that discourages political activism, a dominant PAP on which the middle class depends, and an underdeveloped civil society (Ho 2010, 70–71). Organizationally, the PAP forged a unified apparatus, amending its constitution to rebrand itself a "national movement" in 1982 (Loke 2014, 148). The party systematically coopted intermediary associations, especially trade unions—linchpin to a larger emphasis on isolating opposition parties from potential reservoirs of support.

In 1966, union density in Singapore was about 71 percent, three-fourths of that under the National Trades Union Congress (NTUC, Nam 1969–70, 476). Unionization remains comparatively high and growing, increasing from 23 to 27 percent from 2009 to 2013.[3] The NTUC has expanded to run a host of commercial enterprises—supermarkets, taxis, resorts—pervading even nonmembers' lives. Officially labor leaders draw the line sharply between the NTUC and the PAP. In practice, the connection is "umbilical."[4] Singapore's first postseparation government included six top NTUC leaders as PAP MPs (Nam 1969–70, 477); currently the NTUC secretary-general and four of five assistant secretaries-general are PAP MPs, with seventy-one of eighty-three PAP MPs advisers to unions.[5] Changes to the NTUC constitution in 1978 concentrated power more fully in the secretary-general—thereafter a technocrat hand-picked by the prime minister—including to prevent "undesirable" unionists' holding office in affiliate unions (Heyzer 1997, 391–94). A decade later, five NTUC members who stood as opposition candidates were ousted from their positions. Explained NTUC's secretary-general, Deputy Prime Minister Ong Teng Cheong, "We can't keep inflammable materials in the house and end up fighting fires all the time. If you have a maid in the house and this maid works to break up your family, would you employ her?"[6] Another MP suggested that while an NTUC employee could be a "secret admirer" of an opposition party, to be an "active member" aiming "to bring down your government" would be "disobedience" verging on treason.[7] No longer are unions likely to offer independent bases for a challenge.

With such measures crystallizing, the first several elections postseparation were bland affairs. The nadir was in 1968, returning the PAP unopposed in fifty-one of fifty-eight seats. No opposition candidate polled even 20 percent (Bellows 1970, 115–16). Campaign periods thereafter were as short as eight days, with little advance notice. High disproportionality from gerrymandering and majoritarian voting meant, too, opposition parties could regularly exceed one-quarter of votes, yet win no seats. Hence, the PAP's first electoral losses since Barisan days, starting with a 1981 by-election, then two seats in 1984 and four in 1991, were unpleasant surprises. Lee Kuan Lew fretted about a "freak election result" should voters merely registering a protest vote inadvertently oust the PAP. A 1984 task force parsed reasons for the PAP's decline, offering recommendations for new leadership and a new style (Yap, Lim, and Leong 2009, 364–65). The PAP decided to refrain from needless by-elections—whereas previously it had used them to nudge out one PAP leader and emplace another midterm (Ortmann 2014, 733–36, 739–41)—since the "people got used to the idea that once the government is in power, why not put a few opposition in."[8]

However loath to concede seats, the PAP recognized the value of debate. "Distressed" in 1968 by the virtual collapse of challenger parties, lest lack of a "loyal opposition" foster distortion, the PAP's Central Executive Committee (CEC) proposed fostering a stand-in from its own left wing. Backbenchers formed an "'opposition' group" to enhance debate—although the PAP remained disinclined to encourage criticism or "molly-coddle an opposition into existence" (Bellows 1970, 119–23). One MP from that period noted that the system, ended once other parties reentered parliament, offered a chance to speak up on issues affecting their constituents.[9] Otherwise, MPs are not expected to play substantial policy roles. The office of backbencher is part-time; most on the PAP side (less the opposition[10]) maintain professional careers while in parliament (Ho 2000, 93–99).

To give MPs more of a legislative role and enliven policymaking, Goh Chok Tong resuscitated that ersatz opposition approach in 1987, establishing a system of PAP-backbencher government parliamentary committees (GPCs). GPCs gather input and feedback from the public and experts to demonstrate scrutiny and accountability, although their role is largely advisory. After another electoral decline in 1991, Goh declared the PAP would act more like a conventional governing party: GPCs would become closed-door, internal party committees. Rather than risk embarrassing their own ministers, the PAP would leave it to the real opposition to take the lead in posing questions (Singh 1992, 132–33). Explained PAP MP Lau Teik Soon, GPCs do permit at least "tinkering on the edges" of policies and "raising questions," though a minister might "whack" a too-insistent backbencher.[11] Cross-aisle consultation remains near-verboten, but vertical is fairly common; MPs can also introduce new issues. One PAP MP explained that the party whip is to direct PAP MPs' vote, not their voice.[12]

While the PAP seeks policy input, structural changes have ensured its electoral advantage. Most consequentially, a 1988 constitutional amendment replaced a portion of single-member constituencies (SMCs) with three-member (later up to six-member) group representation constituencies (GRCs), each with at least one seat reserved for an ethnic minority. Some citizens vote now for a single candidate and others for a several-candidate ticket—a unique-to-Singapore "party block vote" (Li and Elklit 1999, 204). Each MP serves a designated ward, tantamount to an SMC. GRCs raise the bar for opposition parties. Having fewer total contests effectively shuts out smaller parties, and GRCs are difficult even for larger opposition parties, given the need to find sufficient credible candidates, including from minority groups. A single weak link can sink the ticket—and attacks typically focus on that person. The higher deposit required adds another obstacle (Tan 2013, 636; Au 2010, 104–6). Even PAP MPs complain of "bigger and bigger and weirder and weirder-looking" GRCs.[13] GRCs ensure all parties are multiracial, and all races represented, but minorities were not previously significantly underrepresented. Pre-1965, for instance, around 40 percent of PAP MLAs were from minority groups (Nam 1969–70, 474–75), and it was not clear that Singaporeans voted on racial lines (Tan 2013, 635). Critics complain that GRCs entrench ethnic voting and stigmatize ethnic minority MPs by bringing them to parliament by quota rather than "straight fights"—the PAP did not nominate another minority candidate to an SMC until 2011 (Maruah 2013, 15–16, 21; Li and Elklit 1999, 201, 212–13).[14]

GRCs expand the scope, too, for gerrymandering. The Electoral Boundaries Review Committee, under the office of the PM, who appoints members, announces usually late-breaking constituency boundaries. (Its 2015 report came out in late July, for elections in early September.) Even dramatic changes require no public explanation, and boundary maps are expensive—over SGD400 for one GRC in 2006 (Lam 2006, 94; Tan, Ong, and Teo 2004, 57–60). The initial delineation of GRCs in 1988 eliminated eight of the PAP's ten previously most-marginal districts; public outcry forced a lighter touch next time (Mutalib 2002, 666; Fetzer 2008, 142–46). Still, in 2015, in one of two SMCs eliminated, the Workers' Party (WP) had won 49 percent in the preceding election.[15] Redelineation has preserved token opposition strongholds such as Potong Pasir, however. Uncertain boundaries challenge parties. An SMC in which a party (including the PAP) has been canvassing may be absorbed into a GRC, or a housing estate may be moved to a new constituency. One PAP MP noted that population resettlement and boundary changes not only transformed his initially rural district, but hurt his margins, allowing him no chance to help voters before they cast votes.[16] On the plus side,

GRCs' ethnic and gender mix (since the norm now is to include women, Tan 2014b) benefits those residents who prefer to approach, say, a Malay-speaking or female MP.

Beyond remaking constituencies, the PAP also introduced nonconstituency members of parliament (NCMPs) in 1984 and nominated members of parliament (NMPs) in 1990 to obviate citizens' inclination to vote opposition MPs into office or join opposition parties to enter parliament. The government offers NCMP slots to "top losers" among opposition candidates (above a 15 percent floor). Some votes, thus, essentially count double: for a PAP candidate who wins and an opposition candidate who also serves (Li and Elklit 1999, 205). NCMPs are accountable to no constituency, and some opposition politicians are reluctant to accept an appointment through which the Elections Department, not voters, places them in parliament.[17] As of 2016, the constitution mandates at least twelve non–ruling party representatives—elected MPs plus NCMPs—all now with full voting rights.[18] NMPs, in contrast, are nonpartisan individuals (currently up to nine), intended to raise the quality of debate and increase participation. Although selected to represent identity-based or functional constituencies, not all have acted accordingly, and they lack ready structures for input or accountability. Yet the strategy redirects activist voices from more disruptive channels (Rodan 2009, 440–42, 446–48, 454–58; Ho 2000, 90–91).

A final innovation, confirming the PAP's distrust of the opposition, was the Elected Presidency. Amendments in 1991 granted Singapore's largely ceremonial president new authority, including veto power should a future government seek to tap into national financial reserves. A miniscule number of Singaporeans meet the tight eligibility criteria. In practice, the office is primarily "custodial and reactive," and apart from 2011, when the PAP-endorsed candidate won by a margin of less than 1 percent, contests usually generate little enthusiasm (Tan 2011, 123–24, Tan 2014a, 377–78, Mutalib 1994).[19]

Campaigns since the 1960s have become zealously regulated. In 2001, for instance, the WP was unable to contest a GRC because the party leader had their nomination form notarized before he finalized the roster and listed the candidates;[20] in 2011, submitting their nomination form less than a minute late disqualified a team of independents.[21] Each campaign poster (subject to rules on size, content, and placement) requires an official sticker from the Elections Department, issued on Nomination Day. (Opposition teams assiduously report PAP violations.)[22] Complementing televised cross-party forums, all parties with a minimum number of candidates receive time in proportion to the number of seats they are contesting to introduce themselves on mainstream television during election campaigns. The PAP, which stands in all, benefits the most (Au 2011, 72). In 2015, social media posts on both sides pushed the boundaries of a "cooling off" day mandated in 2011 to avoid "risk of disorder." And rallies are especially tightly structured. Police distribute officially designated sites by lot, one day in advance. While the process improved in 2015, previously parties sent proxies for election agents to queue overnight at police headquarters throughout the campaign. Stipulations require marshals, a ten-foot buffer between audience and stage, and a cordoned-off zone for officials (Lam 2006, 90–93). Still, rallies remain a comparatively low-cost, high-impact campaign mainstay for opposition parties. In 1991, for instance, the PAP held only five rallies; the WP and the Singapore Democratic Party (SDP) each held fourteen over a ten-day campaign (Singh 1992, 63–64).

Compulsory voting and restrictions' having obviated the get-out-the-vote costs of the 1950s, campaign expenses remain remarkably low, apart from deposits to stand, which are forfeit if a candidate or team receives under one-eighth of votes cast. The comparison with Malaya during merger is revealing: just over SGD1/vote in campaign expenditures for the PAP in Singapore in 1963 versus SGD3.40/vote for the Alliance in 1964 (Pang 1971, 31–32). Now, a strictly enforced cap of SGD4 per voter limits expenditures. Costs are increasing, but no party yet approaches the limit. (It helps that all rely overwhelmingly on volunteer labor.) Total costs tallied to SGD2.6 million in 2006, SGD5.5 million in 2011, and SGD7.1 million in 2015: SGD2.16/voter PAP, SGD0.73/voter opposition.[23] Candidates must submit publicly accessible election returns within one month, with receipts for any expense over SGD10 (see Ufen 2015, 579–81). Deposits, though, have skyrocketed, pegged since 1988 to 8 percent of an MP's allowance, multiplied by the seats in a GRC. The rate increased from SGD500 in 1955–72; to SGD1,500 in 1980–84, when the PAP started losing ground; to SGD4,000 in 1991, under the new formula; to SGD8,000 in 2001 and SGD16,000 in 2011, dropping to SGD14,500 in 2015. Whereas Malaysia's BN outspends opposition candidates, the PAP deters them from standing at all, diminishing the appearance of dissent.

Logistics aside, elections serve more as feedback channels and referenda on performance than opportunities for leadership change (see also Seeberg 2014, 1266–67). Singapore's polls themselves are clean: ballots are secret, the reforms in the 1950s to stanch vote buying and pressure tactics worked, and procedural irregularities are rare. Nevertheless, that ballots have numbered counterfoils sustains rumors that votes are not securely secret. (The opposition waffles between complaining about this feature and avoiding mentioning it, lest they scare off potential voters.) PAP warnings, too, remind voters that however unknowable their individual vote, polling data allow narrow pinpointing of precinct-level results. Taken together, these worries foster a form of what Stokes calls "perverse accountability": "when parties know, or can make good inferences about, what individual voters have done in the voting booth and reward or punish them conditional on these actions" (2005, 316). Stokes emphasizes vote buying, but her logic extends: the PAP benefits from the impression that it can hold voters accountable.

The PAP has likewise shackled civil society—a defining feature of its regime. After 1959, the party grew less open to outside policy input. Interest groups retained some channels for policy influence,[24] generally via behind-the-scenes lobbying, but the PAP did not even make all pending legislation public and proscribed activities such as mass rallies or media campaigns, let alone industrial actions (Chan 1976b, 36–43). The PAP promotes a "civic society," to support rather than challenge the state, emphasizing public order, civility, and citizens' responsibilities rather than rights (Chua 2000b, 63; Lee 2002, 99). It craves consistent feedback, but its effort at "encouraging and structuring grievances" aims to defuse challenges, not reshape or redistribute power (Bellows 1970, 101). In 1991, the PAP's George Yeo spoke of Singapore's need to "prune judiciously" the "banyan tree" of a government that stifled the growth below; however, the democracy underneath may be little more than a "bonsai tree," argues Michael Barr, "kept as a little display for show" (2014a, 35–36).

Curbs on civil society represent a key reason for Singapore's differing position from Malaysia's on the electoral-authoritarian spectrum. Early on, the countries' civil societies were not appreciably different: both had similar sorts of organizations, structuring laws, and breadth of activists and objectives, whatever their key issues. Neither state had an especially vibrant civil society in the early years after separation. However, the character of participation changed with the shift from a comparatively light colonial touch (apart from that on the more militant left) to the heavier-handed PAP. Citizens became "passive clients of the new PAP-governed state" in a polity self-styled as both immature and vulnerable (Tan 2007, 17, 19).

Singapore maintained an array of communal, religious, and other associations. Chan counted over nineteen hundred registered in the 1970s, many ethnic based, most focused on culture or religion, but few really autonomous of a state intent on reducing their salience as communal providers or protectors (1976a, 79–86). Thirty years on, Singapore had six thousand registered societies, but still only a "small and beleaguered cluster" of political or advocacy ones (Ooi and Shaw 2004, 77). Some voluntary welfare organizations partner with the state; the organizations achieve their service-provision objectives and the PAP diffuses potential discontent, while evading direct responsibility (Chua 2000b, 71). However, fewer advocacy-oriented NGOs operate in Singapore than Malaysia, beyond several noteworthy interlocutors on such issues as gender, migrant workers, and conservation.

Especially important, unlike in Malaysia, organizational links between political parties (especially opposition parties) and NGOs are rare. The Societies Act curtails civil or professional organizations' political activities, effectively proscribing alliances. With the line between law and norm blurred, NGOs generally eschew partisan politics (Tan 2011, 127–28; 2007, 32). Hence, for instance, NGO Maruah recoiled at the idea of a joint conference with the National Solidarity Party (NSP) on the death penalty, although their perspectives align.[25] (The same trepidation applies less to links with the PAP.[26]) Even organizations that register as "political associations" cannot participate collectively in elections or issue endorsements (Chia 2012, 34–36). The result is reduced opportunity for parties to widen their societal linkages.[27] NGO activists have served as NMPs, however; the scheme seems intended, in part, to circumvent opposition parties (Rodan 2009, 450).

Critically, the government has combined a general admonition to avoid "politics" outside political parties with a vague delineation of what falls "out of bounds" ("OB markers"). As Prime Minister Goh explained in 1995 in taking to task local writer Catherine Lim for publishing an op-ed critical of his administration, only "well-meaning people who put forth their views in a very well-meaning way will receive a very gentle and very well-meaning reply"; those who mock the government will meet with a "very, very hard blow from the Government in return."[28] The premise is that the political can be "quarantined and sanitized" (Tan 2000, 103–4). Yet where the OB markers are remains unclear, nor is enforcement consistent; to be safe, citizens self-censor.

More broadly, whereas Malaysia entered a period of civil societal efflorescence by the 1980s, the PAP channeled Singapore's increasingly restive population instead toward new institutions. The party really had no choice but to embrace a participatory turn, however superficial. Singaporeans had expanding access to alternative news and ideas, the growing complexity of problems governments address called for input to forestall gaffes, consultation allowed the PAP to spread blame for failures while still claiming credit for what goes right, and collaboration with voluntary organizations distributed the burden of shouldering an increasing array and intensity of welfare needs (Tan 2003, 14–15). The dominant domain for these efforts has been the PAP's own "grass roots": the approximately 1,800 organizations of the People's Association, discussed in chapter 4 and below. But also germane have been a series of initiatives specifically to elicit and channel voice. These efforts aim for "administrative incorporation": to enhance scrutiny and accountability, without politicizing decision making, stimulating collective action, or disciplining elites (Rodan 2018, 39–40). One variant includes large-scale, periodic initiatives such as "Singapore 21," launched in 1997 to fortify "heartware" via a series of discussions on contemporary dilemmas (Lee 2002,

105–8), and "Our Singapore Conversation," a set of over 660 semistructured forums started in 2012, involving 47,000 people, with the premise of understanding what the PAP could do better (Tan, K. P. 2015, 162). What impact the suggestions generated remained unclear; the initiative did not end with policy recommendations but seemed primarily aimed at channeling criticism away from parliamentary challenges or independent organizations (Rodan 2018, 108–11). Another variant involves permanent or recurrent channels, especially the Feedback Unit (now REACH). First mooted following the PAP's 1984 electoral decline—widely attributed to the party's needing to pay more heed to public opinion and selling its policies—the Feedback Unit aimed to give a fuller picture than bad news–averse grassroots leaders and compliant mass media do (Yap, Lim, and Leong 2009, 368–69).

REACH bears closer attention, as it embodies the PAP's blending of technocratic management with personal outreach, encouraging citizens to partner with rather than challenge the party. Such efforts are key to the PAP's cultivation of nonideological, nonconfrontational, atomized politics—a process that not only sustains PAP dominance but tempers the regime writ large. What was then the Feedback Unit started in 1985 with dialogue sessions of around 20 people, mostly PAP-leaning, chaired usually by an MP. Its initial pool included over 4,500 contributors, including those with strongly critical views (seemingly solicited more to gauge public reaction than for policy input); the number of sessions increased from fewer than 20 in 1986 to over 60 in 2003 (Tan, Ong, and Teo 2004, 12–17, 34–35). The agency also receives letters—in its first nine months, over fifteen hundred from the public and grassroots organizations—and introduced electronic feedback channels[29] in the mid-1990s that came to account for 90 percent of feedback (Tan, Ong, and Teo 2004, 32, 46–47, 51). It works also with "strategic partners": the NTUC, clan associations and chambers of commerce, educational institutions, and a suite of ethnicity-specific "self-help" organizations launched in the 1980s–90s (Tan, Ong, and Teo 2004, 32–37).

The effort has grown. "Tea sessions" introduced in 1992 developed into annual consultations with each of fourteen major groups (defined by ethnicity, gender, age, and so on), usually including an MP. Other feedback groups meet monthly to discuss some matter of interest, then convene for an annual conference. Consultations now tend both to precede and follow policymaking, extending to large public forums on key issues (Tan, Ong, and Teo 2004, 37–38, 40–48, 61–63). The PAP convenes committees, too, in crises—for instance, hastily organized sessions after 9/11 among the Malay-Muslim community—and some ministries or statutory boards maintain their own feedback groups, such as demographic-specific Media Development Authority programming committees.[30] However, even the feedback agency's own assessments have deemed transparency a weak point: while most respondents find the channels provided accessible and adequate, fewer are convinced the government listens, and the vast majority wish the government would acknowledge what feedback it uses or rejects (Tan, Ong, and Teo 2004, 83, 96–97).

These efforts are more about preempting problems than opening up; the Singapore government still eschews political liberalism. Yet its coercion is, in Cherian George's terms, "calibrated for maximum effectiveness at minimum cost," giving the appearance of agreement and abating moral outrage (2007, 133, 140). The PAP relies on "instrumental acquiescence" to a regime likely to continue delivering benefits, carefully fostered normative consensus and sense of shared national purpose, and legitimation from multiparty elections. But it also deploys skillful, selective duress for deterrent and punitive purposes.

Exemplifying this pattern is the PAP's achievement of press control absent nationalization or brute suppression (George 2007, 133–35). Control of mass media gave the PAP an early (and enduring) advantage. From 1963 to 1965 alone, Lee Kuan Yew banned or delicensed eleven student and union publications; new regulations in 1966 then prevented publication of "protected information" (Nam 1969–70, 475–76).[31] The state has forced critical publications to close (for example, the *Singapore Herald* in 1971) and detained journalists and editorial staff, requires annual licenses for printing presses, and enforces strict censorship laws (Amnesty 1980, 41). The government advances its own position through its monopoly on mainstream media and actively recruits senior journalists as PAP candidates (Mutalib 2003, 299–306). By 1995, a majority of Singaporeans found the media insufficiently critical of the government; only 17.1 percent deemed its coverage of opposition parties fair or objective (Mutalib 2003, 303). Opposition parties issue publications, but several have incurred defamation suits, hassles with publishers, or similar problems (Gomez 2001). Now, increasingly lively online media oblige newspapers to be more fair, to seem credible (Au 2010, 107). Regulators have adapted, sensitive to the economic implications of exercising more than a "light touch" online. They still limit political speech, but in less visible ways (George 2007, 137–39).

Yet other laws hold Singaporeans back, particularly the Internal Security Act, the Official Secrets Act, and the Societies Act, which amplify lower-key deterrents. One result has been "patently negligible" public participation on policy issues among educated youths, according to surveys from the 1970s through the 1990s (Mutalib 2003, 357–58). By now, as the SDP's Chee Soon Juan notes, "The idea that public assemblies equal chaos has been deeply etched into the minds of Singaporeans" (2012, 95).

Opposition parties and activists face additional constraints. The Public Entertainments and Meetings Act requires that opposition MPs procure licenses to give certain speeches, even in their own wards. PAP MPs are not affected, as the law exempts activities by or for the government (Gomez 2006, 109–17). The SDP's Chee, for example, was imprisoned for speaking without a license in 1998, though the debate he sparked was an impetus for the launch of the Speakers' Corner (Chee 2012, 108–10).[32] The Defamation Act poses another (oft-deployed) deterrent. The WP's Tang Liang Hong, for example, fled into exile in 1997 to escape defamation charges (Ganesan 1998, 231–32).[33] Bankruptcy, which suits under these laws may cause, renders a politician ineligible for office until discharged. For instance, a dubious 1986 conviction barred the WP's Joshua Jeyaretnam from running for election for five years, effectively removing him from parliament for a decade. Within a month of his return to Parliament in 1997, the government again sued him for libel. He lost the case, then was declared bankrupt for being one day late with an installment toward his SGD100,000 fine, barring him from contesting until 2008.[34] In Parliament, too, usually only one member of the eight-MP Committee of Privileges, which conducts hearings on alleged misconduct, is from the opposition.[35]

Major crackdowns are rare but have been harsh. An Amnesty International mission to Singapore in 1978 to investigate political prisoners still detained from 1963's Operation Coldstore[36] confirmed the "sustained psychological pressure" to which detainees were subjected, including to extract self-incriminating "confessions" (Amnesty 1980, 2). Although releases outnumbered arrests in the late 1960s, new waves of political detention came in 1970 and 1974–76 (Amnesty 1980, 15–17, 32–33). The last major onslaught was 1987's "Marxist conspiracy" (Operation Spectrum, coinciding with Malaysia's Operation Lalang), under which the government detained twenty-two Catholic-linked activists without trial under the Internal Security Act (Tan 2007, 31–32). A number of them had been working with the WP (though not members), having helped Jeyaretnam with his 1984 campaign, then stayed on to produce the party newsletter.[37] The 1987 arrests confirmed the PAP's new generation leaders to be "in the same mould" as the old guard (Chan 1989, 86–87).

Taken together, these strategies suggest an enduring, progressively refined PAP effort to make politics seem "a matter of management" coordinated under paternalistic, benevolent leaders (Chan 1979, 13), with sharp penalties for overstepping. The PAP encourages participation, not challenge. Over time, it has trained the public toward these modes and underlying assumptions. Hence, for instance, the WP's mantra that it does not "oppose for the sake of opposing" (WP 2007, 6), as the PAP accuses. The proscription, diminution, or discouragement of ideological or identity-based claims—by decimating the left, maintaining murky "OB markers" and studiously mixed constituencies, and segregating advocacy organizations from parties—has further obviated what are primary axes for countermobilization in Malaysia. The PAP has adroitly delegitimated opposition parties' presenting more than a mannered, technocratic approach, and one that asks voters to decide not who has the better ideas, but who is the more reliable provider.

Development of Political Parties

However effectively the PAP had eliminated the ideological threat from the left by the mid-1960s, the party still faced the challenge of maintaining a functioning party while constituting a governing power. Already by 1971, the PAP faced complaints of being out of touch and rumors of factional splits, especially as idealistic, younger members came up against party leaders' more "problem-solving" approach.[38] Those affected by costs of living that outpaced wages came to resent the PAP—especially its English-educated leadership—and its antivice and cleanliness campaigns, housing policies, and Western leanings.[39] Undergraduates, too, an articulate and influential group, were increasingly hostile to Lee and the PAP by the early 1970s, not least as Deputy Prime Minister Toh Chin Chye became the University of Singapore's vice-chancellor in 1968.[40] Ideologically, the PAP shifted gears, from anticolonialism, to merger and "Malaysian Malaysia," to "survival" after 1965, emphasizing socioeconomic progress; its ideological profile then grew hazier (Pang 1971, 72–77, Mauzy and Milne 2002, 38).

Meanwhile, the PAP fortified its structure. The cadre system instituted in 1958 remains: after rigorous vetting of about one hundred individuals MPs recommend each year, a CEC panel appoints new cadre members. Their total number is secret but was around one thousand in 1998 (Mauzy and Milne 2002, 41). The secretary-general heads the CEC, which overlaps substantially with the cabinet and remains the central decision-making body (Abdullah 2016, 531–32). Even ordinary membership requires having done grassroots work, to weed out opportunists. In 2000, ordinary members numbered around fifteen thousand (Mauzy and Milne 2002, 41).[41] The Young PAP, formed in 1986 for men or women aged 17–25, focused largely on policy issues; it replaced the youth wing active in the 1950s but defunct by the 1960s (Chan 1989, 84).[42] The Women's Wing followed in 1989, emphasizing gender and family issues—though declining to press for gender equality—replacing the Women's League Barisan siphoned off in 1961 (Mauzy and Milne 2002, 42; Lyons 2005, 241). The party also has the PAP Policy Forum, to which each branch nominates two representatives; it functions as a "ground-up think tank" informing policy discussions.[43] And the General Elections Committee prints campaign materials and ranks constituencies according to the level of competition expected, sending "heavyweights" where they will be most useful (Singh 1992, 63).

Party income comes from (low) party dues, most retained at the branch level, as well as levies on MPs and donations (from religious organizations, festival-related groups, and so forth), primarily in election years or for specific events. Publications yield some income, too, although the party curtailed selling advertisements to avoid pestering supporters.[44] Party branches surrender revenues to headquarters, which returns a per-voter allocation to cover campaign costs.[45] PAP kindergartens, initially a revenue source, remain a distinctive branch-level feature as a social service—most alternatives were private, church run, and more expensive—and for party outreach. Most Singaporean children attend them. Originally, the initiative to launch one came from the MP, who rented premises at a discount and constructed the facility with branch resources. Fees, while low, still made the branch money, even when shared with headquarters. Branches added child care centers in the late 1980s to compensate for diminished income with an aging population and, hence, fewer kindergarteners.[46] The party-linked charitable PAP Community Foundation took over management in 1986 and channels funds from kindergartens back to the community (Mauzy and Milne 2002, 44; Yap, Lim, and Leong 2009, 400–1). Expanding kindergartens, child care centers, and child-related subsidies remains a key way the PAP courts young parents—a critical vote segment (Welsh 2016, 125).

The 1950s and 1960s were marked by changes in PAP branch structure. The PAP deliberately maintains a weak party bureaucracy, primarily of paid officials who implement CEC decisions. To avoid personality cults or another takeover, the CEC appointed branch committees starting in 1957, reintroducing elections only a decade later. In 1968, the party abolished twelve district committees that mediated between the CEC and branches in favor of monthly meetings of branch committees and cadres, mostly to receive top-down orders (Pang 1971, 26–28, 34, 59). In 1976, the PAP tasked eight MPs with reorganizing the party. MPs no longer needed to be so self-reliant, population demographics had shifted, and Lee and other leaders worried about entrenched cliques and disorganized operations at the party's base. Assuming a more corporate structure, the party grouped branches under eight new district committees to facilitate coordination. Headquarters took control of party finances and accounting. Branches remained self-sufficient and semiautonomous, but with no say in candidate selection and with minimal policy input (Yap, Lim, and Leong 2009, 397–400; Singh 1992, 40; Mauzy and Milne 2002, 43). Goh Chok Tong worked to reinvigorate the party further in the 1990s, engaging branch leaders and augmenting their role in political socialization, promoting government policies at the grass roots, and channeling feedback (Worthington 2003, 30–31).

Already by the 1970s, the PAP projected a revamped identity. The party's twenty-fifth anniversary publication was fully in English, discarding former deference to other vernaculars, presenting an image of upwardly mobile professionals.[47] Yet party membership lagged sociologically: a 1971 study tallied the largest share as craftsmen and laborers, followed by salespeople (almost half hawkers); more workers were blue-collar than white-collar, and 13.8 percent were unemployed. Fewer than one-fourth identified as trade unionists, and despite the PAP's early embrace of gender equality, under 10 percent were women (Pang 1971, 55–58). PAP discourse sustained a sense of remove: PAP leaders stood apart and let brokers make "government policies more comprehensible to the masses" (Seah 1979, 279). Language was clearly part of the issue, with the bulk of PAP members and volunteers still Chinese-speaking and less well-educated than the overwhelmingly English-educated party leadership. The government decided that "a dependence on this particular group, however useful and enthusiastic they may have been, may not be beneficial in the long run" (Seah 1979, 280; also Pang 1971, 39). By the early 1990s, chastised by voters, the PAP reversed course to woo the Chinese-educated more assiduously (Singh 1992, 74–77).

Leadership became a centerpiece of the PAP's transformation. Initially, recruitment was highly informal—typically just being invited by Lee or another PAP leader. Party leaders identified candidates by their party activities and vote-capturing ability, seeking mass appeal. By 1970, that started to change; the PAP began recruiting a different sort of new "talent" in earnest. What mattered most now was what the candidate would add to the party's image and capacity. Educational qualifications became preeminent: the share of MPs with tertiary education increased from 14.3 percent in 1957 to 39.6 percent in 1968. Higher education is now the norm.[48] Many candidates lacked strong ties to voters or the party (Pang 1971, 39–42). Yet MPs ran branches, serving as chairman (or adviser, if they were a minister) and either organizing elections or appointing branch committee members, not all of whom were cadres. They picked their own teams, looking for loyalty and skill in organization and mobilization. MPs residing elsewhere depended especially on reliable committee members on the ground (Chan 1976a, 116–17, 124–25).[49]

Leadership succession—both pushing out the "old guard" and sourcing increasingly technocratic new blood—became a preoccupation by the early 1970s. (It is again now, as the party readies a new "4G," fourth-generation, leadership.) Lee saw both the problems elsewhere of leaders who hung on too long and the unsuitability of most first-generation leaders for an ever more complex government apparatus (Yap, Lim, and Leong 2009, 359, 391). A 1976 task force spot-checked younger leadership recruits and presented Lee with data on their affect, capacities, and attitude. The PAP then introduced psychological tests for potential candidates, including a Shell Oil–designed system to assess their analytical and big-picture capacities, imagination, and other abilities and a multistage process of tea parties with and interviews by PAP leaders. Candidates now pass through six weeding-out "sieves" (Bellows 2009, 34–35; Yap, Lim, and Leong 2009, 393–97). When party leaders instituted this system in 1980, they asked eleven MPs to retire (which some bitterly resisted, wounding the PAP at the polls). By 1985, the new generation dominated the CEC and parliament. Only Lee himself remained of the cabinet old guard by 1988 (Mauzy and Milne 2002, 45–46).

Lee explained that new leadership recruits should be not party "foot soldiers," but "generals"—in practice, mostly civilian and military technocrats, regardless of political experience. By the 1980s, PAP ranks were sufficiently permeated with "scholar-soldiers" to cause image problems (Mauzy and Milne 2002, 47–48). To promote oneself as a candidate is suspect; rather, the party "taps" those it wants. Still, some are promoted or mentored by a particular party member. For instance, senior PAP minister Ya'acob Mohamed, approaching retirement in the 1970s, wanted Wan Hussin Zoohri to succeed him, given their similar base among teachers and unions. First interviewed in 1976, then selected to stand in 1980, Wan Hussin shadowed Ya'acob for a month or so, getting to know the constituency.[50] Or an MP might encourage a promising individual to volunteer with the party, then be groomed from there (thus being among those who start by working at the branch level). Others may "understudy" a senior MP to acclimate to political work before being fielded.[51] About 20–25 percent of MPs "get retired" each election, requiring constant renewal. Most are allowed to stand at least twice, however, lest it appear that the party made a mistake.[52] Increasingly, PAP ranks assumed the appearance of a "mandarinate—a class of scholar-bureaucrats and scholar-officers—imbued with a sense of their own superior ability and endowed with the energy, resources, and political backing" to pervade every sector (Chan 1989, 81).

The PAP's increasingly elitist, technocratic mien complicates its emphasis on personal connection and service. And yet, as detailed below, that focus persists: overqualified MPs still perform incessant groundwork, complemented by a professionalized party that itself plays an expanded role in local-level governance. Not only the PAP's control of policy levers, but its long duration—sufficient to acclimate voters and challengers to its vision and praxis—reinforce the regime the PAP has crafted.

Challenges by and for the Opposition

While opposition parties have persisted, their shifting context has pressed them to institutionalize and evolve, especially once a smattering of opposition MPs entered parliament in the 1980s. New parties have arisen periodically, sometimes ephemerally or only shortly before elections, but are seldom enduring. The PAP poses a key hindrance, as it "tolerates the existence but not the effectiveness of political competition" (Chan 1976a, 228). Opposition stalwarts include the WP and the SDP; the Singapore People's Party (SPP) has also held office, but as essentially a one-man show.

The PAP's economic success makes it difficult for opposition parties to carve out appealing, distinct positions. Aiming more to differentiate themselves from the PAP than from each other, parties increasingly converge on a similar, PAP-emulating vision in their platforms and praxis.[53] Most lean toward a "nonconflictual stance," suggesting they have internalized the notion that excessive partisanship is "detrimental" (Ortmann 2010, 165–69). Voters have trouble distinguishing among parties, beyond iconic leaders, or may understand their differences more in terms of approach (for example, that the WP is "rational" and the SDP, "confrontational") than specific platforms (IPS 2011, 5; Tan 2007, 7–8). Moreover, PAP rhetoric paints all opposition parties as essentially the same, even as they articulate ever clearer policy positions to undercut critiques of opposing blindly.[54] They do vary moderately in policy prescriptions, but lack sharp ideological differences—all promote more democracy and lower costs of living, and criticize PAP elitism. The leader of a new party, SingFirst, dismissed his opposition counterparts in 2015: "frankly, they are all the same."[55] Leaders—and specifically, leadership struggles—loom larger than policy positions; personal rivalries have been the bane of all the major, and most minor, opposition parties.

Polling results across elections suggest about 40 percent to be PAP "true believers" and 25 percent firmly anti-PAP; the rest are the wavering "middle ground" (da Cunha 2012, 36). While data are fairly scarce, a 2007 survey found 83 percent considered the PAP "a credible party," compared with 49 percent for the WP (the highest among opposition parties), 34 percent for the Singapore Democratic Alliance, and 16 percent for the SDP (Tan and Wang 2007, 7–8). Even so, polling data suggest nearly 80 percent of Singaporeans deem opposition representation in parliament important (Tan 2007, 3). But the trend over time seems toward a higher level of "authoritarian detachment": as of 2006, only 9.2 percent agreed with the idea of discarding parliament and letting "a strong leader decide things"; that share was 21.4 percent in 2014. Similarly, the share agreeing that only one party should be allowed to contest elections rose from 7.5 percent in 2006 to 21.6 percent in 2014—notwithstanding increasing attendance at opposition rallies and other markers of stepped-up, more pluralistic participation in the 2000s (Koh, Tan, and Soon 2007, 13–14).[56] Meanwhile, the appeals even of opposition parties (the SDP, for example) that tend to see their base as educated, English-speaking voters, particularly those sufficiently well off not to be "lured by sweeteners" from the PAP, frequently invoke a degree of precarity and downplay a middle-class image, for instance, by use of Chinese dialects or in the issues they emphasize.[57]

Fundraising remains a hurdle, though donations are increasing.[58] The Political Donations Act limits anonymous donations (which most donors prefer) to a maximum of SGD5,000/year. Parties have had to submit to periodic inspection since the early 1970s (Au 2010, 109; Chan 1976a, 219). Opposition parties rely largely on selling inexpensive party newspapers (technically, unlicensed hawking), also offering a chance to meet voters. Sales have picked up in recent years, constituting a more substantial, if still fairly paltry, funding source.[59] Online appeals now supplement, too. Having MPs (even NCMPs) in office helps party finances, as the party members may tithe their allowance—for the SDP, 50 percent for a part-time MP or 30 percent if full-time.[60] However, that allowance—currently about SGD16,000 monthly (15 percent that much for NCMPs)[61]—covers all the MP's expenses beyond one legislative assistant. Needing to choose, the WP focuses on constituency work rather than invest in paid researchers.[62]

It is also hard for opposition parties to secure permits for events. When the WP wanted to hold a cycling event in 2007, for example, the police denied the request. The Minister of State for Home Affairs' explanation underscored the impossibility of the situation: "[WP supporters] may be behaving well but there may be other people who may disagree with your point of view and there could be quarrels and debates on the ground, attracting other people" (quoted in Au 2010, 109). The WP has complied with the law; the SDP, unable to procure permits for talks or block parties, let alone outdoor protests, has at times turned to civil disobedience. Opposition parties are otherwise limited, really, to "walkabouts," usually through housing estates, apart from the occasional forum in a hired venue.[63]

Most parties make rallies their campaign centerpieces, supplementing canvassing at homes, markets, and public transport stations. The 2011 and 2015 general elections in particular saw increasingly boisterous, massive crowds at opposition rallies, particularly for the WP—even though the rallies themselves almost exclusively consisted of sequential speeches, the daytime ones in blazing heat. Generally, speakers divvy up languages (though some code-switch); they may allot issues on which to focus as well (health care, homeownership, immigration, and so on). They remind voters to vote "without fear" and that "healthy debate" is a good thing. Encomia honor key leaders such as Chee Soon Juan and the SPP's Chiam See Tong. In 2015, at least one WP rally ended in a spontaneous march, a rarity in Singapore; each SDP rally concluded with a torturously long queue to have Chee autograph copies of his books. While the PAP buses residents in from housing estates (however still voluntary their participation), the crowds at opposition rallies come on their own, suggesting greater independent initiative taken to attend—then photos and videos make the rounds of social media.[64]

Also, whereas finding and vetting candidates has been a perennial hurdle, more Singaporeans have been coming forward since around 2006 to join opposition parties and stand for office. Contesting has carried risks. The PAP's successful prosecution of two opposition candidates on defamation and incitement charges for statements they made at 1972 election rallies showed increasingly close supervision (Chan 1976a, 220). Later prosecutions and other harassment have sustained that mode. In part tied to such suits, opposition activism has hobbled several candidates' professional careers.[65] Yet "the quality of the individual candidate," including the candidate's charisma and commitment, seems a larger factor in voters' assessments of opposition parties than of the PAP.[66] The key opposition parties have progressively been pushed to seek PAP-candidate clones, stressing similar paper qualifications—even as the PAP itself realizes the need for more empathetic, less homogeneous representatives.

That opposition parties have persisted indicates both elections' real legitimacy and PAP efforts to contain opponents to the electoral field. The first opposition by-election win in 1981 was a turning point; 1991's general election was another. Then, having been in office nine months, Prime Minister Goh sought a mandate from voters. The economy was strong and the government had recently announced a series of popular policy initiatives (Singh 1992, 32–35). Rather than rallies, the PAP relied on house visits and dialogue sessions for a "personal touch," following Goh's promise of a more open, consultative style—but also leaned on threats of withholding public housing amenities and upgrades. The PAP vote dropped slightly, to 61 percent, and the opposition claimed four seats. Among the key explanations for the PAP's decline were public concerns with the process and outputs of PAP policymaking; the PAP's approach, contra Goh's promises, seemed heavy-handed and arrogant. Better technocrats than mobilizers, PAP leaders could not address voters' concerns of the party's not doing enough for them (Singh 1992, 60–61, 97–102). Opposition parties have increasingly capitalized on these vulnerabilities.

Yet Barisan Sosialis, which never regained momentum after merger, remains the PAP's most daunting competitor to date.[67] Six years after its MPs abdicated their seats in favor of extraparliamentary protest in 1966, Barisan returned from "the wilderness," with rough plans for an anti-PAP United Front coalition. But their chances of winning more than a handful of seats were slim[68] and the party divided on the wisdom of rejoining formal politics at all. Chair Lee Siew Choh announced he would stand, rather than eschew an available channel. Over objections from 95 percent of members, Barisan contested.[69] By the early 1970s, only five of thirteen committee members remained active, Barisan's messages ("paraphrased from Radio Peking and Voice of the Malayan Revolution," snarked the British High Commission) lacked resonance among the general public, and its insistence on Singapore's lack of independence had lost its punch.[70] The remnants merged with the WP in 1988 (Singh 1992, 42).

The Singapore Malay National Organisation (usually referred to by its Malay acronym, PKMS), now severed from UMNO, largely petered out, too, weakened by separation from Malaysia and PAP strategy. Although PKMS insisted the PAP had failed the Malay community in education and language, the PAP courted Malay leaders, younger Malays saw little future in opposition politics, and the combination of redelineation, resettlement, and ethnic housing quotas eliminated concentrations of Malay voters. By the 1970s, PKMS was more social organization than political party.[71]

Opposition politics ramped up in earnest in the 2000s. By 2011, the entry of some especially impressive opposition candidates, including some ex-PAP, effectively "broke the PAP's exclusive claim to credibility" and reassured voters that voting opposition "would not be too wild a choice" (Au 2011, 75–76). Opposition parties benefited from better organization, more consistent groundwork, and strong orators, particularly in the WP and the SDP (Au 2011, 80). Meanwhile, the PAP's responding to demands to think more like politicians, who realize designing "good policy" includes "understanding . . . how it will be received on the ground," as Chan Heng Chee admonished in 2012,[72] had opened up new space for opposition candidates to shine by validating other leadership qualities.

The WP has been the main winner. Mocked as "PAP-lite," the party acknowledges its proximity to the PAP, blaming the latter's "subtly entrapping Singaporeans within certain mindset boundaries" (WP 2007, 6–7). Having been largely dormant since Marshall's resignation in 1963, the WP revived in 1971 when lawyer and former judge Joshua Jeyaretnam joined, promising industrialization, collective bargaining, civil liberties, vernacular education, a national health service, and more. The party launched *The Hammer* in May 1972 and organized subcommittees across residential enclaves and public events. Its vote share crept upward from 24 percent in 1972, until Jeyaretnam's 1981 by-election win, by a mere 653 votes. In parliament, the outspoken Jeyaretnam lambasted PAP policies. Returned in 1984—now one of two opposition MPs—he was disqualified two years later (WP 2007, 23–28; Singh 1992, 42; Mutalib 2003, 131–44). Despite subsequent PAP attacks on WP candidates, Low Thia Khiang then won in 1991. His "personal touch with his constituents" (plus irritation with the PAP) has kept him in office since (Mutalib 2003, 148–51).

Nonetheless, a decade on, the party was in turmoil: a defamation suit over a Tamil article in *The Hammer* ended in major damages, Jeyaretnam resigned from the party, and Low replaced him as secretary-general. (Pritam Singh then succeeded

Low in 2018.) Low determined to make the WP "respectable," recruiting "young professionals" and expanding outreach with monthly open houses and people's forums, new media efforts, regional committees for grassroots engagement, and a youth wing, formalized in 2005 (WP 2007, 31–34). For 2006's campaign, armed with young, well-qualified candidates and burgeoning membership, the WP started house visits several years in advance, including outside their core constituencies, then launched task forces in late 2005 for rally logistics, popular mobilization, and campaign paraphernalia. Once boundaries were announced—about six weeks before the election was called—teams of trained volunteers parceled out the ground, aiming to canvass every flat (Lam 2006, 89–90, 94–95). The party presented itself as an alternative government, its manifesto promising, among other planks, to do away with ethnic public housing quotas, the elected presidency, and GRCs.[73] The WP averaged 37 percent where it stood; other parties did less well—which Prime Minister Lee Hsien Loong noted signaled voters wanted a "credible" opposition, with quality candidates (Yap, Lim, and Leong 2009, 543).

The WP expects its members to do significant groundwork, especially the core constituency committee surrounding each MP. To advance requires that one be unpretentious, industrious, and committed; the party aims to weed out those with a self-serving agenda or who interact poorly with residents. Between 2006 and 2011, for instance, the WP canvassed almost every household in East Coast GRC twice, walking the ground weekly, organizing other outreach, and raising funds through *Hammer* and souvenir sales. As elections approached, they added several direct mailings, which candidates funded themselves.[74] By 2011, the WP "was the epitome of discipline," screening its candidates meticulously, offering a lengthy and detailed manifesto, sustaining intensive groundwork, cultivating an image of rationality and respectability, sticking to talking points, and maintaining organizational tightness (Au 2011, 68–69; da Cunha 2012, 225). But the party no longer offered an alternative government, instead presenting itself as "co-driver" to keep its eyes on the road and slap the PAP awake as needed. Or as one of the WP's stars, Leon Pereira, not-so-stirringly proclaimed at a 2015 rally: "Please support us to entrench a respectable opposition in Singapore politics!"[75]

Founded in 1980 by two-time independent candidate Chiam See Tong, the SDP displaced the WP as the main opposition force in 1991 by winning *two* seats, until internal strife set it back (Mutalib 2003, 166, 179). With a strong personal following, Chiam focused on groundwork before the 1984 elections—chatting at coffeeshops, visiting wet markets—while the SDP started to organize public forums (Loke 2014, 164–92). He was elected that year, holding the seat until 2011, emphasizing less dramatic change than simply opposing one-party rule. His 1988 PAP challenger conceded backhandedly, "you can't get a better opposition" than

Chiam: a "good, nice person" with limited oratorical skills or understanding of issues.[76] The PAP chided and ridiculed him, withheld funds for community facilities PAP wards received, and prevented him from holding such constituency events as PAP MPs organized (Mutalib 2003, 186–88).

The SDP grew increasingly centralized, sparking tensions. Matters came to a head when Chee Soon Juan—a plum recruit in 1992—launched a hunger strike after the National University of Singapore fired him. Chiam urged the party to censure Chee; the party demurred and ultimately sacked Chiam. He successfully sued, but left, regardless, in 1996. But the bad press hurt the SDP; two of its MPs lost their seats in 1997.[77] Chee's continuing travails, including being bankrupted by fines in 2005, added to the party's woes (Yap, Lim, and Leong 2009, 537–40). Still, like the WP, the SDP has been gaining ground.

Similar to the PAP, the SDP has a cadre structure, with a CEC elected every two years by the cadres (whom the CEC, in turn, confirms from among ordinary members). Leadership is collective, including the CEC and issue-based teams, supplemented by wings for youth and women.[78] The party newsletter, *The New Democrat* (previously *Demokrat*), the SDP's chief means of communication, sells "thousands" per issue, though a 2006 lawsuit by both Lees over one of its articles nearly bankrupted the SDP.[79] Membership is a few hundred, with about sixty to seventy "seen publicly" for photos and campaigning—respectably large by Singapore opposition party standards and growing since 2006. New-media platforms have offered a lifeline, helping the SDP circumvent media blackouts. But the SDP has also modulated its approach, moving away from civil disobedience, such as small-scale street protests.[80] The SDP previously embraced a more acerbic edge, for instance, accusing the PAP of profiteering, elitism, opportunism, and corruption (Mutalib 2003, 169–71). Anxious now to show it is "not just throwing stones," but poised to be a new government (even if it "still dare not campaign as such"), the party stresses elaborate policy proposals.[81] Its aims include pluralism and equal opportunity, functioning institutional checks and balances, civil liberties, and participatory democracy. Aware of its uncouth reputation, the SDP insists, "We proudly proclaim that ours is not a convenient vehicle for members to get on so that they can achieve their own self-centred goals."[82]

Chiam's political trajectory continued with the SPP, which epitomizes the personalistic party; when Chiam's health declined, his wife, Lina, took his place, still stressing constituency service (Au 2011, 69–71). A fellow candidate offered approvingly that Lina was the only MP he would call "auntie"; she herself strove to "be a mama" to her constituents.[83] Other contenders have likewise emerged in recent years. The Reform Party, which Joshua Jeyaretnam launched in 2008, and then his son, Kenneth, took over upon his death,[84] and the National Solidarity Party have been among the more prominent. Yet neither has made much headway, leaving their participation in elections beyond 2015 uncertain. Volunteers surge around elections, but membership remains low—and for the minority-led Reform Party, tends to follow ethnic patterns.[85] Party hopping has plagued both parties, although strong vote swings against hoppers in 2015 suggest voters dislike the practice (Loke 2016, 80).

Alliances beyond short-term, partial electoral pacts continue to elude Singapore opposition parties—hardly uncommon in electoral-authoritarian settings (Gandhi and Reuter 2013)—despite calls since the 1980s for closer coordination. For instance, the loose Singapore Democratic Alliance was formed among the SPP, the National Solidarity Party, the Singapore Malay National Organisation, and the Singapore Justice Party to pool candidates for GRCs in 2001. The alliance performed credibly in 2006, albeit with a vague manifesto, then fractured over personality and other conflicts (Au 2010, 103–5; 2011, 69–71). The most consequential effort at unity has been a "by-election strategy" from 1991 to 2006: opposition parties collectively contested too few seats to allow a change of government. The underlying assumption was that voters want an opposition check, but not to unseat the PAP. With all parties short on resources and candidates, concentrating on fewer seats made sense, regardless (Singh 1992, 64; Ortmann 2014, 738; Tan 2011, 116–17).

Since 1980, opposition parties have convened once electoral boundaries are announced to allocate constituencies so as to minimize three-cornered fights. The agreement may not be comprehensive, though, and sometimes collapses. In 2015, discussions entailed an informal meeting, then two days of formal negotiations, given overlapping interests, new parties, a bumper crop of qualified candidates, and rivalries. One three-cornered contest remained.[86] Not all opposition activists support this sharing out of seats, since it limits voters' choice, restyles Singapore as a two-party rather than multiparty system, and may deny a party the chance to contest in a constituency it has been cultivating. Decisions generally boil down to history and how many people the party can field—though smaller parties may exaggerate their capacity at the outset to be sure the few people they really can field make the list. This "gentlemen's agreement" system seems to be breaking down, however, as more people are willing to stand and the WP gains relative dominance. Already by 2011, the WP did not stay long at the meeting: its representatives said where they intended to run and its candidates did so. Again in 2015, they expected to "call the shots."[87] By-elections can be especially fraught. In 2013, for example, the SDP had canvassed all but two blocks of Punggol East before it withdrew to make way for the WP, which had "choped" (marked as theirs) the seat by having contested there at the last election.[88]

All told, Singapore's opposition parties lack the ideological differentiation, governing experience, and space to maneuver and build networks that even Malaysia's have; the PAP's more hegemonic electoral authoritarianism poses a stronger check. However, the frontrunners remain meaningful, their fortunes edging upward. As will be shown, though, not only have their candidate profiles and general posture come increasingly to mimic the PAP's, but their way of cultivating support has, as well, further entrenching the regime they challenge.

State, Party, and Political Economy

Given the extent to which the PAP premises legitimacy on performance, development has always been central to its cultivation of support. The PAP's model from the outset was a "mixed economy," with the government's setting overall directions and intervening as needed, including a strong role for relatively autonomous agencies, statutory boards, and government-linked enterprises (Nam 1969–70, 479; Chan 1976a, 26). Pressing welfare needs initially offered the PAP an economic niche; over time, while maintaining overall growth, the party has implanted partisan advantage in ostensibly programmatic policies. Those efforts, particularly state direction of essential niches such as housing and pensions, have rendered nearly all Singaporeans simultaneously clients of the PAP-led state and stakeholders in the current social order, restricting the space available for opposition innovation. Yet at the same time, as Chua Beng Huat explains, successful growth by the 1980s itself weakened "ideological consensus grounded in the common pursuit of economic growth" (Chua 2017, 72), leaving challengers at least marginal entry points for critique.

Singapore's development strategy overlaps broader political goals, including reducing the chance of social unrest from a stratified society (Heyzer 1997, 389). Political and economic elites intertwine; no "insulated, bureaucratic core with the independence to resist particularistic demands" runs the economy, and much of the "governing elite" remains outside the state, in a hybrid blend of bureaucratic, business, and political actors. Even without such a structure, norms conducive to self-discipline and prudent financial regulation have held. But the overlap of private and public introduces vulnerability, particularly given the lack of effective, independent checks—for instance, in the silence surrounding questionable Lee family transactions (Hamilton-Hart 2000, 203–10).[89] Where the members of this state-capitalist class meet is in a mix of bureaucratic agencies, statutory boards, GLCs, and state-owned enterprises (SOEs). The array of parastatals expanded dramatically after separation, from 2,300 in 1967 to 44,958 in 1972, outpacing growth in the (overlapping) bureaucracy (Seah 1976, 57–61). Managing SOEs and GLCs have been hired professionals, not bureaucrats or party functionaries. Internationally competitive, these firms enable both state control and market discipline, while usually avoiding the problematic investments and other pitfalls that damage SOEs' reputation elsewhere (Chua 2017, 98–102).

Political calculations still tinge economic policies. Separation came amid economic growth but high unemployment. Singapore's rise in per capita income from 1959 to 1967, by 42 percent, was second only to Japan's in Asia. As GNP grew 12 percent from 1965 to 1969 and 14 percent from 1970 to 1974, investments, exports, bank deposits, and other indicators soared; the PAP directed almost one-fourth of the national budget toward education; and 1965–68 saw a new home built every forty-five minutes (Nam 1969–70, 478; Chan 1976a, 24). Yet with labor at a disadvantage, despite the PAP's early worker-centered premises and promises, the 1968 Employment Act and Industrial Relations Act empowered management, not labor. It limited the right to strike and gave management sole jurisdiction on a range of issues related to hiring and terms of employment to ensure an investor-friendly, disciplined workforce (Chan 1976a, 26–27). The National Wages Council meets annually for tripartite negotiations, which informal discussions supplement, to resolve problems among management, workers, and government behind the scenes.[90] But the PAP has resisted tying itself to any one class, thwarting class-based politics (Mauzy and Milne 2002, 36–37; Jesudason 1999, 144–45).[91]

Ideologically, the PAP has consistently eschewed a "welfarist" orientation. It frames heavily subsidized education and health care, for instance, as "productive social involvement" (Mauzy and Milne 2002, 94) and argues against handouts to avoid moral hazard—citizens' malingering or taking more than they need. Even the poor pay token rent (around SGD30), notwithstanding whether payment derives from public assistance; the party's approach is to provide a safety net but ensure it is not too evident, lest people become reliant on it.[92] Increasing inequality, especially in recent years, against a promise of "shared prosperity" has forced innovation; the yen for votes clashes with fears of a "dependency mentality." In 1999, Goh acknowledged the gulf in opportunities between upward- and outward-oriented "cosmopolitans" and more parochial, "Singlish"-speaking "heartlanders," expressing concern that "two Singapores" were developing (Tan 2010, 85). Periodically the government announces initiatives such as 2007's Workfare Income Supplement Scheme, to combat structural poverty via wage supplements, or 2014's Pioneer Generation Package, to benefit senior citizens. Thanks to such enhancements, inequality decreased for the first time in a decade in 2008 after a prolonged rise, but it remains high (Tan 2010, 82–84).[93] Preelection budgets have been especially beneficent. The "Grow & Share" package in 2011 came to SGD3.2 billion; the 2015 package quintupled that spending, with tax rebates, civil servant bonuses, transportation vouchers, and more, benefiting around two-thirds of voters.[94]

These efforts fit into a comprehensive framework for state-led industrialization. In the 1960s, the government delegated authority to the Economic Development Board to attract and prepare for international investment. Splintering off from the Economic Development Board were the Development Bank of Singapore and the Jurong Town Corporation, which the government could direct toward state-supporting ends—such as providing below-market-rate housing to lure "foreign talent" in 1997 (Chua 2017, 105–7; Ganesan 1998, 236). Other SOEs similarly emerged from early imperatives, from energy provision to aviation, or from colonial statutory boards, such as the Central Provident Fund (CPF) pension scheme and SOEs for ports, utilities, and telecommunications that allow low-profit domestic provision of essential services (Chua 2017, 105–11). Profits from (purposefully opaque) sovereign wealth funds also permit above-market-rate interest on CPF accounts, without undue risk; relative returns to the CPF, though, have sparked pushback (and resultant policy tweaking) in recent years (Chua 2017, 112–14). Although the state's risk-taking encouraged private sector investment, by 1991, GLCs and the fifteen largest statutory boards made up almost 75 percent of domestic companies; by 1997, they accounted for 60 percent of Singapore's GDP (Worthington 2003, 24–25; Chan 1989, 80). Since 1991, the government has reinvested 50 percent of state investment profits but adds the balance to the national budget, stabilizing the economy and currency, reducing reliance on taxes or multilateral loans, and allowing heavier spending on public services and social transfers (Chua 2017, 118–21).

Within this landscape, the Housing and Development Board (HDB) exemplifies PAP achievement, sociopolitical engineering, and policy partisanization. By 2000, 86 percent of Singaporeans lived in 99-year-leasehold HDB flats, 93 percent of them owner-occupied (Mauzy and Milne 2002, 90). The system facilitates disciplining, homogenization, and proletarianization of the population: inhabitants pay monthly rent, but also accumulate value; they have an incentive to hold steady jobs, but can afford lower wages than were housing not subsidized; the structure of units and estates preserves the multigenerational, nuclear family, including as an alternative to welfarism;[95] and policies promote social integration and surveillance (Chua 2017, 78–86; Hill and Lian 1995, 121–23). The government, in turn, accepts responsibility to maintain, and maintain the value of, nearly a million public housing flats, while still churning out new ones (Chua 2017, 93–96).

The PAP frames housing more in terms of private property than as a right or entitlement (Hill and Lian 1995, 129). As of 1968, purchasers could withdraw their 20 percent down payment and monthly mortgage from the CPF—which for most households, was feasible. The rate of purchase increased from under 14 percent in 1964, to 44 percent in 1968, then 90 percent in 1986. Lower-income groups benefit more, since the largest flats are the least subsidized, but the income ceiling for eligibility was high enough to cover 90 percent of Singaporeans by 1989, giving the HDB a "virtual monopoly" in housing supply. (Excluding the wealthiest preserves their status and a private market.) Toward the goal of 100 percent homeownership by 1997, the government released the income ceiling altogether for resale flats in 1989. Moreover, after five years, leaseholders may sell their flat on the open market and purchase a new, usually larger, subsidized flat; the older, smaller flat then cycles back into the system, reducing demand for new construction. By framing eligibility for first-sale flats in terms of maximum income levels, though, the government obscures the interclass redistribution entailed, pitching the program as facilitated self-help. That said, anyone evicted for being in arrears becomes homeless, and thus remains the state's problem (Chua 1997a, 313–25). Increased political competition, too, has forced the PAP to show the HDB can "take care of" all segments, from the very poor to the fairly wealthy.[96]

Although a linchpin now to PAP support, housing provision was initially far more fraught. The Land Acquisition Act of 1966, on which the program rests, lets the state itself determine compensation in the interest of reducing speculation (Chua 1997a, 314). By 1968, the government had evicted 26 percent of households in public housing from their previous residence (Hassan 1976, 246). Acquisition was on a "moral high ground"; providing housing demonstrated commitment to improving Singaporeans' material condition, the low compensation offered justified in terms of owners' not having enhanced that land. The state expanded its landholdings from about 40 percent at independence to around 85 percent of Singapore, used for residential,[97] commercial, industrial, and infrastructural development (Chua 1997a, 315; 2000a, 50–51).

The HDB has remade not just the physical, but also the societal landscape, disrupting mobilizable cleavages. When Chan Heng Chee compared five Singapore constituencies in 1969–71, some were rural, others urban; demographic and occupational makeup varied; and the extent to which traditional associations and leaders held sway, the balance of partisan allegiance, and so forth differentiated districts (1976a, 42–78). Just a few years later, she found the "rural-urban dichotomy rather meaningless" and similar cultures across localities (Chan 1976c, 424, 435). Already by then, the HDB had made its mark, the spatial redistribution from resettlement affecting 40 percent of the population (Chan 1976a, 29). Ethnic patterns especially changed: the government formalized an initially unpublicized 20 percent Malay quota in 1989 (Hill and Lian 1995, 126). Constituencies are not identical today. Older estates tend to have a higher share of elderly residents; at least 15 percent of the population lives in (usually more expensive) private housing, with those neighborhoods unevenly distributed island-wide; and some districts are particularly posh, rural, or industrial. But overall, in sharp contrast to Malaysia, Singapore is comparatively homogeneous, removing one obvious way parties might distinguish themselves and their appeals, given geographically defined constituencies. That homogeneity also means it matters less that few MPs live in HDB estates, and very few in the constituency they represent.

The HDB's scope and nature convey political value. Estate upgrading and amenities have been election "carrots"[98] since the early 1990s, focusing voters' attention on parochial concerns. Even though Goh's initial threats to deny opposition voters services in 1991 backfired—he appeared vindictive and arrogant, and the SDP retained the seat—he still cut PAP constituency service in opposition-held estates, directing those voters to the parties they elected, albeit relenting on closing PAP-run kindergartens (Singh 1992, 133–34). The following year, Goh announced that all HDB estates over eighteen years old in PAP constituencies would be upgraded over the next fifteen years. He justified such selective spending as funded by "surplus" the PAP government had generated, which a different government might not have produced.[99]

The PAP escalated the practice of offering constituencies menus of improvements to be made (with public, not party funds) should the PAP be elected, even when the seeming "electoral bribery" at issue in obliging voters to make an economic rather than political decision provoked backlash (Worthington 2003, 43; Tan 2011, 117). On the table in 1997 were, for example, a SGD5 million swimming pool for the Brickworks area and SGD30 million in town improvements in Aljunied—with microtargeting of votes by precinct to decide the sequence of upgrading, even where the PAP won (Lam 2006, 137–38). Promises in 2001 tallied over SGD11 billion: estate upgrading, new development at Punggol, extension of the metro system, and improvements in Potong Pasir calibrated to whether the PAP won or merely narrowed the SDP's margin. In 2006, carrots included SGD100 million in upgrading for Hougang (under the WP since 1991) and SGD80 million for Potong Pasir if the PAP won (Lam 2006, 137–38). When in 2009 those two constituencies finally topped the upgrading queue, their PAP "grassroots advisors," not their opposition MPs, delivered the announcement (Tan 2011, 119). (Likewise, when the HDB opened a new block in Punggol East, it invited only the PAP grassroots adviser, not the WP MP—though they reminded her to see to cleanup.[100]) In 2011, the PAP not only dangled improvements for nearly every ward, but highlighted a drop in property values in opposition wards—claims data-crunching bloggers contested (Au 2011, 82–83).

Also at stake are more mundane "community improvement" resources. PAP-linked Citizens' Consultative Committees (CCCs, more below) must channel requests for these funds, disbursed by the Community Improvements Projects Committee in the Ministry of National Development.[101] From January 1992 through April 1995, seventy-seven of eighty-one wards received these funds; the four excluded were Singapore's four opposition wards (Chua 1997b, 146), although the Projects Committee has granted the occasional opposition-ward CCC request.[102] Praising the greater progress of PAP than opposition areas, PAP MP Ong Chit Chung cited both block upgrading and the sort of improvements these funds support: "major playgrounds, residents' corners, cosy corners, sheltered linkways, running tracks, indoor playlands, amphitheatres, floral clocks, upgrading of lift lobbies, town landmarks and illuminated signboards."[103]

Opposition parties can do little to counter such threats, beyond deploring the tactic and managing their constituencies competently (Au 2010, 108). Unlike Malaysian state-level opposition governments, which can generate funds at least to mitigate BN withholding, opposition MPs in Singapore cannot circumvent most PAP penalties. As one SDP activist sighed in 2015, opposition parties promise checks and balances and policy alternatives; the PAP promises mass transit and HDB upgrading.[104] Singapore's size, however, limits the scope for sanctions against any given ward. If the PAP denies one ward a new school, for instance, children there can walk to the next school over. Making those who vote opposition wait for upgrading is among the few collective punishments in the PAP's toolbox,[105] given its targeted effects and limited negative externalities. Even for those voters penalized, the damage is temporary and remediable at the next election with a change of vote.

Since the 1990s, worried about its margins, the PAP has come to rely on increasingly nuanced inducements, entailing blatant partisanization of what are, in fact, state programs, to coax electoral support, at risk of "being perceived as engaging in myopic pork-barrel reciprocity and tacit retaliation" (Tan 2010, 90). Yet opposition parties remain hard-pressed to do more than cavil at the margins. The extent to which the PAP has melded social engineering, political consolidation, and economic growth through its emphasis on vastly inclusive, deeply permeating programs such as CPF and HDB has reshaped the terrain of electoral contest. It allows the PAP to claim full credit for core economic policies, barring challengers entirely—regardless of the fact that these are state, not party, initiatives. Over time, by aligning citizens' interests with its own, the PAP has developed a strategy that has shifted "politics" toward fixation on "maximum material benefit for the self" (Tan 2007, 21). That the effort undercuts the PAP's own ideologies of meritocracy and incorruptibility offers opposition parties new grounds for challenge, but still on the PAP's terms.

Local Government

As in Malaysia, local governance constitutes a regime cornerstone. Having eliminated elected local government in 1959, but later recognizing a need to connect more directly with voters, the PAP reintroduced local authorities in the 1980s in the form of unelected, MP-chaired town councils, complemented by the People's Association (PA, introduced in chapter 4) network. Explains Jon Quah, "Even though there is no *de jure* local government in Singapore, [these bodies] constitute the *de facto* local government as they perform the functions of local government and illustrate the decentralization process"—although they represent deconcentration of responsibility, not devolution of authority (2001, 1–2). The shift has recentered electoral competition around the local level, reducing politics to "basic issues of efficient estate management, cost of living, and public assistance" (Ooi and Shaw 2004, 71–72). Emphasizing what MPs do locally "effectively turns the general election into a number of local elections, focusing on local issues"; the choice is between an opposition voice at the national level and PAP beneficence at the local level (Li and Elklit 1999, 209–10). Opposition candidates not only need to convince voters to want that alternative voice nationally, but also that they will not suffer locally for the choice. They do so by mimicking the PAP: building up party machines similarly credible in local governance.

Prime Minister Goh Chok Tong's 1996 promise with which this book began, that those who vote for the opposition would be living in "slums" before long, encapsulates the PAP's local election strategy. The tactic countered the opposition's "by-election strategy": the issue for voters became not just who won overall, to represent their interests in parliament, but in a given constituency. This emphasis on local governance centers around service provision—a focus that dates to the 1950s. By the 1980s, however, the contemporary state could readily provide for citizens in need, and institutionalization stepped up individual-level outreach to the community level. Even in opposition wards, the PAP has a material advantage: opposition MPs are not PA "grassroots advisors"; the PAP appoints, instead, a past or future candidate, or an MP from another constituency. Opposition MPs explain their exclusion but cannot be confident voters understand the extent to which they are sidelined. As in Malaysia, MPs have limited policymaking role; absenteeism is common.[106] PAP candidates drawn from outside the party may play a lesser role, too, in their local branch. Over time, MPs "have become more oriented towards local community development and constituency service provision"; although still "'ritualistic' legislators," they are expected to be "asset builders" and "community leaders" in their constituencies (Ho 2000, 74, 99). The model risks sidelining citizens' autonomous effort and fostering dependency, however, raising expectations that the state will take care of ever more areas in which citizens might otherwise mobilize themselves (Ooi and Shaw 2004, 79).

The PA is essential to the local election strategy. More expansive than in the 1960s, but still focused on a mix of communication with the grass roots, social service provision, and social and recreational activities, the network includes community centers/clubs (CCs), each with a management committee; citizens' consultative committees; community development councils; and residents' committees; plus a range of more focused organizations, with some amount of duplication of functions and overlapping personnel.[107] Although not formally under the PAP, the PA serves "to blur the line between government and party" (Mauzy and Milne 2002, 43). The PA's total annual cost in 1970 was around SGD4 million, with a staff of over one thousand (versus one hundred in 1960).[108] The budget for 2016 approached SGD900 million, an increase of over one-third since 2014,[109] suggesting how central the PAP deems this part of its apparatus. The partisan benefits of the PA—with the PM as chair and another minister as deputy—are obvious and intended. A British High Commission Report in 1971 noted the value of the PA's activities and its already "pervasive role" in Singaporeans' lives.[110] The PA had grown by then from running 30 to 188 community centers. Around a dozen ran kindergartens, assessing token fees. Citizens made "an inevitable identification" among the PA, the PAP, and the government, especially with much of MPs' constituency contact and government service provision handled "through and in" CCs. All told, although CCs were "not used for overt political indoctrination," there was "an inextricable web of close connection" between PA and PAP; the PA and CCs contributed substantially to the PAP's "genuine widespread support."[111]

In the "symbiotic" relationship between the PA and the PAP,[112] the PA serves as the government's "mouthpiece" and broker. PA volunteers learn about policies enacted or changes in programs, then they pass those updates along to local residents. Barring opposition MPs as grassroots advisers is on these grounds: the PAP, as government, "cannot trust" such MPs to communicate its policies effectively.[113] The issue first arose in 1981, with Jeyaretnam's election: the government changed the rule to appoint a non-MP. The opposition has disputed the political neutrality of the PA since, raising issues related to grassroots advisers in parliament at least ten times from 1981 to 1997. When the PA suggested opposition MPs may be unable to help promote even "anti-dengue and active ageing" policies in 2011, the public was openly skeptical.[114] The logic gets convoluted. For instance, the chairman of Potong Pasir's Community Development Council, Chiam's twice-defeated PAP opponent, explained that the PM's nominating him need not be assumed "political," but that "naturally, the ruling party feels more comfortable to have its own people working in a project which it initiated." Meanwhile, the post offered a chance to "win the hearts of the people," which would "hopefully translate into votes." (The opponent was annoyed, though, that his "efforts had gone to waste": residents assumed they were the MP's doing.)[115] Some opposition supporters do work with the PA. Officially, membership is open to all—but the PAP also speaks, for instance, of the grass roots' having been "infiltrated" by the WP around East Coast GRC in 2015.[116]

Notably, though, while infusing "new blood" has been a concern for the PA, as for the PAP, recruitment is challenging (Seah 1985, 189). A greater number of survey respondents have said they would *not* want to serve in PA-linked grassroots organizations than would, with younger respondents especially disinclined. (A significantly higher number were willing to serve in NGOs, so the issue is not mere aversion to groups.) That pattern has persisted over time (Ooi, Tan, and Koh 1999, 133–35; Ooi 2009, 185–86). Individuals may accrue some perks from volunteering, but they are minimal. At best, grassroots service might confer preference in getting one's children enrolled in the neighborhood school or a (coveted) closer-in parking space, as well as the chance to be "on the MP's rolodex." Priority in HDB flats may once have been a benefit, but purportedly is not now. Opposition parties are unable to offer even these advantages.[117]

The PA has developed incrementally. It took several years to recover from the staff revolt the PAP's 1961 split (see chapter 4) occasioned. The experience led the PAP to include a larger role for constituents in community work. As detailed in chapter 4, Community Center Management Committees, introduced in 1964, were the first step. Running parallel to the administrative Management Committees were Citizens' Consultative Committees (CCCs) in each constituency, launched in 1965. The PAP was at pains to paint CCCs as "nonpolitical," but about one-third of members initially were PAP members and CCCs cooperated closely with PAP branches. Indeed, the party seemed keen to have CCCs handle community outreach in lieu of branches.[118] Relying on coopted local leaders boosted PAP legitimacy while validating the individuals in question (regardless of educational or professional qualifications), stalled development of alternate power bases, and kept potential recruits out of opposition parties (Nam 1969–70, 473; Chan 1979, 5; Tan 2003, 7, 18; Ooi 2009, 176).

The next structures added were Residents' Committees (RCs), in 1978, to boost neighborliness, social control, ethnic harmony, and links between residents and government, and to keep watch generally. Unlike CCCs, RCs are limited to local residents. HDB blocks are divided into zones, each with an RC for five hundred to two thousand housing units. MPs (or grassroots advisers, in opposition wards) select members and liaise with RCs. (Private housing estates may form counterpart area subcommittees under the local CCC.) RCs allow citizens to participate in governance without entering politics and to resolve grievances before the opposition can exploit them. As the organizations closest to the ground, RCs tend to be the conduit through which organizations higher up in the PA transmit programs downward. RCs themselves, though, have a hierarchical structure and limited accountability; these are not membership organizations or answerable to residents, nor can the government enforce its demands aggressively among their voluntary participants. Turnover also tends to be fairly high. Like the rest of the PA, RCs are politicized: Jeyaretnam complained in 1983 that RCs in his constituency boycotted him—and some RC members refused to help PAP candidates in 1991.[119]

Next to launch were Community Development Councils (CDCs), in 1997. CDC leaders, generally MPs, are only from the PAP, since the PAP does not let opposition MPs disburse government funds. CDCs facilitate administrative devolution of government functions such as social services. The first CDC boundaries left opposition-held Potong Pasir and Hougang separate and the rest of Singapore collapsed into seven CDCs, for a range per CDC of under nineteen thousand to over three hundred thousand voters, and between one and thirteen MPs.[120] The diminutiveness of opposition CDCs hinted at their political purpose. As Potong Pasir's (PAP) CDC chair explained, that small size gave residents "direct access" to really get to know him, and allowed the CDC to better "show its warmth."[121] By 2001, however, the government had reduced the nine CDCs to five, subsuming PAP and opposition wards. This consolidation aimed to allow CDCs to function more as unelected "local governments," each with a full-time mayor (a PAP MP)[122] and professional staff. While their roles have adjusted over time, CDCs have come to focus primarily on distributing government aid to the needy, coordinating services, and helping retrenched workers. Although financed through the PA and government, CDCs also fundraise, promoting philanthropy and self-help. They launched with an annual grant of SGD1 per resident, plus SGD3–4 matching funds for every dollar raised.[123]

The 1997 election campaign left even some mayors confused about CDCs' role. In launching CDCs that year, the government had announced their purpose as nation building and broadening participation. As the election approached, Goh warned that opposition wards would lose CDC benefits that residents of PAP wards would enjoy: those who voted PAP would "benefit from schemes like Edusave merit bursaries and scholarships, and their elderly parents will be taken care of." Otherwise, they would "not get these programmes and their families and estates will be left behind while others progress."[124] Even though the government later backtracked on its threats, as CDCs' role in social service provision expanded, concerns arose that these would be politicized.[125]

Overlapping this PA network and making explicit parties'—not just the affiliated PA's—role in local administration are Town Councils (TCs), first proposed in 1985, then rolled out fully in 1988. TCs have taken over management and maintenance of HDB estates, allowing local areas to develop their own character, with more flexibility than HDB allows. They let residents participate in local decision-making, and MPs lead (Quah 2001, 14–16).[126] An MP, regardless of party, chairs each TC, nominating six to thirty councilors who receive a small allowance; professional estate managers and contractors handle actual management, funded by the subsidies the government would otherwise give HDB and by resident fees (Quah 2001, 16–20). With a GRC or multiconstituency TC (for example, the WP's Aljunied–Hougang–Punggol East Town Council, AHPETC), one MP may chair with other MPs as deputies, or leadership may rotate.

Well before the advent of TCs, MPs played active roles in developing local infrastructure, especially in less-established areas. MPs could request funds, for instance, for piped water, to install streetlamps, and to improve roads.[127] TCs resuscitate that model, allowing enterprising MPs to make their mark or develop town character. One MP used TC funds to introduce cycle paths. Others focus on upgrading markets, improving landscaping, or building walkways. TCs' number and reach change with constituency boundaries, though, complicating a sense of identification with the town. In 1997, for instance, introduction of new GRCs reduced twenty-three TCs to sixteen.[128] TCs allow the MP to intervene directly and claim credit, as with constituency development funds in Malaysia, but specifically also press residents to choose between party machines as their functional local administration.

Opposition MPs face hurdles in running TCs. They cannot count even on basic facilities like office space in HDB estates—when the WP took over Hougang TC, the HDB terminated the contract for its office and required they build a new one (WP 2007, 29–30). The PAP subsequently also took over services like lift maintenance and the estate management computer system, becoming fully independent of the HDB. Those changes brought cost savings and an excuse to post the party logo in every HDB lift, but also significant hassles when a TC transferred to opposition control. The PAP sold the TC software it developed to a PAP-owned company, which terminated its contract with Aljunied TC when the WP came in.[129] Moreover, the companies that bid for PAP TCs' management contracts avoid opposition ones.[130] In 1988, the eight PAP TCs all enlisted the same estate management company, while the ninth, the SDP's Potong Pasir, functioned without an agent (Ooi 1990, 26). The WP complains that managing agents still seem unwilling for "political rather than professional" reasons to work in non-PAP TCs. Party self-management is less feasible, too, since the HDB no longer handles essential services and accounting. The WP's Low Thia Khiang complains that a party may need to "build an army of civil servants first" in order to take over a TC and start operations within the requisite ninety days.[131] Amendments to the Town Council Act that limit new MPs' access to surplus funds accumulated by previous MPs from different parties offer voters further incentive to retain mostly PAP incumbents (Tan 2011, 118). The PA has even appropriated facilities—for example, twenty-six amphitheaters and basketball courts in Aljunied in

2015[132]—previously under TC jurisdiction, so (WP) MPs cannot use them. A PAP challenger for the GRC explained PAP politicians' exemption: they "do not attend grassroots events in their constituencies in their capacity as PAP members but as grassroots advisors who might be 'more aware of the policies and issues faced by residents.'"[133]

A key reason for and effect of TCs' introduction has been to allow the government to change the standard to which voters hold MPs accountable. The PAP urges voters to choose who they think will run the TC well, with mismanagement as "retribution" for a bad choice of MP (Ooi 1990, 7). This criterion forces MPs to emphasize municipal service rather than political ideas, parliamentary performance, or national vision, and purposefully socializes voters to understand politics in those terms. One incumbent PAP MP, for instance, argued in a rally speech that the opposition cares only about making fiery speeches in parliament, and is less interested in local problems and visiting residents. For his part, he dealt with matters from cleanliness to neighbors' spats. Another from the same GRC admonished the SDP not to "use the elections as a political soapbox." Even the minister anchoring the GRC noted that while the opposition "look down on us" and lack local plans, he will handle drains, rat burrows, and mosquitos, and "be there for you."[134] These arguments present the PAP machine as more competent than opposition alternatives and delegitimates "politics"—contesting ideologies and platforms—among legislators.

Both PAP and opposition MPs complain that TCs' functions could be more sensibly organized. Were the goal better management of public housing, TCs could be farmed out (again) to a statutory board. At the cusp of TCs' introduction, HDB managed 620,467 residential units, organized through forty-three area offices, and most residents were satisfied (Ooi 1990, 13–18). Residents do seem to assess TC performance in determining their vote, although data are mostly anecdotal. If accurate, opposition parties could simply take the PAP on with a vision for local, not national, politics—although doing so would embrace a government-as-management regime.[135] Instead, a daring 2015 suggestion by the National Solidarity Party's Hazel Poa, that politicians simply hire appropriate staff, then be assessed more by their contributions in parliament than their estate management, made headlines.[136]

Cynics argue that in establishing TCs, the PAP hoped "for the opposition to fall flat on its face in a most spectacular style should it make a shoddy job of running the town."[137] In practice, they have performed credibly.[138] Running TCs has offered opposition MPs a chance to build a power base useful for other political work, raised their profiles, and allowed both PAP and opposition MPs to "dispense a form of political patronage" in hiring staff.[139] (Salaried TC posts may offer—according to Minister for National Development Lim Hng Kiang, querying the SDP in 1993—"jobs for the boys." If so, the tendency seemingly affects both sides about equally; at the time, just over 40 percent of PAP councilors and a handful of council staff were party members, which some PAP MPs acknowledge they prefer.[140]) The PAP runs TCs in conjunction with the PA network; opposition MPs have established their own grassroots associations to help, emulating the model of relying on a partisan machine extending beyond the party proper, however much doing so strains resources and forecloses other foci.

For instance, once elected in 1991, Low Thia Khiang established the Hougang Constituency Committee for welfare and recreational activities; then in 1992, the Hougang Constituency Education Trust for needy children. He intended the efforts to be part of a move toward "positive engagement," or being "more constructive and relevant to the lives of the people, and less confrontational" (WP 2007, 29–30). Soon after the 2011 elections, the WP launched the Aljunied Constituency Committee (AJCC) as a "grassroots" body for their GRC. MP Pritam Singh specified that unlike PA organizations that barred opposition MPs, theirs would be open to all: "it is not a Trojan horse for Workers' Party membership (and God forbid, contracts/job opportunities/preferential placements for [school] admission etc.). Joining any political party is a purely personal choice. You are not going to see us handing out WP membership forms at AJCC events!"[141] The WP's grass roots partnered with community organizations to distribute monthly food aid, organize holiday celebrations, and more. In 2014, the WP also launched the Workers' Party Community Fund to parallel the PAP Community Foundation (but with a fraction of the PAP Community Foundation's funding). The foundation, Low explained, would "draw a clear line between political work and social and charitable work" in assisting the "underprivileged."[142] The WP admitted, though, it lacked "the luxury of resources available to the PAP," including for "material perks" (WP 2007, 6–7). Indeed, shortly before the election, the PA for Aljunied and Hougang announced the purchase of two buses, costing SGD600,000, two-thirds of it from the PAP Community Foundation, for use as volunteer-staffed mobile community medical clinics. (A PAP branch chair, also a grassroots leader, insisted wooing voters "was not a consideration."[143])

Opposition parties fold their proposed structure and bid into their electoral pitch. Hence, a combined 2015 SPP/Democratic Progressive Party team promised residents a community service cooperative if they won.[144] And running in a 2016 by-election, the SDP acknowledged it could not compete with the PAP's resources, but reassured voters they would not lose benefits. The SDP would offer a legal clinic, financial counseling, children's programs, and more, enabled by the "deep pockets" of SDP backers in other constituencies, pro bono legal help from supporters, and sponsors for needy families and scholarships. As a "small token," the SDP distributed groceries during the campaign, knowing the PAP would follow. The message: if voters choose the SDP, two parties will serve them, as the PAP will respond in kind.[145]

Developing the PA network and TCs has enabled the PAP to shift the electoral ground from ideology and policy visions to local administration via partisan machine, more starkly and formally than in Malaysia. Doing so presses opposition parties not only to devote disproportionate resources and energy to mundane management, but to prove simply that they can do precisely what the PAP does but better, even without access to the same state resources and other advantages PAP MPs enjoy. Rather than contest this model—perhaps impossible, since residents *do* rely on competent HDB estate management, and the MP *is* legally responsible for handling that—opposition parties have adapted to the PAP's premise. By now, altering this core aspect of the regime, in which parties themselves function as pseudogovernments, would require radical reconfiguration on either side.

Linkages with Voters

The PAP and opposition parties' service orientation sustains purposely clientelistic rather than programmatic linkages with voters, however much voters also know, and parties tout, their policy record and proposals. (Election rally speeches can dive deep into the weeds of, say, health care funding.) To enable this approach, the PAP has planted its own "grass roots": the dense PA network. At the same time, as in Malaysia, individual politicians build personal relationships with voters. They maintain the illusion of clientelism—of support rendered by dint of a personal connection. Even bereft of party resources or access to constituency development funds, contemporary opposition parties mimic the PAP with an approach opposition parties pioneered (recall David Marshall or Barisan Sosialis) but largely let slide between Barisan's denouement and the 2000s. In the past, the PAP accused opposition parties of being "hungry ghosts," referencing a holiday in which spirits return for one lunar month, then vanish. Increasingly now, both opposition parties and the PAP work the ground incessantly, supplementing national-level legislative work and constituency-level municipal management with individual outreach.[146] Notes a PAP MP, an MP's strength "lies with his grassroots work."[147]

As in Malaysia, it is especially at this level that opposition parties have gained traction. The WP's Low, for example, has been "known to be to be one of the most hardworking MPs when it came to constituency work" (da Cunha 2012, 202–3); a PAP MP speculates that what made the difference for both Low and SPP's Chiam was that "people know them," and "if you know the guy, unless he has done really bad things, they say, 'Oh, let him in another term.'"[148] On the PAP side, too, some

MPs credit a personal more than party vote, believing people vote for their "sincerity" and eagerness "to help them in their problems."[149] The backlash against what some voters see as coldly rational, arrogant technocrats in recent elections has led the PAP to choose some candidates from a new mold—with social activist backgrounds, or who have proved themselves more through grassroots work than educational qualifications. To assert their humanity, many PAP rally speakers now weave in personal narratives of early hardship and uplift—thanks, of course, to opportunities PAP governance provided.[150] However paradoxically, in urban, highly developed Singapore, cultivating the impression of warmth, approachability, and reliability has become all the more salient to tip the balance.

The PAP has always stressed personal interaction, but given slipping margins, it has focused increasingly on "EQ" (emotional intelligence) since the 1980s (Yap, Lim, and Leong 2009, 368–69). Initially, more such interaction took the form of overt patronage. Early opposition MPs insinuated that the PAP had formed the Works Brigade "to provide jobs for unemployed PAP members," David Marshall tried to sue the PAP for "political nepotism," and Lee Kuan Yew's case against Ong Eng Guan (see chapter 4) included his employing unqualified PAP members in exchange for support (Chan 1976a, 130). PAP MPs acknowledged having "looked after" key constituents. One noted, for instance, that having given local hawkers jobs and places in school from 1968 to 1972, he could count on those "friends" to help him win.[151] By the 1970s, as the PAP reorganized and consolidated, the party machine no longer provided jobs "on a large scale," and "spoils" grew rarer among party volunteers. Even so, party leaders worried that "the day of the ideologically motivated party member and activist is over and that nearly all expect some favours granted by the party" (Chan 1976a, 130–31).

Pressing a less material connection, the PAP urged MPs in 1970 to "identify themselves with the masses";[152] that imperative intensified. A longtime MP mused, "Back in the seventies, you can put up a monkey and you get elected, provided you come from the right party. It is no longer true now, now people look at the candidate."[153] Nor can an MP be merely competent; voters may reject one with "a grumpy face" as "just an IQ."[154] Another was advised on nomination in 1984 that an MP's first priority is to improve the lives of voters in the local area; next most important, for Malay MPs, is to attend to Malay society.[155]

Echoing survey results in Malaysia (albeit to a less extreme extent), polling data confirm voters' greater interest in MPs' presence and personal engagement than in their policymaking role. A 1996 *Straits Times* survey found only 12 percent of respondents prioritized MPs' being vocal and active in parliament, well below their managing constituency matters (39 percent) or being friendly and approachable (25 percent). In other words, "the public image of MPs in their constituency is probably more important than what they actually do within parliament"

(Ho 2000, 102). It is perhaps telling that famously polite and humble Tharman Shanmugaratnam was the PAP's top vote getter in 2015 (Loke 2016, 70). Rising inequality and straitened social mobility have amplified frustration with perceived PAP elitism,[156] even as opposition parties seek PAP-like candidates (Tan, K. P. 2008, 20–23).

Cultivating that personal following is exceptionally labor-intensive. One PAP MP, for instance, a still-working professional, has weekly meet-the-people sessions (generally around 7 p.m. to midnight), monthly agency briefings and committee meetings, weekly block visits or dialogue sessions, and activities in the constituency most weekends, alongside parliamentary sessions and a "whole bunch of stuff" that arises in between. Another spends every weekend and almost every weeknight in her constituency, meeting with grassroots leaders, holding events, and organizing block-by-block dialogue sessions.[157] The PAP stopped constituency walkabouts after independence but reinstated them in 1982, given too-little-known new leaders (Mauzy and Milne 2002, 43). Meet-the-people sessions have persisted throughout, with incumbents who neglected them being dropped (Chan 1979, 5).

Weekly meet-the-people sessions offer a way for MPs—PAP or opposition—to be relevant to the average Singaporean.[158] They blunt the edge of rational technocracy and promote a "petitionary culture" to develop "politically useful, loosely patronal relationships between the PAP government, grassroots leaders, members and ordinary Singaporeans" (Tan 2003, 9). The sessions render the MP "a clearinghouse for complaints and agitation" and reveal failings in bureaucratic channels (Howard 2000, 100–102), although government agencies generally respond well to MPs' interventions, regardless of party. Meet-the-people sessions also fortify the party: branch officers play meaningful roles and parties recruit and build camaraderie among volunteers, socializing them toward party norms (Ong 2015, 375–78). NCMPs do not generally hold meet-the-people sessions—opposition parties cannot do so in PAP wards—though PAP grassroots advisers in opposition wards may, via the PA. *All* elected MPs now hold meet-the-people sessions, however. WP MP Lee Li Lian even held hers as usual the night before she expected to give birth.[159]

Meet-the-people sessions follow a fairly standard format, regardless of party. They are well publicized in newsletters and on posters and cards. Residents arrive, register, and wait. In GRCs, MPs usually hold their own meet-the-people sessions, in their designated ward, though residents might instead attend a neighboring session. In a PAP ward, consultations are indoors, often in a kindergarten. Opposition sessions used to be indoors, too, until HDB barred MP offices from ground-floor "void decks" in 1992; lacking the alternative spaces to which PAP MPs have access, opposition MPs secured HDB's permission to erect temporary structures for meet-the-people sessions (Ong 2015, 381). Hence, an opposition session is likely to be outdoors in a void deck.

Meet-the-people sessions require teams of weekly volunteers to set up then restack chairs, direct and register attendees, speak with residents (if the MP cannot meet individually with all), translate, distribute aid, and prepare letters for the MP to sign. The MP may chat informally with residents at times while party volunteers handle consultations; others spend the full period meeting one-on-one. Party wings may help, as may volunteers from other constituencies—especially for opposition parties with few wards. Party activists serving as welfare officers might follow up with residents at their homes. The process is highly personal, patient, and intensive, though not private. Between forms completed on the spot and letters typed for immediate dispatch, each intervention passes through several hands, precluding favoritism.

Issues vary among the thirty to fifty people an MP might meet in a night. Questions about housing are prevalent, but also concerns about parking or traffic violations, noisy neighbors, medical assistance, taxation, immigration and work permits, finding jobs, and securing spots in crèches or schools. Certain problems have diminished, like helping resettled farmers acquire hawkers' licenses. Some are not really appropriate, like inquiries about extravagant phone bills, but the MPs will help if they can. (One resident was incredulous that her MP could not intervene in a court case, insisting an MP surely outranks a judge.) Many questions concern welfare. At PAP meet-the-people sessions, needy residents may receive on-the-spot assistance (groceries and vouchers, from private donors and the NTUC), as well as referrals to the government's ComCare social assistance program, though not cash. (Volunteers limit handouts: the team might help someone from another ward just once, then notify that person's home constituency, or refer a local resident who comes often and is not working to an agency, instead.) The WP distributes rice to low-income families monthly. Some issues require multiple visits; some residents visit with many issues.

Elvin Ong calculates over 135,000 letters generated per year through meet-the-people sessions, if each MP writes letters for an average of thirty residents weekly (2015, 362). Some agencies now seem to expect letters with requests, as a sort of vetting. These letters are unlikely to override any rules but may grease the works; residents expect MPs to be "rule benders," explains a party activist. On some issues or with some agencies, no letter could "move the needle"; other times, a request might "unclog the pipeline." Sometimes it matters which MP it is. And even if a letter works no magic, at least "it was somebody else said no."

Much meet-the-people session work simply directs residents to the appropriate agency or organization or connects them with a network of employers. The experience keeps the MP apprised of issues in the community, both unique personal concerns and systematic problems recommending a policy tweak (see Lindberg 2010, 136). While under 9 percent of respondents in a national survey had communicated views on policies to the government, the channel deemed most effective for doing so was the meet-the-people session (Ooi, Tan, and Koh 1999, 137–39), and MPs frustrated by issues they encounter bring those concerns to parliament (Ong 2015, 374). Still, as with TCs, the purpose of the sessions seems more political than functional. Muses Ong, "why would [the PAP government] develop an institution that purports to solve a constituent's problem by writing appeal letters to itself?" (2015, 362).

Door-to-door canvassing is the other dominant strategy for developing linkages, initially more for the PAP (including separately qua PA) but increasingly for all parties, all the time.[160] In the 1980s–1990s, the large number of uncontested constituencies made these visits more vital: walkover elections do not offer a chance to learn what residents want during campaigning or keep the grass roots energized. MP Bernard Chen, for instance, made the rounds every two weeks for a quarter century, with a "hit rate" of 40–50 percent.[161] The pace increased further around 2006; weekly walkabouts year-round are now common.

The work is laborious. An organized plan of attack selects specific HDB blocks;[162] the volunteers and politician(s) may split up, ensuring at least some linguistic mix. (Door decorations often recommend the language to use.) They move methodically down and through the building. A large team not only keeps more of the party machinery in practice but signals strong support. For the PAP, volunteers may proceed first, to alert residents of the impending visit. Participants wear matching T-shirts, at a minimum (generally party-branded). The PAP prefers all-white outfits; other parties have semiregulation khakis. The SDP, for instance, trains volunteers on their behavior, messages, and outfits; teams begin walkabouts with a briefing on key issues and questions to ask (including whether their MP has visited, in PAP wards), then end with a debriefing. One team member may be designated photographer. Although visits are timed for when residents are likely to be home (usually evenings and weekends), many doors remain closed. If no one is home or responds, the team may leave a flier and newsletter, perhaps joining other parties', then moves on. If someone answers the door, the team greets them in the appropriate language, if possible, presents the flier (and perhaps a party pen), and asks if they have questions or concerns. A volunteer takes down their information on paper or via smartphone app. The team may offer information on their policies or party, or on upcoming events or new developments in the area; the emphasis depends on whether the visitor is a sitting MP or an aspirant building his or her base. If it is the PA making rounds, their focus may be estate maintenance. Those volunteers should refer to the MP as "grassroots adviser," but often default to "MP" in practice; one explained, "MP" is easier for residents to grasp. (Using the title is legal, so long as the MP does not canvass for votes.)

Some residents want to talk—though some have unreasonable or impossible requests, or complain about neighbors or immigrants,[163] or forswear interest in politics. A few listen patiently to a pitch; fewer accept information about volunteering themselves. The aim is to stimulate feedback: problems they have, changes they recommend. MPs elicit a greater share of substantive questions, echoing those of meet-the-people sessions (and including similar issues whether visiting as PAP or PA): issues with childcare, public transport, local facilities—but also mosquitos, smokers, rats. Still, even an MP might get a response at fewer than half the homes visited, with significant feedback from only a handful of residents. Walkabouts can be a useful tool for gauging support, but given the share of unopened doors or more polite than revealing responses, they are heuristic at best. Opposition party workers note that surveys fare little better: people resist answering. Moreover, opposition parties may have relatively little capacity to help, lacking the PAP's resources and influence.

And parties and candidates may not be sure where they are actually standing or what blocks that constituency will include. Late-breaking boundary changes can render useless much of the footwork teams invest. Members may still assist fellow opposition parties in neighborhoods they have canvassed, especially in the case of a by-election, but are more likely to focus their energy on their own party's areas. The strategy is "micro-local," explained a candidate-to-be, requiring an early start; residents "want to see you at least twice" before the election. He started over two years in advance in the constituency in which he hoped to stand, without being certain of his nomination.

Complementing door-to-door visits are other constituency events. The PA or opposition grass roots organizes a range of activities for residents, in which the MP participates.[164] Different MPs have different styles: some stress recreational offerings, such as line dancing or sporting events; some prefer "chit-chat sessions" or teas. Other events include charity fundraisers, expeditions across the border to Malaysia ("durian politics," for bonding over the beloved fruit), launches of new facilities, and so forth. RCs may collaborate on a health-screening event or seminar. The WP's Low is known for attending wakes and sending funeral wreaths; he and at least one protégé have found doing so highly effective at creating loyal supporters. Malay MPs might attend four or five weddings in a "normal" day (but over a dozen is possible), slipping SGD10–20 into their handshake. One PAP MP distributes fruit monthly to constituents, to encourage healthier lifestyles. An MP may join a Malay organization to distribute alms during Ramadan, or break the fast with constituents. Some MPs organize free tutoring for needy students, which doubles as a way to keep volunteers occupied. MPs attempt to remember names and where residents live, for as many residents as possible. They might treat a group of, say, taxi drivers at a coffee shop chat. WP events may serve food donated by individuals or companies, if not self-funded through ticket sales. (Increased budgets have helped the PA undercut WP ticket prices.) Social media are an increasing part of outreach: voters expect MPs to maintain an online presence and respond to (constant) messages. Yet a virtual presence merely supplements, but cannot replace, actually being there.

This painstaking process builds support but diminishes time for research or discursive space for broader perspectives. It also makes even volunteering, let along being a candidate or MP, a potentially daunting time commitment, particularly for opposition supporters: volunteers may work several nights per week, helping with meet-the-people sessions, newsletter sales, door-to-door visits, policy work, or logistics. However unreasonable these goalposts, given parties' imbalanced resources or even access to public space, experience has trained voters to expect an omnipresent MP, and challengers to walk the ground harder, not to propose different terms on which to be assessed. Easing back on fruitless face time risks being read as "sour grapes."[165] Politicians across parties are by now habituated to cultivate clientelistic linkages.

Vectors for Change

The PAP itself cautions of the need to remake party and leadership to fit new times and has retooled its recruitment, presentation, and approach significantly since the 1950s. Its cadre structure and less stringent competition leave the PAP nimbler than Malaysia's UMNO. Yet opposition parties have adjusted, too, to new rules, such as the PAP's reframing parliamentary elections as local government ones. As these parties increasingly (re-)cast themselves in the PAP's mold—as "credible," non–boat rocking, competent managers, asking only to whittle around the edges of the PAP edifice—meaningful regime change becomes less likely through change of leadership, even beyond how unlikely an opposition win is. If anything, change via PAP recalibration may be more likely. Overall, the emphasis in Singapore now, in contrast to before the merger, is on what Garry Rodan (2012, 314–15) terms "consensus" ideologies of representation: of incorporating stakeholders and expertise into a problem-solving effort, absent contestation[166]— consider, for instance, the WP's "co-driver" approach. Recognizing the extent of Singaporeans' acclimatization to the political culture of PAP-led electoral authoritarianism, opposition parties have largely come to adopt the same premises for legitimacy and accountability, reinforced through a simulacrum of PAP praxis on the ground.

Despite the PAP's achievements, evidence suggests less contentment than income level would predict. The 2011 election in particular demonstrated mounting dissatisfaction and anxiety, mostly tied to "livelihood uncertainties" (Cheung 2015, 1–3). Income inequality is the second highest among developed countries; wages remain stagnant at the lower end, anchored by available foreign workers; the population is among the world's fastest-aging; and an increasing share are now "working poor." Frustration against those with privileged backgrounds, as well as "foreign talent," suggests eroding faith in meritocracy and upward mobility (Cheung 2015, 3–8). Rather than win back those votes with new ideas, the PAP has poured in money and time, courting the WP's still-scant holdings and fighting off further losses with promises of neighborhood amenities and house calls—a plan surely unsustainable over the long term.

Meanwhile, surveys suggest, too, increasing desire for political pluralism among higher occupational classes and more affluent, better-educated younger voters (Koh 2015, 42). Performance legitimacy may have "run its course" (Koh 2015, 47; also Chua 1995, 10–11), though Singaporeans still expect a heavy government role in meeting basic needs (Koh 2015, 45–49). Longtime politicians, too, suggest more Singaporeans question policies than in the past, beyond bread-and-butter issues.[167] Opposition parties hope to capitalize on that interest. However, most present themselves now "as a permanent opposition, aiming at most to secure more seats in Parliament" (Tan 2011, 120). The WP's Sylvia Lim captures this approach in referring to *alternative*, not *opposition* parties, invoking a play on the PAP's *civic* versus *civil* society. Opposition parties "happen, at the time, not to be in formal positions of power" but "oppose the PAP *per se* . . . on every issue." The WP, in contrast, aligns with the PAP on some issues; *alternative* captures its "constructive spirit" in offering options for selected policies (Lim 2007, 240). Meanwhile, the PAP has effectively contained "politics" to parties, sidelining the ideas-generating and coalition-fortifying possibilities of civil-societal alliances. Opposition parties are quick to affirm that to "oppose for the sake of opposing"—which seems to include offering a new political vision, beyond targeted policy critiques—is irresponsible and delegitimizing, as opposition leaders from Chiam in 1991 to today's WP stress (Mutalib 2003, 179).

As in Malaysia, changing the regime requires changing the way politicians and voters perform politics. The PAP has cultivated since the 1960s a "petitionary" politics, at the expense of a politics of bargaining and conflict, asking citizens simply to trust in PAP leaders' expert judgment (Chan 1976a, 232–33). This emphasis on technical expertise and qualifications "has transmuted MPs into bureaucrats" (Hill and Lian 1995, 181–82), even as they turn their glamorous pedigrees to checking drains and ringing doorbells. Opposition parties have largely accepted this framework to evade ridicule and because if the question is who leaps faster to smile and assist, they stand a chance. Rather than becoming less clients of the state as the country develops, Singaporeans are becoming increasingly so. Opposition parties find in that cultivated helplessness an opening: they, too, can serve.

Remaking patterns of access and influence in Singapore reflects the far more hegemonic position of the PAP vis-à-vis Malaysia's BN. Both regimes have changed politicians' behavior, among government and opposition legislators alike; both have pressed citizens to prioritize parochial concerns and meso-particularistic club goods as well as personal outreach; and both purposely confound party and state. But in Singapore, the PAP, with a far tighter grip on parliament and a mind-set shaped by early ideological battles, has devalued opposition parties and electoral politics altogether. The PAP's admonition that those interested in politics join a party and stand for election is intended and understood to repudiate protest—among parties, the PAP expects to win and confirm legitimacy in the process, given how it has structured the game.

Meanwhile, civil society does not play the same role in Singapore as in Malaysia of raising issues, generating policy alternatives, training leaders, and bridging parties, except inasmuch as the PAP uses its own inorganic "grass roots" as a partisan farm team. Notes Alex Au, it is "striking . . . how little interaction there is between opposition parties and civil society in Singapore," a hesitation among activists shaped by fear of losing funding or influence, where the state substantially mediates both, as well as memory of past repression. The WP, too, seems cautious of interaction; the SDP, willing to collaborate, is rebuffed (Au 2010, 113–14).

Opposition (especially WP) inroads, then, have not pierced the PAP's "ideational hegemony"; even the SDP, having challenged the PAP's "core philosophies" by emphasizing civil liberties and still failed to win seats, has recognized the need to play more nearly by PAP rules. The SDP's candidates still include some deemed "antiestablishment" for past activities, however well-credentialed; the WP's lineup is on par with the PAP's (Abdullah 2017, 495, 502–3). And the WP's internalization of PAP ideology comes through in its "appropriation of terms such as 'rational' and 'responsible,'" assuming Singaporeans' complaints center around material grouses, not clashing ideas (Abdullah 2017, 504).

Redressing weaknesses, the PAP has emphasized progressively more clientelistic than programmatic linkages. But its doing so has, perversely, opened new grounds for challenge, in contrast with the near-impermeability of PAP programs. Until recently, opposition parties sprang from hibernation as elections approached, dusting off their platforms. Persistent opposition pockets—constituencies in which an opposition stalwart could rebuff PAP threats and appeals, election after election, clustered mostly in eastern Singapore—raise questions about why *these* areas and *these* people, as opposition gains edge upward. Common responses suggest historical patterns. Hougang, for one, became home to poorly compensated, distressed, resettled farmers in the 1980s, many of them Teochew. Claims that dialects make the difference,[168] though, seem stretched (or at least, less relevant now than previously), with their use diminishing; inasmuch as language does matter, the PAP has also been flaunting dialects more. Some areas where the PAP is especially strong, as on the west side, were industrial zones, undergirded by PAP-loyal unions. Other areas have a high concentration of recent immigrants, who tend to be pro-PAP. That young voters seem to lean more heavily opposition than older voters does not explain the regional pattern; most areas in question are not especially new estates. Part of the answer may be that voters in areas that have been consistently contested are more accustomed to the process and less worried about the secrecy of their ballot; many areas of Singapore were rarely or never contested from the 1960s to 2015. But much seems simply the cachet among voters of well-known personalities on opposition tickets.[169]

Cultivating a personal vote may be something the PAP learned from the opposition, rather than vice-versa—hence the PAP's scramble to downplay the elitism so long a source of pride. However, in a highly developed, complex society, this sort of appeal doubles as a weapon of the weak. Asking voters to choose who they know, not the ideas they deem best, embraces and perpetuates an exclusive, but not impenetrable, regime. How specifically this mix of partisanized policies, empowered partisan machines, and clientelistic linkages plays out differs between Singapore and Malaysia. But in both, the combination maintains space and hope for opposition parties, but only once they embrace—and further entrench—the scheme of governance in place.

DRIVERS OF STASIS AND CHANGE

Will the Pattern Hold?

Maverick Singaporean scholar-diplomat Tommy Koh proposed in 1998 that whereas Singapore under Lee Kuan Yew evoked a banyan tree, strong and over-spreading, the era under Goh Chok Tong suggested a tembusu tree, equally sturdy, but casting a narrower shadow.[1] I suggest that we focus instead below the canopy, on the ground. A mangrove offers a better analogy: adaptable, resilient, with powerful roots. Studies of electoral authoritarianism—of any regime type, really—tend to focus on the treetop, trunk, and branches: the institutional rules and overarching executive. But the ground level matters just as much. Elections may be skewed, but the incumbent's quest for a mandate requires a strategy to cultivate the roots. Over the long term, coaxing compliance is more appealing than coercion—blocking out rainfall and light—especially if the goal is not merely remaining in office, but persisting comfortably. The optimal strategy is to craft structures and habits that implant a party-state. Part of that effort entails shaping voters' interests, expectations, and understandings of politics, acculturating them to authoritarianism. Challengers must court those same voters; less empowered discursively or materially, these contenders may offer a new vision, but have no choice but to work within the framework already laid. When this state of play extends over decades, their milieu shapes opposition parties, like voters and the dominant party itself. A political culture crafted in and for electoral authoritarianism sets in, less readily reshaped than the ranks of leaders.

The foregoing discussion aims to revise our understanding of regimes and regime transitions—and, particularly, what a genuine transition might entail. It recommends that we consider a mix of structural, political-cultural, ideological, and praxis-oriented angles to understand and assess regimes and political change. Most important, the approach and findings recommend not overprivileging national-level and formal factors, recognizing the extent to which informal institutions, norms, and subnational dynamics are also defining (see Aspinall and Berenschot 2019, 10–11). Over time, the workings of politics under electoral authoritarianism may shift the contest from one of policy or ideology, with scope for genuinely distinct platforms and voter choice, toward less differentiable issues of mundane management and microlevel accessibility and acquisition.

Any regime entails some degree of path-dependence. As Pérez-Liñán and Mainwaring have proposed, "parties develop interests, norms, and preferences that typically favor some continuity in regime legacies. They have a reservoir of inherited interests, normative principles, policy preferences, and operational rules—an institutional 'common sense'—that provides a historical underpinning to their strategic considerations" (2013, 394). Interests and attendant praxis, in this view, are malleable but sticky, and both endogenously and exogenously derived. In the case of electoral authoritarianism, the dominant party sustains itself over the long term not just through coercion and manipulation—though these practices also continue—but by aligning voters' electoral preferences with its own. In the process, but surely less purposefully, these strategies shape opposition parties' profiles, goals, and strategies, as well; they learn to compete within the system that is, rather than as if in the system they seek. But as such, these competitors become as likely to perpetuate as to disrupt the patterns of governance and linkages of electoral authoritarianism. To say hybrid regimes remain resilient in Singapore and Malaysia does not require that their dominant parties remain emplaced, but that the model of governing, accountability, and legitimacy the system has fostered has permeated to the roots, such that its reconstitution will require far more than an election.

Fusion of Party and State

A change of government may have fairly modest effects. Even within a given party, complete overhaul is hardly automatic. Describing the Liberal Democratic Party's 2009 loss in Japan, for example, Krauss and Pekkanen note that it is "not just defeat per se, or defeat providing a stimulus to change, that will lead to institutional change but, rather, the way that defeat disrupts time-dependent processes" (2011, 282). In the case of both Malaysia and Singapore, those "time-dependent processes" have achieved more nearly hegemonic status than have initial ideologies or other grounds on which voters and policymakers make decisions. In both states, one party or coalition's decades of unbroken control of national offices, policy legacies, and state machinery, reinforced by fusion of administrative levels and efforts to remake expectations and rewards on the ground, has shaped political culture so as to preserve the regime even beyond the dominant party's tenure, as we now see in Malaysia.

The prevalence of clientelistic linkages and practices need not signal state weakness; legislative office always entails both formal and informal duties, and strong state institutions may favor provision of private as well as public goods (cf. Lindberg 2010, 135, 138). Formal duties, enumerated in constitutions, standing orders, and other rules, may include legislation, executive oversight, and constituency representation and service; informal duties, more often read from legislators' behavior and statements, relate to norms about accountability relationships expected of any occupant of that elected office (Lindberg 2010, 135). Formal and informal interact, however. As we see in Singapore, assignation of new formal roles, as through constitutional amendment, may efficiently and enduringly revamp bases for accountability and legislators' balance among routines. Likewise in Malaysia, Democratic Action Party MP Liew Chin Tong explains (before his coalition's ascent), entrenched norms both result from and reinforce the strong state: "MPs are compelled to perform duties which are supposed to be carried out by state assemblymen or local councillors, so long as they get to meet and greet the voters. Such a political climate created by the ruling party and the bureaucracy does not encourage MPs to focus on their actual work of policy-making. To the bureaucrats and ruling party, Parliament is merely a 'rubber stamp' to legitimise their decisions."[2]

Furthermore, overlap between state and party facilitates manipulation of elections. Beyond the simple desire to retain control, the dominant party may define and understand threats to its own power as threats to the system. Fusion of party and state *is* purposeful and instrumental—but it is also almost unavoidable when there has been only one party in office and that party has created the postcolonial state. That dominant party may itself either approximate internal hegemony or be more pluralistic. Yet the nature of political parties—whether they are cadre-based or mass-based—seems to matter less to the character of linkages than does the wider institutional structure, however much how candidates are selected shapes who needs to be impressed or to whom a legislator is really accountable.

Differentiation and Alignment

The result is a fusion of party and state, not only in terms of function—the impossibility of discerning what voters should credit to the state, and what to the party in office—but also ideologically and discursively. Stable electoral authoritarianism promotes and requires an at least perceived alignment of interests between leaders and led, encouraging and fostered by partisanized programs and industrious outreach. Seen from another perspective, within parties we also find processes of differentiation and coordination. Parties are key and structure the system, but the specific personalities within parties matter, too; alignment is multivalent.

Opposition parties remain meaningful parts of the system, both in their own right and as foils to prompt institutional and political-cultural innovation. And, of course, these parties can make headway, particularly at the more granular, subnational level. In these two states, some opposition parties are as long-established as the parties so durably in government. These parties need to differentiate themselves from the dominant party, but face a dilemma in distinguishing themselves from each other, given the benefits of coordination. Hence, they are likely to converge in terms of machinery and strategy, even if and when parties delineate themselves through ideology or policies.

Meanwhile, we see a mashup of channels and accountability. The regime lays deep roots in structuring state-society relations, within and beyond parties and their machines, curtailing space for a truly independent civil society. The result is an intermeshing of civil society and party politics, on the one hand, such that the public sphere writ large becomes pervasively partisan unless specifically restrained, and clientelist linkages between politicians and constituents that curb or contain voters' expectations, on the other. The latter process nudges bases of legitimacy toward the manageable, micro level, possibly reducing dominant parties' need to control mobilization or expression, but may advantage opponents, too, by shifting contests from party to personality.

Importantly, this order may yield real benefits for voters. Clientelist linkages encourage development of especially diligent, forthcoming, approachable legislators who know that voters may hold *them*, and not just their party or the local machine, accountable. They need not, and often cannot, merely coast in their parties' wake. Their intervention constitutes a sort of para-philanthropy, of supplementing missing, inadequate, or hard-to-access state services and aid with essentially privatized provision, or rebranding state policies as if from the party, coordinated by and through pervasive machines.

This lens foregrounds, too, the importance of party structure and embeddedness for regime resilience. Parties in these states do not fit the classic model of vehicles to aggregate interests and channel them upwards. Instead, they serve functions of representation, to a limited extent, but more of distribution: their credibility rests on their record and promise as patrons, in an instrumental as well as affective sense (see van de Walle 2003, 314). Having adapted to the system that is, these parties may be ill-prepared to introduce or thrive in a genuinely different one, even if and when they take the reins. Indeed, Pakatan has moved sluggishly at best even at reforming easily changed features it used to fault, transferring to itself what used to be the BN's unfair advantage.[3] Nor should one presume voters can readily see around a thicket of norms, or prioritize a presumed (but uncertain) path toward the greater general benefit at possible personal cost. In other words, until the linkages at the system's base shift, such that voters expect and pursue different modes of governance, even willing new leaders will be hard-pressed to reform the system to which they, and the voters on whom they rely, have become acculturated.

What Comparison Suggests

By focusing on structural innovation at the local level, supplementing national-level electoral and other tactics, electoral-authoritarian regimes discipline the public and opposition parties, gradually permeating political culture and everyday political praxis. The implications of these patterns shape politician-voter linkages, premises for accountability and assessing alternatives, and the range of players with stakes in the system-that-is. By focusing too much on who is in power at the top, one risks missing how the system truly functions on the ground, given the way voters, politicians, and parties alike develop in the context of, and respond to the incentives and constraints of, long-term structures and norms. But the comparison between Singapore and Malaysia allows further nuance.

First, we can see a broad distinction at the systemic level by comparing Singapore's unitary system to Malaysia's federal one. Contemporary Malaysia lacks the third tier of government in which previously smaller or more niche parties gained experience and followers. However, state governments do give some space both for voters to "try out" a new party at a subnational level and for localized issues, priorities, or bases for legitimacy to hold sway. The nature of Malaysian federalism—highly centralized in terms of policy jurisdiction, resources, and authority—limits the scope for state power, however, increasing the incentives for the parties in control of states to appropriate local-authority resources and power, including by sustaining party-appointed local councilors. Opposition parties in Singapore lack this option of representation at a subnational level, separate from national contests—nor does Singapore have the sort of patterned demographic variation that gives rise in Malaysia to distinct sets of preferences and interests across states. While creation of town councils supposedly fosters differentiation, the range is narrow.

More broadly, Singapore's regime is more hegemonic than Malaysia's, facilitating more far-reaching restructuring of the formal distribution of power.

(Importantly, that hegemonic authority is partly endogenous to this distribution of power.) Structurally, it is not that parties in government have effectively arrogated local authorities for their own partisan advantage, as in Malaysia. Rather, Singapore's PAP has remade the rules, formally fusing national and local tiers of government through MP-led town councils. Moreover, Singapore's hegemonic electoral-authoritarian regime has been able far more substantially to suppress civil society and dissociate its organizations from partisan political activity than has Malaysia's competitive regime. Doing so significantly constrains the extension of parties, especially from capturing issue- or identity-based segments through civil-societal proxies or partners; the party proper, then, constitutes the machine, supplemented only by each party's intrinsically partisan AstroTurf "grass roots." This mix of not just stronger interparty competition but also weaker linkages between opposition parties and civil society surely deepens authoritarian acculturation, suggesting why the PAP (or by logical extension, hegemonic authoritarian regimes generally) remains less vulnerable to defeat than the BN.

Finally, this comparison offers insight into the implications of different types of political parties for governance. A cadre party such as the PAP is more disciplined, offering less space or need to develop a personal base and less scope for differentiation in the nature of that personal base. The goal is far more to capture vote share on the ground than within the party. Mass parties offer more latitude and incentive for base building, factions, and muddied messaging. Given that distinction, we might expect more meso-particularism in Singapore and micro-particularism in Malaysia. What is perhaps especially notable, then, is the similarity in strategies across these two regimes and their differently organized parties. Both regimes offer collective patronage to woo votes, channeling and branding state resources in ways that are politically useful (through the New Economic Policy and its successor schemes in Malaysia or the Housing and Development Board in Singapore, for instance). Both carve out a role for the parties one tier up the chain in local governance. And, especially, both regimes carefully cultivate a "personal touch" through clientelist linkages, extending beyond the constituency service one might "normally" expect for a supplementary personal vote.

Vectors for Change

This ground-up lens is not to suggest that electoral authoritarianism is forever. But change is difficult. Aspinall and Berenschot (2019, 2–4) note, for instance, the lack of any clear force to "drive out clientelist politics," even after an authoritarian regime's decisive fall, and the mix, at best, of programmatic with clientelistic appeals as governments come to supplement rather than supplant the latter.

Few if any key players may really be satisfied with the system that is, but it is en-trenched—an equilibrium to which parties, politicians, and voters have adapted. To change it would require overcoming hurdles to collective action. Even an up-surge in protest voting or calls for reform leaves open the question of how to en-sure real restructuring when parties and voters alike understand and have learned to navigate the system in place—a system that sets particularistic material inter-ests in stark opposition to shared programmatic reforms. Yet again, the explana-tion here is not monocausal: complex systems change through complex paths. Even just the margins, though, matter.

First, parties, like their analysts, might usefully retrain their gaze—and at least some (especially Pakatan) politicians in Malaysia, less Singapore, are doing so. These political entrepreneurs are discouraging reliance on legislators as service providers and instead encouraging attention to policymaking and programs. We see glimmers of the same process in suggestions that Singapore's town councils be depoliticized to make devolution more efficient and allow MPs to focus on bigger-picture issues—but for now, those suggestions have come more from me-dia commentators and others than from parties themselves, likely leery of lead-ing voters to assume they are simply not up to the task. Until voters shed the ex-pectations toward which they have been groomed over the past three decades, no party can afford to be the one to refuse to play by the prevailing rules, lest it be shut out of the game altogether. This effort shifts voters' attention from the ground—legislators' relatability and short-term performance on their home turf—to scaled-up or longer-term goals. Both types of indicators, associated with clientelistic or programmatic linkages, respectively, are rational reasons for a vote, but the first suggests passing judgment on or nudging the incumbent; the second assesses the system as a whole.

Second, much as Scott predicted a half-century ago (1969, 1146–47), economic growth and transformation does disrupt clientelist relationships, not via some normative teleology, but given, for instance, increasing market complexity, in-frastructure needs, and mobility. Demographic shifts that alter voters' need for reliable state services, administrative changes, permutations in the international environment, and other factors may matter as well (for example, Noble 2010). The PAP goes out of its way to encourage reliance on, for instance, employer net-works and connections to help job-seeking meet-the-people session supplicants find employment. Such services are clearly useful in an economically mutable and increasingly unequal society but also encourage beneficiaries to understand their MP as their link to a job. The voter may then hold the legislator accountable for finding them employment, not for proposing a policy remedy to a systemic prob-lem for which their own joblessness is an indicator. The issue is not merely the fact of pseudo-patronage jobs, but what that provision does for premises for accountability and political legitimacy—political-cultural effects likely to outlive any specific boon. At a more basic level, if fewer voters in either country were sufficiently poor or marginalized as to require immediate handouts, or sufficiently educated and capacitated as to be able to deal directly with government agencies, public utilities, the courts, and the like, demand for clientelism would likely diminish—though that, already, neither country is drastically underdeveloped, yet these practices persist, should curb our expectations of such "developmental" transformation.

Third, the revival of ideology, whether of Islam, socialism, or another dogma, may elevate other priorities and mandate different, perhaps more programmatic, linkages. The current system in both countries assumes what drives voters is fundamentally not ideology but uniform, predictable, satiable material preferences, overlaid with an emotional valence, so that at least enough voters to tip the balance vote for the candidate they know and trust, counting on a well-tuned apparatus that combines concrete support with affective ties. If, for instance, Malaysia's PAS revamps in a way that sidesteps current rules, if the populist alternatives jostling politics in neighboring states make headway in either Malaysia or Singapore, or if a new left-wing challenge gains purchase amid the stark inequity and precarity of contemporary capitalism, voters may come to prefer something different, regardless of the incumbent parties' persistent efforts to control the agenda. Yet even if sufficient voters do weigh legitimacy differently and a party meets their mark, there is no assurance that the system as a whole can or will be remade in light of that premise—that the regime will actually change—anytime soon.

Fourth and finally, the machine may fail: its incapacity to meet popular interests may force a change, whether for lack of resources or of the dense human networks required, the falling away or enervation of the extraparty support involved, or inability to adapt to new challenges. For the dominant party to lose an election does not indicate how this collapse happened; the alternatives in the wings are part of and products of the system now in place. Rank corruption in particular allowed Najib to drag UMNO from office, yet UMNO has largely stayed the course, plotting a comeback regardless of its former leader's personal fate, nor has Pakatan plunged aggressively into institutional reform—not least since going too far, too fast, might well pivot anti-Najib protest voters back to the BN (Weiss 2020). An electoral loss is likely necessary, but not sufficient, to remake both the formal rules and the informal norms sustaining an entrenched regime.

The usual suspects in the transitology and regimes literature still loom large: electoral manipulation, straitened civil liberties, splashed-out patronage, squabbling challengers. But these reveal more about why a dominant party keeps winning than whether a regime has changed or what might induce it to do so. Remaking access to office, patterns of influence, decision-making processes, and the other attributes of a regime writ large requires more than just a change of leaders. Another party, already acclimated to the system that is in place, in practice even if not in principle, may either find it convenient to maintain elements of that order or may be unable to do otherwise, lest voters still hold them accountable to a standard they have long been socialized to expect. The roots of the system confer resilience, the more so the longer they have penetrated undisturbed.

Notes

1. PARTIES, MACHINES, AND PERSONALITIES

1. Warren Fernandez, "PAP Stance on Upgrading Opposition Wards," *Straits Times* (Singapore), 23 December 1996.

2. However ironic in retrospect, the main threats he identified to that competitive system were Singapore's weak economy and uncertain prospects.

3. Dominant parties are found across regime types—for instance, liberal-democratic Japan's LDP. Dunleavy recommends defining dominant parties per meeting three simultaneous criteria: voters' perception of their exceptional efficacy, their laying claim to a protected core within the ideological spectrum, and their appealing to more voters than their rivals (2010, 23–24). Curbing information and association helps a party sustain that niche and image, hence the greater share of dominant parties among illiberal regimes.

4. My reference to "political culture" differs from that of a "requisites of democratization" literature. While that literature homes in on, for instance, the adaptability of Muslim, Confucian, or other societies to democratic norms, or on "traditional" loyalties unconducive to a vibrant civil society or strong parties (Hinnebusch 2006, 375–76), I operationalize culture as a dynamic process: *acculturation* toward a particular mode of politics. Others have noted the difficulty of sustaining a broader argument on the compatibility of "Asian values" and liberalism (e.g., Rodan 1997, 166–69); my argument does not require such an assumption.

5. As Grzymala-Busse notes, durability entails not just duration, but also turmoil and likely persistence (2010, 1279).

6. This book complements several years' comparative research into political networks and resource flows in the context of Southeast Asian elections, in collaboration with Edward Aspinall, Allen Hicken, and Paul Hutchcroft.

7. This pattern is a variant on what Cox and McCubbins term *morselization* (2001, 47), or carving up the "carcass" of government policies into smaller projects distributed per "a political rather than an economic logic."

8. What are now the Malaysian states of Sabah and Sarawak, on the island of Borneo, were administered separately from Malaya. They joined the federation in 1963, with Singapore.

9. This pattern is not unique, though impetuses vary. Taiwan, for instance, substituted appointment for election of township executives in 1997 as part of postdemocratization constitutional changes, in an effort to check organized crime and vote buying (Jacobs 1997, 156).

10. In contrast, across Africa, for instance, clientelism tends not to be channelled through party machines (LeBas 2011, 35).

11. While likely inefficient and conducive to corruption, clientelist linkages are not antithetical to a sincere commitment to growth; Jesudason (1997, 148) describes a model of "developmental clientelism" combining an orientation prioritizing high growth and stability with cronyism and rent seeking.

12. Interview, Khairy Jamaluddin, 6 March 2015, Washington, DC.

13. Commissioned survey, conducted by the Merdeka Center for Opinion Research; $n = 1,110$.

14. Interview, Jeannette Chong-Aruldoss, 11 January 2016, Singapore.

15. Restraints on campaign practices may remain, too. For instance, worries about "overheated elections" and corruption have justified maintaining regulations that protect South Korean party elites from challengers (Mobrand 2015).

16. Clientelism, for instance, is an informal institution; abuse of power is more likely to be simply noninstitutional behavior.

17. While Levitsky and Way (among other scholars) label Singapore borderline authoritarian, the regime fits awkwardly with their definition (2010, 6–7, 34) given its limited coercion or fraud, and because opposition parties operate openly and earnestly; their leaving many seats uncontested has reflected both constraints and strategy. Levitsky and Way place pre-2018 Malaysia, too, among "the most *formally* authoritarian" of competitive authoritarian regimes, as measured by laws on the books (2010, 321). Howard and Roessler categorize Singapore as competitive until 2001, then hegemonic (2006, 369).

18. I use the term *cadre party* here as Singaporean parties commonly do: as having a limited, vetted set of full members; a *mass party*, in contrast, is one open to all members (or all who meet ethnic, religious, or other criteria). These uses differ from Duverger's original social-class distinction, in which cadre parties cater to the higher echelons, and mass parties, to the working class (Gunther and Diamond 2003, 170–71).

19. Self-interest played a role: among those minorities were Europeans and Eurasians.

2. REGIMES AND RESILIENCE RECONCEPTUALIZED

1. Under SNTV, voters select only one candidate and may not rank other candidates in case their first choice is eliminated.

2. A short-lived anti-LDP coalition government enacted the shift to encourage small parties to combine, lessen the entrenched advantages of the LDP, and spur interparty contests rather than the often patronage-laden, personalistic competition SNTV fosters by rendering party mates rivals (Krauss and Pekkanen 2011, 16–17; Reed, Scheiner, and Thies 2012, 356, 361). While the party as a whole stood to benefit from introducing single-member districts, specific MPs resisted change, consistently sinking proposals for anything but "microlevel" electoral reforms (McElwain 2008, 32–33).

3. Once in office, this coalition negotiated with the LDP to introduce MMM rules in 1994. The Diet also partially addressed urban-rural malapportionment and passed campaign finance reforms (Krauss and Pekkanen 2011, 22–25).

4. In part for fear of international backlash, the ruling KMT responded to prodemocracy protests with elections in the 1990s rather than a serious crackdown (Levitsky and Way 2010).

5. However commonly done, labeling one-time electoral interactions (e.g., vote buying) as clientelism risks stretching the concept (Hilgers 2011, 568).

6. Other parties had or have kōenkai but rely more on party-based mass organizations or labor unions than does the LDP (Krauss and Pekkanen 2011, 18).

7. Diet factions (*keiretsu*)—led by senior party veterans who trade political and financial benefits for exclusive, public support in their quest for party/government leadership—grew entrenched in that same early period of the LDP. A key factor was that around one-third of national resources distributed to localities were in a public works fund lacking objective criteria; MPs benefited from having access to lobby the center for consideration. Factions and kōenkai are mutually reinforcing (Krauss and Pekkanen 2011, 18, 100–2, 277–82; Hutchcroft 2014, 181). Taiwan (especially the KMT) likewise has fixed, named factions, "forming a chain of dyadic relationships linking leaders to voters," similarly traceable to the particular history of state-society relations (Bosco 1992, 157–58).

8. Many African unaffiliated or swing voters vote on incumbents' performance, too (Weghorst and Lindberg 2013).

3. THE CONVOLUTED POLITICAL PATH TO MALAYSIA

1. The MCP pursued a democratic republic via "bourgeois democratic revolution" through the end of World War II, then a people's republic via armed struggle. Peaceful negotiation in the mid-1950s gave way to a return to militancy in 1961 (Hara 2016, 132–34). In talks with the United Kingdom, Malaya, and Singapore in 1955, MCP leader Chin Peng requested that his party be legally recognized and able to compete; he was rebuffed (Chin Peng 2003, 377). He also offered to end the insurgency if the Alliance coalition could wrest control over internal security and defense from the British. Tunku Abdul Rahman promised to try; the deal expedited Britain's grant of independence so as to cut short the conflict. Claiming denial of a follow-up meeting with the Tunku (as Malaysia's first prime minister is commonly called), the MCP reneged (Cheah 2006, 639).

2. Singapore was concerned, too, over the effect of Bruneian A. M. Azahari's revolutionary movement on Malays in Singapore and Malaya. National Archives Singapore, Oral History Centre (NAS OHC), interview, Richard Corridon, 6 August 1981, accession no. 000044/10.

3. The earliest such efforts were ad hoc committees, then a standing municipal body, at the turn of the nineteenth century in Penang, with members selected (or partly elected) by and from among an elite slice of the population; formal municipal elections followed, Straits Settlements–wide, in 1857 (Sim and Koay 2015a).

4. The National Archives (TNA): CO 717/186/11, memo and enclosure from Gurney to Higham, 1 March 1950.

5. For instance, the attorney general's office wondered if Malaya should set up an elections commission as in India, prompting a survey of practice across the Commonwealth: TNA: CO 1030/24, Elections Commission for Federation of Malaya elections, correspondence and minutes, January/February 1955.

6. The sultan of Kedah, for one, expressed "certain doubts generally" about elections. TNA: CO 717/186/11, extract from Proceedings of the Tenth Meeting of the Conference of Rulers, 22–23 February 1950.

7. *Penghulu* have been civil service appointees since the late 1980s–90s, but both the relevant sultan and the UMNO district head have retained significant informal say. Interview, Saifuddin Abdullah, 22 December 2015, Kuala Lumpur.

8. TNA: CO 717/190/2, Legal report by attorney general, "The Local Authorities Elections Ordinance, 1950. Ordinance No. 52 of 1950," 15 May 1951; Norris 1980, 10–13; Hawkins 1953, 156.

9. "Twenty-Two Towns," *Straits Budget*, 4 June 1950; TNA: CO 717/186/11, despatch from Gurney to Griffiths, 9 April 1950.

10. TNA: CO 717/186/11, extract from Legislative Council Proceedings, 14 June 1950.

11. TNA: CO 1022/296, "Village and Town Councils in Malaya" [19 May 1952]; Strauch 1981, 126–28. By the end of 1954, terrorist incidents had declined to an average of one per week; two years later, civilian deaths still totaled over 2,300, almost three-fourths of them Chinese, plus over 6,200 guerrillas, over 90 percent Chinese. By 1957, Britain adjudged the Malayan government able to manage the situation with British/Commonwealth backup (Cowen 1958, 64).

12. Per a proud essay in the MCA newsletter, "These new villages may appropriately be described as 'babies' (in the diplomatic sense) of the MCA. It is thus the duty of the MCA to help these new villages to 'grow up' and take their proper place in the Malaysian nation" (Teh 2007 [1971], 3). The MCA *did* help—for instance, "prodding the Alliance" to begin including new villages in rural development plans in 1962 (Milne 1963, 81).

13. TNA: CO 1022/296, notes from paper by Secretary for Chinese Affairs, Johore, "Village Councils"; Bill for Village Councils Ordinance, 1952 and cover letter from

Hannyngton, 9 April 1952; Report of the Select Committee on the Village Councils Bill, 1952, Leg Co Tabled Paper for 23/4/52, No. 40 of 1952, Federation of Malaya; "Malaya Rural Slums to Go," *Daily Telegraph*, 3 May 1952; CO 717/186/11, despatch from Gurney to Griffiths, 9 April 1950.

14. TNA: CO 1022/298, Report on Local Government by H. Bedale, minutes.

15. Supplemental legislation governed Sarawak (the Local Authority Ordinance of 1948) and Sabah (the Local Government Ordinance of 1961), as well as Kuala Lumpur (the Federal Capital Act 1960) (WDC 2008, 20).

16. TNA: CO 1022/296, enclosures to letter from MacGillivray, 4 February 1953.

17. TNA: DO 187/32, Terence J. O'Brien, "Child's Guide to North Borneo Political Party Life," [15 July 1963].

18. TNA: CO 1030/219, savingram no. 55/54, from high commissioner, 13 January 1954.

19. TNA: CO 717/186/11, "Elections in Johor," 12 October 1950.

20. TNA: CO 1030/219, Elections to Councils of State and Settlement Councils, record of meeting, 10 February 1954, Kuala Lumpur.

21. TNA: 1030/223, extract from Federation of Malay a Monthly Political Report for February 1955.

22. "An Election Scandal," *Straits Budget*, 4 November 1954.

23. TNA: CO 1030/233, despatch no. 311/55, from MacGillivray, High Commissioner, 16 March 1955; TNA: CO 717/186/11, Report of the Select Committee of the Council of State, Johore, Council Paper No. 7/1950; e.g., "Alliance Triumph," *Straits Budget*, 14 October 1954; Tinker 1956, 269.

24. TNA: CO 717/186/11, memo and enclosure from Gurney to Higham, 1 March 1950; CO 1022/296, "Village and Town Councils in Malaya" [19 May 1952]; Cowen 1958, 53.

25. TNA: FCO 141/7413, "A Note on Electoral Arrangements in the Federation of Malaya with Particular Regard to the Racial Composition of the Population," 21 March 1955; Rabushka 1970, 348–49.

26. TNA: CO 1030/309, Petition to the High Commissioner et al., from UMNO and MCA, 14 February 1954; "Convention to Petition Rulers," *Straits Budget*, 18 February 1954; petition to the High Commissioner, et al., 19 March 1954, and subsequent correspondence, April/May 1954.

27. TNA: CO 1030/309, telegram no. 62 from Secretary of State for Colonies, 15 May 1954.

28. TNA: CO 1030/309, "Membership of Malaya Legislative Council," *Times* (London), 15 May 1954.

29. TNA: CO 1030/309, telegram no. 418 from Templer, 26 May 1954; telegram no. 465 from MacGillivray, 14 June 1954; telegram no. 488 from MacGillivray, 20 June 1954; CO 1030/310, letter from MacGillivray, 25 June 1954; and subsequent correspondence regarding nominated association members.

30. TNA: CO 1030/310, UMNO-MCA Alliance press release, 7 July 1954.

31. TNA: CO 1030/314, memorandum from Devaser, 19 August 1953. The MCA likewise worried reserving seats for non-Malays would aggravate communalism. TNA: CO 717/186/12, Malacca Branch of the MCA, Memorandum on Proposed Electoral Scheme for the Federal Legislative Council and for State and Settlement Legislatures, 19 May 1951.

32. TNA: CO 1022/299, letter from Lennox-Boyd to Wyatt, 30 January 1952; Radio Malaya press statement transcripts, January 1952; report on the Introduction of Elections in the Municipality of George Town, Penang, 1951 [cover memo dated 7 March 1952]; CO 717/186/12, "Note on Municipal Elections in Malaya" [August 1951].

33. TNA: CO 717/186/12, Radio Malaya press statement D. Inf. 6/51/5 (BCST), 1 June 1951; Radio Malaya press statement, 21 June 1951.

34. TNA: CO 717/186/12, Radio Malaya press statement, 27 June 1951.

35. TNA: CO 717/186/12, Malacca government press statement, 2 June 1951.

36. TNA: CO 1022/299, report by G. Hawkins, Supervisor of Elections, "Elections in Malaya."

37. For instance, TNA: CO 1022/296, *Local Councils* (leaflet), Kuala Lumpur: Department of Information, Federation of Malaya, December 1952.

38. "The Voter in K.L.," *Straits Times*, 7 July 1951.

39. TNA: CO 717/186/12, extract from Monthly Review of Chinese Affairs, Issue No. 53, Copy No. 7, June 1951.

40. TNA: CO 717/186/12, extract from Ex. Co. Mins. of Meeting, 3 July 1951.

41. "The Voter in K.L.," *Straits Times*, 7 July 1951; "K.L. Seeks a Wider Franchise," *Straits Times*, 28 June 1951.

42. "The Voiceless and Voteless," *Straits Budget*, 2 August 1951.

43. TNA: CO 1022/299, report by G. Hawkins, Supervisor of Elections, "Elections in Malaya"; CO 717/186/12, extract from Monthly Review of Chinese Affairs, issue no. 53, copy no. 7, June 1951. These arguments of Chinese disinterest, by policymakers and analysts alike (e.g., Carnell 1954, 232) seemed to conflate grievance and exclusion with apathy; many of the same observers also noted greater Chinese support for the banned MCP.

44. TNA: CO 717/186/12, extract from *Monthly Review of Chinese Affairs*, issue no. 53, copy no. 7, June 1951.

45. TNA: CO 1030/223, despatch no. 311/55, from MacGillivray, High Commissioner, 16 March 1955; extract from Federation of Malaya Monthly Political Report for February 1955.

46. TNA: FCO 141/7413, "Report of the Committee appointed to examine the question of Elections to the Federal Legislative Council," Kuala Lumpur: Government Press, 1954; Watherston, "A Note on Electoral Arrangements in the Federation of Malaya with Particular Regard to the Racial Composition of the Population," 21 March 1955.

47. TNA: FCO 141/7413, Letter from MacGillivray to MacKintosh, 13 April 1955; Tinker 1956, 260.

48. TNA: FCO 141/7413, telegram no. 338, 17 June 1955, and no. 438, 28 July 1955; despatch no. 958/55, 8 August 1955; Tinker 1956, 277–79.

49. TNA: FCO 141/7413, telegram no. 438, 28 July 1955; despatch no. 958/55, 8 August 1955.

50. For instance, after some Malays left UMNO for Singapore's multiracial People's Action Party in the mid-1950s, UMNO floated the idea of a pro-merger alliance with the People's Action Party in 1959. Lee Kuan Yew was receptive, but not other party leaders. By 1964, UMNO leaders in Kuala Lumpur were stirring up communalism in Singapore (ending in race riots), fearing that if too many Malays embraced the People's Action Party, UMNO Singapore would fail. NAS OHC, interview, Lee Khoon Choy, 20 April 1981, accession no. 000022/42; NAS OHC, interview, Othman Wok, 20 January and 17 February 1982, accession no. 000133/8, /13.

51. Chinese stood to gain from the Malayan Union plan but failed to organize in favor, nor did any other organized political groups, due either to disinterest or caution (Cowen 1958, 52; Khong 2003, 136–37).

52. Interview, Mahathir Mohamad, 10 October 2016, Putrajaya.

53. TNA: CO 537/2174, ref. no. (2A) in M.U. Secret 92/7, 10–12 January 1947; CO 1022/183, extract from PMR no. 9, September 1951 (orig. 55404/6/1951).

54. Fundraising efforts to support six Singaporean Malays sentenced to death for rioting in 1950 catalyzed that branch. TNA: CO 1022/183, extract from PMR, September 1951, April 1952, May 1952.

55. Launched in 1945 and part of UMNO for the latter's first three months in 1946, the Malayan Nationalist Party "ceased overt existence" upon several leaders' arrest in late 1948 for alleged communist sympathies (Tinker 1956, 275).

56. TNA: CO 1022/183, extract from PMR, May 1952; CO 537/6020, extract from Political Summary, August 1950; Chin Peng 2003, 155.

57. TNA: CO 537/6020, extract from Federation of Malaya Political Report, February 1950 (orig. 5298/22/50); CO 537/6020, extract from PMR, 27 September 1950.

58. TNA: CO 537/6020, letter from Gurney, 19 May 1950.

59. Interview, Musa Hitam, 28 July 2015, Kuala Lumpur.

60. TNA: CO 537/2174, ref. no. (2A) in M.U. Secret 92/7, 10–12 January 1947.

61. TNA: DO 35/9922, savingram no. 129, 17 June 1958; Weiss 2006, 62.

62. TNA: CO 537/6020, extract from PMR no. 5/50-31/5/50.

63. TNA: DO 35/9922, savingram no. 129, 17 June 1958.

64. TNA: CO 537/6020, extract from Federation of Malaya Political Report, February 1950 and May [1950] (orig. 5298/22/50).

65. TNA: CO 537/7297, extract from PMR 4/1951 [1951].

66. TNA: CO 537/6020, letter from Onn to Gurney, 26 June 1950. Malays had participated actively in anticommunist efforts, through the Malay regiment and police forces (Wade 2009, 15). Onn also proposed in a rather snarky "little billet-doux" that the British send the Band of the Federation of Malaya Police to perform across the United Kingdom to educate the British people about Malaya. Colonial officials looked into the proposal, but nothing seems to have come of it. TNA: CO 537/6020, letter from Onn to Griffiths and subsequent correspondence, late 1950.

67. TNA: CO 1022/183, extract from PMR, July 1952; Malay and Indonesian Affairs (undated).

68. "Siti Ramah: A Women's Movement Leader's Sacrifice for Merdeka," 26 August 2010, http://malaysiandigest.com/archived/index.php/15-features/personality/24950-siti -rahmah-a-womens-movement-leaders-sacrifice-for-merdeka.html (accessed 29 September 2017).

69. TNA: CO 717/186/11, despatch from Gurney to Griffiths, 9 April 1950.

70. TNA: CO 537/620, letter from Gurney, 19 May 1950; TNA: CO 717/186/11, "Proposal to Permit the United Malays National Organisation to Elect Candidates to Seats in the Federal Legislative Council," [1950].

71. TNA: CO 537/7297, extract from PMR no. 1, 31 January 1951.

72. TNA: CO 537/2174, ref. no. (2A) in M.U. Secret 92/7, 10–12 January 1947.

73. TNA: CO 537/7297, extract from PMR no. 1, 31 January 1951; CO 537/7297, extract from PMR 2/1951.

74. TNA: DO 35/9922, despatch from Tory, 7 September 1959.

75. TNA: CO 537/620, extract from PMR no. 7/1950, 26 July 1950.

76. TNA: DO 35/9922, despatches from Tory, 18 July 1958 and 7 September 1959; Weiss 2006, 75–76.

77. Interviews, Chong Ton Sin, 24 December 2015, 2 January 2016, Petaling Jaya.

78. Interview, Syed Husin Ali, 5 August 2015, Petaling Jaya.

79. That stipulation delayed registration—although colonial authorities themselves noted the ruling's indefensibility. TNA: DO 35/9919, extract from Malayan Fortnightly Summary no. 11 (17–30 January 58), 31 January 1959; extract from Malayan Fortnightly Summary no. 12 (30/1–13/2/58), 14 February 1958; extract from Penang Summary no. 21, 30 July 1958; extract from savingram no. 168, Malayan Fortnightly Summary, 1 August 1958; extract from savingram no. 241, Penang Fortnightly Summary no. 24, 21/9– 18/10/58; Weiss 2006, 93–99.

80. TNA: DO 35/9919, extract from savingram no. 241, Penang Fortnightly Summary no. 24, 21/9–18/10/58.

81. Interview, Syed Husin Ali, 5 August 2015, Petaling Jaya; Cheah 2006, 640.

82. TNA: DO 35/9918, savingram no. 170, 21 October 1959; TNA: DO 35/9918, extract from Malayan Fortnightly Summary, 1–13 March 1960.

83. TNA: DO 35/9918, extract from savingram no. 238, 23/10/58.

84. TNA: DO 187/56, Jesselton, "Sabah: Political Parties: Brief for Visit of Minister of State for Commonwealth Relations, August 1964," 19 August 1964.

85. Interview, Rahman Dahlan, 1 August 2016, Putrajaya.

86. TNA: DO 187/32, Memorandum for Submission to the Inter-Governmental Committee on Malaysia, 29 August 1962; Terence J O'Brien, "Child's Guide to North Borneo Political Party Life" [15 July 1963]; Crouch 1996, 50–51.

87. TNA: DO 187/32, Terence J O'Brien, "Child's Guide to North Borneo Political Party Life" [15 July 1963].

88. TNA: CO 537/2174, letter from Onn Jaafar to Edward Gent, 17 February 1947.

89. "Chinese, Eurasians, Indians Join UMNO," *Straits Budget*, 23 February 1950.

90. TNA: CO 537/7297, extract from PMR 4/1951.

91. *Merdeka* then remained the slogan until the party's twentieth-fifth anniversary celebration in 1971, when it was dropped in favor of "Unity, Loyalty, Service." TNA: FCO 24/1156, Letter from Dunn to Sullivan, 12 May 1971.

92. TNA: CO 537/7297, extract from PMR 7/1951, PMR 2/1951.

93. TNA: CO 537/7297, letter from Gurney to Higham, 29 August 1951.

94. TNA: CO 1030/315, "Statement Issued by the Central Executive Committee of Party Negara," 26 April 1954; Party Negara, Statement of Policy, 23 May 1954.

95. TNA: CO 1030/315, Onn bin Jaafar, Radio Malaya Press Statement, 5 July 1955.

96. TNA: CO 1030/313, "Memorandum Submitted by the Labour Party of Malaya to the Alliance Merdeka Mission," 29 December 1955; minute by Cahill, 5 January 1956.

97. TNA: CO 1030/312, Special Branch report, "Tunku Abdul Rahman: President of U.M.N.O." [14 March 1955]. Divvying up Alliance executive seats in 1958—ultimately six UMNO, five MCA, three MIC—the Tunku argued that if MCA representation were lower, UMNO would have to bear more coalition expenses, which it could ill afford. TNA: DO 35/9922, despatch from Tory, 18 July 1958.

98. TNA: FCO 141/7413, Watherston, "A Note on Electoral Arrangements in the Federation of Malaya with Particular Regard to the Racial Composition of the Population," 21 March 1955.

99. TNA: DO 359922, despatch from Tory, 7 September 1959.

100. TNA: CO 717/186/12, Malacca Branch of the MCA, "Memorandum on Proposed Electoral Scheme for the Federal Legislative Council and for State and Settlement Legislatures," 19 May 1951.

101. "K.L. Elections: Women Will Have a Big Say," *Straits Times*, 10 August 1951. That a property qualification for voting included in Singapore's 1948 Municipal Elections Ordinance was almost immediately abolished, in part because its effect was to disenfranchise housewives, indicates a similar concern there to encourage women's vote. "Twenty-Two Towns," *Straits Budget*, 4 June 1950.

102. TNA: CO 1030/307, despatch from Templer, 4 May 1954 and Director of Intelligence's statement, 21 July 1956; CO 1030/306, letter from MacGillivray, 1 June 1955.

103. TNA: CO 537/7297, letter from Onn to Gurney, 6 January 1951.

104. TNA: CO 537/7297, letter from Gurney, 17 January 1951.

105. TNA: CO 537/7297, extract from PMR 7/1951.

106. "The Alliance Wins Again," *Straits Budget*, 4 November 1954.

107. Resettlements aimed to kickstart export-oriented agriculture; slow migration to ill-prepared cities; create a progressive, proactive "new rural elite"; and reduce poverty. Criteria for selection included age (21–45), being married and landless, and following ethnic and Pahang-state-specific quotas (Lhériteau 2005, 317–29). Women could not apply directly to be settlers, though FELDA eventually came to recognize them as co-owners rather than merely wives or daughters (Rashila 2005, 132).

108. In Sarawak, the district officer—a civil servant—managed security, police, medical care, immigration, and more through the 1960s, connecting closely with the (indirectly elected) legislative council. It was not until after 1970 that politicians became more involved; by then, local elections had ceased (interview, Leo Moggie, 13 January 2016, Kuala Lumpur).

109. A small but important incident: the Tunku ordered the national flag to be displayed at the end of the Emergency, 31 July 1960. George Town's Socialist Front–led council refused. The Penang state government amended the Municipal Ordinance, granting itself power to compel the council to conform on issues of state or national importance (Sim and Koay 2015b, 16).

110. That said, the Alliance performed better in Penang and Ipoh's 1961 local elections than in 1959's parliamentary elections there (Smith 1962, 154).

111. District officers appoint *ketua kampung*, with input from the party and local MP. Interview, Nur Jazlan Mohamed, 6 January 2015, Kuala Lumpur.

112. The government added *Rukun Tetangga* (Neighborhood Watch) in the 1970s, to involve "all able-bodied male adults in neighbourhood security" (Cheah 2002, 132).

113. Interview, Saifuddin Abdullah, 22 December 2015, Kuala Lumpur; Funston 2016, 41, 133n22. More recently, Pakatan Rakyat–led opposition state governments appointed some non–party member *ketua kampung* and JKKK members, but generally where they lacked strong party leaders. Interview, Ronnie Liu, 20 July 2015, Petaling Jaya.

114. Interview, Musa Hitam, 28 July 2015, Kuala Lumpur.

115. TNA: FCO 141/13006, Secretariat, North Borneo, Paper for the Malaysia Commission of Enquiry No. 4/62, 29 March 1962.

116. Interview, Teng Chang Yeow, 3 January 2015, George Town, Penang; Ho 1992, 7–9.

117. TNA: FCO 141/13006, Secretariat, North Borneo, Paper for the Malaysia Commission of Enquiry No. 4/62, 29 March 1962.

118. Interview, Syed Husin Ali, 5 August 2015, Petaling Jaya.

119. Interview, Chong Ton Sin, 24 December 2015, Petaling Jaya; Chin and Por 2018.

120. Interviews, Musa Hitam, 28 July 2015, Kuala Lumpur; and Leo Moggie, 13 January 2016, Kuala Lumpur.

4. EDGING TOWARD SOVEREIGN SINGAPORE

1. A proposal for "civil centres" to house child welfare clinics, libraries, and more, "tactfully directing the growing enthusiasm into the proper channels" without incurring debts to "rich merchants" as funders, went unfulfilled—but foreshadowed later community centers. The National Archives (TNA): CO 717/182/5, memorandum by chairman, Rural Board, Singapore, 29 March 1949; letter from Gimson to Higham, 25 April 1949.

2. TNA: CO 717/182/5, letter from Gimson to Higham, 25 April 1949; CO FCO 141/14970, Council of Ministers Paper no. (58)86; joint memorandum: District Council Elections, 10 February 1958; Singapore Government Press Statement, text of talk by M. P. D. Nair over Radio Malaya, 5 March 1958; Director of Information Services, "Political Parties Participation in District Elections" [30 April 1958]; telegram no. 198, 27 May 1958.

3. TNA: CO 953/6/6, letter from Hill to Scarlett, 20 April 1951.

4. TNA: CO 1022/320, "The Colony of Singapore: Report of Special Commissioner, Dr. L. C. Hill, C.B.E. on the Reform of Local Government," 29 November 1951; "'Scrap S.I.T.' Plan to Be Discussed," *Straits Times*, 16 February 1952.

5. TNA: CO 1022/91, letter from Paskin to Nicoll, 9 December 1952; minute from Paskin to Lloyd, 5 March 1953.

6. "Governor Explains How Council Will Be Formed," *Straits Times*, 16 May 1947, p. 1.

7. The report invoked the Legislative Council of the Straits Settlements, inaugurated in 1921, which included two members elected by British members of the Singapore and Penang Chambers of Commerce so as to align "merchants" with government, per Raffles's founding vision. TNA: FCO 141/16888, P. A. B. McKerron et al., "Report of the Committee appointed by His Excellency the Governor of Singapore to make recommendations for the reconstitution of the Legislative Council of the Colony," Singapore: Government Printing Office, August 1946; Colony of Singapore, Supplement to the Government Gazette, 18 July 1947, Singapore Legislative Council Elections Ordinance, 1947; "Governor Explains How Council Will Be Formed," *Straits Times*, 16 May 1947.

8. TNA: CO 953/1/7, minute by Morris, 30 August 1948.

9. TNA: CO 953/1/7, extract from Legislative Council Proceedings, 15 June 1948; G. Hawkins, "Comments on the Bill to amend the Singapore Legislative Council Elections Ordinance," 1 June 1948.

10. "'Members' for Singapore," *Straits Budget* 18 October 1951.

11. TNA: CO 1022/92, despatch by Paskin, 4 May 1953; letters from Lloyd to Jackson, 11 May 1953, and Waddington, 16 June 1953.

12. National Archives Singapore, Oral History Centre (NAS OHC), interviews, S. Rajaratnam, 20 July 1982, accession no. 000149/09; Tan Chee Khoon, 22 March 1986, 000645/01; Pang 1971, 18–19; Yap, Lim, and Leong 2009, 264–74.

13. TNA: CO 953/1/7, G. Hawkins, "Report on Singapore Elections, 1947–1948," no. 5 of 1948, 23 July 1948; FCO 141/16888, telegram no. 820, 25 October 1947; P. A. B. McKerron et al., "Report of the Committee appointed . . . for the Reconstitution of the Legislative Council of the Colony," Singapore: Government Printing Office, August 1946; Carnell 1954, 216.

14. TNA: FCO 141/16888, G. Hawkins, "Electoral Registration in Singapore. Factors Affecting Response of Voters," 1947.

15. TNA: FCO 141/16888, telegram no. 214, 23 March 48; "63 Per Cent Voters Go to Poll," *Sunday Times*, 21 March 1948; http://www.singapore-elections.com/general-election /1948/, accessed 3 January 2017; TNA: CO 953/1/7, G. Hawkins, "Report on Singapore Elections, 1947–1948," no. 5 of 1948, 23 July 1948.

16. TNA: CO 537/5959, extract from Singapore Political Situation Report for July [1950], orig. 55404/4/50.

17. TNA: CO 1022/384, extract from Singapore Political Reports for November 1951 and December 1951; Carnell 1954, 218.

18. Elections had been suspended in the interim—the incumbents' terms were extended—while the Rendel and other committees completed their work. http://www .singapore-elections.com/city-election/1953/, accessed 5 January 2017.

19. TNA: CO 1030/713, Council of Ministers, "Returning Officer's Report on the City Council Elections—December 1957," Council of Ministers Paper No. (58)56, 25 January 1958.

20. TNA: CO 1030/702, savingram no. 116, 27 December 1957.

21. Ibid.

22. TNA: CO 1030/638, despatch from Goode, 12 June 1959.

23. "Votes for Cash Gangs Threaten S'pore Election," *Straits Times*, 10 November 1953. That year, too, City Council sought to stiffen the residency requirement for candidates to

disqualify "birds of passage," after one from India absconded to escape criminal prosecution. TNA: CO 1022/384, General Department, "Colonial Constitutional Note: Residential Qualifications for Members of the Singapore City Council," December 1953.

24. NAS OHC, interview, Fong Sip Chee, 8 July 1980, accession no. 000024/12.

25. NAS OHC, interview, 10 August 1982, accession no. 000215/11.

26. Secret (or triad) societies had long supported new immigrants and helped organize Chinese-community life but were suppressed after 1890. Dialect- and class-based associations took over some functions, then the Straits Chinese Business Association and Singapore Chinese Chamber of Commerce, launched in 1900 and 1906, respectively, assumed economic and community leadership functions (Chan 1976, 82–84). For more on Singapore's early associational life, see Weiss 2006, chap. 3.

27. TNA: FCO 141/14783, minute by Goodwin, 4 January 1958; note by Goode, 2 January 1958.

28. TNA: CO 1030/702, savingram no. 116, 27 December 1957. Meanwhile, the PAP was delayed in electing its first mayor after winning City Council due to rowdy supporters who packed the council chamber.

29. TNA: CO 1022/384, "Report of the Committee appointed to enquire into the Registration of Electors and the Conduct of the Elections," 27 July 1953.

30. TNA: CO FCO 141/14860, S. H. D. Elias et al., "Report of the Commission of Inquiry into Corrupt, Illegal or Undesirable Practices at Elections," Singapore: Government Printing Office, 1958.

31. TNA: CO 1030/639, Council of Ministers, "The Legislative Assembly Elections (Amendment) Bill," CM Paper No. (58)797, 17 November 1958.

32. TNA: CO 1030/639, Council of Ministers, "Compulsory Voting," CM Paper No. (58)76, 17 November 1958; also telegrams, notes, memos, 19–29 April 1958.

33. For example, TNA: FCO 141/14860, "Tan Feng-ming" (translation/summary), *Sin Chew Jit Poh*, 23 January 1958; Patricia Morgan, "A Compulsory Voting Shock for Lim," *Straits Times*, 28 January 1958; "Matters of Moment," *Singapore Tiger Standard*, 29 January 1958; "Chamber Backs Compulsory Voting," *Singapore Standard*, 1 February 1958; "Europeans Favour Compulsory Vote," *Straits Times*, 5 February 1958.

34. TNA: CO 1030/639, Council of Ministers, "Compulsory Voting," CM Paper No. (58)76, 17 November 1958. Already by 1951, over one-third of registered voters were untraceable (Carnell 1954, 217).

35. TNA: CO 1030/639, Council of Ministers, "Compulsory Voting," CM Paper No. (58)76, 17 November 1958; FCO 141/14860, Singapore Government Press Statement, text of speech by the chief minister, Tun Lim Yew Hock, 26 January 1959.

36. "'Must Vote' Penalties Are Attacked," *Sunday Times*, 28 December 1958, p. 11.

37. TNA: CO 1030/639, letter from Goode, 15 April 1959.

38. TNA: CO 1030/639, minute by Hennings, 4 February 1959.

39. TNA: CO 1030/639, letter from Goode, 15 April 1959; TNA: FCO 141/14860 [Goode], note on discussion with the chief minister, 3 April 1958.

40. TNA: CO 1030/704, Special Branch report, ref: OF 1508, "Workers' Party Public Protest Meeting Against Proposed Introduction of Compulsory Voting and Postponement of the Legislative Assembly Elections," 28 March 1958.

41. NAS OHC, interview, Gerald De'Cruz, 4 June 1982, accession no. 000105/20; TNA: FCO 141/14860, Note from Goode, 24 January 1958.

42. "Compulsory Vote? Yes" *Straits Times*, 10 March 1958, pp. 1–2; "Call for Compulsory Polls," *Singapore Standard*, 4 August 1958.

43. "The Lib-Socs Support Compulsory Voting," *Straits Times*, 13 March 1958, p. 4.

44. TNA: CO 1030/639, savinggram no. 142, 18 December 1958.

45. "Inche Hamid: 'Serious Action if Compulsory Vote Is Approved,'" *Straits Times* 24 April 1958, p. 1; "'Must Vote' Law to Force 700,000 Electors," *Straits Times*, 28 November 1958, p. 4.

46. TNA: CO 1030/639, savinggram no. 142, 18 December 1958.

47. "Preparing for Elections," *Straits Times*, 7 January 1959.

48. Europeans in particular stayed home, for fear of disturbances (which did not materialize). TNA: CO 1030/638, despatch from Goode, 12 June 1959.

49. TNA: CO 1030/638, despatch from Goode, 12 June 1959.

50. TNA: CO 1030/638, Singapore Information Office press release, 31 May 1959; despatch from Goode, 12 June 1959.

51. TNA: CO 1030/318, letter and attachment from Nicoll to Martin, 21 February 1955; TNA: FCO 141/14598, memo from R. N. Broome, "Note on Political Parties in the Coming Election," 15 November 1954; NAS OHC, interview, John Anthony Moore Ede, 2 November 1983, accession no. 000322/06

52. NAS OHC, interview, Jumabhoy Mohamed Jumabhoy, 8 August 1983, accession nos. 000318/05, 000318/08.

53. NAS OHC, interview, Rajabali Jumabhoy, 22 July 1981, accession no. 000074/15; Bellows 1967, 128.

54. TNA: CO 1030/318, letter and attachment from Nicoll to Martin, 21 February 1955; NAS OHC, interview, Chan Kum Chee, 10 October 1983, accession no. 000341/09.

55. TNA: CO 1030/323, Singapore Local Intelligence Committee, Political Report for the Period 31 December 1955–17 January 1956; letter from Chan Kum Chee to party members, 12 January 1956.

56. NAS OHC, interview, Lee Geck Seng, 8 March 1980, accession no. 000009/08. David Marshall—not a fan—quipped that: "in England, they say, 'My Lord, the Mayor'; in Singapore, we say, 'My God! The Mayor.'" NAS OHC, interview, 27 September 1984, accession no. 000156/15.

57. Ong Eng Guan, "City Council Work," *PAP 4th Anniversary Celebration Souvenir*, November 1958, p. 25.

58. TNA: CO 1030/713, despatch from governor [Goode], 27 November 1957.

59. "New Tasks for the P.A.P.," in *Our First Ten Years: P.A.P. 10th Anniversary Souvenir*, 1964, p. 126.

60. TNA: CO 1030/318, letter and attachment from Nicoll to Martin, 21 February 1955.

61. TNA: CO 1030/702, Singapore government press statement, "Text of a Talk by the Minister for Culture, Mr. S. Rajaratnam—The Challenge of Our Times," 12 September 1959.

62. TNA: CO 1030/713, despatch from governor [Goode], under savingram no. 111, 27 November 1957; Intel report, "Singapore City Council Elections," 7 March 1958; CO 1030/702, savingram no. 116, 27 December 1957.

63. NAS OHC, interview, Fong Sip Chee, 1 July 1980, accession no. 000024/10.

64. NAS OHC, interview, Gerald De'Cruz, 25 September 1981, accession no. 000105/10.

65. "'No More Pacts with the PAP'" *Singapore Standard*, 9 January 1958.

66. For example, re: M. P. D. Nair: TNA: CO 1022/384, extract from Singapore Weekly Digest, no. 45/53, 7 November 1953; "Mr. Jumabhoy Is Given a Walk-Over in City Ward," *Straits Times*, 5 November 1953.

67. TNA: CO 1030/638, despatch from Goode, 12 June 1959.

68. J. J. Puthucheary, "Political Role of the Trade Union" *Petir* III:6, 4 January 1960, pp. 4–5.

69. "Union Jacks Removed," *Times* (London), 9 January 1958. Governor Goode chalked Ong's gestures up to "youthful exuberance" and the PAP's claim to "roots in the common

people"; overall, he found Ong had "all the markings of an outstanding leader." TNA: CO 1030/713, telegram no. 10, 22 January 1958.

70. TNA: CO 1030/318, letter and attachment from Nicoll to Martin, 21 February 1955.

71. TNA: FCO 141/14598, memo from Broome to CS, 2 October 1954; FCO 141/14598, memo from R. N. Broome, "Note on Political Parties in the Coming Election," 15 November 1954.

72. NAS OHC, interview, 25 September 1981, accession no. 000105/10.

73. Marshall thought it never exceeded four hundred. NAS OHC, interview, 25 September 1984, accession no. 000156/06.

74. NAS OHC, interviews, Jumabhoy Mohamed Jumabhoy, 21 November 1981, accession no. 000112/05; 8 August 1983, 000318/08; 10 December 1983, 000318/45; TNA: CO 1030/713, despatch from governor [Goode], 27 November 1957.

75. NAS OHC, interview, Gerald De'Cruz, 4 June 1982, accession no. 000105/20.

76. NAS OHC, interview, Jumabhoy Mohamed Jumabhoy, 22 October 1983, accession no. 000318/16.

77. NAS OHC, interview, 25 September 1984, accession no. 000156/07.

78. Ibid.

79. TNA: CO 1030/698, telegram no. 183 from Goode, 13 November 1958; SPA platform and membership form, 29 December 1958; Thomas 2015, 53–70, 81. The SPA then joined with UMNO, the MCA, and the MIC as the Singapore Alliance in mid-1963, but communal peninsular-party links alienated the coalition in Singapore; the (again reorganized) grouping won no seats and was virtually defunct by 1965 (Chan 1976, 193; Bellows 1967, 125).

80. "Lib-Socs Will Not Fight Labour Front," *Singapore Standard*, 11 March 1958.

81. A questionable election donation to an LF minister, which the PAP played up, was especially damaging (Thomas 2015, 57–70, 78–79, 87–94; Bellows 1967, 125; NAS OHC, interview, Teo Kah Leong, 3 December 1993, accession no. 001431/04).

82. TNA: CO 1030/704, Singapore Workers' Party, *Constitution* [1957].

83. NAS OHC, interview, David Marshall, 27 September 1984, accession no. 000156/15.

84. TNA: CO 1030/704, savingram no. 106, 12 November 1957.

85. TNA: CO 1030/704, report by Blades on discussion with Marshall, 14 January 1958; FCO 141/14785, letter from Marshall, 8 January 1958.

86. *The Workers' Party: 50th Anniversary Commemorative Book*, 1957–2007, pp. 21–23.

87. The PRS aimed to unite Singapore's Malays but cooperate across communities. Beset by weak leadership and ideological conflict, the PRS aligned with Barisan but remained small (Yap 2016, 11–18).

88. TNA: FCO 141/14598, memo from Blades, 14 October 1954.

89. NAS OHC, interview, Teo Seng Bee, 15 January 1987, accession no. 000736/03.

90. TNA: FCO 141/14598, memo from R. N. Broome, "Note on Political Parties in the Coming Election," 15 November 1954.

91. MCA and UMNO leaders spoke at the PAP's launch, despite their differences. TNA: CO 1030/316, supplement no. 1 to Singapore PIJ 1955, "People's Action Party," 21 June 1955.

92. TNA: FCO 141/15320, e.g., savingram no. 1544, 23 December 1957; Pang 1971, 1.

93. TNA: FCO 141/14598, memo from Blades, 14 October 1954. The name was a poser: organizers considered "Socialist Party" but wanted "People" in the title; they avoided "Singapore" since they aimed for a united Malaya, but including "Malayan" might antagonize supporters from UMNO and the MCA; they wanted to be an active party, so went with "Action." NAS OHC, interview, Lee Geck Seng, 23 February 1980, accession no. 000009/02.

94. TNA: CO 1030/702, Singapore government press statement, "Text of a Talk by the Minister for Culture, Mr. S. Rajaratnam—The Challenge of Our Times," 12 September 1959.

95. *People's Action Party 1st Anniversary Celebration Souvenir*, 27 November 1955, p. 1, 11.

96. Goh Keng Swee, "Our Economic Future," *PAP 4th Anniversary Celebration Souvenir*, November 1958, pp. 12–15.

97. Lee Kuan Yew, "Labour and Trade Unions" (from a 1 March 1959 rally speech), *The Tasks Ahead: P.A.P.'s Five-Year Plan, 1959–1964*, Part 2 [1959].

98. NAS OHC, interview, Lee Geck Seng, 13 March 1980, accession no. 000009/09; Ong Eng Guan, "Since I Became the First Mayor of Singapore," *PAP 4th Anniversary Celebration Souvenir*, November 1958, pp. 16–17.

99. TNA: FCO 141/14784, Toh Chin Chye, "The People Behind the P.A.P.," *Petir* II:5, May 1959, p. 11.

100. TNA: CO 1030/316, supplement no. 1 to Singapore PIJ 1955, "People's Action Party," 21 June 1955.

101. NAS OHC, interview, Lee Geck Seng, 23 February 1980, accession no. 000009/04.

102. NAS OHC, interview, Fong Sip Chee, 1 July 1980, accession no. 000024/08.

103. NAS OHC, interview, Ong Chang Sam, 26 July 1980, accession no. 000010/02.

104. Lee Kuan Yew, "Mr. Lee Kuan Yew Replies," *Petir* III:5, 19 December 1959, p. 4; TNA: CO 1030/713, telegram no. 10, 22 January 1958. The WP's Marshall, too, criticized media, for instance, complaining of Radio Singapore's limiting access to election broadcasts. "Don't Try to Keep Us Off Air, Marshall Warns," *Straits Times*, 15 April 1959, p. 4.

105. Goh Keng Swee, "Rectification of the English-Educated," parts I and II, *Petir* III:7, 22 January 1960, pp. 7–8 and III:9, 9 March 1960, pp. 4–5.

106. NAS OHC, interviews, Othman Wok, 17 February 1982, accession no. 000133/13; Haji Ya'acob bin Mohamed, 29 November 1986, 000747/09; TNA: CO 1030/638, despatch from Goode, 12 June 1959.

107. TNA: FCO 141/14783, memo and report from Corridon, 10 July 1956. The PAP's manifesto, for instance, barred polygamy—a bold move. NAS OHC, interview, Shirin Fozdar, 39 September 1983, accession no. 000336/14.

108. NAS OHC, interview, Lee Geck Seng, 23 February 1980, accession no. 000009/03.

109. "Policies of the Government and the Party Decided Collectively, says Toh," *Petir* III:13, 14 July 1960, p. 4.

110. Lee himself disputes that such a vote happened, insisting that had Ong wanted the position, Lee "would have happily given it to him." "Did Lee Become PM by One Vote?" *Straits Times*, 20 September 2009.

111. NAS OHC, interview, Peter Low Por Tuck, 11 January 1980, accession no. 000002/10; 16 January 1980, 000002/11; Chan 1989, 73.

112. NAS OHC, interviews, Lee Geck Seng, 8 March 1980, accession no. 000009/08; 13 March 1980, 000009/09; S. V. Lingam, 25 February 1980, 000014/03; Peter Low Por Tuck, 9 January 1980, 000002/03; Tay Kum Sun, 9 January 1980, 000011/01.

113. NAS OHC, interview, Fong Sip Chee, 1 July 1980, accession no. 000024/07.

114. Ibid.

115. NAS OHC, interview, Lee Khoon Choy, 23 June 1981, accession no. 000022/48.

116. NAS OHC, interview, Lee Geck Seng, 23 February 1980, accession no. 000009/04.

117. TNA: CO 1030/713, despatch from governor [Goode], 27 November 1957.

118. NAS OHC, interview, S. Rajaratnam, 5 August 1982, accession no. 000149/25.

119. "A New Slant on Job Security?" *Singapore Standard*, 21 March 1958.

120. TNA: FCO 141/14784, "30th May 1959—The End of an Era," *Petir* II:5, May 1959, p. 1; NAS OHC, interview, Lee Khoon Choy, 26 May 1981, accession no. 000022/42. *Petir* appeared weekly from mid-1959 through the 1960s; currently, it comes out quarterly (https://www.pap.org.sg/petir-the-lightning).

121. NAS OHC, interview, S. V. Lingam, 8 March 1980, accession no. 000014/04.

122. TNA: FCO 141/14783, Special Branch, "People's Action Party Thanksgiving Party," 28 January 1958.

123. NAS OHC, interviews, Fong Sip Chee, 28 October 1980, accession no. 000024/22; Lee Geck Seng, 8 March 1980, 000009/08.

124. TNA: CO 1030/316, extract from Singapore Local Intelligence Committee— Political Report for the Period 16–29 October 1954. Five years later, they conceded that *Petir* "does not provide any encouraging evidence for the theory that the P.A.P. is a monolithic crypto-Communist, anti-Western and Chinese chauvinist organ of dictatorship" (TNA: CO 1030/702, letter from West to Hennings, 7 December 1959).

125. NAS OHC, interview, Richard Corridon, 20 March 1982, accession no. 000044/14.

126. TNA: CO 1030/316, letters from Lee K. Y., 23 June 1956, 29 June 1956.

127. TNA: FCO 141/14783, Special Branch report on the Fourth Annual Conference of the People's Action Party held at the Singapore Badminton Hall, 4 August 1957; Chan 1989, 73.

128. "Lee's Group Is Back in Power," *Singapore Standard*, 21 October. 1957; TNA: FCO 141/14783, Special Branch report on the Special Party Conference of the People's Action Party held at the Singapore Badminton Hall, 20 October 1957

129. TNA: CO 1030/713, despatch from governor [Goode], 27 November 1957.

130. TNA: FCO 141/15320, extract from Monthly Intelligence Report No. 8, 29 May 1957.

131. TNA: CO 1030/702, letter from Turnbull to Lennox Boyd, 7 November 1957; FCO 141/17160, memo no. 244 from Selkirk to Sandys, 5 October 1962.

132. TNA: FCO 141/14783, memorandum from governor [Goode], 27 February 1958.

133. NAS OHC, interviews, S. V. Lingam, 8 March 1980, accession no. 000014/05; Fong Sip Chee, 15 July 1980, 000024/15.

134. Ong Pang Boon, "On the Question of the Selection of Cadres," *Petir* III:13, 14 July 1960, p. 8. Probably under 3 percent thereafter were cadre rather than ordinary members (Pang 1971, 23–24).

135. TNA: FCO 141/17160, report from Moore to Maulding, 12 July 1962 (Poh 2016, 241). The PAP had lost another by-election three months earlier to now-independent Ong Eng Guan. These defections involved intense left-wing intraparty lobbying to win over enough Assembly members to tip the balance. NAS OHC, interview, Dennis Bloodworth, 21 May 1982, accession no. 000166/16.

136. "Outlook Leftish," *Economist*, 1 January 1958. Lim became PAP assistant secretary-general in 1956 but was then detained from that October through 1959.

137. NAS OHC, interview, Lim Kim San, 17 April 1985, accession no. 000526/17, 000526/18.

138. NAS OHC, interviews, Lim Hock Siew, 12 July 1985, accession no. 000215/23; Peter Low Por Tuck, 18 January 1980, 000002/14, /15; Ong Chang Sam, 18 September 1980, 000010/08; Bellows 1967, 134.

139. Dennis Bloodworth suggests Barisan lured them with promises of civil service positions and perks. NAS OHC, interview, 27 May 1982, accession no. 000166/17.

140. A decade later, despite the government's arrests, raids on party headquarters and branches, suppression of secondary associations, and other efforts, Barisan still had about seven thousand members and close to thirty branches, though in a weak position to contest elections (Chan 1976, 195–201; Mutalib 2003, 83; Seah 1973, 24–27, Mauzy and Milne 2002, 42; TNA: CO 1030/1196, savingram no. 304, 17 August 1961).

141. NAS OHC, interview, Dennis Bloodworth, 27 May 1982, accession no. 000166/17.

142. NAS OHC, interviews, Dennis Bloodworth, 21 May 1982, accession no. 000166/16; Lee Geck Seng, 27 March 1980, 000009/11; TNA: FCO 141/17160, report from Moore to Maulding, 12 July 1962.

143. TNA: FCO 141/17160, letter from Goh to Moore, 29 January 1963; FCO 141/17161, *Singapore: Barisan Sosialis (Socialist Front) Party*, correspondence/minutes.

144. TNA: FCO 141/17161, Declaration of Meeting of Conveners of the Barisan Sosialis, 3 September 1961.

145. TNA: CO 1030/1196, telegram from Selkirk, 27 July 1961.

146. TNA: CO 1030/1196, savingram no. 283, 4 August 1961 (including text of 30 July 1961 statement by Lee Siew Choh and Sheng Nam Chin).

147. NAS OHC, interview, Dennis Bloodworth, 21 May 1982, accession no. 000166/16.

148. NAS OHC, interview, Lim Hock Siew, 12 July 1985, accession no. 000215/23.

149. Interview, Poh Soo Kai, 25 July 2016, Cheras; NAS OHC, interviews, Peter Low Por Tuck, 18 January 1980, accession no. 000002/15; Ong Chang Sam, 13 September 1980, accession no. 000010/12.

150. The PAP also affiliated informally with a range of less radical grassroots bodies—the Wooden Dwellers Association, the Country People's Association, cultural organizations, and so on. NAS OHC, interview, Fong Sip Chee, 15 July 1980, accession no. 000024/15.

151. Some areas where Barisan support was highest, such as Aljunied and Potong Pasir, remain opposition-leaning.

152. Interview, Poh Soo Kai, 25 July 2016, Cheras. Their hostility to the Tunku and his government made it harder for Barisan to attract prominent Malay members. NAS OHC, interview, Dennis Bloodworth, 27 May 1982, accession no. 000166/17.

153. The choices were approval or choosing federation on the same terms as either Penang and Malacca (without local control over education and labor, and possibly with their much stricter qualifications for citizenship) or the Borneo territories (still unclear). "No" was not an option; blank or unclear ballots were counted as yeses (Milne 1963, 80–81; TNA: FCO 141/17160, telegram no. 318, 3 July 1962).

154. TNA: FCO 141/17160, Report from Moore to Maulding, 12 July 1962.

155. TNA: FCO 141/17161, Speech by Lim Chin Siong on the 1st Anniversary Celebration of Barisan Sosialis, 11 November 1962.

156. TNA: FCO 141/17160, telegrams no. 43, 31 January 1962, and no. 315, 29 June 1962.

157. TNA: FCO 141/17160, telegrams no. 318, 3 July 1962; no. 324, 5 July 1962; and a flurry of telegrams that week.

158. TNA: FCO 141/17160, memo no. 244 from Selkirk to Sandys, 5 October 1962.

159. TNA: FCO 141/17160, memo by Moore to Wallace, of conversation with Lee Kuan Yew, 16 November 1962; E. M. West, "Note of a Meeting with Mr. Lee Kuan Yew," 30 November 1962.

160. See https://data.gov.sg/dataset/resident-population-by-ethnicity-gender-and-age-group, accessed 12 June 2019.

161. NAS OHC, interview, Ong Chang Sam, 13 September 1980, accession no. 000010/08.

162. NAS OHC, interview, 25 September 1983, accession no. 000341/06.

163. TNA: CO 1030/713, telegram no. 10, 22 January 1958.

164. TNA: CO 1030/638, savingram no. 138, 12 December 1958.

165. TNA: CO 1030/638, despatch from Goode, 12 June 1959.

166. *People's Action Party 1st Anniversary Celebration Souvenir*, 27 November 1955, p. 11–12.

167. Ong Eng Guan, "City Council Work," *PAP 4th Anniversary Celebration Souvenir*, November 1958, pp. 24–26.

168. NAS OHC, interview, Gerald De'Cruz, 4 June 1982, accession no. 000105/22.

169. NAS OHC, interview, Lee Geck Seng, 8 March 1980, accession no. 000009/08.

170. NAS OHC, interview, S. Rajaratnam, 5 August 1982, accession no. 000149/25.

171. TNA: 1030/318, letter from Nicoll, 21 February 1955.

172. NAS OHC, interview, S. V. Lingam, 25 February 1980, accession no. 000014/03.

173. CCMCs replaced similar bodies eliminated in 1959.

174. Among the PAP's first acts was dismissing an Asia Foundation employee in charge of CCs, to avoid CCs' being used for foreign governments' "propaganda" (or "disreputable pastimes" like mahjong). K. M. Byrne, "Our Community Centres" *Petir* III:15, 7 September 1960, p. 3.

175. Bellows 1970, 106–7; Chan 1976, 136–37; NAS OHC, interview, Lee Wai Kok, 28 December 1982, accession no. 001394/02.

176. TNA: FCO 24/925, P. M. Kelly, "National Youth Leadership Training Institute," 7 April 1970.

177. TNA: CO 1022/384, extract from Singapore political report for December 1951.

178. "After the Elections," *Straits Times*, 3 December 1951.

179. TNA: CO 1030/713, Council of Ministers, "Returning Officer's Report on the City Council Elections—December 1957," CM Paper No. (58) 56, 25 January 1958.

180. NAS OHC, interview, 2 November 1983, accession no. 000322/06.

181. NAS OHC, interviews, 21 November 1981, accession no. 000112/05; 8 August 1983, 000318/05.

182. NAS OHC, interview, 22 October 1983, accession no. 000318/16.

183. NAS OHC, interview, Lee Geck Seng, 23 February 1980, accession no. 000009/03; 8 March 1980, 000009/08; 13 March 1980, 000009/09; 14 March 1980, 000009/10.

184. NAS OHC, interview, Lee Geck Seng, 14 March 1980, accession no. 000009/10.

185. Goh Keng Swee, "My Election," *Petir* III:7, 22 January 1960, pp. 4–5.

186. NAS OHC, interview, Lim Hock Siew, 10 August 1982, accession no. 000215/11.

187. NAS OHC, interview, S. Rajaratnam, 12 July 1982, accession no. 000149/07.

188. NAS OHC, interview, 16 January 1980, accession no. 000002/11.

189. NAS OHC, interview, 17 February 1982, accession no. 000133/13.

190. NAS OHC, interview, S. Rajaratnam, 6 August 1982, accession no. 000149/27. Moreover, he realized, in hindsight, that he had won largely thanks to the groundwork of procommunist campaign workers, who treated him "as a pawn" in the course of the campaign.

191. NAS OHC, interview, Lee Khoon Choy, 20 April 1981, accession no. 000022/26; Comber 1994, 106; Tan, K. Y. L. 2008, 301.

192. His inspiration might have been either Citizens' Advice Bureaus he saw in London or the autobiography of Indian chief minister Mirza Ismail (Comber 1994, 112).

193. NAS OHC, interview, Fong Sip Chee, 8 July 1980, accession no. 000024/12.

194. Chan 1976, 106–7; "Union Jacks Removed," *Times* (London), 9 January 1958; NAS OHC, interview, Fong Sip Chee, 1 July 1980, accession no. 000024/09.

195. NAS OHC, interview, Ng Kah Ting, 2 March 1982, accession no. 000139/09.

196. NAS OHC, interview, Lee Khoon Choy, 23 June 1981, accession no. 000022/48.

197. Ibid.

198. NAS OHC, interview, 22 October 1983, accession no. 000318/18.

199. TNA: FCO 141/14784, "Pre-Election Exercises," *Petir* II:3, March 1959, p. 1.

200. TNA: FCO 141/17161, Chan Sun Wing, "Why I Quit" (transcript of speech), 13 August 1961.

201. TNA: FCO 141/17160, memo from Bloom to Radford, Moore, Selkirk, 6 December 1962.

202. TNA: FCO 141/17160, M. Revell, report, "Lee Kuan Yew's Tours of Rural Constituencies," 29 March 1963.

203. That a British base accounted for 15–20 percent of GNP tempered the virulence of anticolonialism (Bellows 1967, 135–36).

204. TNA: FCO 141/17160, Johnny Ho Huok Sing, report, "Visit of Singapore's Prime Minister to H. M. Naval Base, Singapore," 2 April 1963.

205. TNA: FCO 141/17160, note from Moore to Higham, 8 April 1963.

5. COMPETITIVE AUTHORITARIANISM IN MALAYSIA

1. The government investigated at least thirty-three individuals or organizations for sedition in 2013–14 alone (Funston 2016, 94).

2. The BN lost its amendment-approving two-thirds supermajority in 2008.

3. The latter became a plum patronage job. Personal conversation, Michael Ong, 19 May 2015, Canberra. Pakatan has promised to increase parliament's role in key appointments, but as of this writing, authority remains with the prime minister.

4. Interview, Mohamad Ariff Md. Yusof, 7 March 2019.

5. Azril Annuar, "History Made as Undi 18 Bill Passed with Bipartisan Support," *Malay Mail*, 16 July 2019.

6. A rare exception: Deputy Minister Saifuddin Abdullah proposed an amendment to the University and University Colleges Act via the UMNO Supreme Council, circumventing the disapproving minister; Saifuddin was censured, but the amendment passed. Interview, Saifuddin Abdullah, 16 June 2014, Kuala Lumpur (KL).

7. Interview, Gan Ping Sieu, 17 July 2014, KL.

8. Interviews, P. Kamalanathan, 12 July 2014, Rawang; Lee Kah Choon, 2 January 2015, Bayan Lepas; Khairy Jamaluddin, 6 March 2015, Washington, DC.

9. Interview, Ahmad Fauzi Zahari,15 June 2015, KL.

10. Interview, Toh Kin Woon, 12 June 2015, George Town, Penang.

11. Election-watch initiative Pemantau, a project of election-reform coalition Bersih, tallied numerous violations before and during the most recent election—even though Pakatan Harapan won—and offered detailed recommendations for improvement (Pemantau 2018).

12. For instance, "EIP: M'sia's Polls Law, Boundaries Worst in World," *Malaysiakini*, 21 February 2015.

13. Interview, Nurul Izzah Anwar, 8 January 2015, KL; "EC Denies Redelineation Being Done in Favour of Certain Parties," *Malaysiakini*, 19 September 2016.

14. The National Archives (TNA): FCO 24/483, letter from Duncan to Mound, 15 November 1968.

15. Funston 2016, 48; Andrew Lo, "Bloated Civil Service," *Star*, 3 February 2017. So substantial a state-dependent middle class makes strict scrutiny of public funds less likely (Greene 2007, 271–74); indeed, the BN successfully implanted a "political rationale" into the bureaucracy (Washida 2019, 76).

16. Interviews, Shaharuddin Badaruddin, 7 April 1999, Wangsa Maju; ABIM group, 7 January 2015, Bangi; Mohamad Raimi Ab Rahim, 1 January 2016, Petaling Jaya (PJ).

17. Interview, Ibrahim Ali, 9 January 2015, KL; Abdillah 2016, 16.

18. Heng 1996, 44; TNA: FCO 25/1155, letter from Dunn to Sullivan, 22 April 1971.

19. Interviews, Teng Chang Yeow, 3 January 2015, George Town; Steven Sim, 9 January 2015, PJ; Chong Sin Woon, 20 March 2015, KL; Toh Kin Woon, 2 June 2015, George Town; Shahrir Samad, 3 August 2015, KL; Ng 2005, 193–98, 2003, 94–100.

20. Interview, Ahmad Fauzi Zahari, 15 June 2015, KL.

21. Interview, Lee Kim Sin, 7 January 2015, Bangi.

22. Interview, Shahrir Samad, 3 August 2015, KL.

23. Interview, Tian Chua, 18 June 2014, KL.

24. Susan Loone, "Penang Fisherfolk Want Cash Aid to Avoid Leakages," *Malaysiakini*, 26 June 2018.

25. Interviews, Toh Kin Woon, 12 June 2015, George Town; and Teng Chang Yeow, 3 January 2015, George Town.

26. Interview, Shahrir Samad, 3 August 2015, KL.

27. British estimates were higher: around three hundred thousand; TNA: FCO 24/483, letter from Duncan to Mound, 15 November 1968.

28. "Umno Signing Up Thousands of New Members Monthly," *New Straits Times*, 31 July 2017.

29. Puteri formed to counteract sharp declines in youth support. Pemuda's age cap is 40; Puteri's, 35.

30. Interview with Ahmed Shabery Cheek, 31 July 2015, KL.

31. TNA: FCO 24/1156, letter from Clift to Sullivan, 26 January 1971.

32. TNA: FCO 24/483, letter from Duncan to Mound, 15 November 1968.

33. Interview, Wan Saiful Wan Jan, 6 August 2015, KL.

34. Funston 2016, 83; "Delegates Bribed RM200, Alleges Dr M," *New Straits Times*, 15 September 2006.

35. "Dakwaan Dr. M satu tuduhan liar," *Utusan Online*, 13 September 2006.

36. Most peripheral component parties, including all of BN Sarawak, hived off after the BN's 2018 loss, though the Alliance core persists; what the coalition will comprise for the next election remains uncertain as of this writing.

37. When the Sarawak United People's Party joined the coalition, for instance, it was on written agreement ensuring the states' rights–oriented party a deputy chief minister post with veto power (lost in 2011) and nondiscriminatory policies. TNA: FCO 24/809, report, "Malaysia: Malay-dominated Central Government Wins Uneasy Control of Sarawak," 17 July 1970.

38. TNA: FCO 24/483, letter from Duncan to Mound, 15 November 1968.

39. Interview, Teng Chang Yeow, 3 January 2015, George Town.

40. TNA: FCO 24/479, confidential conversation record of lunch meeting of Lord Shepherd et al. and "members of various Malaysian political parties," [June?] 1969.

41. Initially maintaining editorial independence, the *Star* increased circulation from around twelve thousand to one hundred thousand within five years; it became a key funding source for the MCA. Interview, Hng Hung Yong, 1 August 2016, PJ; Crouch 1996, 86.

42. Hoping to coordinate smaller-scale efforts among Chinese investors confronting Malay-focused large state enterprises, the MCA also incorporated party-controlled holding companies in several states by the early 1980s, with limited success (Heng 1997, 271–73).

43. TNA: FCO 24/1156, letter from Dunn to Sullivan, 20 January 1970.

44. Interview, Sim Tong Him, 1 August 2015, Kota Melaka.

45. Interview, Ong Kian Ming, 16 July 2014, KL.

46. Interview, S. Arutchelvan, 19 June 2014, KL.

47. Ibid.

48. Interviews, Tian Chua, 18 June 2014, KL; Rafizi Ramli, 16 July 2014, KL; Sim Tze Tzin, 20 July 2014, PJ; DAP activist, December 2014, KL.

49. Interview, Ahmad Shabery Cheek, 31 July 2015, KL.

50. Interview, Mahathir Mohamad, 10 October 2016, Putrajaya.

51. Interview, Mujahid Yusuf Rawa, 7 August 2016, KL.

52. Interview, Tian Chua, 18 June 2014, KL.

53. After a five-party joint appeal, two of the 1969–70 detainees were released unconditionally in October 1970. TNA: FCO 24/801, letter from Dunn to Sullivan, 2 October 1970.

54. TNA: FCO 25/1155, memo from Dunn to Sullivan, 29 January 1971; letter from Wilkes to Sullivan, 22 September 1971; "Malaysians Fined for Sedition," *Guardian*, 12 May 1971. *Utusan Melayu*'s editor and senior subeditor were likewise convicted and fined

under the Sedition Act at around the same time for reporting on a speech by Musa Hitam. TNA: FCO 25/1155, letter from Dunn to Sullivan, 24 June 1971.

55. TNA: FCO 25/1155, memo from Wong to Clift, 8 June 1971.

56. TNA: FCO 24/809, telegram from Walker, 29 May 1970; letter from Grubb to Sullivan, 1 July 1970.

57. What is offered may be quite creative: payments for displaying BN flags, for example, or for having the flag marked with a number drawn after the election (field notes, 11 March 1999, Sabah), or vouchers redeemable for cash *if* the BN wins that seat (Teo 2014, 73). In Sarawak, government and opposition parties alike hire brokers to buy votes among groups like longhouse residents and oil palm workers; the BN has spent far more, but imprecise monitoring means candidates "have to expect" brokers to play both sides (interview, DAP politician, April 2016, Sarawak). Opposition rejoinders mix indignation at these practices' prevalence with regret at their own insufficient resources.

58. MARA's primary foci are economic/vocational assistance and education, particularly via a network of bumiputera-only tertiary institutions. Usman Awang put this history to verse in 1991, perplexingly: http://www.mara.gov.my/en_US/pengenalan -sejarah.

59. TNA: FCO 24/483, letter from Duncan to Mound, 15 November 1968.

60. Interview, Ibrahim Ali, 9 January 2015, KL.

61. Andrew Lo, "Bloated Civil Service," *Star*, 3 February 2017; "Now That Malaysia Has a New Government, the Real Work Begins Reforming the Country," *The Conversation*, 23 May 2018.

62. "Full Text of PM's Speech at the Bumiputera Economic Empowerment Programmes Launch," *Star*, 14 September 2013.

63. Interviews, Lee Khai Loon, 3 January 2015, Seberang Jaya; Lee Kim Sin, 7 January 2015, Bangi; Nik Nazmi Nik Ahmad, 15 July 2015, PJ. Origin stories differ. The most plausible is that the Alliance introduced *penyelaras* after 1969 to sustain engagement in PAS-held seats in Terengganu (interview, Ahmad Shabery Cheek, 31 July 2015, KL). Selangor introduced *ADUN angkat* in 2008—ADUN "adopted" BN-held state constituencies to service alongside their own—but soon replaced them with *penyelaras* (Yeoh 2012, 35; interview, Ronnie Liu, 20 July 2015, PJ). One BN ex-*penyelaras* said he received no set allocation but could recommend projects for the prime minister's office to fund (interview, Ding Kuong Hiing, 25 April 2016, Meradong).

64. Interview, Ahmad Shabery Cheek, 31 July 2015, KL.

65. "PM: More Money for BN MPs Next Year," *Malaysiakini*, 16 August 2015.

66. Agriculture Minister Ismail Sabri Yaakob asserted that if Keadilan's Wan Azizah Wan Ismail won a 2015 by-election, "she will not even get past my office lobby . . . [her district] will be left behind. She cannot do anything because development is mainly under the federal government" (Looi Sue-Chern, "No Approval for Funds, Projects if Wan Azizah Wins, Ismail Sabri Tells Voters," *Malaysian Insider*, 1 May 2015).

67. Interviews, UMNO ADUN, 3 January 2015, Seberang Jaya; UMNO adviser, 23 December 2015, KL.

68. The state government can "negotiate" on who the federal government appoints as district officer, as the chief minister may otherwise delay the process (Loh 2010, 133, 137; Ong Kian Ming, personal communication, 1 November 2017).

69. Interviews, Tian Chua, 18 June 2014, KL; Ong Kian Ming, 16 July 2014, KL; Sim Tze Tzin, 20 July 2014, PJ and 23 December 2014, Subang Jaya; Peter Chong, 31 December 2014, PJ; Sivarasa Rasiah, 8 January 2015, PJ; Hatta Ramli, 6 August 2015, Ampang Jaya.

70. Ben Tan, "No Allocations for BN Reps, Says Johor MB," *Malay Mail*, 12 May 2018.

71. "Equal Funds for Johor Reps a Good Move, Says Liew," *Free Malaysia Today*, 31 May 2018.

72. Allison Lai, "Wee Questions Allocation for MPs," *Star*, 8 June 2018; "Dewan Rakyat Chaotic on Elected Reps' Allocation Issue," *Sun*, 1 April 2019.

73. Interviews, Yap Soo Huey, 4 January 2015, George Town; Steven Sim, 9 January 2015, PJ.

74. Interview, Nik Nazmi Nik Ahmad, 15 July 2015, PJ.

75. Interviews, Mujahid Yusuf Rawa, 15 June 2015; Shamsul Iskandar, 16 June 2015, KL.

76. TNA: FCO 24/479, confidential conversation record of lunch meeting of Lord Shepherd et al. and "members of various Malaysian political parties," [June?] 1969.

77. Interview, Lee Kah Choon, 2 January 2015, Bayan Lepas.

78. TNA: FCO 24/809, telegram from Lewis, 29 May 1970.

79. See http://www.br1m.info/about-br1m/.

80. Interviews, Tan Seng Keat, 31 December 2015, KL; Wan Saiful Wan Jan, 6 August 2015, KL.

81. Interview, Nur Jazlan Mohamed, 6 January 2015, KL. A parallel is Mexico's anti-poverty PRONASOL (National Solidarity Program), introduced in the early 1990s amid the PRI's declining public sector patronage resources and, hence, electoral support. PRONASOL assistance helped ease the transition to free-market policies, but its pattern of funding also helped the PRI counter the appeal of opposition parties (Greene 2007, 106–7).

82. Interview, Shahrir Samad, 3 August 2015, KL.

83. "PM: Government Will Phase Out BR1M," *New Straits Times*, 26 August 2018.

84. Suggested an informant, the inspiration may have been a 2005 PAS plan for death benefits to court older voters.

85. Speech by Lim Guan Eng, 29 June 2013, https://www.penang.gov.my/en/dmedia /2591-penang-economic-conference; https://www.facebook.com/cmlimguaneng/posts /1558901477473281; "A Different Sort of 'AES,'" *The Rocket*, 15 December 2012; interviews, Lim Guan Eng, 3 January 2015, Butterworth; Keadilan service center staff, Penang, 2 January 2015.

86. See https://www.selangor.gov.my/index.php/pages/view/2534 for details on what is now Initiatif Peduli Rakyat (Caring for the People).

87. Government of Selangor 2010; interview (and field notes), Rodziah Ismail, 5 August 2016, Shah Alam.

88. N. Faizal Ghazali, "What's Wrong with PAS Logo on S'gor Gov't Aid Envelopes?" *Malaysiakini*, 29 October 2017.

89. For example, http://www.wongchen.com/2017/07/executive-summary-faq-selangor -governments-audit-freezing-community-spending-p104-kelana-jaya/; regular updates at https://www.facebook.com/wongchenpkr/.

90. Joseph Sipalan, "Najib Tells Sibu: You Help Me, I Help You," *Malaysiakini*, 13 May 2010. (BN lost, barely.)

91. Interview, Rahman Dahlan, 1 August 2016, Putrajaya.

92. Interview, Ahmad Shabery Cheek, 31 July 2015, KL.

93. Field notes, 8 March 1999, Sabah. She also warned against accepting preelection drinks or candy from UMNO, which might be spiked so they sleep through election day.

94. A DAP-linked NGO complements these efforts among Christian communities, organizing retreats and exposure trips, sponsoring small improvements and services, and bringing a group of pastors to visit Putrajaya and the Selangor legislature. Their argument is less specifically "vote DAP," though, than to encourage questioning the system (interviews, DAP politicians, December 2014, KL and April 2016, Sarawak).

95. Interviews, Teresa Kok, 31 December 2014, KL; Oscar Ling,18 June 2015, KL; Sim Tze Tzin, 29 July 2015, PJ; Sim Tong Him, 1 August 2015, Kota Melaka; Wong Ling Biu, 23 April 2016, Sarikei; Ting Tze Fui, 24 April 2016, Meradong. Keadilan Sarawak chair Baru Bian offered his rural constituency similar infrastructure, backed by an NGO, but

presented these more as personal than party initiatives. He estimated having delivered nearly MYR2 million in projects (interview, 21 April 2016, Kuching).

96. A separate 1971–72 royal commission considered local authorities' duties, resources, opportunities, and compensation (Norris 1980, 66–69).

97. Penang Institute, "Local Government in Malaysia: Types, Functions, Organisation, Members and Budget," http://penanginstitute.org/v3/resources/articles/statistics/676-local -government-in-malaysia-types-functions-organisation-members-and-budget, accessed 31 October 2017. I use "local council/councilor" for the gamut of local authorities.

98. Interview, Peter Chong, 31 December 2014, PJ.

99. Interview, Rajiv Rishyakaran, 18 July 2014, PJ.

100. Local Government Act 1976, s. 10.

101. The system also underrepresents women—merely 12.9 percent of councilors in 2005—though the 9th Malaysia Plan (2006–10) aimed for 30 percent women in public sector "decision-making positions" (WDC 2008, 30; EPU 2006, 288).

102. Aeria 2005, 126; interviews, Teresa Kok, 31 December 2014, KL; Saifuddin Abdullah, 22 December 2015, KL.

103. WDC 2008, 25–28, 58; Goh 2005, 62–69; Aeria 2005, 129–30; interviews, DAP staffer, 13 July 2014, KL; Peter Chong, 31 December 2014, PJ; Lee Kah Choon, 2 January 2015, Bayan Lepas; Yap Soo Huey, 4 January 2015, George Town; Tan Jo Han, 11 June 2015, PJ; Toh Kin Woon, 12 June 2015, George Town; Nik Nazmi Nik Ahmad, 15 July 2015, PJ; Shahrir Samad, 3 August 2015, KL.

104. Interviews, Gan Ping Sieu, 17 July 2014, KL; Rajiv Rishyakaran, 18 July 2014, PJ; Peter Chong, 31 December 2014, PJ; Chong Sin Woon, 20 March 2015, KL; Tan Jo Han, 11 June 2015, PJ.

105. Interviews, DAP staffer, 13 July 2014, KL; Teresa Kok, 31 December 2014, KL; Sim Tong Him, 1 August 2015, Kota Melaka.

106. Interview, Nur Jazlan Mohamed, 6 January 2015, KL.

107. States rely on a narrow range of indirect taxes and duties, plus federal capitation and road grants.

108. Interview, Saifuddin Abdullah, 22 December 2015, KL.

109. Hunter 2013; interview, Jahara Hamid, 3 January 2015, Seberang Jaya.

110. Interviews, Lee Khai Loon, 3 January 2015, Seberang Jaya; Yap Soo Huey, 4 January 2015, George Town; Lee Kim Sin, 7 January 2015, Bangi; Steven Sim, 9 January 2015, PJ; Ariff Sabri Abdul Aziz, 3 August 2015, PJ; Saifuddin Abdullah, 22 December 2015, KL.

111. Interviews, Teh Yee Cheu, 2 January 2015, George Town; Khairy Jamaluddin, 6 March 2015, Washington, DC.

112. "Villages under the Opposition Will Receive Allocation—DPM," *Malaysiakini*, 28 June 2018; "JKKK to Be Rebranded as MPKK—Rina," *Malaysiakini*, 28 June 2018.

113. Selangor has a small public service commission, formed in 1960, from which it can fill junior positions, but higher-level offices remain federal positions; a similar civil service in Penang merged with the federal system in the 1970s (Yeoh 2012, 25).

114. Field notes, C4 forum, 9 January 2015, PJ; interview, Steven Sim, 9 January 2015, PJ.

115. Interviews, Lim Guan Eng, 3 January 2015, Butterworth; Ronnie Liu, 20 July 2015, PJ.

116. Interview, Elizabeth Wong, 13 January 2015, Shah Alam.

117. Interview, Sivarasa Rasiah, 8 January 2015, PJ.

118. Interview, Tan Jo Han, 11 June 2015, PJ.

119. Interviews, Darell Leiking, 16 June 2015, KL; Oscar Ling, 18 June 2015, KL.

120. Interview, Gan Ping Sieu, 17 July 2014, KL.

121. Collaboration across parties is rare, but not between a same-party MP and ADUN. Interviews, Sim Tze Tzin, 23 December 2014, PJ; Lee Kah Choon, 2 January 2015, Bayan Lepas.

122. Interview, Teh Yee Cheu, 2 January 2015, George Town.

123. Parti Sosialis Malaysia is a partial exception: it builds presence and legitimacy by grass-roots work and runs a service center but emphasizes assisting groups such as plantation workers, squatters, and trade unions over more mundane welfare activities (interview, S. Arutchelvan, 19 June 2014, KL).

124. Interviews, Lee Kim Sin, 7 January 2015, Bangi; Shamsul Iskandar,16 June 2015, KL; Yong Siew Wei, 23 April 2016, Sarikei.

125. Interview, P. Kamalanathan, 12 July 2014, Rawang.

126. Interviews, Teng Chang Yeow, 3 January 2015, George Town; Sivarasa Rasiah, 8 January 2015, PJ; Darell Leiking, 16 June 2015, KL.

127. On service center costs: interviews, P. Kamalanathan, 12 July 2014, Rawang; Peter Chong, 31 December 2014, PJ; Zairil Khir Johari, 1 January 2015, George Town; Teh Yee Cheu, 2 January 2015, George Town; Nur Jazlan Mohamed, 6 January 2015, KL; Khairy Jamaluddin, 6 March 2015, Washington, DC; Nik Nazmi Nik Ahmad, 15 July 2015, PJ; Shahrir Samad, 3 August 2015, KL.

128. On service centers and legislators' intercession: interviews, Saifuddin Abdullah, 16 June 2014, KL; Tian Chua, 18 June 2014, KL; P. Kamalanathan, 12 July 2014, Rawang; Rafizi Ramli, 16 July 2014, KL; Rajiv Rishyakaran, 18 July 2014, PJ; Khairy Jamaluddin, 6 March 2015, Washington, DC; Akademi Kapten Hussein group, 19 March 2015, PJ; Toh Kin Woon, 12 June 2015, George Town; Keadilan service center staff, 2 January 2015, Penang; Teh Yee Cheu, 2 January 2015, George Town; Jahara Hamid, 3 January 2015, Seberang Jaya; Lee Khai Loon, 3 January 2015, Seberang Jaya; Yap Soo Huey, 4 January 2015, George Town; Sim Tong Him, 1 August 2015, Kota Melaka; Rodziah Ismail, 5 August 2016, Shah Alam.

129. Even the British continued to pick winners, to the extent they could. When UMNO sacked the "outstanding" but impecunious Musa Hitam in 1969, British officials scurried to find funding and a place for him to study in the United Kingdom for a year, outbidding rival offers from the United States and Australia. TNA: FCO 24/483, telegram from Duff to McMinnies, 14 August 1969; letter from Duncan to Aiers, 15 August 1969; letter from Cotton to Francis, 9 October 1969; intervening correspondence.

130. Interview, Khairy Jamaluddin, 6 March 2015, Washington, DC.

131. Interview, Mahathir Mohamad, 10 October 2016, Putrajaya.

132. On visibility and being present and active in the community: interviews, Saifuddin Abdullah, 16 June 2014, KL; Tian Chua, 18 June 2014, KL; P. Kamalanathan, 12 July 2014, Rawang; Rafizi Ramli, 16 July 2014, KL; Zairil Khir Johari, 1 January 2015, George Town; Jahara Hamid, 3 January 2015, Seberang Jaya; Lee Khai Loon, 3 January 2015, Seberang Jaya; Sivarasa Rasiah, 8 January 2015, PJ; Steven Sim, 9 January 2015, PJ; Ahmad Fauzi Zahari, 15 June 2015, KL; Mujahid Yusuf Rawa,15 June 2015, KL; Nik Nazmi Nik Ahmad, 15 July 2015, PJ; Ronnie Liu, 20 July 2015, PJ; Leo Moggie, 13 January 2016, KL; Ting Tze Fui, 24 April 2016, Meradong; Ding Kuong Hiing, 25 April 2016, Meradong; Hng Hong Yong, 1 August 2016, PJ; Rahman Dahlan, 1 August 2016, Putrajaya; Rodziah Ismail, 5 August 2016, Shah Alam.

133. Ong 1976, 408–9; interviews, Mahdzir Ibrahim, 25 December 2014, KL; Khalid Samad, 4 August 2015, Shah Alam.

134. Interview, Jamilah Ibrahim, 24 February 1999, Kota Bharu.

135. http://www.parlimen.gov.my/takwim-dewan-rakyat.html?uweb=dr, accessed 6 November 2017.

136. Interviews, Rafizi Ramli, 16 July 2014, KL; Khairy Jamaluddin, 6 March 2015, Washington, DC.

137. Commissioned survey by Merdeka Center, $n = 1,110$.

138. Field notes, 25 December 2014, Full Gospel Tabernacle, PJ.

139. On cash grants: interviews, Saifuddin Abdullah, 16 June 2014, KL; S. Arutchelvan, 19 June 2014, KL; Rafizi Ramli, 16 July 2014, KL; Rajiv Rishyakaran, 18 July 2014, PJ; Sim Tze Tzin, 23 December 2014, Subang Jaya; Keadilan service center staff, 2 January 2015, Penang; Lee Kah Choon, 2 January 2015, Bayan Lepas; Jahara Hamid, 3 January 2015, Seberang Jaya; Kamarul Bahrin Shah Rj Ahmad Baharuddin Shah, 15 January 2015, KL; Mujahid Yusuf Rawa, 15 June 2015, KL; Ahmad Fauzi Zahari, 15 June 2015, KL; Nik Nazmi Nik Ahmad, 15 July 2015, PJ; Ronnie Liu, 20 July 2015, Petaling Jaya; Sim Tong Him, 1 August 2015, Kota Melaka; Ariff Sabri Abdul Aziz, 3 August 2015, PJ; Hatta Ramli, 6 August 2015, Ampang Jaya; Leo Moggie, 13 January 2016, KL; Baru Bian, 21 April 2016, Kuching; Wong Ling Biu, 23 April 2016, Sarikei; Ting Tze Fui, 24 April 2016, Meradong; Ding Kuong Hiing, 25 April 2016, Meradong.

140. TNA: FCO 24/809, letter from Grubb to Sullivan, 16 June 1970.

141. Interview, 3 January 2015, Butterworth.

142. On these services: interviews, Baru Bian, 21 April 2016, Kuching; Sivarasa Rasiah, 8 January 2015, PJ; Mujahid Yusuf Rawa,15 June 2015, KL; Yap Soo Huey, 4 January 2015, George Town.

143. Interview, Khalid Samad, 4 August 2015, Shah Alam.

144. Interviews, DAP staffer, 13 July 2014, KL; Ong Kian Ming, 16 July 2014, KL.

145. "PKR's 'Culture of Cronyism' Threatens Reformasi, Claims Youth Leader," *Malaysiakini*, 28 August 2018.

146. Interviews, Tian Chua, 18 June 2014, KL; Sim Tze Tzin, 20 July 2014, PJ.

147. Interview, Mahdzir Ibrahim, 25 December 2014, KL.

148. Rashila 2005, 137; interview, Jamilah Ibrahim and Arniwati Sabirin, 24 February 1999, Kota Bharu.

149. Interview, Jahara Hamid, 3 January 2015, Seberang Jaya.

150. Interviews, Akademi Kapten Hussein group, 19 March 2015, PJ; Ahmad Shabery Cheek, 31 July 2015, KL; Rahman Dahlan, 1 August 2016, Putrajaya; Puteri UMNO group, 12 October 2016, KL.

151. Interview, Ariff Sabri Hj Abdul Aziz, 3 August 2015, PJ.

152. MIC launched its Putera (Youth) wing, alongside a less visible women's counterpart, only in 2007. Interviews, P. Kamalanathan, 12 July 2014, Rawang; Murugesan, 16 January 2015, KL; http://puteramic.com/Aboutus/, accessed 31 October 2017.

153. Its Unit Amal (Action Unit) has also managed logistics and provided security for opposition events (Liow 2011, 670–75, 681–85).

154. Interviews, Nik Nazmi Nik Ahmad, 15 July 2015, PJ; Rodziah Ismail, 5 August 2016, Shah Alam.

155. Interviews, Lee Kah Choon, 2 January 2015, Bayan Lepas; and Teng Chang Yeow, 3 January 2015, George Town.

156. Interview, Keadilan service center staff, 2 January 2015, Penang.

157. Interview, Nurul Izzah Anwar, 8 January 2015, KL.

158. Worried about the limits to that loyalty with only a three-seat majority in Kelantan in 2004, Nik Aziz required a controversial, misogynistic oath of each PAS ADUN: that they would divorce their wives if they defected (interview, Khalid Samad, 4 August 2015, Shah Alam). Facing criticism, PAS dropped the divorce clause in 2018 (Nazurah Ngah, "Pas to Drop Controversial 'Divorce Clause' From Party Oath of Allegiance," *New Straits Times*, 10 February 2018).

159. Interview, Wan Saiful Wan Jan, 6 August 2015, KL. The "progressives" who left PAS for Amanah in 2015 were among those likely holding substantial party funds, given their professional networks.

160. Interview, Ahmad Fauzi Zahari, 15 June 2015, KL.

161. Interview, Lee Kah Choon, 2 January 2015, Bayan Lepas.

162. Interview, Low Khere Chiang, 27 April 2016, Batu Kitang.

163. Interview, DAP staffer, 13 July 2014, KL.

164. Interview, Mujahid Yusuf Rawa, 15 June 2015, KL.

165. Interview, Musa Hitam, 28 July 2015, Kuala Lumpur.

166. Interviews, Khairy Jamaluddin, 6 March 2015, Washington, DC; Akademi Kapten Hussein group, 19 March 2015, PJ; Ahmad Fauzi Zahari, 15 June 2015, KL; Puteri UMNO group, 12 October 2016, KL.

167. Interview, Chong Sin Woon, 20 March 2015, KL.

168. Interview, Gan Ping Sieu, 17 July 2014, KL.

169. Interviews, PKR politicians, July 2014, January 2015, and June 2015, Selangor.

170. Interview, Yap Soo Huey, 4 January 2015, George Town.

171. Interviews, Yap Soo Huey, 4 January 2015, George Town; Wong Ling Biu, 23 April 2016, Sarikei.

172. Interview, Teng Chang Yeow, 3 January 2015, George Town.

173. Interview, Nur Jazlan Mohamed, 6 January 2015, KL.

174. Interview, Chew Mei Fun, 12 January 2015, Putrajaya.

175. Interviews, Rajiv Rishyakaran, 18 July 2014, PJ; Rahman Dahlan, 1 August 2016, Putrajaya.

176. Interview, Saifuddin Abdullah, 16 March 2015, KL.

177. Interview, P. Kamalanathan, 12 July 2014, Rawang.

178. Interview, Rajiv Rishyakaran, 18 July 2014, PJ.

179. Interviews, Tian Chua, 18 June 2014, KL; Rafizi Ramli, 16 July 2014, KL; Sim Tze Tzin, 20 July 2014, PJ; Lee Khai Loon, 3 January 2015, Seberang Jaya; Yap Soo Huey, 4 January 2015, George Town; Suaram group, 4 January 2015, George Town; Steven Sim, 9 January 2015, PJ; Elizabeth Wong, 13 January 2015, Shah Alam; postelection reform committee staff, 12 February 2019, KL; Cynthia Gabriel, 15 March 2019, PJ.

180. Interview, Lim Kah Cheng, 1 January 2015, George Town.

181. Interviews, Yap Soo Huey, 4 January 2015, George Town; also Sim Tze Tzin, 20 July 2014, PJ; Sivarasa Rasiah, 8 January 2015, PJ. Earlier efforts at meet-the-people sessions, at least in Penang, saw poor attendance by councilors, administrators, and public alike (Rüland 1990, 465).

182. Interview, Saifuddin Abdullah, 16 June 2014, KL. That said, Saifuddin was hardly the UMNO norm, and was only reelected after joining Pakatan.

183. Terence Gomez, "Controversy over GLCs: Terence Gomez Responds to Daim Zainuddin," *Aliran*, 26 January 2019; also Syed Jaymal Zahiid, "Study: Political Appointments at State GLCs, Patronage Continue under Pakatan," *Malay Mail*, 2 September 2018; Gomez 2018.

184. Interview, Pakatan politician, October 2018, Canberra, Australia.

185. "Bersatu VP Says 'Stupid' Not to Use Gov't Resources, Gets Standing Ovation," *Malaysiakini*, 30 December 2018.

186. Ong 1976, 421n13; interviews, Khalid Samad, 4 August 2015, Shah Alam; Ronnie Liu, 20 July 2015, PJ; and Keadilan ADUN, July 2015, PJ.

187. Interviews, Sim Tze Tzin, 23 December 2014, Subang Jaya; Zairil Khir Johari, 1 January 2015, George Town; Teh Yee Cheu, 2 January 2015, George Town.

188. Coalition for Good Governance press conference, 31 December 2014, PJ.

189. The short-lived Pakatan government in Perak restored elections for the state's 817 *ketua kampung* (village heads); after ADUN defections, the BN took over the state government and sacked the lot (Yeoh 2012, 14).

190. In reality, Malays now outnumber non-Malays in forty-three of forty-nine cities. Ong Kian Ming, "Restore local elections to increase accountability, to better reflect local representation and to increase transparency," media statement, 25 January 2015.

191. Lim Guan Eng, "Follow Penang: BN must explain why they refuse to restore the 3rd vote," transcript of speech, 6 May 2011, Penang; https://www.penang.gov.my/en/dmedia/1547-local-government-election-forum (accessed 3 August 2017).

192. Qishin Tariq, "'No' to Penang Local Government Elections," Star, 15 August 2014.

193. Interviews, Lim Kah Cheng, 1 January 2015, George Town; Yap Soo Huey, 4 January 2015, George Town; and Suaram group, 4 January 2015, George Town; Yeoh 2012, 51.

194. Instead of seventy-two promised NGO and professional representatives, the peak was seventeen, in 2008–09 (Rodan 2018, 195).

195. Interviews, Derek Fernandez, 8 January 2015, PJ; Tan Jo Han, 11 June 2015, PJ; Ronnie Liu, 20 July 2015, Petaling Jaya.

196. Interviews, Lim Kah Cheng, 1 January 2015, George Town; Lim Guan Eng, 3 January 2015, George Town; and Yap Soo Huey, 4 January 2015, George Town.

197. Joseph Kaos Jr., "No-Go for Local Council Polls," Star, 11 December 2008.

198. Interview, Gan Ping Sieu, 17 July 2014, KL.

199. Interview, Tian Chua, 18 June 2014, KL.

200. Interviews, Chong Sin Woon, 20 March 2015, KL; Puteri UMNO group, 12 October 2016, KL.

201. Interview, Teng Chang Yeow, 3 January 2015, George Town.

6. HEGEMONIC ELECTORAL AUTHORITARIANISM IN SINGAPORE

1. Lee rejected a 1966 Constitutional Commission proposal to add a council of state or ombudsperson to protect minority interests (Nam 1969–70, 468–69).

2. Interview, Sidek Saniff, 2 July 2015, Singapore.

3. Xue Jianyue, "Union Membership Growing at Faster Rate: NTUC," Today, 21 August 2014.

4. National Archives Singapore, Oral History Centre (NAS OHC), interview, Lawrence Sia, 11 December 2007, accession no. 003244/20.

5. Joanna Seow, "PAP MPs and Ministers to Be More Involved in Labour Movement," Straits Times, 21 November 2017; Joanna Seow, "Melvin Yong and Desmond Choo to Move Up as NTUC Assistant Secretaries-General," Straits Times, 23 February 2018.

6. "Opposition All Weeded Out: NTUC Chief," Straits Times, 7 November 1988.

7. NAS OHC, interview, Lawrence Sia, 12 November 2007, accession no. 003244/13.

8. NAS OHC, interview, Bernard Chen Tien Lap, 16 January 2002, accession no. 002530/10.

9. NAS OHC, interview, Teo Chong Tee, 6 June 2005, accession no. 002934/06.

10. The Workers' Party's Chen Show Mao retired and Sylvia Lim resigned upon election in 2011, for instance, as did Lee Li Lian in 2013.

11. NAS OHC, interview, 17 May 1997, accession no. 001871/29.

12. PAP MP 1, interview, July 2014, Singapore; PAP MP 3, interview, September 2015, Singapore.

13. NAS OHC, interview, Dixie Tan, 8 April 2003, accession no. 002749/17.

14. Indeed, a Malay member of an early GRC faced criticism of being "under the armpit" of his Chinese teammates (interview, Sidek Saniff, 2 July 2015, Singapore).

15. "Breaking News—EBRC Report Released," Online Citizen, 24 July 2015.

16. NAS OHC, interview, Teo Chong Tee, 6 June 2005, accession no. 002934/06.

17. For instance, the WP's Lee Li Lian in 2015. "Lee Li Lian, Dennis Tan, Leon Perera Elected as NCMPs," Straits Times, 17 September 2015.

18. "Everything You Need to Know about the Key Changes on S'pore's Political System in 60 Seconds," *Mothership*, 27 January 2016.

19. The next election, in 2017, was a walkover; only Malays could contest—rumor had it, to exclude 2011's near-winner.

20. Interview, Eric Tan, 21 July 2016, Singapore. The PAP finalizes its lineup last minute, too. For instance, they may shift a rookie from an intended seat on nomination day if a strong challenger stands there, to deny the opposition the chance to react. The party prepares "many sets" of nomination papers, just in case. NAS OHC, interview, Lew Syn Paw, 5 May 2002, accession no. 002385/08.

21. Ko Siew Huey, "Why an Opposition Team Missed Deadline," *Online Citizen*, 27 April 2011.

22. Field notes, September 2015, Singapore.

23. "S$5.5m Spent on GE2011," *Channel News Asia*, 15 June 2011; "GE2015 Spending: PAP Candidates Spend $5.3m while the Eight Opposition Parties' Expenses Totaled $1.8m," *Straits Times*, 29 October 2015.

24. For instance, medical and religious groups weighed in on family planning.

25. Simply considering inviting SDP leader Chee Soon Juan to join a panel in 1999 sparked angst among the organizers: doing so might broach "partisan politics" and "cause unnecessary alarm" (Ng 2002, 124–25; interviews, Chee Soon Juan, 7 July 2014, Singapore; Martyn See, 1 July 2015, Singapore; Jeannette Chong-Aruldoss, 11 January 2016, Singapore).

26. Interview, Jolovan Wham, 6 July 2015, Singapore. Still, Wham's NGO collaborated closely with NCMP Lina Chiam, helping her prepare speeches on foreign-worker housing and human trafficking.

27. Churches offer a possible, emerging exception. In 2015, PAP-connected church networks appeared to spread rumors via WhatsApp and social media of opposition candidates' support for marriage equality. In actuality, only SDP and the Reform Party reject sexual-orientation discrimination, and SDP had not expressed the policy position insinuated (field notes, 9–10 September 2015, Singapore; interview, SPP activist, January 2016, Singapore).

28. "PM: Debate Welcomed but Govt Will Rebut Malicious Arguments," *Straits Times*, 24 January 1995.

29. These include online straw polls, though the PAP insists it does not govern by poll.

30. Interview, Suzaina Kadir, 9 July 2014, Singapore.

31. The *Straits Times* purportedly moved its headquarters from Singapore to Kuala Lumpur in the 1960s for greater freedom of expression (Nam 1969–70, 475).

32. The Speakers' Corner allowed permit-free speech, so long as speakers were citizens and registered with the police; rules have since been relaxed slightly (Lee 2002, 110–11).

33. Claims in the other direction are rare but happen. Chiam See Tong, for instance, represented by Jeyaretnam, successfully sued two PAP ministers for slander in 1980 (Loke 2014, 125–7).

34. NAS OHC, interview, Joshua Benjamin Jeyaretnam, 22 June 2007, accession no. 002932/12.

35. Gomez 2006, 123–25; and for the current roster: https://www.parliament.gov.sg /about-us/structure/select-committees/committee-of-privileges (accessed 25 November 2019).

36. Most had been released by the early 1970s.

37. Interview, Tan Tee Seng, 5 January 2016, Singapore. Some of these "old left" former detainees are now again active in opposition parties, especially SDP; one, Wong Souk Yee, became secretary-general.

38. The National Archives (TNA): FCO 24/1198, letter from Manning to Chick, 31 December 1971.

39. TNA: FCO 24/1199, letter from Kelly to Chick, 29 March 1971.

40. TNA: FCO 24/883, letter from Fuller to Muro, 10 June 1970; Weiss 2011, 177–80.

41. Chan, though, puts PAP membership at 43,000 in 1971, even with the party's having made little effort at recruitment post-1961 (1976a, 127).

42. The wing's own propaganda implies young Singaporeans' discomfort with the PAP: it sought not numbers, but youth willing to commit "and to be openly identified with the PAP." *PAP Youth in Action: 1986–1991*, People's Action Party, September 1991, p. 60. A truly awful Young PAP recruitment video in 2014 (https://mothership.sg/2014/05/the-ypap-made-a-video-they-want-to-re-ignite-the-passion/, accessed 28 June 2019), entertaining but likely counterproductive, sparked both parodies and suspicions of sabotage.

43. Interview, Malminderjit Singh, 11 July 2016, Singapore.

44. NAS OHC, interview, Lau Teik Soon, 28 April 1997, accession no. 001871/18; Pang 1971, 29–31.

45. Interview, PAP MP 1, July 2014, Singapore.

46. NAS OHC, interviews, Lau Teik Soon, 28 April 1997, accession no. 001871/18; Chay Wai Chuen, 5 April 2007, 003144/01; Cheong Eric Yuen Chee, 12 April 2004, accession no. 002838/16

47. PAP, *Petir: 25th Anniversary Issue*, 1979.

48. Kor Kian Beng, "Just One MP a Poly Grad: Is There a Ceiling, Student Asks?" *Straits Times*, 2 August 2008.

49. MPs' staff otherwise are parliamentary, not party positions—perhaps a legislative assistant to help with research, preparing questions and speeches, and reviewing bills and a personal assistant for scheduling and mail. Interviews, PAP MP 1, July 2014, Singapore; Malminderjit Singh, 11 July 2016, Singapore.

50. Interview, Wan Hussin Hj Zoohri, 25 June 2015, Singapore.

51. NAS OHC, interview, Lew Syn Paw, 5 May 2002, accession no. 002385/07.

52. Interviews, PAP MP 1, July 2014, Singapore; PAP MP 2, July 2015, Singapore; NAS OHC, interview, Dixie Tan, 8 April 2003, accession no. 002749/17.

53. On parties' differentiation: interviews, Kenneth Jeyaretnam, 24 June 2014, Singapore; Chee Soon Juan, 7 July 2014, Singapore; Ravi Philemon, 8 July 2014, Singapore; Lee Li Lian, 29 June 2015, Singapore; Bryan Lim, 2 July 2015, Singapore; Kenneth Paul Tan, 10 July 2015, Singapore. Field notes, "SDP at 35" event, 21 June 2015, Singapore.

54. Excessive wonkishness—reflected in impractically long, detailed platforms—may not help; SDP's Chee self-deprecatingly notes the challenge of reducing a 105-page report to a 140-character tweet.

55. Interview, Tan Jee Say, 8 July 2015, Singapore.

56. It would be easy to read too much into these data. Malaysians had markedly higher levels of support for getting rid of parliament—29 percent in 2011 and 26 percent in 2014 (Chu et al. 2016, 24–25)—only to oust their government in 2018.

57. Interview, SDP activist, 18 April 2016, Singapore.

58. Interview, Chee Soon Juan, 7 July 2014, Singapore; Au 2011, 86.

59. Au 2010, 109; interview, Ravi Philemon, 8 July 2014, Singapore.

60. Interview, Bryan Lim, 18 April 2016, Singapore.

61. Salaries started to increase significantly in 1972, with the premise that attracting good people requires paying competitive market rates (Bellows 2009, 36).

62. Interview, Lee Li Lian, 30 June 2014, Singapore.

63. Interview, Chee Soon Juan, 7 July 2014, Singapore; field notes, "SDP at 35" event, 21 June 2015, Singapore; Au 2010, 110–11.

64. Field notes, WP, SDP, SPP rallies, 6, 7, 8, 9 September 2015, Singapore.

65. John Tan, interview, 22 July 2015, Singapore.

66. Gerald Giam, email correspondence, 10 January 2016.

67. The fathers of at least two current PAP MPs, Janil Puthucheary and Ong Ye Kun, were Barisan members—the father of the former was an Operation Coldstore detainee; of the latter, an MP.

68. Gerald de Cruz, "The Barisans Limp Back into the Election Arena with a Bold Front," *New Nation*, 28 March 1972.

69. Arthur Richards, "Time Not Ripe, Says Barisan's Mr. No," *Straits Times*, 30 March 1972; "Barisan Sosialis to Contest Next Election," *Straits Times*, 25 March 1972; Chan 1976a, 217–18.

70. TNA: FCO 95/1346, letter from Wong to Smith, 30 March 1972.

71. TNA: FCO 24/1199, letter from Kelly to Chick, 29 March 1971; Chan 1976a, 207–10; Mutalib 2003, 206–14.

72. Phua Mei Pen, "S'pore 'Now Needs Politicians,'" *Straits Times*, 31 March 2012.

73. Yap, Lim, and Leong 2009, 537; interview, Eric Tan, 21 July 2016, Singapore.

74. Interviews, Daniel Goh, 30 June 2014, Singapore; Eric Tan, 21 July 2016, Singapore; da Cunha 2012, 204.

75. Field notes, 6 September 2015, Singapore.

76. NAS OHC, interview, Kenneth Chen Koon Lap, 19 December 2001, accession no. 002325/06; Mutalib 2003, 167–69, 183–84; Loke 2014, 192–93.

77. SDP, *The Singapore Democrats: 30th Anniversary Commemorative Magazine*, 2010, n.p.; Mutalib 2003, 185–91.

78. Interview, Chee Soon Juan, 7 July 2014, Singapore.

79. SDP, *The Singapore Democrats: 30th Anniversary Commemorative Magazine*, 2010, n.p.; Mutalib 2003, 169.

80. Interviews, Chee Soon Juan, 7 July 2014, Singapore; John Tan, 22 July 2015, Singapore; Bryan Lim, 2 July 2015, Singapore; field notes, "SDP at 35" event, 21 June 2015, Singapore; Au 2010, 104.

81. Interview, SDP activist, July 2015, Singapore.

82. SDP, *The Singapore Democrats: 30th Anniversary Commemorative Magazine*, 2010, n.p.

83. Field notes, SPP rally, 9 September 2015, Singapore.

84. The Reform Party still foregrounds Joshua Jeyaretnam's name and photo; many older Singaporean fans seem unaware he left WP.

85. Interview, Kenneth Jeyaretnam, 24 June 2014, Singapore.

86. Loke 2016, 76–77; Ong 2016, 188–91; interview, John Gan Eng Guan, 14 October 2016, Singapore.

87. Interviews, Kenneth Jeyeratnam, 24 June 2014, Singapore; Lee Li Lian, 30 June 2014, Singapore; Chee Soon Juan, 7 July 2014, Singapore; John Tan, 22 July 2015, Singapore; SPP activist, July 2015, Singapore; Bryan Lim, 18 April 2016, Singapore.

88. Interviews, Bryan Lim, 2 July 2015, Singapore; John Tan, 22 July 2015, Singapore.

89. Exemplifying the narrowness of Singapore's political/economic inner circle is the position of the Lee family—including Hsien Loong's wife's helming Temasek and brother's leadership of telephone company Singtel, then GLC Fraser & Neave (Barr 2014b, 13–14, 108).

90. NAS OHC, interview, Ee Boon Lee, 18 July 2006, accession no. 003045/03; Ho 2010, 73–74.

91. Some efforts, such as an elitist, essentialist early 1980s "graduate mothers scheme," have backfired spectacularly, sparking social mobilization and PAP backpedaling.

92. Interviews, Gillian Koh, 9 July 2015, Singapore; Malminderjit Singh, 11 July 2016, Singapore.

93. Analysts dispute inequality data, given the variety and nature of government transfers. An alternative perspective is that the floor is rising, but so is the ceiling (interview, Gillian Koh, 9 July 2015, Singapore).

94. Details at www.mof.gov.sg/growandshare/index.htm (accessed 28 June 2019); Welsh 2016, 126.

95. In part due to HDB purchase restrictions (no young singles, single parents . . .), the share of families in nuclear households increased from 70 percent in 1957 to 75 percent in 1970 (Hassan 1976, 247).

96. Interview, Gillian Koh, 9 July 2015, Singapore.

97. In the 1980s, the state also began to sell parcels of land, also with ninety-nine-year leases, to private-condominium developers, reducing the burden on HDB as housing supplier. Efforts to modulate HDB resale prices, appease upwardly mobile young professionals, and stave off price-escalating private-market speculation have caused ongoing tensions and course corrections (Chua 2000a, 52–55).

98. Crowds shouted, "We are not rabbits!" at the mention of PAP goodies at 2015 rallies (for example, SPP rally, 8 September 2015, Singapore).

99. "Upgrading: PAP Sends Out Open Letter to S'poreans," *Straits Times*, 29 December 1996.

100. Interview, 30 June 2014, Singapore.

101. "Sniffing Out the Grassroots Divide in Aljunied," *Straits Times*, 24 June 2011.

102. Chiang Yin Pheng, "Money from Govt Fund to Improve Two Opposition-Held Wards," *Straits Times*, 2 September 1995; "Grassroots Groups Plan Upgrades in WP Wards," *Straits Times*, 21 January 2014.

103. Cephah Tan, "Are Town Councils Doing The Job They Were Meant To?" *Straits Times*, 16 April 1993.

104. Field notes, 9 September 2017, Singapore.

105. NAS OHC, interview, Bernard Chen Tien Lap, 16 January 2002, accession no. 002530/10.

106. "MPs' Disappearing Act," https://singaporearmchaircritic.wordpress.com/2014/07/16/mps-disappearing-act/, accessed 15 November 2017.

107. Initially under the Community Development Ministry, CCCs and RCs shifted to the PA in 1993 ("RCs and CCCs Now Come Under PA's wing," *Straits Times*, 27 July 1993).

108. TNA: FCO 24/1228 [P. M. Kelly], report, "The People's Association," February 1971.

109. "WP's Sylvia Lim Asks If People's Association Has Drifted from Mandate," *Today*, 14 April 2016.

110. The High Commission forwarded the report to Saigon; the South Vietnamese government even sent teams to observe the PA's CCs.

111. TNA: FCO 24/1228 [P. M. Kelly], report, "The People's Association," February 1971.

112. NAS: OHC, interview, Lau Teik Soon, 30 April 1997, accession no. 001871/19. To volunteers themselves, it may be T-shirts that most clearly demarcate teams: they cannot wear PAP shirts in PA spaces or when joining the MP qua PA grassroots adviser (interview, Eunice Chia-Lim, 27 June 2014, Singapore).

113. Interview, Eunice Chia-Lim, 27 June 2014, Singapore. These positions are remarkably consistently (and unironically) represented, complete with fairly uniform terminology (for example, of "trust" and "mouthpieces").

114. Janice Heng, "Should Opposition MPs Be Grassroots Advisers?" *Straits Times*, 23 September 2011.

115. Leslie Koh, "Chiam Can Set Up Own CDC to Challenge Me, Says Andy Gan," *Straits Times*, 20 December 1997.

116. Interview, PAP volunteer, June 2014, Singapore.

117. Interview, Gillian Koh, 9 July 2015, Singapore; NAS OHC, interview, Lau Teik Soon, 28 April 1997, accession no. 001871/18.

118. TNA: FCO 24/1228 [P. M. Kelly], report, "The People's Association," February 1971; Pang 1971, 78; Chan 1976a, 144–45; Seah 1985, 188.

119. Singh 1992, 41, 63; Vasoo 1994, 54–63; Hill and Lian 1995, 125, 179–80; Quah 2001, 10–14; Ooi 2009, 179; "Some MPs Form Groups to Look After Needs of Private Estates," *Straits Times*, 25 November 1994.

120. Joanne Lee, "Hougang, Potong Pasir to Form Their Own CDCs," *Straits Times*, 12 May 1997.

121. Leslie Koh, "Chiam Can Set Up Own CDC to Challenge Me, Says Andy Gan," *Straits Times*, 20 December 1997.

122. The minimum annual mayoral salary in 2015 was SGD660,000; each mayor also received an allowance as MP (SGD192,500 in 2015), plus three drew ministerial pay of at least SGD418,000 ("Super Guardians of Singapore," 18 September 2015, http://sg50election .blogspot.my/2015/09/what-does-mayor-in-singapore-do-and-how.html?m=1, accessed 15 November 2017).

123. Ganesan 1998, 232–33; Quah 2001, 22–27; Mauzy and Milne 2002, 96–98; Tan 2003, 16–17; Ooi and Shaw 2004, 71; Ooi 2009, 178; Chua Mui Hoong, "'Local Parliaments' with Full-Time Mayors Soon," *Straits Times*, 20 March 2000; "CDCs: A Brief History, *Straits Times*, 12 January 2008.

124. Cherian George, "Opposition MPs Should Get a Role in CDCs," *Straits Times*, 27 April 1997; Peh Shing Huei and Ken Kwek, "CDC: In Search of a Clear Role," *Straits Times*, 24 June 2006.

125. Braema Mathi and Lydia Lim, "Will CDCs 'Politicise' Social Services?" *Straits Times*, 1 April 2000.

126. Private housing falls outside TCs.

127. NAS OHC, interview, Lawrence Sia, 12 November 2007, accession no. 003244/13.

128. Leong Ching Ching and Joanne Lee, "Town Councils Gearing Up for Handover Changes," *Straits Times*, 24 January 1997; Ooi and Shaw 2004, 70–71.

129. Walter Fernandez, "PAP Town Councils to Handle Essential Services," *Straits Times*, 27 February 1996; Walter Fernandez, "PAP Town Councils To Be Totally Independent of HDB," *Straits Times*, 24 March 1996; Robin Chan, "Key Issues in Review of Town Council Ops," *Straits Times*, 12 January 2013; Au Waipang, "PAP Mis-AIMed, Faces Blowback, Part 2," *Yawning Bread*, 29 December 2012.

130. WP activist, interview, June 2015, Singapore.

131. "Take Politics Out of Town Council Transfers: WP's Low," Straits Times, 13 February 2015. Both PAP and WP have used managing agents owned by party members: Esmaco for PAP; FMSS for WP ("Getting Political," *Straits Times*, 7 May 2013).

132. Au Waipang, "Sack HDB, Disband People's Association," *Yawning Bread*, 24 August 2011.

133. "Grassroots Organisations 'Meant to Serve Government of the Day,'" *Today*, 9 September 2015.

134. Field notes, PAP rallies, 7, 8 September 2015, Singapore. The minister, Vivian Balakrishnan, also compared the opposition to an interloper, trying to disrupt a happy marriage, and insisted that opposition "checks and balances" are really "paralysis and gridlock."

135. Bertha Henson, "Are Town Councils a Boost for Opposition Parties?" *Straits Times*, 4 July 1993.

136. "MPs' Primary Role Should Come in Parliament: Hazel Poa," *Today*, 16 August 2015.

137. Bertha Henson, "Are Town Councils a Boost for Opposition Parties?" *Straits Times*, 4 July 1993.

138. AHPETC came under attack shortly before the 2015 election over its management and accounting. Widely viewed as an attempt to discredit the WP, the allegations may have earned WP sympathy. The PAP seemed a "playground bully" and politicized the civil service (Howard Lee, "Politicising the AHPETC Saga, and Why ST Got It Wrong," *Online Citizen*, 16 July 2015; also Sue-Ann Chia, "Perception of Bias Dents Report's Credibility," *Straits Times*, 3 July 2010; Charissa Yong and Tham Yuen-C, "Town Councils: Finding a Balance," *Straits Times* 22 November 2014).

139. Bertha Henson, "Are Town Councils a Boost for Opposition Parties?" *Straits Times*, 4 July 1993.

140. Chua Mui Hoong, "Town Council Posts: Are They Given to Reward Party Members?," *Straits Times*, 8 May 1993; Chua Mui Hoong et al., "Who Should Fill Town Council Jobs?," *Straits Times*, 24 July 1993.

141. Pritam Singh, "Straits Times: Sniffing Out the Grassroots Divide in Aljunied," 24 June 2011, https://singapore2025.wordpress.com/2011/06/24/straits-times-sniffing-out-the-grassroots-divide-in-aljunied/ (accessed 8 November 2017).

142. Andrew Loh, "Workers' Party Sets Up Community Fund for Social Programme," *Online Citizen*, 2 June 2014; "WP Activists Help Party Grow a Grassroots Network," *Today*, 19 September 2015; interview, Eric Tan, 21 July 2016, Singapore.

143. "Aljunied, Hougang Residents to Get Free Health Screening from Mobile Clinics," *Straits Times*, 12 July 2015.

144. They lost, but established it, regardless. Interview, Abdillah Zamzari, 5 January 2016, Singapore; Chong Zi Liang, "Help Scheme in Bishan, Toa Payoh," *Straits Times*, 4 January 2016.

145. Interview, SDP activist, April 2016, Singapore; Singapore Democrats, "We Are One, We Are Bukit Batok," 22 April 2016, http://yoursdp.org/news/sdp_39_s_social_programmes_we_are_one_we_are_bukit_batok/2016-04-22–6118 (accessed 15 November 2017).

146. Interview, Bryan Lim, 2 July 2015, Singapore.

147. NAS OHC, interview, Lau Teik Soon, 12 May 1997, accession no. 001871/23.

148. NAS OHC, interview, Bernard Chen Tien Lap, accession no. 002530/10.

149. NAS OHC, interview, Teo Chong Tee, 3 May 2005, accession no. 002934/03.

150. Field notes, PAP rallies, 7, 8 September 2015, Singapore.

151. NAS OHC, interview, Joseph Francis Conceicao, 23 May 2006, accession no. 003055/01.

152. PAP, *15th Anniversary Celebration Souvenir*, 1970, p. 62.

153. NAS OHC, interview, Bernard Chen Tien Lap, 21 January 2002, accession no. 002530/10.

154. NAS OHC, interview, Kenneth Chen Koon Lap, 21 January 2002, accession no. 002325/07.

155. NAS OHC, interview, Abdullah Tarmugi, 11 July 2007, accession no. 003179/03.

156. See https://jesscscott.wordpress.com/2015/08/25/elitism-quotes/ (accessed 15 November 2017).

157. Interviews, 3 July 2014, 6 September 2015, Singapore.

158. On MPS, letter writing, et al.: field notes, PAP meet-the-people sessions, 7 July 2014 and 22 June 2015; WP meet-the-people session, 29 June 2015; interviews, Eunice Chia-Lim, 27 June 2014, Singapore; Daniel Goh, 30 June 2014, Singapore; and Gillian Koh, 9 July 2015, Singapore; NAS OHC, interview, Bernard Chen Tien Lap, accession

no. 002530/11; Lau Teik Soon, 28 & 30 April 1997, 001871/17 & 20; "WP Activists Help Party Grow a Grassroots Network," *Today*, 19 September 2015; http://www.wp.sg/david -marshall-and-the-dawn-of-meet-the-people-sessions-in-singapore/, accessed 15 November 2017.

159. Field notes, 30 June 2014, Punggol East.

160. On door-to-door canvassing: field notes, PAP walkabout, 25 June 2015; Reform Party walkabouts, 26 June 2014, 6 July 2014; SDP walkabouts, 2 July 2015, 9 September 2015; interviews, Eunice Chia-Lim, 27 June 2014, Singapore; Lee Li Lian, 30 June 2014, Singapore; Ravi Philemon, 8 July 2014, Singapore; Tan 2003, 9.

161. NAS OHC, interview, 16 January 2002, accession no. 002530/10.

162. Opposition parties can seldom access private condominiums—just HDB estates and private houses.

163. Frustration with surging immigration, of both migrant workers and permanent residents, has been an increasingly hot issue over the last two electoral cycles. Approximately one in four residents is now "foreign," putting new strains—that opposition parties exploit—on housing prices, public transit, and other facilities and prompting new curbs on permanent residents' housing options (Chua 2017, 90–93).

164. On these activities: field notes, 28 June 2015, Punggol; interviews, Eunice Chia-Lim, 27 June 2014, Singapore; Daniel Goh, 30 June 2014, 29 June 2015, Singapore; Lee Li Lian, 30 June 2014, Singapore; Sidek Saniff, 2 July 2015, Singapore; PAP MP 1, July 2014, Singapore; PAP MP 2, July 2015, Singapore; PAP MP 3, September 2015, Singapore; Eric Tan, 21 July 2016, Singapore.

165. Interview, SPP activist, January 2016, Singapore.

166. Alternatives modes are democratic (accountable to fellow citizens), localist (group based), or populist (without intermediation between elite and masses).

167. Interview, Wan Hussin Hj Zoohri, 25 June 2015, Singapore.

168. For example, Low's own assessment; see "PM Told Not to See Results As Rejection of His Style of Govt," *Straits Times*, 2 September 1991.

169. Interviews, Daniel Goh, 29 June 2015, Singapore; Eric Tan, 21 July 2016, Singapore.

7. DRIVERS OF STASIS AND CHANGE

1. "Goh between the Lees," *Straits Times*, 12 September 2009.

2. Liew Chin Tong, "The Role of an MP," *Malaysian Insider*, 27 December 2013.

3. To be fair, part of Pakatan's challenge is not only a generic one of establishing politics on new grounds, plus having a majority too slim to push through the constitutional amendments all sorts of other reforms require, but the fact that Mahathir, a key architect of the old order, has kicked off the effort, joined by a flock of BN-system habitués.

Bibliography

Abdillah Noh. 2016. "Political Change and Institutional Rigidity in Malaysia: Is There a Way Out?", ISEAS Working Papers #2, Singapore: ISEAS Yusuf Ishak Institute.

Abdullah, Walid Jumblatt. 2016. "Assessing Party Structures: Why Some Regimes Are More Authoritarian Than Others." *Australian Journal of International Affairs* 70 (5):525–40, http://dx.doi.org/10.1080/10357718.2016.1151859.

Abdullah, Walid Jumblatt. 2017. "Bringing Ideology In: Differing Oppositional Challenges to Hegemony in Singapore and Malaysia." *Government and Opposition* 52 (3):483–510, http://dx.doi.org/10.1017/gov.2015.30.

'Abidin Muhriz, Tunku. 2012. "A New Dawn for the Dewan Negara? A Study of Malaysia's Second Chamber and Some Proposals for Reform." IDEAS Report, Institute for Democracy and Economic Affairs.

Aeria, Andrew. 1997. "The Politics of Development and the 1996 Sarawak State Elections." *Kajian Malaysia* XV (1&2):57–83.

Aeria, Andrew. 2005. "Sarawak: State Elections and Political Patronage." In *Elections and Democracy in Malaysia*, edited by Mavis Puthucheary and Norani Othman, 118–52. Bangi: Universiti Kebangsaan Malaysia Press.

Afif bin Pasuni. 2015. "Terengganu and Kelantan Elections: The Separation and Convergence of Blurred Identities." In *Coalitions in Collision: Malaysia's 13th General Elections*, edited by Johan Saravanamuttu, Lee Hock Guan, and Mohamed Nawab Mohamed Osman, 235–48. Singapore: ISEAS.

Alagappa, Muthiah. 1995. "The Anatomy of Legitimacy." In *Political Legitimacy in Southeast Asia: The Quest for Moral Authority*, edited by Muthiah Alagappa, 11–30. Stanford, CA: Stanford University Press.

Amnesty International. 1980. *Report of an Amnesty International Mission to Singapore: 30 November to 5 December 1978*. London: Amnesty International Publications.

Aspinall, Edward. 2010. "Indonesia: The Irony of Success." *Journal of Democracy* 21 (2):20–34, http://dx.doi.org/10.1353/jod.0.0157.

Aspinall, Edward. 2014. "When Brokers Betray: Clientelism, Social Networks, and Electoral Politics in Indonesia." *Critical Asian Studies* 46 (4):545–70, http://dx.doi.org/10.1080/14672715.2014.960706.

Aspinall, Edward, and Ward Berenschot. 2019. *Democracy for Sale: Elections, Clientelism, and the State in Indonesia*. Ithaca, NY: Cornell University Press.

Aspinall, Edward, and Mada Sukmajati, eds. 2016. *Electoral Dynamics in Indonesia: Money Politics, Patronage and Clientelism at the Grassroots*. Singapore: NUS Press.

Au, Alex Waipang. 2010. "The Ardour of Tokens: Opposition Parties' Struggle to Make a Difference." In *Management of Success: Singapore Revisited*, edited by Terence Chong, 100–120. Singapore: ISEAS.

Au, Alex Waipang. 2011. "Parties and Personalities: Staying Together (or Not) Under Fire." In *Voting in Change: Politics of Singapore's 2011 General Election*, edited by Kevin Y. L. Tan and Terence Lee, 68–89. Singapore: Ethos Books.

Barkan, Joel D. 2008. "Legislatures on the Rise?" *Journal of Democracy* 19 (2):124–37, http://dx.doi.org/10.1353/jod.2008.0020.

Barr, Michael D. 2014a. "The Bonsai under the Banyan Tree: Democracy and Democratisation in Singapore." *Democratization* 21 (1):29–48, http://dx.doi.org/10.1080/13510347.2012.706606.

Barr, Michael D. 2014b. *The Ruling Elite of Singapore: Networks of Power and Influence.* London: I. B. Tauris.

Baskin, Mark. 2010. "Constituency Development Funds (CDFs) as a Tool of Decentralized Development." 56th Commonwealth Parliamentary Conference, Nairobi, 10–19 September.

Bedale, Harold. 1953. Establishment, Organisation and Supervision of Local Authorities in the Federation of Malaya. Kuala Lumpur: Government Press.

Bellows, Thomas J. 1967. "The Singapore Party System." *Journal of Southeast Asian History* 8 (1):122–38, http://dx.doi.org/10.1017/S0217781100003513.

Bellows, Thomas J. 1970. *The People's Action Party of Singapore: Emergence of a Dominant Party System.* New Haven, CT: Yale University Southeast Asia Studies.

Bellows, Thomas J. 2009. "Meritocracy and the Singapore Political System." *Asian Journal of Political Science* 17 (1):24–44, http://dx.doi.org/10.1080/02185370902767581.

Bosco, Joseph. 1992. "Taiwan Factions: Guanxi, Patronage, and the State in Local Politics." *Ethnology* 31 (2):157–83.

Brownlee, Jason. 2007. *Authoritarianism in an Age of Democratization.* New York: Cambridge University Press.

Bruhn, Kathleen, and Kenneth F. Greene. 2007. "Elite Polarization Meets Mass Moderation in Mexico's 2006 Elections." *PS: Political Science & Politics* 40 (1):33–38, http://dx.doi.org/10.1017/S1049096507070060.

Brun, Diego Abente. 2014. "Introduction: Evaluating Political Clientelism." In *Clientelism, Social Policy, and the Quality of Democracy*, edited by Diego Abente Brun and Larry Diamond, 1–14. Baltimore: Johns Hopkins University Press.

Butler, Daniel M., Christopher F. Karpowitz, and Jeremy C. Pope. 2012. "A Field Experiment on Legislators' Home Styles: Service versus Policy." *Journal of Politics* 74 (2):474–86, http://dx.doi.org/10.1017/S0022381611001708.

C4 Center. [2018]. *The FELDA Crisis.* Petaling Jaya, Malaysia: Center to Combat Corruption and Cronyism.

Calvo, Ernesto, and María Victoria Murillo. 2014. "Partisan Linkages and Social Policy Delivery in Argentina and Chile." In *Clientelism, Social Policy, and the Quality of Democracy*, edited by Diego Abente Brun and Larry Diamond, 17–38. Baltimore: Johns Hopkins University Press.

Carnell, Francis G. 1954. "Constitutional Reform and Elections in Malaya." *Pacific Affairs* 27 (3):216–35, http://dx.doi.org/10.2307/2753019.

Case, William. 2005. "Southeast Asia's Hybrid Regimes: When Do Voters Change Them?" *Journal of East Asian Studies* 5 (2):215–37, http://dx.doi.org/10.1017/S1598240800005750.

Case, William. 1996. "Can the 'Halfway House' Stand? Semidemocracy and Elite Theory in Three Southeast Asian Countries." *Comparative Politics* 28 (4):437–64, http://dx.doi.org/10.2307/422052.

Case, William. 2011. *Executive Accountability in Southeast Asia: The Role of Legislatures in New Democracies and Under Electoral Authoritarianism.* Policy Studies 56. Honolulu: East-West Center.

Chan Heng Chee. 1975. "Politics in an Administrative State: Where Has the Politics Gone?" In *Trends in Singapore*, edited by Seah Chee Meow, 51–68. Singapore: Singapore University Press. Original edition, 1974.

Chan Heng Chee. 1976a. *The Dynamics of One Party Dominance: The PAP at the Grassroots.* Singapore: Singapore University Press.

Chan Heng Chee. 1976b. "The Political System and Political Change." In *Singapore: Society in Transition*, edited by Riaz Hassan, 30–51. New York: Oxford University Press.

Chan Heng Chee. 1976c. "The Role of Parliamentary Politicians in Singapore." *Legislative Studies Quarterly* 1 (3):423–41, http://dx.doi.org/10.2307/439506.

Chan Heng Chee. 1979. "In Middle Passage: The PAP Faces the Eighties." Occasional Paper #26, Department of Political Science, University of Singapore.

Chan Heng Chee. 1989. "The PAP and the Structuring of the Political System." In *Management of Success: The Moulding of Modern Singapore*, edited by Kernial Singh Sandhu and Paul Wheatley, 70–89. Singapore: ISEAS.

Chandra, Kanchan. 2004. *Why Ethnic Parties Succeed: Patronage and Ethnic Head Counts in India*. New York: Cambridge University Press.

Chandra, Kanchan. 2014. "Patronage, Democracy, and Ethnic Politics in India." In *Clientelism, Social Policy, and the Quality of Democracy*, edited by Diego Abente Brun and Larry Diamond, 156–73. Baltimore, MD: Johns Hopkins University Press.

Cheah Boon Kheng. 2002. *Malaysia: The Making of a Nation*. Singapore: ISEAS.

Cheah Boon Kheng. 2006. "The Left-wing Movement in Malaya, Singapore and Borneo in the 1960s: 'An Era of Hope or Devil's Decade'?" *Inter-Asia Cultural Studies* 7 (4):634–49, http://dx.doi.org/10.1080/14649370600983196.

Chee Soon Juan. 2012. *Democratically Speaking*. Singapore: Chee Soon Juan.

Cheema, G. Shabbir, and S. Ahmad Hussein. 1978. "Local Government Reform in Malaysia." *Asian Survey* 18 (6):577–91, http://dx.doi.org/10.2307/2643227.

Cheeseman, Nic. 2010. "African Elections as Vehicles for Change." *Journal of Democracy* 21 (4):139–53, http://dx.doi.org/10.1353/jod.2010.0019.

Cheeseman, Nic, and Marja Hinfelaar. 2009. "Parties, Platforms, and Political Mobilization: The Zambian Presidential Election of 2008." *African Affairs* 109 (434):51–76, http://dx.doi.org/10.1093/afraf/adp070.

Cheeseman, Nic, and Miles Larmer. 2013. "Ethnopopulism in Africa: Opposition Mobilization in Diverse and Unequal Societies." *Democratization* 22 (1):22–50, http://dx.doi.org/10.1080/13510347.2013.809065.

Cheung, Paul. 2015. "Introduction: Is Life Getting Better in Singapore?: Issues on Social Inequality." In *Inequality in Singapore, Singapore*, edited by Faizal Bin Yahya, 1–11. Singapore: World Scientific Publishing.

Chia, Roderick. 2012. *Democracy and Civil Society in Singapore: The Politics of Control*. Singapore: Singaporeans for Democracy.

Chin, James. 2001. "Unequal Contest: Federal-State Relations under Mahathir." In *Mahathir's Administration: Performance and Crisis in Governance*, edited by Ho Khai Leong and James Chin, 28–61. Singapore: Times Books International.

Chin, James. 2006. "New Chinese Leadership in Malaysia: The Contest for the MCA and Gerakan Presidency." *Contemporary Southeast Asia* 28 (1):70–87, http://dx.doi.org/10.1355/cs28-1d.

Chin, James. 2014. "Second-class Bumiputera? The Taming of the Dayak and Kadazandusun of East Malaysia." In *Misplaced Democracy: Malaysian Politics and People*, edited by Sophie Lemière, 109–27. Petaling Jaya, Malaysia: Strategic Information and Research Development Centre.

Chin, James Ung-Ho. 2002. "Malaysia: The Barisan National Supremacy." In *How Asia Votes*, edited by John Fuh-sheng Hsieh and David Newman, 210–33. London: Chatham House.

Chin Peng (Ong Boon Hua). 2003. *Alias Chin Peng: My Side of History*. Singapore: Media Masters.

Chin, Victor, and Por Heong Hong. 2018. *Five Tigers* (documentary film). Malaysia: Freedom Film Network.

Choo Ng Kwee. 1969. "Community Centres and Local Leaders in Singapore." *Community Development Journal* 4 (2):99–105.

Chu, Yun-han, Yu-tzung Chang, Min-Hua Huang, and Mark Weatherall. 2016. "Reassessing the Popular Foundation of Asian Democracies: Findings from Four Waves of the Asian Barometer Survey." Working Paper Series No. 120, Asian Barometer & Globalbarometer.

Chua Beng Huat. 1995. *Communitarian Ideology and Democracy in Singapore*. New York: Routledge.

Chua Beng Huat. 1997a. "Not Depoliticized but Ideologically Successful: The Public Housing Programme in Singapore." In *Understanding Singapore Society*, edited by Ong Jin Hui, Tong Chee Kiong, and Tan Ern Ser, 307–27. Singapore: Times Academic Press.

Chua Beng Huat. 1997b. *Political Legitimacy and Housing: Stakeholding in Singapore*. London: Routledge.

Chua Beng Huat. 2000a. "Public Housing Residents as Clients of the State." *Housing Studies* 15 (1):45–60, http://dx.doi.org/10.1080/02673030082469.

Chua Beng Huat. 2000b. "The Relative Autonomies of the State and Civil Society." In *State-Society Relations in Singapore*, edited by Gillian Koh and Ooi Giok Ling, 62–76. Singapore: Oxford University Press.

Chua Beng Huat. 2010. "The Cultural Logic of a Capitalist Single-party State, Singapore." *Postcolonial Studies* 13 (4):335–50, http://dx.doi.org/10.1080/13688790.2010.518347.

Chua Beng Huat. 2017. *Liberalism Disavowed: Communitarianism and State Capitalism in Singapore*. Ithaca, NY: Cornell University Press.

Cobbold, C. F. 1962. Report of the Commission of Enquiry into North Borneo and Sarawak. London: Stat. Office.

Comber, Leon. 1994. "David Marshall and 'Meet the People'—Singapore 1955–56." *Asian Studies Review* 18 (2):105–12, http://dx.doi.org/10.1080/03147539408713000.

Comber, Leon. 2012. *Singapore Correspondent: Political Dispatches from Singapore (1958–1962)*. Singapore: Marshall Cavendish.

Cowen, Zelman. 1958. "The Emergence of a New Federation in Malaya." *Tasmanian University Law Review* 1 (1):46–67.

Cox, Gary W., and Mathew D. McCubbins. 1986. "Electoral Politics as a Redistributive Game." *Journal of Politics* 48 (2):370–89, http://dx.doi.org/10.2307/2131098.

Cox, Gary W., and Mathew D. McCubbins. 2001. "The Institutional Determinants of Policy Outcomes." In *Presidents, Parliaments, and Policy*, edited by Stephan Haggard and Matthew D. McCubbins, 21–63. New York: Cambridge University Press.

Croissant, Aurel, and Olli Hellmann. 2017. "Introduction: State Capacity and Elections in the Study of Authoritarian Regimes." *International Political Science Review* 39 (1):3–16, http://dx.doi.org/10.177/01925121170066.

Crouch, Harold. 1996a. "Malaysia: Do Elections Make a Difference?" In *The Politics of Elections in Southeast Asia*, edited by R. H. Taylor, 114–35. Cambridge: Woodrow Wilson Center Press and Cambridge University Press.

Crouch, Harold A. 1996b. *Government and Society in Malaysia*. Ithaca, NY: Cornell University Press.

Curless, Gareth. 2016. "'The People Need Civil Liberties': Trade Unions and Contested Decolonisation in Singapore." *Labor History* 57 (1):53–57, http://dx.doi.org/10.1080/0023656X.2016.1140623.

da Cunha, Derek. 2012. *Breakthrough: Roadmap for Singapore's Political Future*. Singapore: Straits Times Press and NUS.

Dancz, Virginia H. 1987. *Women and Party Politics in Peninsular Malaysia*. New York: Oxford University Press.

Davidson, Jamie S., and Erik Mobrand. 2017. "Rule Making and Rule Breaking: Electoral Corruption in East Asia." In *Handbook of Corruption in Asia*, edited by Ting Gong and Ian Scott, 69–82. New York: Routledge.

Davis, L. H. N. 1953. Report of the Committee on Town and Rural Board Finances. Kuala Lumpur: Government Press.

Diamond, Larry. 2002. "Thinking about Hybrid Regimes." *Journal of Democracy* 13 (2):21–35, http://dx.doi.org/10.1353/jod.2002.0025.

Distelhorst, Greg, and Yue Hou. 2017. "Constituency Service under Nondemocratic Rule: Evidence from China." *Journal of Politics* 79 (3):1024–40, http://dx.doi.org/10.1086/690948.

Donno, Daniela. 2013. "Elections and Democratization in Authoritarian Regimes." *American Journal of Political Science* 57 (3):703–16, http://dx.doi.org/10.1111/ajps.12013.

du Toit, Pierre, and Nicola de Jager. 2014. "South Africa's Dominant-Party System in Comparative Perspective." *Taiwan Journal of Democracy* 10 (2):93–113.

Dunleavy, Patrick. 2010. "Rethinking Dominant Party Systems." In *Dominant Political Parties and Democracy: Concepts, Measures, Cases and Comparisons*, edited by Matthijs Bogaards and Francoise Boucek, 23–44. London: Routledge.

Election Commission. 2013. Summary of the EC's Clarifications on the Issues of the Electoral Roll and the Improvement of Electoral Process. Putrajaya: Election Commission Malaysia.

Enloe, Cynthia H. 1975. "The Neglected Strata: States in the City-Federal Politics of Malaysia." *Publius* 5 (1):151–70, http://dx.doi.org/10.2307/3329432.

EPU. 2006. *Ninth Malaysia Plan, 2006–2010*. Putrajaya: Economic Planning Unit, Prime Minister's Department.

Faisal S. Hazis. 2009. "The Politics of Development in Sarawak." *Akademika* 77:91–111.

Faisal S. Hazis. 2015. "Patronage, Power and Prowess: Barisan Nasional's Equilibrium Dominance in East Malaysia." *Kajian Malaysia* 33 (2):1–24.

Farish A. Noor. 2014. *The Malaysian Islamic Party PAS 1951–2013: Islamism in a Mottled Nation*. Amsterdam: Amsterdam University Press.

Fenno, Richard F. 1977. "US House Members in Their Constituencies: An Exploration." *American Political Science Review* 71 (3):883–917, http://dx.doi.org/10.2307/1960097.

Fetzer, Joel S. 2008. "Election Strategy and Ethnic Politics in Singapore." *Taiwan Journal of Democracy* 4 (1):135–53.

Funston, John. 2016. "UMNO—From Hidup Melayu to Ketuanan Melayu." In *The End of UMNO? Essays on Malaysia's Dominant Party*, edited by Bridget Welsh, 30–147. Petaling Jaya, Malaysia: SIRD.

Gandhi, Jennifer, and Ora John Reuter. 2013. "The Incentives for Pre-Electoral Coalitions in Non-Democratic Elections." *Democratization* 20 (1):137–59, http://dx.doi.org/10.1080/13510347.2013.738865.

Ganesan, Narayanan. 1998. "Singapore: Entrenching a City-state's Dominant Party System." *Southeast Asian Affairs* 99:229–43.

GCCP. 2015. GCCP: Towards A People-centred Parliament. Malaysia: Gabungan Cadangan Penambahbaikan Parlimen.

George, Cherian. 2007. "Consolidating Authoritarian Rule: Calibrated Coercion in Singapore." *Pacific Review* 20 (2):127–45, http://dx.doi.org/10.1080/09512740701306782.

Giersdorf, Stephan, and Aurel Croissant. 2011. "Civil Society and Competitive Authoritarianism in Malaysia." *Journal of Civil Society* 7 (1):1–21, http://dx.doi.org/10.1080/17448689.2011.553401.

Goh Ban Lee. 2005. "The Demise of Local Government Elections and Urban Politics." In *Elections and Democracy in Malaysia*, edited by Mavis Puthucheary and Norani Othman, 49–70. Bangi: Universiti Kebangsaan Malaysia Press.

Goh Ban Lee. 2007. *Counselling Local Councils*. Petaling Jaya, Malaysia: FOMCA/ERA.

Golden, Miriam A. 2003. "Electoral Connections: The Effects of the Personal Vote on Political Patronage, Bureaucracy and Legislation in Postwar Italy." *British Journal of Political Science* 33:189–212, http://dx.doi.org/10.1017/S0007123403000085.

Gomez, Edmund Terence. 2012. "Monetizing Politics: Financing Parties and Elections in Malaysia." *Modern Asian Studies* 46 (5):1370–97, http://dx.doi.org/10.1017/S0026749X12000200.

Gomez, Edmund Terence. 2014. "Malaysia's Political Economy: Ownership and Control of the Corporate Sector." In *Misplaced Democracy: Malaysian Politics and People*, edited by Sophie Lemière, 245–81. Petaling Jaya, Malaysia: Strategic Information and Research Development Centre.

Gomez, Edmund Terence. 2018. *Minister of Finance Incorporated: Ownership and Control of Corporate Malaysia*. Petaling Jaya, Malaysia: SIRD.

Gomez, James. 2001. "Publish and Perish: The Censorship of Opposition Party Publications in Singapore." In *Publish and Perish: The Censorship of Opposition Party Publications in Singapore*, edited by James Gomez, 12–24. Singapore: National Solidarity Party.

Gomez, James. 2006. "Restricting Free Speech: The Impact on Opposition Parties in Singapore." *Copenhagen Journal of Asian Studies* 23 (1):105–31.

Government of Selangor. 2010. *Governing Selangor: Policies, Programmes and Facts*. Shah Alam, Selangor, Malaysia: Pejabat Setiausaha Kerajaan Negeri Selangor.

Greene, Kenneth F. 2007. *Why Dominant Parties Lose: Mexico's Democratization in Comparative Perspective*. New York: Cambridge University Press.

Greene, Kenneth F. 2010. "The Political Economy of Authoritarian Single-Party Dominance." *Comparative Political Studies* 43 (7):807–34, http://dx.doi.org/10.1177/0010414009332462.

Grzymala-Busse, Anna. 2010. "Time Will Tell? Temporality and the Analysis of Causal Mechanisms and Processes." *Comparative Political Studies* 44 (9):1267–97, http://dx.doi.org/10.1177/0010414010390653.

Gunther, Richard, and Larry Diamond. 2003. "Species of Political Parties: A New Typology." *Party Politics* 9 (2):167–99, http://dx.doi.org/10.1177/13540688030092003.

Hadiz, Vedi R. 2003. "Reorganizing Political Power in Indonesia: A Reconsideration of So-called 'Democratic Transitions.'" *Pacific Review* 16 (4):591–611, http://dx.doi.org/10.1080/0951274032000132272.

Haggard, Stephan, and Robert R. Kaufman. 2012. "Inequality and Regime Change: Democratic Transitions and the Stability of Democratic Rule." *American Political Science Review* 106 (3):495–516, http://dx.doi.org/10.1017/S0003055412000287.

Haggard, Stephan, and Robert R. Kaufman. 1995. *The Political Economy of Democratic Transitions*. Princeton, NJ: Princeton University Press.

Hamilton-Hart, Natasha. 2000. "The Singapore State Revisited." *Pacific Review* 13 (2):195–216, http://dx.doi.org/10.1080/095127400363550.

Hara, Fujio. 2016. "The Malayan Communist Party As Recorded in the Comintern Files." ISEAS Working Papers 1, Singapore: ISEAS Yusof Ishak Institute.

Harper, T. N. 1999. *The End of Empire and the Making of Malaya*. New York: Cambridge University Press.

Hassan, Riaz. 1976. "Public Housing." In *Singapore: Society in Transition*, edited by Riaz Hassan, 240–68. New York: Oxford University Press.

Hawkins, Gerald. 1953. "First Steps in Malayan Local Government." *Pacific Affairs* 26 (2):155–58.

Heitshusen, Valerie, Garry Young, and David M. Wood. 2005. "Electoral Context and MP Constituency Focus in Australia, Canada, Ireland, New Zealand, and the United

Kingdom." *American Journal of Political Science* 49 (1):32–45, http://dx.doi.org/10
.2307/3647711.

Hellman, Olli. 2013. "The Developmental State and Electoral Markets in East Asia: How
Strategies of Industrialization Have Shaped Party Institutionalization." *Asian Survey* 53 (4):653–78, http://dx.doi.org/10.1525/AS.2013.53.4.653.

Helmke, Gretchen, and Steven Levitsky. 2006. "Introduction." In *Informal Institutions and
Democracy: Lessons from Latin America*, edited by Gretchen Helmke and Steven Levitsky, 1–30. Baltimore: Johns Hopkins University Press.

Heng Pek Koon. 1996. "Chinese Responses to Malay Hegemony in Peninsular Malaysia
1957–96." *Tonan Ajia Kenkyu [Southeast Asian Studies]* 34 (3):32–55.

Heng Pek Koon. 1997. "The New Economic Policy and the Chinese Community in Peninsular Malaysia." *The Developing Economies* 35 (3):262–92.

Heyzer, Noeleen. 1997. "International Production and Social Change: An Analysis of the
State, Employment and Trade Unions in Singapore." In *Understanding Singapore
Society*, edited by Ong Jin Hui, Tong Chee Kiong, and Tan Ern Ser, 374–95. Singa-
pore: Times Academic Press.

Hicken, Allen. 2006. "Stuck in the Mud: Parties and Party Systems in Democratic Southeast Asia." *Taiwan Journal of Democracy* 2 (2):23–46.

Hicken, Allen. 2011. "Clientelism." *Annual Review of Political Science* 14 (1):289–310,
http://dx.doi.org/10.1146/annurev.polisci.031908.220508.

Hilgers, Tina. 2008. "Causes and Consequences of Political Clientelism: Mexico's PRD in
Comparative Perspective." *Latin American Politics and Society* 50 (4):123–53.

Hilgers, Tina. 2011. "Clientelism and Conceptual Stretching: Differentiating among
Concepts and among Analytical Levels." *Theory and Society* 40 (5):567–88, http://
doi.org/10.1007/s11186-011-9152-6.

Hill, Michael, and Lian Kwen Fee. 1995. *The Politics of Nation Building and Citizenship in
Singapore*. New York: Routledge.

Hilley, John. 2001. *Malaysia: Mahathirism, Hegemony and the New Opposition*. New York:
Zed.

Hinnebusch, Raymond. 2006. "Authoritarian Persistence, Democratization Theory and the
Middle East: An Overview and Critique." *Democratization* 13 (3):373–95, http://dx
.doi.org/10.1080=13510340600579243.

Hirschman, Charles. 1986. "The Making of Race in Colonial Malaya: Political Economy
and Racial Ideology." *Sociological Forum* 1 (2):330–61.

Ho Khai Leong. 1992. "The Malaysian Chinese Guilds and Associations as Organized Interests in Malaysian Politics." Working Paper #04, Department of Political Science,
National University of Singapore.

Ho Khai Leong. 1998. "Accountability in the Malaysian Bureaucracy: Politics and Administration." Working Paper #18, Department of Political Science, National University of Singapore.

Ho Khai Leong. 2000. *The Politics of Policy-Making in Singapore*. Singapore: Oxford University Press.

Ho Khai Leong. 2010. "Political Consolidation in Singapore: Connecting the Party, the
Government and the Expanding State." In *Management of Success: Singapore Revisited*, edited by Terence Chong, 67–79. Singapore: ISEAS.

Holland, Alisha C., and Brian Palmer-Rubin. 2015. "Beyond the Machine: Clientelist Brokers and Interest Organizations in Latin America." *Comparative Political Studies*
48 (9):1186–223, http://dx.doi.org/10.1177/0010414015574883.

Howard, Judith. 2000. "The Social Psychology of Identities." *Annual Review of Sociology*
26:367–93, http://dx.doi.org/10.1146/annurev.soc.26.1.367.

Howard, Marc Morjé, and Philip G. Roessler. 2006. "Liberalizing Electoral Outcomes in Competitive Authoritarian Regimes." *American Journal of Political Science* 50 (2):365–81, http://dx.doi.org/10.1111/j.1540-5907.2006.00189.x.

Hunter, Murray. 2013. "Village Security and Development Committees (JKKK): Frontline in Malaysia's Next General Election." *Eurasia Review*, August 19.

Hutchcroft, Paul. 2014. "Linking Capital and Countryside: Patronage and Clientelism in Japan, Thailand, and the Philippines." In *Clientelism, Social Policy, and the Quality of Democracy*, edited by Diego Abente Brun and Larry Diamond, 174–203. Baltimore: Johns Hopkins University Press.

Hutchinson, Francis. 2013. "Hidden Counter-Revolution: A History of the Centralisation of Power in Malaysia." ISEAS Perspective #06, Singapore: ISEAS.

Hutchinson, Francis E. 2015. "Centre–State Relations and Intra-Party Dynamics in Malaysia: UMNO and the Case of Johor." *Asian Journal of Political Science* 23 (2):111–33, http://dx.doi.org/10.1080/02185377.2015.1055774.

IPS. 2011. "IPS Post-Election Forum 2011." Institute of Policy Studies, National University of Singapore.

Jacobs, J. Bruce. 1997. "Democratisation in Taiwan Revisited." *Asian Studies Review* 21 (2–3):149–57, http://dx.doi.org/10.1080/03147539708713169.

Jayasuriya, Kanishka, and Garry Rodan. 2007. "Beyond Hybrid Regimes: More Participation, Less Contestation in Southeast Asia." *Democratization* 14 (5):773–94, http://dx.doi.org/10.1080/13510340701635647.

Jesudason, James V. 1997. "The Developmental Clientelist State: The Malaysian Case." *Humboldt Journal of Social Relations* 23 (1 & 2):147–73.

Jesudason, James V. 1999. "The Resilience of One-Party Dominance in Malaysia and Singapore." In *The Awkward Embrace: One-Party Domination and Democracy*, edited by Hermann Giliomee and Charles Simkins, 127–72. Amsterdam: Harwood Academic Press.

Jomo K. S., and E. T. Gomez. 2000. "The Malaysian Development Dilemma." In *Rents, Rent-Seeking and Economic Development: Theory and Evidence in Asia*, edited by Mushtaq H. Khan and Jomo K. S., 274–303. New York: Cambridge University Press.

Jones, Rodney W. 1972. "Linkage Analysis of Indian Urban Politics." *Economic and Political Weekly* (17 June):1195–203.

Kailitz, Steffen. 2013. "Classifying Political Regimes Revisited: Legitimation and Durability." *Democratization* 20 (1):39–60, http://dx.doi.org/10.1080/13510347.2013.738861.

Kaur, Amarjit. 1998. *Economic Change in East Malaysia: Sabah and Sarawak since 1850.* Houndmills, UK: Palgrave Macmillan.

Key, V. O. 1964. *Politics, Parties, and Pressure Groups*, 5th ed. New York: Thomas Y. Crowell. Original edition, 1942.

Khong Cho-Oon. 1995. "Singapore: Political Legitimacy through Managing Conformity." In *Political Legitimacy in Southeast Asia: The Quest for Moral Authority*, edited by Muthiah Alagappa, 108–35. Stanford, CA: Stanford University Press.

Khong Kim Hoong. 2003. *Merdeka! British Rule and the Struggle for Independence in Malaya, 1945–1959*. Petaling Jaya, Malaysia: SIRD. Original edition, 1984.

Khoo Boo Teik. 2016. "Networks in Pursuit of a 'Two-Coalition System' in Malaysia: Pakatan Rakyat's Mobilization of Dissent between Reformasi and the Tsunami." *Southeast Asian Studies* 5 (1):73–91, http://dx.doi.org/10.20495/seas.5.1_73.

Khor Yu Leng. 2015. "The Political Economy of FELDA Seats: UMNO's Malay Rural Fortress in GE13." In *Coalitions in Collision: Malaysia's 13th General Elections*, edited by Johan Saravanamuttu, Lee Hock Guan, and Mohamed Nawab Mohamed Osman, 91–121. Singapore: ISEAS.

Kimball, Walter B. 1968. "Singapore's People's Association." *Studies in Intelligence* 12 (4):47–55.

Kitschelt, Herbert. 2000. "Linkages between Citizens and Politicians in Democratic Polities." *Comparative Political Studies* 33 (6/7):845–79, http://dx.doi.org/10.1177 /001041400003300607.

Koh, Gillian. 2015. "The Emergent in Governance in Singapore." In *Inequality in Singapore,* edited by Faizal Bin Yahya, 41–52. Singapore: World Scientific Publishing.

Koh, Gillian, Tan Ern Ser, and Debbie Soon. 2007. "Asian Barometer Country Report: Singapore." Working Paper Series No. 147.

Koh Lay Chin. 2011. "The Challenges of Being an MP." In *Understanding the Dewan Rakyat,* edited by Deborah Loh and Jacqueline Ann Surin, 81–87. Petaling Jaya, Malaysia: ZI Publications.

Krauss, Ellis S., and Robert J. Pekkanen. 2011. *The Rise and Fall of Japan's LDP: Political Party Organizations as Historical Institutions.* Ithaca, NY: Cornell University Press.

Kua Kia Soong. 1994. "The Malaysian Parliament: More Questions than Answers." *Aliran Monthly* 14 (1):32–33.

Kuhonta, Erik Martinez. 2008. "The Paradox of Thailand's 1997 'People's Constitution': Be Careful What You Wish For." *Asian Survey* 48 (3):373–92, http://dx.doi.org/AS .2008.48.3.373.

Lafaye de Micheaux, Elsa. 2017. *The Development of Malaysian Capitalism: From British Rule to the Present Day.* Translated by Sandie Zanolin. Petaling Jaya, Malaysia: SIRD.

Lai Seck Ling. 1997. "Corak Pengundian di Kalangan Pengundi Cina di Kawasan Dewan Undangan Negeri (DUN) Seri Kembangan: Di Antara *Straight-ticket Voting* dan *Split-ticket Voting*" [Voting Patterns among Chinese Voters in Seri Kembangan State Legislative Constituency: Between Straight-ticket Voting and Split-ticket Voting]. Academic Exercise, Department of Political Science, Faculty of Social Sciences and Humanities, Universiti Kebangsaan Malaysia.

Lam, Dana. 2006. *Days of Being Wild: GE 2006, Walking the Line with the Opposition.* Singapore: Ethos Books.

Lam Peng Er. 2011. "The End of One-Party Dominance and Japan's Emergence as a 'Common Democracy.'" In *Political Systems, Party Systems and Democratization in East Asia,* edited by Lye Liang Fook and Wilhelm Hofmeister, 133–55. Hackensack, NJ: World Scientific.

Landé, Carl H. 1977. "Introduction: The Dyadic Basis of Clientelism." In *Friends, Followers and Factions: A Reader,* edited by Steffen W. Schmidt, James C. Scott, Carl Landé, and Laura Guasti, xiii–xxxvii. Berkeley: University of California Press.

Landé, Carl H. 1983. "Political Clientelism in Political Studies: Retrospect and Prospects." *International Political Science Review* 4 (4):435–54.

LeBas, Adrienne. 2011. *From Protest to Parties: Party-Building and Democratization in Africa.* Oxford: Oxford University Press.

Lee, Cassey. 2013. "Malaysia's 13th GE: A Tale of Two Manifestos." ISEAS Perspective 24, Singapore: ISEAS.

Lee, Edwin. 1968. "The Emergence of Towkay Leaders in Party Politics in Sabah." *Journal of Southeast Asian History* 9 (2):306–24.

Lee Hock Guan. 2015. "Mal-apportionment and the Electoral Authoritarian Regime in Malaysia." In *Coalitions in Collision: Malaysia's 13th General Elections,* edited by Johan Saravanamuttu, Lee Hock Guan, and Mohamed Nawab Mohamed Osman, 63–89. Singapore: ISEAS.

Lee, Terence. 2002. "The Politics of Civil Society in Singapore." *Asian Studies Review* 26 (1):97–117.

Leifer, Michael. 1964. "Communal Violence in Singapore." *Asian Survey* 4 (10):1115–21, http://dx.doi.org/10.2307/2642213.

Lemarchand, René, and Keith Legg. 1972. "Political Clientelism and Development: A Preliminary Analysis." *Comparative Politics* 4 (2):149–78, http://dx.doi.org/10.2307/421508.

Leong, Keith Yu Keen. 2012. *The Future of Pakatan Rakyat: Lessons from Selangor.* Kuala Lumpur: Institute for Democracy and Economic Affairs.

Levitsky, Steven, and Lucan A. Way. 2010. *Competitive Authoritarianism: Hybrid Regimes after the Cold War.* New York: Cambridge University Press.

Lhériteau, Claire. 2005. "FELDA and the Manipulation of Land Policy in Malaysia." In *Elections and Democracy in Malaysia*, edited by Mavis Puthucheary and Norani Othman, 313–32. Bangi: Universiti Kebangsaan Malaysia Press.

Li, Jinshan, and Jørgen Elklit. 1999. "The Singapore General Election 1997: Campaigning Strategy, Results, and Analysis." *Electoral Studies* 18:199–216, http://dx.doi.org/10.1016/S0261-3794(98)00027-4.

Lim Hong Hai. 2005. "Making the System Work: The Election Commission." In *Elections and Democracy in Malaysia*, edited by Mavis Puthucheary and Norani Othman, 249–91. Bangi: Universiti Kebangsaan Malaysia Press.

Lim Kit Siang. 1971. *Athi Nahappan Report on Local Authorities* (press statement). 10 December. Accessed 3 August 2017, https://bibliotheca.limkitsiang.com/1971/12/10/athi-nahappan-report-on-local-authorities/.

Lim, Regina. 2008. *Federal-State Relations in Sabah, Malaysia: The Berjaya Administration, 1976–85.* Singapore: ISEAS.

Lim, Sylvia. 2007. "The Future of Alternative Party Politics: Growth or Extinction?" In *Renaissance Singapore? Economy, Culture, and Politics*, edited by Kenneth Paul Tan, 239–52. Singapore: NUS Press.

Lindberg, Staffan I. 2009. "Democratization by Elections: A New Mode of Transition?" In *Democratization by Elections: A New Mode of Transition*, edited by Staffan I. Lindberg, 1–21. Baltimore: Johns Hopkins University Press.

Lindberg, Staffan I. 2010. "What Accountability Pressures Do MPs in Africa Face and How Do They Respond? Evidence from Ghana." *Journal of Modern African Studies* 48 (1):117–42, http://dx.doi.org/10.1017/S0022278X09990243.

Liow, Joseph Chinyong. 2006. *Piety and Politcs: Islamism in Contemporary Malaysia.* New York: Oxford University Press.

Liow, Joseph Chinyong. 2011. "Creating Cadres: Mobilization, Activism and the Youth Wing of the Pan-Malaysian Islamic Party, PAS." *Pacific Affairs* 84 (4):665–86, http://dx.doi.org/10.5509/2011844665.

Lipscy, Phillip Y., and Ethan Scheiner. 2012. "Japan under the DPJ: The Paradox of Political Change without Policy Change." *Journal of East Asian Studies* 12 (3):311–22, http://dx.doi.org/10.1017/S1598240800008043.

Lipset, Seymour Martin, and Stein Rokkan. 1967. "Cleavage Structures, Party Systems, and Voter Alignments: An Introduction." In *Party Systems and Voter Alignments: Cross-National Perspectives*, edited by Seymour M. Lipset and Stein Rokkan, 1–64. New York: Free Press.

Lockard, Craig A. 1967. "Parties, Personalities and Crisis Politics in Sarawak." *Journal of Southeast Asian History* 8 (1):111–21.

Loh, Deborah, and Koh Lay Chin. 2011. "MP Watch: Who Replied, Who Didn't, and Why." In *Understanding the Dewan Rakyat*, edited by Deborah Loh and Jacqueline Ann Surin, 55–62. Petaling Jaya, Malaysia: ZI Publications.

Loh, Francis Kok Wah. 1997. "Understanding Politics in Sabah and Sarawak: An Overview." *Kajian Malaysia* 15 (1&2):1–14.

Loh, Francis Kok Wah. 2003a. "Developmentalism versus Reformism: The Contest for Bukit Bendera, 1999." In *New Politics in Malaysia*, edited by Francis Kok Wah Loh and Johan Saravanamuttu, 158–77. Singapore: ISEAS.

Loh, Francis Kok Wah. 2003b. "Towards a New Politics of Fragmentation and Contestation." In *New Politics in Malaysia*, edited by Francis Kok Wah Loh and Johan Saravanamuttu, 253–82. Singapore: ISEAS.

Loh, Francis Kok Wah. 2005. "Strongmen and Federal Politics in Sabah." In *Elections and Democracy in Malaysia*, edited by Mavis Puthucheary and Norani Othman, 70–117. Bangi: Universiti Kebangsaan Malaysia Press.

Loh, Francis Kok Wah. 2008. "The BN National Security State and the ISA." *Aliran Monthly* 7.

Loh, Francis Kok Wah. 2010. "Restructuring Federal-State Relations in Malaysia: From Centralised to Co-operative Federalism?" *Round Table* 99 (407):131–40, http://dx.doi.org/10.1080/00358531003656180.

Loke Hoe Yeong. 2014. *Let the People Have Him: Chiam See Tong: The Early Years*. Singapore: Epigram Books.

Loke Hoe Yeong. 2016. "Parties, Personalities and Protagonists." In *Change in Voting: Singapore's 2015 General Election*, edited by Terence Lee and Kevin Y. L. Tan, 66–82. Singapore: Ethos Books.

Lowi, Theodore J. 1967. "Machine Politics—Old and New." *The Public Interest* 9:83–92.

Luna, Juan Pablo, Fernando Rosenblatt, and Sergio Toro. 2014. "Programmatic Parties: A Survey of Dimensions and Explanations in the Literature." In *Politics Meets Policies: The Emergence of Programmatic Political Parties*, edited by Nic Cheeseman, Juan Pablo Luna, Herbert Kitschelt, Dan Paget, Fernando Rosenblatt, Kristen Sample, Sergio Toro, Jorge Valladares Molleda, Sam van der Staak, and Yi-ting Wang, 1–41. Stockholm: International Institute for Democracy and Electoral Assistance.

Lust, Ellen. 2009. "Competitive Clientelism in the Middle East." *Journal of Democracy* 20 (3):122–35, http://dx.doi.org/10.1353/jod.0.0099.

Lust-Okar, Ellen. 2005. *Structuring Conflict in the Arab World: Incumbents, Opponents, and Institutions*. New York: Cambridge University Press.

Lyons, Lenore. 2005. "A Politics of Accommodation: Women and the People's Action Party in Singapore." *International Feminist Journal of Politics* 7 (2):233–57, http://dx.doi.org/10.1080/14616740500065139.

Machado, K. G. 1974. "From Traditional Faction to Machine: Changing Patterns of Political Leadership and Organization in the Rural Philippines." *Journal of Asian Studies* 33 (4):523–47, http://dx.doi.org/10.2307/2053123.

Magaloni, Beatriz. 2006. *Voting for Autocracy: Hegemonic Party Survival and Its Demise in Mexico*. New York: Cambridge University Press.

Magaloni, Beatriz. 2010. "The Game of Electoral Fraud and the Ousting of Authoritarian Rule." *American Journal of Political Science* 54 (3):751–65, http://dx.doi.org/10.1111/j.1540-5907.2010.00458.x.

Magaloni, Beatriz. 2014. "Defining Political Clientelism's Persistence." In *Clientelism, Social Policy, and the Quality of Democracy*, edited by Diego Abente Brun and Larry Diamond, 253–62.

Manderson, Lenore. 1977. "The Development of the Pergerakan Kaum Ibu UMNO, 1945–1972." PhD diss., Asian Civilizations, Australian National University.

Maruah. 2013. *Defending the Legitimacy of Singapore Elections: MARUAH Position Paper on the GRC System*. Electoral System Review Paper #2, Singapore.

Maryanov, Gerald S. 1967. "Political Parties in Mainland Malaya." *Journal of Southeast Asian History* 8 (1):99–110, http://dx.doi.org/10.1017/S0217781100003495.

Mauzy, Diane K., and R. S. Milne. 2002. *Singapore Politics under the People's Action Party.* London: Routledge.

Maznah Mohamad. 2015. "Fragmented but Captured: Malay Voters and the FELDA Factor in GE13." In *Coalitions in Collision: Malaysia's 13th General Elections,* edited by Johan Saravanamuttu, Lee Hock Guan, and Mohamed Nawab Mohamed Osman, 123–57. Singapore: ISEAS.

McElwain, Kenneth Mori. 2008. "Manipulating Electoral Rules to Manufacture Single-Party Dominance." *American Journal of Political Science* 52 (1):32–47, http://dx.doi.org/10.1111/j.1540-5907.2007.00297.x.

Mersat, Neilson Ilan. 2009. "'Blue Waves versus Political Tsunami': Sarawak and the 2008 Malaysian General Election." *Akademika* 77:113–32.

Mietzner, Marcus. 2017. "Authoritarian Elections, State Capacity, and Performance Legitimacy: Phases of Regime Consolidation and Decline in Suharto's Indonesia." *International Political Science Review* 39 (1):83–96, http://dx.doi.org/10.1177/019251211687139.

Milne, R. S. 1963. "Malaysia: A New Federation in the Making." *Asian Survey* 3 (2):76–82, http://dx.doi.org/10.2307/3023678.

Milne, R. S. 1986. "Malaysia—Beyond the New Economic Policy." *Asian Survey* 26 (12):1364–82, http://dx.doi.org/10.2307/2644552.

Milne, R. S., and K. J. Ratnam. 2013 [1974]. *Malaysia—New States in a New Nation: Political Development of Sarawak and Sabah in Malaysia.* New York: Routledge.

Milner, Anthony, Abdul Rahman Embong, and Tham Siew Yean. 2014. "Introduction." In *Transforming Malaysia: Dominant and Competing Paradigms,* edited by Anthony Milner, Abdul Rahman Embong, and Tham Siew Yean, 1–17. Singapore: ISEAS.

Mobrand, Erik. 2015. "The Politics of Regulating Elections in South Korea: The Persistence of Restrictive Campaign Laws." *Pacific Affairs* 88 (4):791–811, http://dx.doi.org/10.5509/2015884791.

Mohd Azizuddin Mohd Sani. 2009. "The Emergence of New Politics in Malaysia: From Consociational to Deliberative Democracy." *Taiwan Journal of Democracy* 5 (2):97–125.

Morlino, Leonardo, Björn Dressel, and Riccardo Pelizzo. 2011. "The Quality of Democracy in Asia-Pacific: Issues and Findings." *International Political Science Review* 32 (5):491–511, http://dx.doi.org/10.177/0192512111418334.

Muhamad Fuzi Omar. 2008. "Parliamentary Behaviour of the Members of Opposition Political Parties in Malaysia." *Intellectual Discourse* 16 (1):21–48.

Musolf, Lloyd, and J. Fred Springer. 1977. "Legislatures and Divided Societies: The Malaysian Parliament and Multi-Ethnicity." *Legislative Studies Quarterly* II (2):113–36, http://dx.doi.org/10.2307/439560.

Mustafa Izzuddin. 2004–5. "Ideological Decentralization: A Comparative Study of Young PAP and UMNO Youth." B. Soc. Sci. thesis (Honours), Political Science, National University of Singapore.

Mutalib, Hussin. 1994. *Singapore's Elected Presidency and the Quest for Regime Dominance.* Working Paper #9, Department of Political Science, National University of Singapore.

Mutalib, Hussin. 2002. "Constitutional-Electoral Reforms and Politics in Singapore." *Legislative Studies Quarterly* 27 (4):659–72, http://dx.doi.org/10.2307/3598663.

Mutalib, Hussin. 2003. *Parties and Politics: A Study of Opposition Parties and the PAP in Singapore.* Singapore: Eastern Universities Press.

Nahappan, Athi. 1970. Report of the Royal Commission of Enquiry to Investigate into the Workings of Local Authorities in West Malaysia. Kuala Lumpur: Jabatan Chetak Kerajaan.

Nam Tae Yul. 1969–70. "Singapore's One-Party System: Its Relationship to Democracy and Political Stability." *Pacific Affairs* 42 (4):465–80, http://dx.doi.org/10.2307/2754128.

Ng Beoy Kui. 2001. "Vulnerability and Party Capitalism: Malaysia's Encounter with the 1997 Financial Crisis." In *Mahathir's Administration: Performance and Crisis in Governance*, edited by Ho Khai Leong and James Chin, 161–87. Singapore: Times Books International.

Ng Tien Eng. 2003. "The Contest for Chinese Votes: Politics of Negotiation or Politics of Pressure?" In *New Politics in Malaysia*, edited by Francis Kok Wah Loh and Johan Saravanamuttu, 87–106. Singapore: ISEAS.

Ng Tien Eng. 2005. "Re-shaping Party Platforms: The Dong Jiao Zong." In *Elections and Democracy in Malaysia*, edited by Mavis Puthucheary and Norani Othman, 184–204. Bangi: Universiti Kebangsaan Malaysia Press.

Ng, Tisa. 2002. "Party Politics Dealing with Disagreement." In *Building Social Space in Singapore: The Working Committee's Initiative in Civil Society Activism*, edited by Constance Singam, Tan Chong Kee, Tisa Ng, and Leon Perera, 119–32. Singapore: Select Publishing.

Noble, Gregory W. 2010. "The Decline of Particularism in Japanese Politics." *Journal of East Asian Studies* 10 (2):239–73, 10.1017/S1598240800003453.

Nonini, Donald M. 2015. *"Getting By": Class and State Formation among Chinese in Malaysia*. Ithaca, NY: Cornell University Press.

Norris, M. W. 1980. *Local Government in Peninsular Malaysia*. Westmead, UK: Gower.

Norris, Pippa. 1997. "The Puzzle of Constituency Service." *Journal of Legislative Studies* 3 (2):29–49, http://dx.doi.org/10.1080/13572339708420508.

Oakley, Alysson Akiko. 2018. "Anatomy of Authority: Informal Political Networks and the Mobilization of Indonesia's Elite." PhD diss., Johns Hopkins University, School of Advanced International Studies.

Ong, Elvin. 2015. "Complementary Institutions in Authoritarian Regimes: The Everyday Politics of Constituency Service in Singapore." *Journal of East Asian Studies* 15 (3):361–90, http://dx.doi.org/10.1017/S1598240800009115.

Ong, Elvin. 2016. "Opposition Coordination in Singapore's 2015 General Elections." *The Round Table* 105 (2):185–94, http://dx.doi.org/10.1080/00358533.2016.1154385.

Ong Kian Ming. 2005. "Examining the Electoral Roll." In *Elections and Democracy in Malaysia*, edited by Mavis Puthucheary and Norani Othman, 292–315. Bangi: Universiti Kebangsaan Malaysia Press.

Ong, Michael. 1976. "The Member of Parliament and His Constituency: The Malaysian Case." *Legislative Studies Quarterly* 1 (3):405–22, http://dx.doi.org/10.2307/439505.

Ong, Michael. 1987. "Government and Opposition in Parliament: The Rules of the Game." In *Government and Politics in Malaysia*, edited by Zakaria Haji Ahmad, 40–55. New York: Oxford University Press.

Ooi Giok Ling. 1990. *Town Councils in Singapore: Self-Determination for Public Housing Estates*, IPS Occasional Paper No. 4. Singapore: Times Academic Press.

Ooi Giok Ling. 2009. "State Shaping of Community-Level Politics: Residents' Committees in Singapore." In *Local Organizations and Urban Governance in East and Southeast Asia: Straddling State and Society*, edited by Benjamin L. Read and Robert Pekkanen, 174–90. New York: Routledge.

Ooi Giok Ling, and Brian J. Shaw. 2004. *Beyond the Port City: Development and Identity in 21st Century Singapore*. New York: Prentice Hall.

Ooi Giok Ling, Tan Ern Ser, and Gillian Koh. 1999. "Political Participation in Singapore: Findings from a National Survey." *Asian Journal of Political Science* 7 (2):126–41, http://dx.doi.org/10.1080/02185379908434151.

Ortmann, Stephan. 2010. *Politics and Change in Singapore and Hong Kong: Containing Contention.* New York: Routledge.

Ortmann, Stephan. 2014. "The Significance of By-elections for Political Change in Singapore's Authoritarian Regime." *Asian Survey* 54 (4):725–48, http://dx.doi.org/10.1525/as.2014.54.4.725.

Pang Cheng Lian. 1971. *Singapore's People's Action Party: Its History, Organization and Leadership.* Singapore: Oxford University Press.

Pemantau. 2018. *Election Observation Report of the 14th Malaysian General Election.* Petaling Jaya, Malaysia: Bersih & Adil Network.

Pempel, T. J. 2010. "Between Pork and Productivity: The Collapse of the Liberal Democratic Party." *Journal of Japanese Studies* 36 (2):227–54, http://dx.doi.org/10.1353/jjs.0.0178.

People's Association. 1973. *Kindergarten.* Information Series no. 4, Singapore: People's Association.

Pérez-Liñán, Aníbal, and Scott Mainwaring. 2013. "Regime Legacies and Levels of Democracy: Evidence from Latin America." *Comparative Politics* 45 (4):379–97, http://dx.doi.org/10.5129/001041513X13815259182785.

Persson, Anna L., and Bo Rothstein. 2019. "Lost in Transition: A Bottom-up Perspective on Hybrid Regimes." *Annals of Comparative Democratization* 17 (3): 10–12.

Poh Soo Kai. 2016. *Living in a Time of Deception.* Petaling Jaya, Malaysia: Pusat Sejarah Rakyat.

Poulgrain, Greg. 2014. *The Genesis of Konfrontasi: Malaysia, Brunei and Indonesia, 1945–1965.* Petaling Jaya, Malaysia: SIRD.

Pye, Lucien W. 1965. "Introduction: Political Culture and Political Development." In *Political Culture and Political Development,* edited by Lucien W. Pye and Sidney Verba, 3–26. Princeton, NJ: Princeton University Press.

Quah, Jon S. T. 2002. "Decentralization in Singapore: From Residents' Committees to Community Development Councils." Working Papers #25, Political Science, National University of Singapore.

Quah, Jon S. T., and Stella R. Quah. 1989. "The Limits of Intervention." In *Management of Success: The Molding of Modern Singapore,* edited by Kernial Singh Sandhu and Paul Wheatley, 102–27. Singapore: ISEAS.

Rabushka, Alvin. 1970. "The Manipulation of Ethnic Politics in Malaya." *Polity* 2 (3):345–56, http://dx.doi.org/10.2307/3234129.

Rabushka, Alvin. 1973. *Race and Politics in Urban Malaya.* Stanford, CA: Hoover Institution Press.

Rakner, Lise, and Nicolas van de Walle. 2009. "Opposition Weakness in Africa." *Journal of Democracy* 20 (3):108–21, http://dx.doi.org/10.1353/jod.0.0096.

Randall, Vicky, and Lars Svåsand. 2002. "Party Institutionalization in New Democracies." *Party Politics* 8 (1):5–29, http://dx.doi.org/10.1177/1354068802008001001.

Rashila Ramli. 2005. "The Multiple Roles of Rural Malay Women during the 1999 Election: The Case of FELDA J8." In *New Politics in Malaysia,* edited by Francis Kok Wah Loh and Johan Saravanamuttu, 129–40. Singapore: ISEAS.

Read, Benjamin L. 2000. "Revitalizing the State's Urban 'Nerve Tips.'" *China Quarterly* 163 (September):806–20, http://dx.doi.org/10.1017/S0305741000014673.

Read, Benjamin L. 2009. "The Multiple Uses of Local Networks: State Cultivation of Neighborhood Social Capital in China and Taiwan." In *Local Organizations and Urban Governance in East and Southeast Asia,* edited by Benjamin L Read and Robert Pekkanen, 121–57. New York: Routledge.

Read, Benjamin L. 2012. *Roots of the State: Neighborhood Organization and Social Networks in Beijing and Taipei.* Stanford, CA: Stanford University Press.

Reed, Steven R., Ethan Scheiner, and Michael F. Thies. 2012. "The End of LDP Dominance and the Rise of Party-oriented Politics in Japan." *Journal of Japanese Studies* 38 (2):353–76, http://dx.doi.org/10.1353/jjs.2012.0037.

Reid, Joseph D. Jr., and Michael M. Kurth. 1992. "The Rise and Fall of Urban Political Patronage Machines." In *Strategic Factors in Nineteenth Century American Economic History: A Volume to Honor Robert W. Fogel*, edited by Claudia Goldin and Hugh Rockoff, 427–45. Chicago: University of Chicago Press.

Remmer, Karen L. 2007. "The Political Economy of Patronage: Expenditure Patterns in the Argentine Provinces, 1983–2003." *Journal of Politics* 69 (2):363–77, http://dx.doi.org/10.1111/j.1468-2508.2007.00537.x.

Rodan, Garry. 1997. "Civil Society and Other Political Possibilities in Southeast Asia." *Journal of Contemporary Asia* 27 (2):156–78, http://dx.doi.org/10.1080/00472339780000111.

Rodan, Garry. 2009. "New Modes of Political Participation and Singapore's Nominated Members of Parliament." *Government and Opposition* 44 (4):438–62, http://dx.doi.org/10.1111/j.1477-7053.2009.01297.x.

Rodan, Garry. 2012. "Competing Ideologies of Political Representation in Southeast Asia." *Third World Quarterly* 33 (2):311–32, http://dx.doi.org/10.1080/01436597.2012.666014.

Rodan, Garry. 2014. "Civil Society Activism and Political Parties in Malaysia: Differences over Local Representation." *Democratization* 21 (5):824–45, http://dx.doi.org/10.1080/13510347.2013.878331.

Rodan, Garry. 2018. *Participation without Democracy: Containing Conflict in Southeast Asia*. Ithaca, NY: Cornell University Press.

Rüland, Jürgen. 1990. "Continuity and Change in Southeast Asia: Political Participation in Three Intermediate Cities." *Asian Survey* 30 (5):461–80, http://dx.doi.org/10.2307/2644839.

Rustam A. Sani. 2008. *Social Roots of the Malay Left*. Petaling Jaya, Malaysia: SIRD.

Sartori, Giovanni. 1976. *Parties and Party Systems*. New York: Cambridge.

Schaffer, Frederic Charles. 2007. *Elections for Sale: The Causes and Consequences of Vote Buying*. Boulder, CO: Lynne Rienner.

Schedler, Andreas. 2002. "The Menu of Manipulation." *Journal of Democracy* 13 (2):36–50, http://dx.doi.org/10.1353/jod.2002.0031.

Schedler, Andreas. 2010. *Transitions from Electoral Authoritarianism*. CIDE Working Paper #22. Mexico City: Centro de Investigación y Docencia Económicas.

Scheiner, Ethan. 2006. *Democracy without Competition in Japan: Opposition Failure in a One-party Dominant State*. New York: Cambridge University Press.

Scheiner, Ethan. 2007. "Clientelism in Japan: The Importance and Limits of Institutional Explanations." In *Patrons, Clients and Policies: Patterns of Democratic Accountability and Political Competition*, edited by Herbert Kitschelt and Steven I. Wilkinson, 276–97. New York: Cambridge University Press.

Scheiner, Ethan. 2012. "The Electoral System and Japan's Partial Transformation: Party System Consolidation without Policy Realignment." *Journal of East Asian Studies* 12 (3):351–79, http://dx.doi.org/10.1017/S1598240800008067.

Schmitter, Philippe C. 2001. "Parties Are Not What They Once Were." In *Political Parties and Democracy*, edited by Larry Diamond and Richard Gunther, 67–89. Baltimore: Johns Hopkins University Press.

Schmitter, Philippe C., and Terry Lynn Karl. 1991. "What Democracy Is . . . and Is Not." *Journal of Democracy* 2 (3):75–88, http://dx.doi.org/10.1353/jod.1991.0033.

Scott, James C. 1968. *Political Ideology in Malaysia: Reality and the Beliefs of an Elite*. New Haven, CT: Yale University Press.

Scott, James C. 1969. "Corruption, Machine Politics, and Political Change." *American Political Science Review* 63 (4):1142–58, http://dx.doi.org/10.1017/S0003055400263247.

Scott, James C. 1972a. *Comparative Political Corruption*. Englewood Cliffs, NJ: Prentice-Hall.

Scott, James C. 1972b. "Patron-Client Politics and Political Change in Southeast Asia." *American Political Science Review* 66 (1):91–113, http://dx.doi.org/10.2307/1959280.

Seah Chee Meow. 1973. *Community Centres in Singapore: Their Political Involvement*. Singapore: Singapore University Press.

Seah Chee Meow. 1976. "The Singapore Bureaucracy and Issues of Transition." In *Singapore: Society in Transition*, edited by Riaz Hassan, 52–66. New York: Oxford University Press.

Seah Chee Meow. 1978. "People's Participation at the Local Level in Singapore." In *People's Participation at the Local Level*, edited by Arnold Wehmhoerner, 7–23. Bangkok: Friedrich-Ebert-Stiftung.

Seah Chee Meow. 1979. "Grassroots Political Participation in Singapore." In *Petir: 25th Anniversary Issue*, 276–81. Singapore: People's Action Party.

Seah Chee Meow. 1985. "Parapolitical Institutions." In *Government and Politics of Singapore*, edited by Jon S. T. Quah, Chan Heng Chee, and Seah Chee Meow, 173–94. Singapore: Oxford University Press.

Seeberg, Merete Bech. 2014. "State Capacity and the Paradox of Authoritarian Elections." *Democratization* 21 (7):1265–85, http://dx.doi.org/10.1080/13510347.2014.960210.

Shamsul Amri Baharuddin. 1997. "The Economic Dimension of Malay Nationalism: The Socio-Historical Roots of the New Economic Policy and Its Contemporary Implications." *The Developing Economies* 35 (3):240–61.

Shefter, Martin. 1977. "Party and Patronage: Germany, England, and Italy." *Politics & Society* 7 (4):403–51, http://dx.doi.org/10.1177/003232927700700402.

Shefter, Martin. 1994. *Political Parties and the State: The American Historical Experience*. Princeton, NJ: Princeton University Press.

Shekhar, Vibhanshu. 2008. "Malay Majoritarianism and Marginalised Indians." *Economic and Political Weekly* 43 (8):22–25.

Shin Kwang-Yeong. 2012. "The Dilemmas of Korea's New Democracy in an Age of Neoliberal Globalisation." *Third World Quarterly* 33 (2):293–309, http://dx.doi.org/10.1080/01436597.2012.666013.

Siddiquee, Noore Alam. 2006. "Paradoxes of Public Accountability in Malaysia: Control Mechanisms and Their Limitations." *International Public Management Review* 7 (2):43–65.

Sim, Steven, and Koay Su-Lyn. 2015a. "History of Local Government Election [sic] in Malaysia." *REFSA Quarterly* 1:6–15.

Sim, Steven, and Koay Su-Lyn. 2015b. "Local Elections Are Part of a Larger Reform Agenda." *Penang Monthly*, 19 March.

Sim, Steven, and Koay Su-Lyn. 2015c. "Revisiting the Athi Nahappan Report: Part 1." *REFSA Quarterly* 1:16–19.

Singh, Bilveer. 1992. *Whither PAP's Dominance? An Analysis of Singapore's 1991 General Elections*. Petaling Jaya, Malaysia: Pelanduk.

Smith, T. E. 1960. "The Malayan Elections of 1959." *Pacific Affairs* 33 (1):38–47, http://dx.doi.org/10.2307/2753647.

Smith, T. E. 1962. "The Local Authority Elections 1961 in the Federation of Malaya." *Journal of Commonwealth Political Studies* 1 (2):153–55, http://dx.doi.org/10.1080/14662046208446966.

Stokes, Susan C. 2005. "Perverse Accountability: A Formal Model of Machine Politics with Evidence from Argentina." *American Political Science Review* 99 (3):315–25, http://dx .doi.org/10.1017/S0003055405051683.

Stokes, Susan C., Thad Dunning, Marcelo Nazareno, and Valeria Brusco. 2013. *Brokers, Voters, and Clientelism: The Puzzle of Distributive Politics.* New York: Cambridge University Press.

Strauch, Judith. 1981. "Chinese New Villages of the Malayan Emergency, A Generation Later: A Case Study." *Contemporary Southeast Asia* 3 (2):126–39.

Suffian, Ibrahim, and Lee Tai De. 2020. "How Malaysia Voted in 2018." In *Toward a New Malaysia? The 2018 Election and Its Aftermath*, edited by Meredith L. Weiss and Faisal Hazis, 17–40. Singapore: NUS Press.

Syed Husin Ali. 1996. *Two Faces: Detention without Trial.* Kuala Lumpur: INSAN.

Szwarcberg, Mariela. 2012. "Uncertainty, Political Clientelism, and Voter Turnout in Latin America: Why Parties Conduct Rallies in Argentina." *Comparative Politics* 45 (1):88–106, http://dx.doi.org/10.5129/001041512802822851.

Tan Ern Ser, and Wang Zhengxu. 2007. "Singapore Country Report: Second Wave of Asian Barometer Survey." Working Paper Series No. 35, Asian Barometer & Globalbarometer.

Tan, Eugene K. B. 2010. "The Evolving Social Compact and the Transformation of Singapore: Going Beyond Quid Pro Quo in Governance." In *Management of Success: Singapore Revisited*, edited by Terence Chong, 80–99. Singapore: ISEAS.

Tan, Kenneth Paul. 2003. "Democracy and the grassroots sector in Singapore." *Space & Polity* 7 (1):3–20, http://dx.doi.org/10.1080/1356257032000086642.

Tan, Kenneth Paul. 2007. "New Politics for a Renaissance City?" In *Renaissance Singapore? Economy, Culture, and Politics*, edited by Kenneth Paul Tan, 17–36. Singapore: NUS Press.

Tan, Kenneth Paul. 2008. "Meritocracy and Elitism in a Global City: Ideological Shifts in Singapore." *International Political Science Review* 29 (1):7–27, http://dx.doi.org/10 .1177/0192512107083445.

Tan, Kenneth Paul. 2011. "The People's Action Party and Political Liberalization in Singapore." In *Political Systems, Party Systems and Democratization in East Asia*, edited by Lye Liang Fook and Wilhelm Hofmeister, 107–31. Hackensack, NJ: World Scientific.

Tan, Kenneth Paul. 2015. "Singapore in 2014: Adapting to the 'New Normal.'" *Asian Survey* 55 (1):157–64, http://dx.doi.org/10.1525/AS.2015.55.1.157.

Tan, Kevin Y. L. 2000. "Understanding and Harnessing Ground Energies in Civil Society." In *State-Society Relations in Singapore*, edited by Gillian Koh and Ooi Giok Ling, 98–105. Singapore: Oxford University Press.

Tan, Kevin Y. L. 2008. *Marshall of Singapore: A Biography.* Singapore: ISEAS.

Tan, Kevin Y. L. 2015. *The Constitution of Singapore: A Contextual Analysis.* Portland, OR: Bloomsbury.

Tan Kim Hong. 2008. "The Labour Party of Malaya, 1952–1972." *Aliran Monthly* (10).

Tan, Netina. 2013. "Manipulating Electoral Laws in Singapore." *Electoral Studies* 32 (4):632–43, http://dx.doi.org/10.1016/j.electstud.2013.07.014.

Tan, Netina. 2014a. "The 2011 General and Presidential Elections in Singapore." *Electoral Studies* 35:374–78, http://dx.doi.org/10.1016/j.electstud.2014.02.001.

Tan, Netina. 2014b. "Ethnic Quotas and Unintended Effects on Women's Political Representation in Singapore." *International Political Science Review* 35 (1):27–40, http://dx .doi.org/10.5509/2016892309.

Tan Yew Soon, Lilian Ong, and Allison Teo. 2004. *Building Bridges: The Story of the Feedback Unit.* Singapore: Feedback Unit, Ministry of Community Development and Sports.

Teh Hock Heng. 2007 [1971]. "Revisiting Our Roots: New Villages." *The Guardian* 4:3.

Templeman, Kharis Ali. 2012. "The Origins and Decline of Dominant Party Systems: Taiwan's Transition in Comparative Perspective." PhD diss., University of Michigan.

Tennant, Paul. 1973. "The Abolition of Elective Local Government in Penang." *Journal of Southeast Asian Studies* 4 (1):72–87, http://dx.doi.org/10.1017/S0022463400016428.

Teo Sue Ann. 2014. "Balik Pulau, Penang: Home Run for the Home Boys." In *Electoral Dynamics in Malaysia: Findings from the Grassroots*, edited by Meredith L. Weiss, 65–79. Petaling Jaya, Malaysia: SIRD.

Thachil, Tariq. 2011. "Embedded Mobilization: Nonstate Service Provision as Electoral Strategy in India." *World Politics* 63 (3):434–69, http://dx.doi.org/10.1017/S0043887111000116.

Thirkell-White, Ben. 2006. "Political Islam and Malaysian Democracy." *Democratization* 13 (3):421–44, http://dx.doi.org/10.1080=13510340600579318.

Thomas, Margaret, ed. 2015. *The Politics of Defeat: Preliminary Chapters and the Secret Diary of Francis Thomas*. Singapore: Ethos Books.

Thomas, Melissa A., and Oumar Sissokho. 2005. "Liaison Legislature: The Role of the National Assembly in Senegal." *Journal of Modern African Studies* 43 (1):97–117, http://dx.doi.org/10.0017/S0o22278X04000631.

TI. 2010. *Reforming Political Financing in Malaysia*. Kuala Lumpur: Transparency International–Malaysia.

Tilman, Robert O. 1963. "Elections in Sarawak." *Asian Survey* 3 (10):507–18, http://dx.doi.org/10.2307/3023452.

Ting, Helen. 2007. "Gender Discourse in Malay Politics: Old Wine in New Bottle?" In *Politics in Malaysia: The Malay Dimension*, edited by Edmund Terence Gomez, 75–106. New York: Routledge.

Tinker, Irene. 1956. "Malayan Elections: Electoral Pattern for Plural Societies?" *Western Political Quarterly* 9 (2):258–82, http://dx.doi.org/10.1177/106591295600900203.

Ufen, Andreas. 2015. "Laissez-faire versus Strict Control of Political Finance: Hegemonic Parties and Developmental States in Malaysia and Singapore." *Critical Asian Studies* 47 (4):564–86, http://dx.doi.org/10.1080/14672715.2015.1082263.

van de Walle, Nicolas. 2003. "Presidentialism and Clientelism in Africa's Emerging Party Systems." *Journal of Modern African Studies* 41 (2):297–321, http://dx.doi.org/10.1017/S0022278X03004269.

Van Zyl, Albert. 2010. "What Is Wrong with the Constituency Development Funds?" *IBP Budget Brief* 3 (10).

Vasil, R.K. 1971. *Politics in a Plural Society: A Study of Non-communal Political Parties in West Malaysia*. Kuala Lumpur: Oxford University Press.

Vasil, Raj. 1988. *Governing Singapore: Interviews with the New Leaders*. Singapore: Times Books International. Original edition, 1984.

Vasoo, S. 1994. *Neighbourhood Leaders' Participation in Community Development*. Singapore: Times Academic Press.

von Soest, Christian, and Julia Grauvogel. 2017. "Identity, Procedures and Performance: How Authoritarian Regimes Legitimize Their Rule." *Contemporary Politics* 23 (3):287–305, http://dx.doi.org/10.1080/13569775.2017.1304319.

Wade, Geoff. 2009. *The Origins and Evolution of Ethnocracy in Malaysia*, ARI Working Paper Series No. 112. Singapore: Asia Research Institute, National University of Singapore.

Wahman, Michael. 2011. "Offices and Policies—Why Do Oppositional Parties Form Pre-electoral Coalitions in Competitive Authoritarian Regimes?" *Electoral Studies* 30 (4):642–57, http://dx.doi.org/10.1016/j.electstud.2011.05.009.

Washida, Hidekuni. 2019. *Distributive Politics in Malaysia: Maintaining Authoritarian Party Dominance*. New York: Routledge.

WDC. 2008. *Redefining Governance: Women's Rights and Participatory Democracy in Local Government*. Petaling Jaya, Malaysia: Women's Development Collective and European Commission.

Weghorst, Keith R., and Staffan I. Lindberg. 2013. "What Drives the Swing Voter in Africa?" *American Journal of Political Science* 57 (3):717–34, http://dx.doi.org/10.1111/ajps.12022.

Weiss, Meredith L. 2006. *Protest and Possibilities: Civil Society and Coalitions for Political Change in Malaysia*. Stanford, CA: Stanford University Press.

Weiss, Meredith L. 2011. *Student Activism in Malaysia: Crucible, Mirror, Sideshow*. Ithaca, NY and Singapore: Cornell SEAP Publications and NUS Press.

Weiss, Meredith L., ed. 2014a. *Electoral Dynamics in Malaysia: Findings from the Grassroots*. Kuala Lumpur and Singapore: SIRD and ISEAS.

Weiss, Meredith L. 2014b. "Of Inequality and Irritation: New Agendas And Activism in Malaysia and Singapore." *Democratization* 21 (5):867–887, http://dx.doi.org/10.1080/13510347.2014.910764.

Weiss, Meredith L. 2015. "The Anti-Democratic Potential of Party System Institutionalization: Malaysia as Morality Tale." In *Party System Institutionalization in Asia: Democracies, Autocracies, and the Shadows of the Past*, edited by Allen Hicken and Erik Kuhonta, 25–48. New York: Cambridge University Press.

Weiss, Meredith L. 2020. "The Road Ahead: How to Transform Malaysia's Regime." In *Toward a New Malaysia? The 2018 Election and Its Aftermath*, edited by Meredith L. Weiss and Faisal S. Hazis, 246–66. Singapore: NUS Press.

Welsh, Bridget. 2013. "Malaysia's Elections: A Step Backward." *Journal of Democracy* 24 (4):136–50, http://dx.doi.org/10.1353/jod.2013.0066.

Welsh, Bridget. 2016. "Clientelism and Control: PAP's Fight for Safety in GE2015." *The Round Table* 105 (2):119–28, http://dx.doi.org/10.1080/00358533.2016.1154390.

Welsh, Bridget, Ibrahim Suffian, and Andrew Aeria. 2007. "Malaysia Country Report: Second Wave of Asian Barometer Survey." Working Paper Series No. 46, Asian Barometer & Globalbarometer.

Wilkinson, Steven I. 2007. "Explaining Changing Patterns of Party-Voter Linkages in India." In *Patrons, Clients and Policies: Patterns of Democratic Accountability and Political Competition*, edited by Herbert Kitschelt and Steven I. Wilkinson, 110–40. New York: Cambridge University Press.

Wilkinson, Steven I. 2014. "Patronage Politics in Post-independence India." In *Patronage As the Politics of South Asia*, edited by Anastasia Piliavsky, 259–80. New York: Cambridge University Press.

Winichakul, Thongchai. 2008. "Toppling Democracy." *Journal of Contemporary Asia* 38 (1):11–37, http://dx.doi.org/10.1080/00472330701651937.

Wong Chin Huat. 2012. "Introduction: Rehearsal of Electoral Fraud in the 13th General Election?: The 16 By-elections since 2008." In *Democracy at Stake? Examining 16 By-elections in Malaysia, 2008–2011*, edited by Wong Chin Huat and Soon Li Tsin, 1–33. Petaling Jaya, Malaysia: SIRD.

Wong Chin Huat. 2015. "How Incompetency in Local Governments Help [sic] to Preserve Political Hegemony in Malaysia." *REFSA Quarterly* 1:25–29.

Wong Chin-Huat, James Chin, and Norani Othman. 2010. "Malaysia—Towards a Topology of an Electoral One-Party State." *Democratization* 17 (5):920–49, http://dx.doi.org/10.1080/13510347.2010.501179.

Worthington, Ross. 2003. *Governance in Singapore*. New York: Routledge.

WP. 2007. *The Workers' Party: 50th Anniversary Commemorative Book, 1957–2007*. Singapore: Workers' Party of Singapore.

Yao, Souchou. 2016. *The Malayan Emergency: Essays on a Small, Distant War*. Copenhagen: NIAS Press.

Yap Hon Ngian 2016. "Imprisoned for 17 Years: In Said Zahari's Own Words." In *Remembering Said Zahari: Patriot and Freedom Fighter*, edited by Yap Hon Ngian, 7–23. Petaling Jaya, Malaysia: Pusat Sejarah Rakyat.

Yap, Sonny, Richard Lim, and Leong Weng Kam. 2009. *Men in White: The Untold Story of Singapore's Ruling Political Party*. Singapore: Singapore Press Holdings.

Yeoh, Tricia. 2012. *States of Reform: Governing Selangor and Penang*. Penang, Malaysia: Penang Institute.

Young, Daniel J. 2009. *Is Clientelism at Work in African Elections? A Study of Voting Behavior in Kenya and Zambia*. Afrobarometer Working Paper no. 106.

Index

Abdul Rahman, Tunku, 59, 60, 62, 67, 68, 80, 94, 108, 111–12, 149–50
Abdul Taib Mahmud, 129
absenteeism, 133
acculturation, 2, 6, 19, 22, 148, 205, 209n4
administrative grassroots engagement, 45–46, 134
administrative incorporation, 162
affirmative action program, 7, 71
Agenda Ekonomi Saksama (Equitable Economic Agenda), 127
Ahmad Boestamam, 64
Ahmad Ibrahim, 90, 115
AHPETC, 239n138
"Albany Regency," 43
Alliance
    clientelism and, 76
    elections and, 53, 54–55, 57–58
    left-wing parties and, 64–65
    local elections and, 10, 72–73
    PAP and, 94
    reconfiguration of, 108
    voter turnout and, 57
Alliance Merdeka Mission, 67–68
All-Malaya Council of Joint Action, 81
Alternative Front (Barisan Alternatif; BA), 119
Amnesty International, 165
Angkatan Belia Islam Malaysia (Malaysian Islamic Youth Movement; ABIM), 112
Angkatan Pemuda Insaf (Movement of Aware Youth), 59, 64
anticolonial sentiment, 85, 90, 93
Anwar Ibrahim, 115–16, 146
Asian Financial Crisis (1997), 31
Aspinall, Edward, 205
Au, Alex, 198

Bahagian Kemajuan Masyarakat (Social Development Division; KEMAS), 130
Balakrishnan, Vivian, 238n134
bankruptcy, 165
Bantuan Rakyat 1Malaysia (1Malaysia People's Aid, BR1M), 127
Bantuan segera (on-the-spot assistance), 143–44

Barisan Alternatif (Alternative Front; BA), 119
Barisan Nasional (National Front; BN)
    civil service and, 135
    constituency services and, 136, 139
    constituting, 116–17
    covert funding and, 126
    developmentalism and, 124
    ideological premise of, 148
    incumbency and, 126–27
    installation of, 108
    institutional makeup and, 109–111
    opposition parties and, 119–21
    patronage and, 129, 131
    Sarawak Alliance and, 66
Barisan Rakyat Jati Sarawak, 66
Barisan Sosialis (Socialist Front)
    challenge to PAP from, 83
    community centers and, 100
    description of, 92–95
    elections and, 72–73, 80, 108
    Operation Coldstore and, 154
    opposition from, 172–73
    ousted PAP members and, 91
    resettlement schemes and, 98
Barnes Report, 75
Barr, Michael, 161
Baru Bian, 144, 228–29n95
Beale, Harold, 52
Bellows, Thomas, 2
Berenschot, Ward, 205
Berjaya, 129, 134
Bersih, 151, 225n11
Bharatiya Janata Party (BJP), 44–45
Bloodworth, Dennis, 222n139
Blythe Committee, 82
Borneo, 49
Borneo Utara National Party, 65
Briggs Plan, 51
British North Borneo (Sabah). See Sabah
Bulan Kebajikan (Welfare Month), 128
bumiputera, 111–12, 122–23
Bumiputera Economic Empowerment program, 123
by-election strategy, 176, 183
Byrne, K. M., 101

cadre party, 20
cadre system, 166
campaigns, curbs on, 120
Case, William, 17
catchall parties, 156
Central Executive Committee (CEC) of PAP, 89, 91, 100, 157, 166
Central Executive Committee (CEC) of SDP, 175
Central Provident Fund (CPF), 179–80, 182
Centre of People's Power (Pusat Tenaga Ra'ayat), 81
Chan Heng Chee, 161, 173, 180
Chan Kum Chee, 96
Chandra, Kanchan, 42
change
    drivers of, 200–8
    vectors for, 148–153, 196–99
charismatic politicians, 12
Chee Soon Juan, 164–65, 171, 175, 234n25
Cheeseman, Nic, 27
Chen, Bernard, 194
Chen, Michael, 117
Chiam See Tong, 171, 174–75, 190, 234n33
Chinese Chambers of Commerce, 75, 84, 87, 112
Chinese National Unity Movement, 113
Chinese networks, 112–13
Chua Beng Huat, 177
Citizens' Consultative Committees (CCCs), 101, 181–82, 185
City Council (Singapore), 79, 85–86, 87, 90, 99, 102–3
civic education initiatives, 56
civil liberties, constraints on, 26, 36
civil society organizations (CSOs), 8, 16–17, 112–13
clientelism
    Alliance and, 76
    demand for, 206–7
    impact of, 24, 203
    incentives for, 36–37
    integral nature of, 22
    literature on, 6
    mobilization and, 43–46
    overview of, 11–14, 36–37
    patron-client ties and, 37–41
    as policy framework, 41–43
    See also patronage
Coalition for Good Governance, 151
coalition formation, 29–30, 113–21
Cobbold, C. F., 49
collective exchanges, 37
Commission of Inquiry on Sarawak and North Borneo, 49

Committee on Town and Rural Board Finances, 52
communal parties, in Malaysia, 61–63
communalism, 87, 95
communism, 96. See also Malayan Communist Party (MCP)
Community center management committees, 185
community centers (CCs), 100–2, 184
Community Development Councils (CDCs), 186
community improvement resources, 181–82
Community Improvements Projects Committee, 181–82
competitive authoritarianism
    hegemonic electoral authoritarianism versus, 18
    vectors for change and, 148–53
compulsory voting, 82–83, 160
consensus ideologies, 196
constituency delineation, 110–11
Constituency Delineation Commission, 55
constituency development funds (CDFs), 41–42, 124–26, 130, 131, 137–38, 143
constituency maldistribution, 110–11, 120
constituency services, 39–41, 75–76, 103, 105–6, 135–39, 141, 152, 181, 190, 206–7
constitutional commission, 80
constitutional dominance, 26
"cooling off" day, 159–60
corruption charges, 72, 207
Council of Trust for the People (Majlis Amanah Raka; MARA), 121
Country People's Association, 98, 223n150
covert funding, 126
Cox, Gary W., 209n7
Crouch, Harold, 17–18

Daim Zainuddin, 115
Davidson, Jamie S., 19
De Cruz, Gerald, 86
de Jager, Nicola, 26
Defamation Act, 165
Democratic Action Party (DAP)
    arrests and, 120
    branch-building and, 144
    challenge for, 118
    constituency services and, 136, 137
    gerrymandering and, 111
    hawkers and, 113
    income for, 126
    local elections and, 151
    MCA and, 73, 112

nominations for office and, 146–47
remaking image, 133
wings of, 145
Democratic Party of Japan (DPJ), 30, 32, 39
Democratic Party (Sabah), 65
Democratic Party (Singapore), 84
Democratic Progressive Party (DPP; Taiwan), 34
Department of Social Welfare, 100
Development Bank of Singapore, 179
developmental clientelism, 209n11
developmentalism, culture of, 121, 124
divorce clause, 231n158
Dong Jiao Zong (United Chinese School
   Teachers and School Committees
   Association; DJZ), 61, 112–13
door-to-door canvassing, 194–95
du Toit, Pierre, 26
Dunleavy, Patrick, 209n3
Duverger, Maurice, 210n18

Economic Development Board, 179
Ede, John, 103
Education Act (1961), 62
Education and Cultural Committee, 89
Elected Presidency, 159
Election Commission (EC; Malaysia), 55,
   110–11
Election Offences Act (1954), 61, 120
elections
   introduction in Malaysia, 50–58
   introduction in Singapore, 78–83
   local, 51–53, 71–73, 131–32, 151–52
   malfeasance in, 81–82
   "open seat," 35
   public enthusiasm and, 56–58
   relative centrality of, 25–27
   state-level, 53
electoral authoritarianism
   clientelism and, 12–13
   dominant parties in, 8
   elections and, 25–27
   local government and, 9–11
   longevity of, 3–4, 6
   parties under, 27–28
   partisan allegiance under, 8–9
   patronage-democracy and, 42
   persistence of, 17–19
   success or failure of regimes of, 28–35
   See also competitive authoritarianism;
      hegemonic electoral authoritarianism
Electoral Boundaries Review Committee, 158
electoral manipulation, 110
electoral rolls, 111

Elias Commission, 78, 82
Emergency Council, 91
Emergency Regulations and Trade Union
   Ordinance, 88
employment
   patronage and, 71
   public sector, 122–23
   unemployment in Singapore, 97, 178
Employment Act (1968), 178
English-language speakers, 89, 95–96
Enloe, Cynthia H., 10
Equitable Economic Agenda (Agenda Ekonomi
   Saksama), 127
ethnic outbidding, 111
ethnicity
   role of in Malaya, 66–67, 111–12
   in Singapore, 95–96

Fan Yew Teng, 120
Federal Capital Act (1960), 72, 132
Federal Elections Committee (Malaysia), 55
Federal Land Development Authority (FELDA),
   70, 124, 128
Federated Malay States, 49
Federation of Indian Organisations (FIO), 62
Federation of Malaya Agreement (1948), 50
Feedback Unit, 163–64
first-mover advantage, 19
formal institutions, 16
Freedom House criteria, 26
Funston, John, 58

General Elections Committee, 166–67
Gent, Edward, 67
George, Cherian, 164
George Town City Council, 52
Gerakan. See Parti Gerakan Rakyat Malaysia
   (Malaysian People's Movement Party;
   Gerakan)
gerrymandering, 55, 111, 120, 157, 158
Ghafar Baba, 114
Ghana, 40
Ghazali Shafie, 112
Gimson, Franklin, 79
GNP, growth in, 178
Goh Chok Tong, 1, 155, 157, 162, 167, 172, 178,
   181, 183, 186, 200
Goh Keng Swee, 89, 93, 103–4
Golden, Miriam, 39
Gomez, Terence, 149
Goode, William, 83–84, 96
government-linked corporations (GLCs), 122,
   123, 149, 177, 179

Greene, Kenneth, 15, 27, 30, 32
group representation constituencies (GRCs),
    158–159, 187, 188, 189, 192
Grow & Share package, 178
Grzymala-Busse Anna, 209n5
Gurney, Henry, 53, 59–60, 67, 69

Hammer, The, 173, 174
hands-on service, 75–76
Harbour Board, 99
Harris Salleh, 129
Hawkers' Association of Penang, 113
Hawkins, G., 79–80
hegemonic dominance, 26
hegemonic electoral authoritarianism,
    competitive authoritarianism versus, 18
Hill, L. C., 79
Hinfelaar, Marja, 27
Hogan, M. J., 54
housing, 179–81
Housing and Development Board (HDB), 1,
    97, 98, 179–81, 182, 185, 186–87, 192–93
Howard, Marc Morjé, 15, 29, 210n17
Hutchcroft, Paul, 4, 12, 42, 43
hybridity, terrain of, 2–7

identity cleavage in Taiwan, 34
immigration, 240n163
Implementation Coordination Unit, 125
incumbent advantage, 28–31
incumbent decline, 33–35
incumbent performance, 31–33
Independence of Malaya Party, 55, 62
India, 33, 42, 44–45
Indigenous Empowerment Organization
    (Pertubuhan Pribumi Perkasa Malaysia),
    112
Indonesia, 31
Industrial Coordination Act (1975), 122
Industrial Relations Act (1968), 178
inequality, 32, 178, 197
informal institutions, 16
Information Bureau, 90
institutional makeup
    in Malaysia, 109–113
    in Singapore, 155–66
Institutional Revolutionary Party (PRI;
    Mexico), 15, 19, 27, 30, 31
Internal Security Act (1960; Singapore 1963),
    65, 83, 120, 164, 165
investment ventures, 61
Ishak Haji Mohamed, 64
Islam, PMIP and, 69

Islamist organizations, 112
Ismail Sabri Yaakob, 227n66

Jabatan Sukarelawan Malaysia, 113
Japan
    Democratic Party of Japan (DPJ), 30, 32, 39
    kōenkai system in, 38–39
    Liberal Democratic Party (LDP), 15, 28, 30,
        32, 38–39, 201
    occupation by, 48
    opposition parties and, 30
    patronage and, 32
Jawatankuasa Kemajuan dan Keselamatan
    Kampung (Village Development and
    Security Committees; JKKK), 73–74, 134
Jayasuriya, Kanishka, 14–15
Jesudason, James V., 209n11
Jeyaretnam, Joshua, 165, 173, 175, 184, 186,
    234n33
Jeyaretnam, Kenneth, 175
Jumabhoy, Jumabhoy Mohamed, 103, 105–6
Jurong Town Corporation, 179

Kaum Ibu. See Pergerakan Kaum Ibu UMNO
    (UMNO Women's Section Movement;
    Kaum Ibu)
Keadilan. See Parti Keadilan Rakyat (People's
    Justice Party; Keadilan)
Kenya, 35, 40
Kenya African National Union party, 35
Kesatuan Melayu Muda (Young Malay Union),
    64, 67
ketua kampung, 73
Key, V. O., 27
Khadijah Sidek, 59
Khir Johari, 114
kōenkai system, 38–39
Koh, Tommy, 200
Konfrontasi, 65, 72, 102
Koperatif Serbaguna Malaysia (KSM), 117
Krauss, Ellis S., 201
Kuomintang (KMT), 12, 27, 34

Labour Front (LP), 79, 81, 83, 85–86, 88, 95
Labour parties
    British, 54–55, 63
    Labour Party of Malaya (LPM), 63–65,
        67–68, 76, 118
    Labour Party of Singapore, 81
    in Malaysia, 57, 63
    state-based (in Malaya), 53
Labour Research Unit, 98
Land Acquisition Act (1996), 180

Landé, Carl, 38
Lau Teik Soon, 157
Lee, K. C., 105, 106
Lee Hsien Loong, 155, 174
Lee Kuan Yew, 80, 82–83, 88–96, 99, 104, 154–57, 164, 169, 191, 200
Lee Li Lian, 192
Lee Siew Choh, 92, 172
left-wing parties, 63–65, 85–88. *See also individual parties*
Legislative Assembly, 80
Legislative Council, 53–55, 79–80, 81
Legislative Council Elections Ordinance (1947), 79–80
Legislative Council of the Straits Settlements, 217n7
Levitsky, Steven, 210n17
Liberal Democratic Party (LDP; Japan), 15, 28, 30, 32, 38–39, 201
Liberal Socialist Party (LSP), 81, 83, 84–85, 87
Liew Chin Tong, 202
Lim, Catherine, 162
Lim, Sylvia, 197
Lim Ah Lek, 117
Lim Chin Siong, 89, 91, 92, 94, 96, 104
Lim Guan Eng, 143, 151
Lim Hng Kiang, 188–89
Lim Hock Siew, 81–82
Lim Keng Yaik, 126
Lim Kit Siang, 73, 137
Lim Yew Hock, 83, 86, 87, 88, 91, 96
Lindberg, Staffan I., 40
Ling Liong Sik, 117
linkages with voters
    in Malaysia, 139–48
    in Singapore, 190–96
livelihood uncertainties, 197
Local Councils Ordinance (1952), 52
Local Elections Ordinance (1950), 51
local government
    elections and, 51–53, 78–79
    machines and, 9–11, 71–74, 99–102
    in Malaysia, 51–53, 131–39
    in Singapore, 78–79, 182–90
Local Government Act (1976), 132
Local Government Elections Enactment (2012), 151
Local Government Elections Working Group, 151
Local Government Integration Ordinance (1963), 79, 99
Loh, Francis, 121
lotteries, UMNO and, 60

Low, Peter, 104
Low Thia Khiang, 173–74, 187, 189, 190, 195

Machinda, 66
Magaloni, Beatriz, 3–4
Mahathir Mohamad, 109, 115–16, 118, 123, 127, 152, 240n3
Mainwaring, Scott, 201
Majlis Amanah Rakat (Council of Trust for the People; MARA), 121
Majlis Pengurusan Komuniti Kampung (Village Community Management Councils; MPKK), 134
Malay Nationalist Party, 64
Malay Rulers, 48–49, 50, 58, 60–61
Malay Union, 86
Malayan Indian Congress (MIC), 51, 62. *See also* Malaysian Indian Congress (MIC)
Malayan Chinese Association (MCA)
    Alliance and, 68, 72
    Chinese view of, 64
    elections and, 50, 55, 80, 85, 87
    Hogan committee and, 54
    launch of, 61–62
    local government and, 73
    neighborhood associations and, 75
    new villages and, 51–52
    UMNO alliance with, 60
    voter turnout and, 57
    See also Malaysian Chinese Association (MCA)
Malayan Communist Party (MCP), 48, 64, 67, 68–69
Malayan Democratic Union, 81
Malayan Democratic United Front, 59
Malayan Emergency, 48, 50, 77
Malayan National Conference (MNC), 54
Malayan People's Party (Partai Ra'ayat Malaya), 63–65, 75. *See also* Parti Rakyat Malaysia (Malaysian People's Party; PRM)
Malayan People's Socialist Front. *See* Socialist Front (Malaysia)
Malayan Union, 58
Malaysia
    civil society organizations (CSOs) in, 16–17
    clientelism in, 11–14
    compared to Singapore, 204–5
    competitive authoritarianism in, 108–53
    local authorities in, 9–10
    municipal elections in, 9–10
    opposition coordination in, 29
    overview of politics of, 2–7

Malaysia *(continued)*
  political history of, 48–76
  reasons for focusing on, 19–21
  Singapore's independence from, 2
Malaysian Anti-Corruption Commission, 123, 124
Malaysian Chinese Association (MCA)
  campaigns of, 112
  constituency services and, 136
  decreased support for, 117
  youth wing of, 145
  See also Malayan Chinese Association (MCA)
Malaysian Chinese Union Declaration, 113
Malaysian Indian Congress (MIC), 117, 145.
  See also Malayan Indian Congress (MIC)
Malaysian Islamic Youth Movement (Angkatan Belia Islam Malaysia; ABIM), 112
Malaysian United Indigenous Party (Parti Pribumi Bersatu Malaysia), 118–19
malfeasance, 81–82, 133
Marshall, David, 86–87, 88, 91, 94, 96, 97, 104–5, 191
Maruah, 162
mass party, 21
Maznah Mohamad, 128
McCubbins, Matthew D., 209n7
McNeice committee, 79
Media Development Authority, 163
media takeovers, 61
meet-the-people sessions, 104–6, 192–94
"mental revolution," 97
"menu of manipulation," 3
Merakyatkan Ekonomi Selangor (People-Based Economy program; MES), 127–28
meso-particularism, 4, 43
Mexico, 15, 19, 30, 31
micromanagement, 1–2
micro-particularism, 4, 43
Middle Road unions, 89, 90–91
Ministry of Housing and Local Government, 132
mixed economy model, 177
mixed-member majoritarian (MMM) voting, 28
mobilization, clientelism and, 43–46
Mobrand, Erik, 19
"moderate" parties, 84–85
Moi, Daniel Arap, 35
morselization, 36, 209n7
Movement of Aware Youth (Angkatan Pemuda Insaf), 59, 64
Muhyiddin Yassin, 118–19
Municipal Commission, 79, 81
Municipal Committee, 78
Municipal Ordinance (1887), 78

Municipal Ordinance of the Straits Settlements, 51
Musa Hitam, 115–16, 230n129
Muslimat, 145
Mustapha Datu Harun, Tun, 65

Nahappan, Athi, 131–32
Nair, Devan, 81–82
Najib Razak, 115, 116, 120, 123, 125, 129, 140, 145, 207
National Action Party (PAN; Mexico), 30
National Association of Perak, 57
National Civics Bureau (Biro Tata Negara), 130
National Consultative Council, 109
National Council for Local Government, 72, 132, 151
National Front (Barisan Nasional; BN). *See* Barisan Nasional (National Front; BN)
National Language Bill (1967), 62
National Operations Council, 109, 132
National Solidarity Party (NSP), 162, 175–76, 188
National Trades Union Congress (NTUC), 92–93, 98, 156
National Trust Party (Parti Amanah Negara), 119
National Wages Council, 98, 178
National Youth Leadership Training Institute, 102
neighborhood associations, 45–46, 74–75
New Democrat, The, 175
New Development Policy, 121
New Economic Model, 121
New Economic Policy (NEP), 115, 121–23, 124, 137
New Order regime (Indonesia), 31
New Vision Policy, 121
Nik Aziz Nik Mat, 146, 231n158
Ningkan, Stephen Kalong, 66
nominated members of parliament (NMPs), 159
nominations for office, 146
nonconstituency members of parliament (NCMPs), 159
nongovernmental organizations (NGOs), 115, 133, 137, 146, 148, 149, 152, 161, 162, 185, 228n94
North Borneo, 52
North Borneo Chinese Associations, 75

Official Secrets Act, 110, 164
1Malaysia Development Berhad (1MDB), 119, 140
1Malaysia People's Aid (Bantuan Rakyat 1Malaysia; BR1M), 127

1MDB debacle, 124
Ong, Elvin, 193, 194
Ong Chit Chung, 182
Ong Eng Guan, 85–86, 89, 96, 99, 104, 105, 191, 222n135
Ong Teng Cheong, 156
Onn Jaafar, 59, 60–61, 62, 67, 69, 112
"open seat" elections, 35
Operation Coldstore, 94, 154, 165
Operation Lalang, 112, 165
Operation Spectrum, 165
opposition challenges, 118–21, 169–77
opposition weakness, 28–31
organizational ties, 74
Othman Wok, 104

Pakatan Harapan (Alliance of Hope) coalition
    BN and, 125
    civil service and, 135
    civil society organizations (CSOs) and, 113
    constituency services and, 138
    ideological premise of, 148
    Keadilan and, 118
    local elections and, 133, 152
    patronage and, 149–50
    success of, 21, 109–10
Pan-Malayan Islamic Association (Persatuan Islam Se-tanah Malaya), 63
Pan-Malayan Islamic Party (PMIP), 57, 62–63, 69, 108. See also Parti Islam seMalaysia (PAS)
Pan-Malayan Labour Party (PMLP), 63
PAP Community Foundation, 167
PAP Policy Forum, 166
Partai Ra'ayat Malaya (Malayan People's Party), 63. See also Parti Rakyat Malaysia (Malaysian People's Party; PRM)
Partai Rakyat Singapura, 93–94, 118
Parti Amanah Negara (National Trust Party), 119
Parti Gerakan Rakyat Malaysia (Malaysian People's Movement Party; Gerakan), 112, 113, 117, 118, 136–37, 151
Parti Islam seMalaysia (PAS), 119, 126, 130, 133, 137, 145, 151
Parti Keadilan Rakyat (People's Justice Party; Keadilan), 111, 116, 118, 139, 144, 145
Parti Kebangsaan Melayu Malay (Malay Nationalist Party), 59
Parti Negara Sarawak, 66
Parti Pesaka, 66
Parti Pesaka Bumiputera Bersatu (United Bumiputera Heritage Party; PBB), 66, 126

Parti Pribumi Bersatu Malaysia (Malaysian United Indigenous Party; Bersatu), 118–19, 148, 149–50
Parti Rakyat Malaysia (Malaysian People's Party; PRM), 63, 64, 65, 75–76, 120
Parti Sosialis Malaysia, 118, 143, 230n123
Parti Sosialis Rakyat Malaysia, 63. See also Parti Rakyat Malaysia (Malaysian People's Party; PRM)
Parti Warisan Sabah (Sabah Heritage Party, Warisan), 118, 119
participatory initiatives, 149
parties
    coalitions and, 113–21
    development of, 166–77
    under electoral authoritarianism, 27–28
    hegemonic electoral authoritarianism and, 166–77
    in Malaysia, 58–69, 113–21
    in Singapore, 83–97
    See also individual political parties
parties and structuring policies, 7–9
partisan political economy, 69–71, 97–99
Party Negara, 53, 57, 62, 67
Party of the Democratic Revolution (PRD; Mexico), 30
patronage
    decline of advantage of, 32–33
    employment and, 71
    machines and, 4
    material resources and, 36
    See also clientelism
patronage-democracy, 42
patron-client ties, 37–41
Pekkanen, Robert J., 201
Pemantau, 225n11
Pemuda UMNO (UMNO Youth), 53, 55, 59, 114, 145
Penang Fishermen's Association, 113
penghulu, 51, 59
Peninsular Malay Union (Persatuan Melayu Semenanjong), 61
penyelaras (coordinator) system, 124–25
People-Based Economy program (Merakyatkan Ekonomi Selangor, MES), 127–28
People's Action Party (PAP)
    after Singapore's separation, 155–58
    Barisan Sosialis and, 94–95
    branch structure of, 167
    City Council and, 79
    civic society and, 161
    clientelism and, 45
    consolidation of, 155

People's Action Party *(continued)*
in context of Singapore's political history, 88–92
description of, 20
economic policies and, 176
elections and, 80, 81, 82–83, 84–86
electoral authoritarianism and, 17
ethnicity and, 96
evolution of, 166–68
formation of, 77
housing and, 179–81
income for, 167
Konfrontasi and, 64–65
leadership succession and, 168–69
linkages with voters and, 190–96
local government and, 10, 182–90
machine politics and, 99–102
mobilization and, 97
opposition parties and, 169–77
outreach of, 103–7
policy platform of, 88
political economy and, 97–99
in power, 2–3, 5
press control and, 164
recruitment and, 168
restructuring of, 89–90, 92
unexpected win of, 95
vectors for change and, 196–99
People's Association (PA), 45, 92, 99–100, 102, 183–86, 187–88, 189, 190
Perak Malay League, 57
Perak Progressive Party, 57
Pereira, Leon, 174
Pérez-Liñán, Aníbal, 201
performance legitimacy, 31–33, 102, 197
Pergerakan Kaum Ibu UMNO (UMNO Women's Section Movement; Kaum Ibu), 59–60. *See also* Wanita UMNO (UMNO Women)
Persatuan Islam Se-tanah Malaya (Pan-Malayan Islamic Association), 63
Persatuan Melayu Semenanjong (Peninsular Malay Union), 61
Persatuan Ulama Se-Malaya (Ulama Association of Malaya), 63
personal linkages, 11–14
Pertubuhan Kebangsaan Melayu Singapura (Singapore Malay National Organisation; PKMS), 87, 173. *See also* Singapore Malay National Organisation (PKMS)
Pertubuhan Pribumi Perkasa Malaysia (Indigenous Empowerment Organization), 112

perverse accountability, 160–61
petitionary culture, 192, 197
Petroleum Development Act (1974), 122
Pioneer Generation Package (2014), 178
Plebeian, 92
Poa, Hazel, 188
policy framework, clientelism as, 41–43
political culture, definition of, 4
political detentions, 93, 94–95
Political Donations Act, 171
political economy
competitive authoritarianism and, 121–31
hegemonic electoral authoritarianism and, 177–82
political legitimacy, 18
political machines
clientelism and, 43–46
description of, 4
electoral authoritarianism and, 5
local government and, 9–11
in Malaysia, 71–74
in Singapore, 99–102
political networks
in Malaysia, 58–69
in Singapore, 83–97
Political Study Centre, 97
preelection coalitions, 29–30
Preservation of Public Security Ordinance (1955), 83
press control, 164
privatization, 32, 34, 123
Progressive Party, 81, 84–85, 96, 102–3
public, formal politics and, 80–83
Public Advisory Bureau (PAB), 105
Public Complaints Bureau, 90
public education for elections, 56
Public Entertainments and Meetings Act, 164–65
public housing development, 7, 98–99
Public Security Ordinance, 91
Public Utilities Board, 97, 99
Pusat Tenaga Ra'ayat (Centre of People's Power), 81
Puteh Mariah, 68
Puteri UMNO, 114, 145
Puthucheary, J. J., 85

Quah, Jon, 183

Radical Party (Malaysia), 51
Rahman Yakub, 126
Rajah, T. T., 91
Rajaratnam, S., 104, 156

rallies, 160, 171–72
Razak, Tun, 132
Razaleigh Hamzah, Tengku, 115, 116, 136
REACH, 163–64. *See also* Feedback Unit
Read, Benjamin, 134
Reform Party, 175–76
Reformasi movement, 118, 152
regimes
    approaching, 14–17
    reconceptualizing, 24–47
Rendel, George, 80
repressive–responsive regime, 17–18
resettlement schemes, 98–99, 180
residents' associations (RAs), 113
Residents' Committees (RCs), 185–86
right-wing parties, 84–85. *See also individual parties*
Rodan, Garry, 14–15, 196
Roessler, Philip G., 15, 29, 210n17
"rotten-door" transition, 47
Rukun Tetangga, 113
Rural Board, 78
Rural Industrial Development Authority (RIDA), 121
Rural Residents' Association, 93
rural weighting, 110

Sabah
    elections and, 52–53, 57
    Federation of Malaya and, 49
    overrepresentation of, 111
    parties of, 65–66
    patronage and, 129–30
Sabah Alliance, 65
Sabah Chinese Association, 65
Sabah National Party (SANAP), 65
safety net, 178
Saifuddin Abdullah, 149
Sarawak
    elections and, 52, 57
    Federation of Malaya and, 49
    overrepresentation of, 111
    parties of, 65–66
    patronage and, 129
Sarawak Alliance, 66
Sarawak National Party, 66
Sarawak United People's Party, 66, 226n37
Schedler, Andreas, 3
Scheiner, Ethan, 32
Scott, James, 43, 44, 206
Sedition Act, 120
Selangor Chinese Assembly Hall, 112
Semangat '46 (Spirit of '46), 115, 118

semiauthoritarianism, 17
semidemocracies, 17
Senegal, 40
Settlement Council Elections Bill, 53
sexual-orientation discrimination, 234n27
Shafie Apdal, 119
Singapore
    civil society organizations (CSOs) in, 17
    clientelism in, 11–14
    compared to Malaysia, 204–205
    hegemonic electoral authoritarianism in, 154–99
    independence of, 2, 49
    local authorities in, 10
    micromanagement in, 1
    municipal elections in, 9–10
    overview of politics of, 2–7
    political history of, 77–107
    reasons for focusing on, 19–21
Singapore Association of Trade Unions, 92, 94, 97
Singapore Chinese Chamber of Commerce, 218n26
Singapore Democratic Alliance, 170, 176
Singapore Democratic Party (SDP), 170, 171, 175, 182, 189–90
Singapore General Employees Union, 92
Singapore Improvement Trust, 98
Singapore Justice Party, 176
Singapore Malay National Organisation (PKMS), 87, 173, 176. *See also* Pertubuhan Kebangsaan Melayu Singapura (Singapore Malay National Organisation; PKMS)
Singapore People's Alliance (SPA), 87, 96
Singapore People's Party (SPP), 170, 176
Singapore Rural Residents' Association, 98
SingFirst, 170
Singh, Pritam, 173–74, 189
single member constituencies (SMCs), 158
single nontransferable vote (SNTV) rules, 28, 34
single-party dominance, 3–4
social cleavages, 33–35
Social Development Division (Bahagian Kemajuan Masyarakat, KEMAS), 130
social media, 196
Socialist Front (Malaysia), 64–65, 72–73, 80, 108, 110, 216n109
Societies Act, 162, 164
South Korea, 210n15
sovereign wealth funds, 179
Spirit of '46 (Semangat '46), 115, 118
Star, The, 117

stasis, drivers of, 200–208
state control over the economy, 32
state-led industrialization, 178–79
state-level elections, 53
state-owned enterprises (SOEs), 177–78, 179
Stephens, Donald (later Fuad), 65
Stokes, Susan C., 160–61
Straits Chinese Business Association, 61, 218n26
Straits Settlements, 49
Street, Drainage and Building Act (1973), 132
strikes, decrease in, 98
Suharto, 31
Syed Ja'afar Albar, 126

Taiwan, 34, 209n9
Tang Liang Hong, 165
tea sessions, 163
Thachil, Tariq, 45
Tharman Shanmugaratnam, 192
Thomas, Francis, 103
Toh Chin Chye, 166
Town and Country Planning Act (TCPA; 1976), 132
Town Council Act, 187
Town Councils (TCs), 186–89, 190, 194
trade unions, 85, 87, 88–93, 97–98, 99, 118, 156
Trades Union Congress, 92

Ulama Association of Malaya (Persatuan Ulama Se-Malaya), 63
UMNO Baru, 115
UMNO Women. *See* Wanita UMNO (UMNO Women)
UMNO Women's Section Movement (Pergerakan Kaum Ibu UMNO), 59–60. *See also* Wanita UMNO (UMNO Women)
Unfederated Malay States, 49
United Bumiputera Heritage Party (Parti Pesaka Bumiputera Bersatu; PBB), 66, 126
United Chinese School Teachers and School Committees Association (Dong Jiao Zong; DJZ), 61, 112–13
United Democratic Party, 63
United Front coalition, 172
United Malays National Organisation (UMNO)
    affirmative action programs and, 7
    Alliance and, 68
    civil society organizations (CSOs) and, 113
    compulsory voting and, 83
    constituency services and, 136, 139
    in context of Malaysian political history, 58–61

corruption charges and, 207
covert funding and, 126
declared illegal, 109
description of, 20–21
elections and, 50, 51, 55, 57–58, 80, 85, 87–88
ethnicity and, 112
evolution of, 114–16
Hogan committee and, 54
local government and, 10, 73
nominations for office and, 146
offshoots from, 118–19
PAP compared to, 17
patronage and, 124
position of, 67
in power, 2–3, 5
rural base and, 74
rural development and, 64
voter linkages and, 140
voter turnout and, 57
wings of, 145
United National Kadazan Organisation (UNKO), 65
United Party, 65
United Pasok Momogun Organisation, 65
United Sabah National Organisation (USNO), 65
United Socialist Front, 87
Universal Declaration of Human Rights, 54
Utusan Melayu, 61

vigilante groups, 101
Village Community Management Councils (Majlis Pengurusan Komuniti Kampung; MPKK), 134
Village Development and Security Committees (JKKK; *Jawatankuasa Kemajuan dan Keselamatan Kampung*), 73–74, 134
Vision 2020, 123
vote buying, 38, 61, 81–82, 161
voter mobilization, 37
voter registration, 56–57, 68, 80–81, 82, 110, 111
voter turnout, 57, 81, 102
voters, connecting with, 74–76, 102–7, 139–48, 190–96
voting, compulsory, 82–83

Wan Azizah Wan Ismail, 227n66
Wan Hussin Zoohri, 169
Wanita UMNO (UMNO Women), 59, 114, 145. *See also* UMNO Women's Section Movement (Pergerakan Kaum Ibu UMNO; Kaum Ibu)

Warisan; *See* Parti Warisan Sabah (Sabah Heritage Party; Warisan)
Washida, Hidekuni, 124
Way, Lucan A., 210n17
weddings, 142, 195
Welfare Month (Bulan Kebajikan), 128
Women's League of the PAP, 92, 166
women's suffrage, 68
Women's Wing of the PAP, 166
women's wings of Malaysian parties, 145
Wong Chen, 128
Wooden Dwellers Association, 223n150
Workers' Charter, 88
Workers' Party Community Fund, 189

Workers' Party (WP), 64, 82–83, 85, 87, 158–59, 170–71, 173–74, 176, 198
Workfare Income Supplement Scheme (2007), 178
Works Brigade, 92

Ya'acob Mohamed, 169
Yao, Souchou, 51
Yeo, George, 161
Yeoh, Hannah, 146
Young Malay Union (Kesatuan Melayu Muda), 64, 67
Young PAP, 166

zero-sum issues, 34